Domenico Scarlatti – Master of Music

Malcolm Boyd

Domenico Scarlatti –
Master of Music

SCHIRMER BOOKS
A Division of Macmillan, Inc.
NEW YORK

Schirmer Books
A Division of Macmillan, Inc.
866 Third Avenue, New York, N.Y. 10022

First published in Great Britain by
George Weidenfeld & Nicolson Limited
91 Clapham High Street
London SW4 7TA

Library of Congress Catalog Card Number: 86-21743

Printed in the United States of America

printing number
1   2   3   4   5   6   7   8   9   10

Library of Congress Cataloging-in-Publication Data

Boyd, Malcolm.
    Domenico Scarlatti—master of music.

    Bibliography: p.
    1. Scarlatti, Domenico, 1685-1757?—Criticism and
interpretation. I. Title.
ML410.S221B7   1987   780'.92'4   86-21743
ISBN 0-02-870291-3

To Jeremy –
un applauso genetliaco

Contents

	PREFACE	ix
1	Italy, 1685–1722	1
2	Operas and Oratorios	32
3	Chamber Cantatas	84
	★	
4	Portugal, *c.* 1723–9	96
5	Serenatas	104
6	Church Music	112
	★	
7	Spain, 1729–57	130
8	Keyboard Works	147
9	Late Vocal Works	195
	★	
10	Scarlatti's Reputation and Influence	205
	APPENDIXES	
I	Some Scarlatti Arrangements	224
II	Scarlatti's Will	236
III	Two Unpublished Sonatas	239
IV	List of Compositions	253
	BIBLIOGRAPHY	276
	NOTES	281
	INDEX	291

Preface

The pioneering work of Alessandro Longo in the early years of this century has been followed by a number of important studies on Domenico Scarlatti which have concentrated on one or other of two particular aspects. Sacheverell Sitwell, Ulisse Prota-Giurleo and Roberto Pagano have made notable contributions to our knowledge and understanding of Scarlatti's life and background, while Walter Gerstenberg, Hermann Keller, Giorgio Pestelli, Joel Sheveloff and others have directed our attention to the various stylistic, historical, textual and contextual problems raised by the keyboard sonatas. Ralph Kirkpatrick's indispensable monograph of 1953 added considerably to what was then known in both these areas, but the author's attempt to deal comprehensively with the vocal works as well was limited by the number of sources available to him and, it must be said, by his own evident lack of interest in them.

Many changes have taken place in the musical world since Kirkpatrick's book was first published. Editions and performances of late Baroque opera are much more numerous than they were then, and the vast repertory of Baroque chamber cantatas, most of which survive only in manuscript or in early printed editions, has been increasingly explored by both singers and scholars. While the number of authenticated keyboard sonatas by Scarlatti has remained more or less constant during this time, the extant vocal music has been augmented by the discovery of no fewer than three complete operas, several chamber cantatas, two masses and other church compositions. It may freely be admitted that, even if the numerous other lost works were eventually recovered, there is no likelihood that the vocal music would ever replace the keyboard sonatas in popular and critical esteem. But Scarlatti can now be seen as a more gifted and versatile composer for voices than has so far been recognized, and therefore as a more complete master of music than has often been supposed.

In order to underline the relationship that exists between Scarlatti's career and the various musical genres in which he worked,

I have grouped the first nine chapters of this book into three sections, dealing in turn with Italy, Portugal and Spain. In each section a biographical chapter is followed by two others covering the music particularly associated with the period in question. Obviously Chapters 5 and 6, dealing respectively with the serenatas and the church music, are more retrospective than the other chapters on the works, but since Scarlatti's activities in both these areas seem virtually to have ceased when he went to Spain it seemed appropriate to place them alongside the chapter on his Portuguese sojourn. The final chapter is even more retrospective, since it attempts to summarize the reputation that Scarlatti and his music have enjoyed since the mid eighteenth century.

I have received generous help from numerous individuals and institutions during the writing of this book. An initial debt to H. C. Robbins Landon for interesting me in the project in the first place has been increased by his continuing support since then. Roberto Pagano, whose encyclopedic knowledge of all things Scarlattian is equalled only by his readiness to share it with others, generously allowed me to read the text of his biographical study prior to its publication in 1985; I have plundered it shamelessly. Among other scholars from whom I received valuable help and advice I must mention in particular Bernd Baselt, Francesco Degrada, Genoveva Gálvez, Thomas Griffin, Loek Hautus, Jean Lionnet, Magda Marx-Weber, Joel Sheveloff and Eleonora Simi Bonini.

A research visit to Madrid in 1984 was made possible by financial help from University College, Cardiff. The music staff of the College library, of Archbishop Marsh's Library, Dublin, and of all the libraries whose abbreviations are listed in Appendix IV helped me either in person or by replying to queries and supplying material, but I must make special mention of the following, whose assistance extended far beyond the call of duty: Padre Modesto-Giovanni Bortoli (Convento San Francesco della Vigna, Venice), Rudolf Elvers (Staatsbibliothek Preussischer Kulturbesitz, West Berlin), Gail L. Freunsch (Library of Congress, Washington), Barbara Glowka (Diözesan-Bibliothek, Münster), Helga Heim (Staats- und Universitätsbibliothek, Hamburg), Macario Santiago Kastner (Fábrica da Sé Patriarcal, Lisbon) and Juan José Rey (Real Conservatorio de Música, Madrid). Joachim Schlichte kindly allowed me to consult the RISM indexes at Kassel.

For translations from Latin and Spanish I am indebted to John Wharton and to Marta Sánchez and Marilyn Schwenk respectively; Anna Maria Gowen solved many linguistic problems in Italian opera librettos and cantata texts. My wife, Beryl, cast a critical and discerning eye over the typescript and David Wyn Jones a no less vigilant one over the proofs.

To all these, and to the several friends and colleagues who have shared their experience of Scarlatti's music with me, I extend my thanks.

M. B. Cardiff, 1986

Bibliographical references. References in the text to the standard work by Ralph Kirkpatrick, *Domenico Scarlatti* (Princeton, 1953), are indicated simply by page numbers. Thus, for example, 'Kirkpatrick (p. 266)' refers the reader to page 266 of Kirkpatrick's book. Other bibliographical references are contained in the notes on pages 281–90.

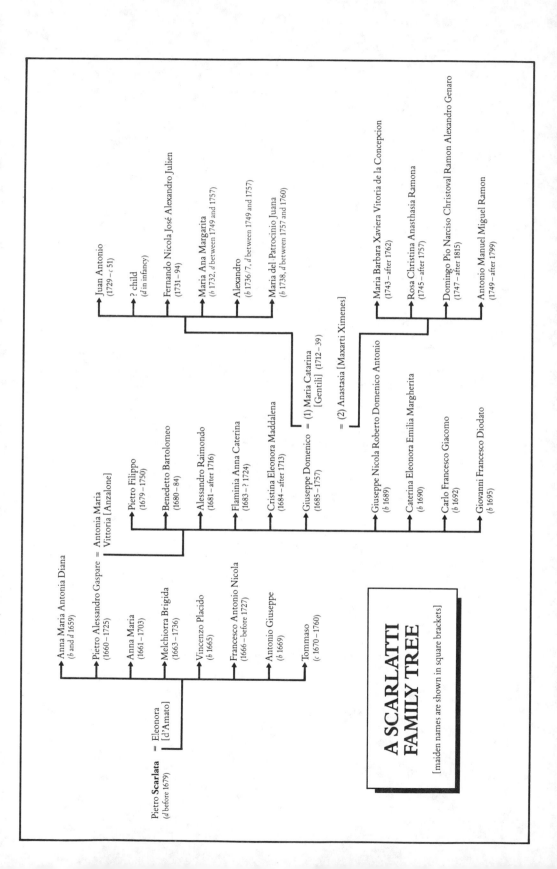

Pietro **Scarlata** = Eleonora
(d before 1679)   [d'Amato]

Anna Maria Antonia Diana
(b and d 1659)

Pietro Alessandro Gaspare = Antonia Maria
(1660–1725)   Vittoria [Anzalone]

Anna Maria
(1661–1703)

Melchiorra Brigida
(1663–1736)

Vincenzo Placido
(b 1665)

Francesco Antonio Nicola
(1666–before 1727)

Antonio Giuseppe
(b 1669)

Tommaso
(c 1670–1760)

Juan Antonio
(1729–c 51)

? child
(d in infancy)

Fernando Nicola José Alexandro Julien
(1731–94)

Maria Ana Margarita
(b 1732, d between 1749 and 1757)

Alexandro
(b 1736/7, d between 1749 and 1757)

Maria del Patrocinio Juana
(b 1738, d between 1757 and 1760)

Pietro Filippo
(1679–1750)

Benedetto Bartolomeo
(1680–84)

Alessandro Raimondo
(1681–after 1716)

Flaminia Anna Caterina
(1683–? 1724)

Cristina Eleonora Maddalena
(1684–after 1713)

Giuseppe Domenico = (1) Maria Catarina
(1685–1757)   [Gentili] (1712–39)

                    = (2) Anastasia [Maxarti Ximenes]

Giuseppe Nicola Roberto Domenico Antonio
(b 1689)

Caterina Eleonora Emilia Margherita
(b 1690)

Carlo Francesco Giacomo
(b 1692)

Giovanni Francesco Diodato
(b 1695)

Maria Barbara Xaviera Vitoria de la Concepcion
(1743–after 1762)

Rosa Christina Anasthasia Ramona
(1745–after 1757)

Domingo Pio Narciso Christoval Ramon Alexandro Genaro
(1747–after 1815)

Antonio Manuel Miguel Ramon
(1749–after 1799)

A SCARLATTI
FAMILY TREE

[maiden names are shown in square brackets]

Domenico Scarlatti – Master of Music

ONE   *Italy, 1685–1722*

The musical family, with exceptional talent running through several generations, has been a familiar phenomenon in all periods of music history. One only has to think of the extraordinary Cremonese families of violin-makers, the Amati and the Guarneri, whose work spanned over two centuries, or, among present-day musicians, of the Menuhins, the Dolmetsches and the Torteliers. In the case of musical artisans and executants such as these the phenomenon occasions little surprise, since the idea of a craft or a practical skill as something passed down from father to son is a familiar one in many walks of life. But the modern stereotype of the creative artist, based as it is mainly on nineteenth- and early twentieth-century figures, suggests someone more likely to be in rebellion against his parents, and families of composers such as the Couperins in France, the Bendas in Bohemia, the Bachs in Germany and the Scarlattis in Italy have not often been paralleled in later times.

This observation has much to tell us about how the activity of composing music was viewed in the Baroque era and about the place of the composer in seventeenth- and eighteenth-century society. It means also that the relationship between father and son among composers is one of particular interest, and as we shall see this is especially so in the case of Domenico Scarlatti.

THE SCARLATTI FAMILY

Musical talent seems to have entered the Scarlatti family through Domenico's paternal grandmother, Eleonora d'Amato, a native of Palermo in Sicily. Although we know nothing about her own musical ability, her family certainly moved among musicians, and she herself was most probably the sister of the priest and composer Vincenzo Amato (or d'Amato), who was born in 1629 and in 1665 became *maestro di cappella* at the cathedral in Palermo.[1] Vincenzo Amato had trained as a priest at the Seminario dei Chierici in Palermo and then devoted himself to the study of music. He published two volumes of sacred compositions (masses and motets) in 1656, and was the composer of an opera, *Isaura*, and an oratorio, *Il martirio di Santa Caterina*. His two Passions, the *St John* and the *St Matthew*, continued in use in Sicily until well into the twentieth century.

On 5 May 1658 Eleonora d'Amato was married to Pietro Scarlata (as his name appears in the marriage register) at the church of San Antonio Magno Abate in Palermo. Little is known about Pietro, Domenico's grandfather, except that he was originally from Trapani, a town on the Sicilian coast about fifty miles west of Palermo. His name does not appear in connection with any musical establishment on the island, and quite possibly he was not a musician at all. That he was, however, marrying into a musical family is confirmed by the presence, as witness to the marriage, of the singer and composer Marc'Antonio Sportonio. Sportonio enjoyed greater renown than any other musician in Sicily. He had studied in Rome with the composer Carissimi and served the Duke of Modena as a singer; in 1655 he helped to organize the earliest opera performance in Palermo, Francesco Cavalli's *Giasone*, in which he sang the role of Delfa.

Pietro Scarlata and his wife lost no time in starting a family, and just nine months after the wedding, on 8 February 1659, a daughter, Anna Maria Antonia Diana, was born; she died the following October. Of the seven children subsequently born to the couple no fewer than five followed a musical career. The two daughters, Anna Maria and Melchiorra Brigida, became singers; Francesco was active as a violinist and composer in Naples and later in London; and the youngest son, Tommaso, spent most of his life as a tenor in Naples, where he lived until he was about ninety. More important than any of these, however, was Alessandro, the second child and the eldest to survive. He was born on 2 May 1660 and baptized Pietro Alessandro Gaspare the following day in the church where his parents had been married almost exactly two years earlier.

Little is known about Alessandro Scarlatti's early years in Sicily, but it is likely that, growing up in a musical family, his talents were directed and fostered by friends and relatives, including Vincenzo Amato and Sportonio. In 1672 conditions of famine and social unrest in Palermo, as well (one may infer) as the relative poverty of the Scarlatti family, led the parents to send the twelve-year-old Alessandro and his two sisters to Rome, where they probably had relatives and where there were better prospects than in Sicily for the employment of their musical gifts.

The Rome in which Alessandro Scarlatti spent his teens, and where his son Domenico was to find employment later on, was one of the major musical centres in Italy. In the sixteenth century Palestrina, Victoria and numerous lesser composers had filled its fine churches with *a cappella* music of the purest and most refined kind, and their example was emulated in archaic, *stile antico* church music by composers active in Rome throughout the seventeenth century, and even into the eighteenth. Alessandro and Domenico were both to make notable contributions to the tradition. Rome was also the cradle of the oratorio, a relatively new genre when Alessandro arrived there, but one which had already been cultivated by a composer of the first rank in Giacomo Carissimi.

Secular music was not neglected. Papal opposition to public theatrical performances, and in particular to the participation of women in them, often made opera production difficult, but prohibitions could be circumvented in private theatres built and supported by the nobility and by wealthy and influential cardinals such as Benedetto Pamphili and Pietro Ottoboni, both of whom not only encouraged opera but even wrote opera librettos themselves. So, too, had Monsignor Giulio Rospigliosi, who as Pope Clement IX (1667–9) authorized the building of Rome's first public opera house, the Teatro Tordinona, opened in January 1671. The young Alessandro Scarlatti would have had few opportunities to attend opera performances there, however, for opposition from Clement IX's successor, Innocent XI, forced its closure in 1674; its doors were not reopened to the public until 1690, when Alessandro's own opera *La Statira* was given there. Under continuing pressure from some of the cardinals, who considered the Tordinona and its surroundings to be a hotbed of crime and immorality, the pope finally ordered its destruction in 1697.

While opera followed a difficult course at Rome in the 1670s, chamber music (both vocal and instrumental) flourished there more vigorously than ever. The *cantata da camera*, or chamber cantata, which Alessandro Scarlatti was to cultivate with particular distinction, was enthusiastically encouraged in the 'academies' of the same patrons who supported opera, and performed in the main by opera singers. Indeed, by 1672 the genre had begun to resemble an operatic scene, with a flexible framework of recitative, arioso and aria. Alessandro would have found much to stimulate his musical imagination in the cantatas then being written by composers such as Carissimi, Pietro Simone Agostini, Mario Savioni and Alessandro Stradella. As for instrumental music, one has only to recall the presence in Rome of the keyboard virtuoso and composer Bernardo Pasquini and (from about the same time as Alessandro Scarlatti) of Arcangelo Corelli, the leading composer of sonatas and concertos, to realize that in this field, too, the Eternal City was pre-eminent.

It was in this stimulating environment that Alessandro Scarlatti spent his formative years. Tradition has it that he studied in Rome with Carissimi; he may even have arrived from Sicily with a letter of introduction to the aged composer from his godfather Marc'Antonio Sportonio, one of Carissimi's former pupils. But Alessandro's studies with him cannot have lasted long, for Carissimi died on 12 January 1674, in his seventieth year. Whether or not the young Sicilian received any other formal education in Rome, and if so from whom, we do not know. There is no record of his having been attached to any of the churches and oratories that provided a musical training for young singers, or of his having attended any of the private schools which then existed. But the mere presence in Rome of so many outstanding musicians and the many opportunities of hearing music performed by the leading virtuosos of the day must in themselves have been an education to him.

It was evidently as a church musician that Alessandro Scarlatti first found employment in Rome. As the researches of Arnaldo Morelli (1984) have shown, he was appointed *maestro di cappella* at the church of San Giacomo degli Incurabili on 16 December 1678 and remained there until November 1682, when he succeeded Antonio Foggia as *maestro* at the church of San Gerolamo della Carità. The post at San Giacomo degli Incurabili may not have been Scarlatti's first appointment, however, if on 12 April 1678, about three weeks before his eighteenth birthday, he found himself in a position to marry a Roman girl, Antonia Maria Vittoria Anzalone. The first of their ten children, Pietro Filippo, was born the following January. By then Scarlatti had written at least one opera, and in 1679 another, *Gli equivoci nel sembiante*, was performed privately in Rome (Pope Innocent XI's decrees discouraging public performances of opera having by then taken full effect). The enormous success of *Gli equivoci*, which was soon repeated in several other Italian cities and even as far afield as Vienna, may be attributed in large part to Domenico Filippo Contini's neatly contrived pastoral libretto and to certain incidents which made its early performances something of a *succès de scandale*.[2] But it also marked Scarlatti as a composer of outstanding promise and earned for him the protection of Queen Christina of Sweden. That cultured and colourful monarch had abdicated her throne in 1654, embraced the Roman Catholic faith and set herself up as one of the most munificent and influential patrons of the arts in a city not short of wealthy Maecenases. The libretto of Scarlatti's third opera, *L'honestà negli amori* (1680), names the composer as her *maestro di cappella*, a title he retained until he left for Naples four years and at least four operas later.

NAPLES (1685–1704)

When Pietro Andrea Ziani, *maestro di cappella* to the court of Naples since 1680, died on 12 February 1684, the Spanish viceroy, the Marchese del Carpio, immediately appointed Alessandro Scarlatti to succeed him. The marquis had known Scarlatti's music at Rome, where he had served as Spanish ambassador to the Vatican until 1683, and Scarlatti for his part was no doubt attracted to Naples by the greater opportunities it offered to an opera composer of growing reputation. The fact that the appointment was made over the head of Francesco Provenzale, who as *maestro onorario* had expected to succeed Ziani, and that it was accompanied by accusations of favouritism resulting from the intrigues of one of Scarlatti's sisters (probably Melchiorra) with court officials, led to scandal, dismissals and resignations. But Scarlatti retained his post and remained as vice-regal *maestro di cappella* until 1702.

Naples had been under Spanish rule since 1503, during which time the self-interest of the Neapolitan nobility had discouraged the formation of a strong bourgeoisie. A growing population (despite recurrent plagues it reached 186,000 in 1700), together with prohibitions on building outside the city walls, tended to emphasize the divisions between rich and poor, and Naples soon acquired a reputation for noise and overcrowded living conditions which has lasted into modern times. It nevertheless emerged as a leading centre for opera in Italy during the eighteen years of Alessandro Scarlatti's first sojourn there. Musical activity was largely in the hands of the Spanish viceroy, who maintained a *cappella* of singers and instrumentalists to provide music for church services and for operas and serenatas in his private theatre. He also took a controlling interest in the public theatre, the Teatro San Bartolomeo, to which opera productions were commonly transferred after being seen at the palace. The viceroy had jurisdiction, too, over three of the four conservatories that specialized in providing musical training for poor or unusually talented boys, on similar lines to the Venetian *ospedali* for girls. Scarlatti's professional connections with these conservatories seem to have been confined to a few weeks in 1689, when he taught (not very diligently, it seems) at the Conservatorio di Santa Maria di Loreto. For most of the time he was kept busy writing or adapting operas for the viceroy, and he also maintained his connections with Roman patrons during these years. In 1687 the Marchese del Carpio died, and was succeeded as viceroy first by Francesco de Benavides y Avila, Count of Santo Stefano, and in 1696 by Luis Francisco de la Cerda, Duke of Medinaceli. Under

Medinaceli performances of operas and serenatas became more lavish than ever, both at the royal palace in Naples and at the summer residence at Posillipo, the small promontory separating the gulf of Naples from the bay of Pozzuoli. In addition, the Teatro San Bartolomeo was enlarged. Scarlatti was fully employed writing operas for all these locations, and by 1705 he could claim to have composed no fewer than eighty-eight works for the stage. This total, however, probably included *rifacimenti* (reworkings) for the Neapolitan stage of the Venetian operas that were so much in vogue at the time.

Alessandro Scarlatti and his wife Antonia had brought five children with them from Rome: Pietro, the eldest, who has already been mentioned; Benedetto Bartolomeo, who died only a few months after his arrival in Naples; Alessandro Raimondo, who in 1717 was still living in Rome; Flaminia Anna Caterina, a gifted singer whose portrait (now lost) was painted by Francesco Solimena; and Cristina Eleonora Maddalena, named after her illustrious godmother, Queen Christina of Sweden. Five more children were added to the family at Naples, the first and most famous being Domenico.

Domenico Scarlatti was born on 26 October 1685 and baptized six days later in the church of Montesanto. The baptism was entered in the register of the Parocchia della Carità as follows:

> 1 November 1685. I, the curate named below [Giuseppe Sorrentino], baptized a male child born on 26 ultimo, the son of Signor Alessandro Scarlati [*sic*] and Signora Antonia Anzalone, man and wife; he was given the names Giuseppe Domenico and was held at the sacred font by Signora D. Eleonora del Carpio, Princess of Colobrano, and by Signor D. Domenico Marzio Carafa, Duke of Maddaloni.[3]

The name Giuseppe may have been chosen as a compliment to the curate who officiated at the baptism, but it was by the name of his godfather that Domenico became known. The choice of godparents gives some indication of the elevated circles in which Alessandro Scarlatti moved in Naples, as he had done also in Rome; little wonder that Cardinal Ottoboni, in the Latin epitaph he wrote for Scarlatti's tombstone, referred to him as 'optimatibus regibusq[ue] . . . carus'. The Duke of Maddaloni was one of the most prominent members of the Neapolitan aristocracy, and he evidently held Scarlatti in high esteem. He had visited Rome with his wife in June 1679 and had either attended a performance of *Gli equivoci nel sembiante* or at least heard about its extraordinary success; the following year he mounted a production of the opera at his own palace in Naples. It may even have been on the duke's recommendation that Alessandro was invited to become *maestro di cappella* at Naples, and his continuing patronage of the composer is indicated by an inscription on the autograph score of the cantata *Vedi Eurilla quel fior* (1725): 'per l'Ecc.^{mo} Duca de Maddaloni'. The infant Domenico was not, however, 'held at the sacred font' by the wife of the viceroy, del Carpio, as has usually been stated. Roberto Pagano has convincingly shown that the Princess of Colobrano at the time was Eleonora Cardines, whose husband, another Domenico Carafa, was closely related to the Duke of Maddaloni.[4] The confusion in the baptismal register probably arose, as Pagano suggests, because the Princess of Colobrano was standing proxy for the vicereine or for her daughter, Caterina.

Nothing whatever is known about Domenico's early life in Naples. It would presumably have been possible for him to win a free place at one of the conservatories, as his almost exact contemporary Nicola Porpora did in 1699, but his name is not to be found in any of the surviving rosters. We may presume that he received a comprehensive musical education from his father, and indeed this much is implied in a letter which Prince Ferdinando de' Medici wrote to Alvise Morosini in 1705 (see p. 12). Certainly by the age of fifteen he must have acquired from somewhere considerable skill as both a keyboard player and a composer, since on 13 September 1701 he was appointed *organista e compositore di musica* in the royal *cappella* of which his father was *maestro*. His salary was 11 ducats 1 tari a month (that of his father being 500 scudi a year, plus whatever he could earn from additional commissions and other duties). Domenico received also a personal allowance from Medinaceli for his services as 'clavicembalista di camera di S[ua] E[ccellenza]'; even at this early age his outstanding gifts as a harpsichord player did not go unrecognized. What the younger Scarlatti's official duties were is not known, and neither do we possess any music which can be dated with certainty to the period of his employment at the Neapolitan court. Some of the chamber cantatas were no doubt written during these years – one of them is actually dated 1699 – and the keyboard sonatas K287–8 and 328 (for organ, not harpsichord) reflect his experience as organist of the royal chapel, even if they were not actually composed at this time. He must also have written and improvised harpsichord music for Medinaceli's private enjoyment.

Only four months after Domenico's appointment his father applied to the viceroy for ten months' leave of absence on full salary for them both. Rather surprisingly, the request was agreed to on 7 January

1702, but when it became known that the new king of Spain, Philip V, was to visit Naples all leave for servants of the viceroy was cancelled. Alessandro was, of course, kept busy during the king's visit, which lasted from 16 April until 2 June; works composed and performed in his honour included the opera *Tiberio imperatore d'oriente* and a serenata, *Cari lidi, amene sponde*. Domenico, for his part, must have made his first acquaintance with the monarch at whose court in Spain he was later to serve for several years. It was not until 14 June that the Scarlattis were free to leave Naples, but by then Medinaceli's harsh quelling of a pro-Austrian conspiracy among the Neapolitan nobility (the famous *congiura di Macchia*) had earned the censure of Madrid, and he had been replaced by a new viceroy, the Duke of Ascalona. No doubt with an eye to the opera season due to begin in November, Ascalona granted the Scarlattis only four months' leave, but, with Medinaceli gone, Alessandro can have felt no strong incentive to return to Naples. When he departed for Florence he was accompanied, as we now know, by the whole of his 'numerosa famiglia'[5] and by the singer Maria Maddalena Musi, who was to take part in Prince Ferdinando's opera performances at Pratolino in the autumn. The intention was obviously to secure employment elsewhere, if it could be found.

On their way to Florence the party spent some weeks in Rome, where Alessandro renewed his contacts with Prince Ruspoli and no doubt with other Roman patrons as well. He was probably also intent on displaying the talents of his most gifted son. Two cantatas by Domenico date from this time and may have been performed in Ruspoli's palace in the Piazza di Santa Maria in Arcolei. In Florence Alessandro's hopes were pinned on his musically gifted patron Prince Ferdinando de' Medici, son of the Grand Duke of Tuscany, Cosimo III. Ferdinando had promoted Alessandro's operas in several north Italian cities and in 1688 had commissioned a new one (probably *La serva favorita*) from him for performance at his villa at Pratolino, near Florence. On 9 August 1702 Ferdinando's thirty-ninth birthday was celebrated with a motet specially commissioned from the elder Scarlatti and performed in the Church of the Santissima Annunziata in Florence, the composer receiving a gold snuff-box for his pains. A few days later another new motet marked the birthday of Grand Duke Cosimo, and in September Alessandro's opera *Flavio Cuniberto* was given in Prince Ferdinando's private theatre at Pratolino.

Domenico presumably participated in all this music-making in one way or another. His cantata *Ninfe belle e voi pastori* was composed at Leghorn, not far away, and could therefore belong to this period, though its style suggests a somewhat later date of composition. But if, as seems likely, Alessandro hoped that Ferdinando would offer him and his son permanent employment at Florence, he was disappointed and was to remain so, although he continued to provide a new opera for Pratolino each year until 1706. The prince was certainly not blind (or deaf) to the Scarlattis' exceptional genius, and quite likely he would have been delighted to have them in his employ; but he was still financially dependent on his father, Cosimo III, who made no secret of his lack of interest in music and his total distrust of musicians – 'reputati gente di cattiva fama', as he once described them.

According to Kirkpatrick (p. 16) Domenico Scarlatti 'seems to have returned [to Naples] within the period of his leave, in other words by November 1702', while his father 'was apparently unwilling to return there' and 'accepted a patently inferior position in Rome'. However, the correspondence between Alessandro and Prince Ferdinando, which has been published since Kirkpatrick wrote those words, suggests otherwise.[6] On 24 November 1702 the composer informed his patron that he had arrived in Rome 'in good health, with that part of my family which came with me'; and on the 16th of the following month he again wrote to Ferdinando, mentioning that he was setting out for Naples the next day. Possibly Domenico had preceded him there, but it seems just as likely that they travelled together, having overstayed their leave by just over a month – a not uncommon occurrence among musicians at the time if the experience of Bach and Handel is anything to go by. Whatever the case, Alessandro did not remain long in Naples. By the end of April 1703 he had returned to Rome, and in December he accepted the post of vice-*maestro di cappella* at Santa Maria Maggiore, in which capacity he assisted the same Antonio Foggia whom he had succeeded at San Gerolamo della Carità twenty years earlier. During the next few years he composed mainly oratorios, church music and chamber cantatas; the only opportunities for theatrical composition were provided by the annual opera performances of Prince Ferdinando at Pratolino.

The reasons for Alessandro's leaving Naples in 1703 are commonly said to have been his financial difficulties (in 1699 he had complained that his salary as *maestro* was in arrears) and the unstable political situation in consequence of the War of the Spanish Succession. Probably both these factors influenced his decision, but if they were the only reasons they would not explain why he allowed Domenico to remain there. Quite possibly Alessandro left Naples with the hope that his son might succeed him as the viceroy's *maestro di cappella*. Francesco Provenzale had been reinstated in 1688, but only as *maestro di camera*, with the task of substituting for the organist Tommaso Pagano during periods of absence or illness. Provenzale was in any case seventy-six years old in 1702, and quite possibly in poor health himself; he could not hope automatically to succeed to the senior post. Francesco Mancini, organist at one of the Neapolitan conservatories, had been called upon to provide the music for two new operas, *Ariovisto* and *Lucio Silla*, during the 1702–3 season at the Teatro San Bartolomeo; he was no doubt given his chance because of Alessandro Scarlatti's failure to return to Naples in time. But for the 1703–4 season Domenico seems to have assumed his father's mantle. The eighteen-year-old musician probably made his début as an opera composer with *L'Ottavia ristituita al trono* and *Il Giustino*, and he also carried out the necessary *rifacimenti* (adaptations) to a Venetian import, *L'Irene*, by Carlo Francesco Pallarolo, first produced in 1695. For the first time in his life Domenico was living and working independently of his father.

It would be pleasant to think that Domenico Scarlatti was chosen as composer for the 1703–4 opera season solely on his merits, or even because of what was expected of him as the son of Alessandro. But the choice probably had more to do with the appointment of Nicola Barbapiccola as impresario of the San Bartolomeo theatre for that season. In 1699 Barbapiccola, a Neapolitan shipowner and a widower, had become the second husband of Domenico's aunt, Anna Maria.[7] Eleven years before this, in 1688, his other aunt, Melchiorra, had married Nicola Pagano, a 'scheming double bass player', as Roberto Pagano calls him,[8] who was also closely involved in opera at Naples. The productions of 1703–4 at the San Bartolomeo were very much a family affair, involving Domenico, who composed or arranged the music, three of his uncles (Nicola Barbapiccola, the impresario; Nicola Pagano, playing the double bass; and Tommaso, who sang tenor) and his younger brother, Giuseppe, who painted the sets. From his comparative isolation in Rome, Alessandro must have observed the activities of his Neapolitan kinsmen with satisfaction, even if the political situation there caused him concern. But, if he hoped that Domenico would succeed him as *maestro di cappella* in Naples, he was again to be disappointed.

Francesco Pacheco de Acuña, Duke of Ascalona and Marquis of Villena, had succeeded Medinaceli as viceroy in February 1702. He evidently continued to hope that Alessandro would return to Naples as *maestro di cappella*, and it was not until December 1703 that a public competition was held to choose his successor. The four competitors, Cristoforo Caresana, Francesco Mancini, Domenico Sarro and Gaetano Veneziano had each to compose a setting of the mass.

Domenico Scarlatti, for some reason, did not compete and Veneziano was adjudged the winner, but it was not until 25 October 1704, after the death of Provenzale, that he was appointed to the post, at a salary of 30 ducats a month. Two months later Sarro was made vice-*maestro*, and at the same time Mancini, Giovanni Veneziano (Gaetano's son) and Domenico Scarlatti were appointed organists. In Scarlatti's case this merely confirmed an appointment he already held, but at the same time he was deprived of the honorarium he had until then received as a chamber musician and his salary was reduced to a mere 6 ducats a month.

There was clearly no reason now for Alessandro to allow his most gifted son to remain in Naples, and it was not long before Domenico resigned his post and joined his father in Rome. Opportunities for advancement there, however, proved to be even more limited than in Naples, and in May 1705 Alessandro sought to secure a post for him in Venice, sending him there in the company of the famous castrato Nicolo Grimaldi, known as 'Nicolino' or 'Nicolini'. They travelled by way of Florence, and possibly hopes were still cherished of finding a suitable post there, for Domenico left with a letter of warm recommendation from his father to Prince Ferdinando de' Medici:

Your Royal Highness,
My son Domenico humbly brings himself, and my heart with him, to the feet of Your Royal Highness, acknowledging the deep respect and most humble obedience we owe to you.

I have forced him to leave Naples where, although there was room for his talent, it was not a talent for that place. I am now sending him from Rome, since Rome has no roof to shelter music, which lives here like a beggar. This son of mine is an eagle whose wings are grown; he should not stay idle in the nest, and I must not hinder his flight.

As the Neapolitan singer Nicolino happens to be travelling from here to Venice, I have determined to send my son with him; and accompanied only by his own ability (which has greatly advanced since he was able to be with me and to share the honour of serving Your Royal Highness personally three years ago), he leaves, like a wanderer, to take whatever opportunities present themselves to make his name; there is none to be expected here in Rome.

I should like him, before he proceeds on his journey to seek his fortune, to appear before Your Royal Highness in order to receive and carry out your most highly esteemed commands, as his and my greatest and most exalted lord, kindest patron and benefactor. It is to my own glory, honour and advantage, as well as to his, that the world should know us as Your Royal Highness's most humble servants.

This thought is a consolation to me and makes me hope for the best possible outcome from my son's pilgrimage, that, having commended him to Divine Providence and Protection as the supreme source of all goodness, I immediately then make my most humble entreaties for the high and most powerful patronage of Your Royal Highness at whose feet I place him, just as I, with the deepest respect and obedience, submit myself for all my life as Your Royal Highness's most humble, devoted and obliged servant,

Rome, 30 May 1705   Alessandro Scarlatti[9]

VENETIAN SOJOURN (1705–7)

Domenico and Nicolino reached Florence early in June 1705 and were received by Prince Ferdinando, who replied to Alessandro Scarlatti's letter in the following terms:

Florence, 8 June 1705

Your son Domenico has truly such a wealth of talent and spirit as to be able to secure his fortune anywhere, but especially in Venice, where ability meets with every esteem and favour.

He came to see me on his way to that city, and gave me your letter full of understandable concern for your son's advancement; whither I, who also regard him most benevolently, sent him, bearing a letter from me to the noble Sig. Alvise Morosini. I shall be delighted if my recommendation bears fruit, and hope you will give me occasion to employ my good offices often to the benefit of you and your family, to whom, finally, I wish Heaven may grant ever greater contentment.[10]

Two days before this letter was written, Domenico had left Florence for Venice with Prince Ferdinando's letter of introduction to Alvise Morosini:

Florence, 6 June 1705

The young Domenico Scarlatti, son of Alessandro, the celebrated composer, following in the footsteps of his gifted parent in that profession – and arousing every expectation, both in view of the excellent guidance he has had from his father and on account of his own great ability – desires to make his talent known and to find for himself a satisfactory position in that city to which he is now travelling, and where his ability should meet with better acceptance and favour. Therefore I, wishing you both [well] in the liveliest possible way – and also desirous of assisting his father, who has served me well on many occasions and earned more than my ordinary gratitude and benevolence – warmly recommend him to Your Honour's kindness, since I could not hope to find in Venice more benign and effective support for him than your protection, motivated as you are by a noble instinct to favour subjects of talent and merit with your most beneficial influence.

Whatever service Your Honour may be so good as to do for this young man, and also on my behalf, will place me in ever greater debt to your kindness and earn my cordial gratitude; meanwhile I . . . pray that Heaven may grant you full and true happiness.[11]

Prince Ferdinando was right to describe Venice as a city where a young and talented musician might expect to make his mark. Even more than in Rome and Naples, there existed there opportunities for employment and for promotion to positions of high prestige in the musical world. Venice was one of Europe's richest trading centres, its merchants supporting an elected legislature, headed by the Doge, and a hereditary nobility whose traditional love of music and the arts permeated the whole life of the city. Gifts and endowments provided funds for the four famous *ospedali* which provided deprived girls and young ladies with an education and upbringing. The *ospedali* also meant employment for many Venetian musicians, who taught the girls to sing and to play musical instruments, often to a very high standard indeed. The composer Giovanni Legrenzi had taught at the Ospedale dei Mendicanti from about 1671 to 1681, and Antonio Vivaldi's first appointment at the Ospedale della Pietà was made not long before Domenico Scarlatti's arrival in the city. Religious services at the *ospedali* were looked upon as social and musical occasions, and as one of the city's most popular tourist attractions.

For many ambitious musicians (including Legrenzi) a post at one of the *ospedali* was seen as a stepping-stone to a more prestigious appointment at the basilica of St Mark. It was not until the mid-sixteenth century that St Mark's had achieved any particular distinction for its music, largely through the efforts of the Netherlander, Adrian Willaert, who was *maestro di cappella* there from 1527 until his death in 1562. Although its importance began to decline again after Monteverdi's period in office there (1613–43), it continued throughout the seventeenth century to be served by some notable *maestri*, including Francesco Cavalli and Legrenzi. By 1700 the prestige of the post was no longer matched by the salary it commanded, and it was often filled by musicians of little distinction. The incumbent in 1705, when Domenico Scarlatti arrived, was Antonio Biffi; he supplemented his income from St Mark's by acting as choirmaster at the Ospedale dei Mendicanti.

While church music at St Mark's was on the decline, secular music, especially opera, continued to flourish in the city. Ever since the opening there of the first public opera house, the Teatro San Cassiano, in 1637, Venice had led the rest of Italy and Europe in the scenic and musical development of opera, and in the early years of the eighteenth century it had not yet yielded its supremacy in *opera seria* to Naples. As both Alessandro Scarlatti and Handel were soon to show, Venice was still an important centre for an opera composer to study his craft and to prove himself in front of the most knowledgeable (if not the most impartial) of opera audiences. In 1705 opera was to be seen in at least four houses built and supported by aristocratic Venetian families, and Domenico could have been present at performances of works by such composers as Albinoni, Giovanni Bononcini, Caldara, Gasparini, Lotti and Pollarolo. Vivaldi had not by then entered on his career as an opera composer.

A great deal of the music-making that went on in Venice, as in Rome and elsewhere, was initiated privately in 'academies' and in the palaces of the nobility. A particular feature of the Most Serene Republic, and one which contributed a great deal to its character and independence, was the presence there of gifted *nobili dilettanti*, represented in musical society by such important figures as Tomaso Giovanni Albinoni and the Marcello brothers, Alessandro and Benedetto. Most Venetian noblemen, however, were content to support music merely as patrons, and this seems to have been the role of Alvise Morosini, to whom Prince Ferdinando had so warmly recommended Domenico Scarlatti. Morosini was presumably a member of the old and illustrious patrician family that in its heyday produced four doges, two cardinals and no fewer than twenty-six procurators of St Mark's. His reply to Prince Ferdinando was courteous and respectful, but not exactly encouraging:

Royal Highness,
    Your Royal Highness increases my devotion by your revered commands in favour of Sig. Domenico Scarlatti, in assisting whom to the best of my poor ability I shall make myself worthy of your valued attention.
    I render most humble thanks to Your Royal Highness for being so kind as to exercise with me that authority which you possess. I shall not neglect, for my part, to study every means of serving you.
    Hoping for further opportunities to make known my respect for you, I take pride in being Your Royal Highness's most humble, devoted and truly obliged,

Venice, 27 June 1705   Alvise Morosini[12]

What exactly Morosini was able to do for Domenico we do not know. In fact, we cannot even be certain how long the young composer remained in Venice; archival sources are silent about his activities and whereabouts until January 1708, by which time he had returned to Rome, and no corroboration has yet been found for Marc Pincherle's statement that Scarlatti was employed as a teacher at one of the Venetian *ospedali*.[13] Certain late eighteenth-century sources indicate, however, that he remained in Venice long enough to become acquainted with two musicians who, in different ways, were to have some influence on his later career as a keyboard player and composer. One of these was Francesco Gasparini, who only a few years earlier, in June 1701, had been appointed *maestro di coro* at the Ospedale della Pietà. According to the English historian Charles Burney, Alessandro Scarlatti 'had so high an opinion of Francesco Gasparini, then a composer and a harpsichord master of great eminence at Rome, that he placed his son, Domenico, while a youth to study under him in that city'.[14] The veracity of Burney's statement has been questioned. There is no further evidence to support it, and Domenico Scarlatti can have spent very little time in Rome before 1701, by which time Gasparini had settled in Venice. It is nevertheless by no means impossible that he did study with Gasparini in one or other of the two cities, more probably Venice. Alessandro was certainly on good terms with Gasparini, as is indicated by the friendly exchange of cantatas which took place in 1712, when they both produced settings of the same text, *Andate, o miei sospiri*. Domenico would surely have lost no time in seeking out Gasparini in Venice, whether as his former teacher or as his father's friend, and we may be certain that Gasparini would have introduced the young Scarlatti to Vivaldi, who had joined the Pietà as violin master at the same time as Gasparini. At the San Cassiano theatre Domenico might have attended no fewer than five new operas by Gasparini between October 1705 and December 1707, and during these years Gasparini was also setting down his ideas on figured bass accompaniment in an important and widely read book, *L'armonico pratico al cimbalo* (Venice, 1708). Some of the precepts it contains, particularly on the employment of the acciaccatura, probably influenced Scarlatti's later keyboard style.

The most important of the musicians Scarlatti met in Venice was his exact contemporary, George Frideric Handel. Handel arrived in the republic in November 1707 and remained there until February 1708.[15] The circumstances of his first meeting with Scarlatti were recalled in a much-quoted passage by Handel's biographer, John Mainwaring: 'Venice was his [Handel's] next resort. He was first discovered there at a Masquerade, while he was playing on a harpsichord in his visor. Scarlatti happened to be there, and affirmed that it could be no one but the famous Saxon, or the devil.'[16] While Mainwaring was probably correct in placing the meeting in Venice, there seem to be no grounds for later suppositions that both composers had been present when Alessandro Scarlatti's opera *Il Mitridate Eupatore* was performed at the Teatro San Giovanni Grisostomo some months earlier. Alessandro had left Rome for Venice towards the end of 1706. In January 1707 he composed a new oratorio there, *Cain, ovvero Il primo omicidio*, for performance during Lent, and the Carnival season saw the production of two new operas, *Il Mitridate Eupatore* and *Il trionfo della libertà*. Domenico was no doubt at hand to assist his father in preparing all these works, and may even have taken part in their performance; but Handel was at this time in Rome, and so could not have heard them. Both the operas were a flop, and it is unlikely therefore that either of them was revived in Venice after Handel's arrival later in the year.

The lack of success, amounting to hostility, that Alessandro Scarlatti's operas met with in Venice should not be attributed to the quality of the music or to the seriousness of the librettos (by Girolamo Frigimelica Roberti), but rather to the composer's behaviour towards the theatre management, which the xenophobic Venetians found arrogant and condescending. No doubt disappointed by his reception in a city where he may have been hoping to find an opening for himself, Alessandro left for Urbino and spent about six months there with his eldest son, Pietro, who held the post of *maestro di cappella* at the cathedral.

On 18 April 1707 Alessandro Scarlatti wrote from Urbino to Prince Ferdinando de' Medici, expressing as forcefully as possible within the social and epistolary conventions of the time his concern at not being in a position to support himself and his 'numerosa famiglia':

> Exalted, royal and true Signore, I must acquaint you with my present condition which, while freeing me from the duties of service at present and leaving me my own master (although exposed to the uncertain providence of humankind), is insufficient to support the heavy burden of a large family who, though possessing every ability, are deprived of the support that would enable them to exercise their gifts to their own benefit, whether because of the difficult times we live in or their own lack of good fortune (the two nearly always go together), or because of the circumstances of my own fate [*o sia per costituzione del mio particolare ascendente*].
> I do not blush, therefore – indeed, I take pride and count myself fortunate in this – that I throw myself at the feet of Your Royal Highness,

as my guardian angel and the perennial fount from which I have so often received the precious water of many exalted and merciful favours. . . .[17]

This letter, to which Ferdinando responded only with bland hopes that Heaven would be kind to the composer and his family, suggests that Domenico had found no position for himself in Venice; Pietro, too, was soon to be called back from Urbino to Naples by his autocratic father. The north Italian cities seem to have proved unlucky for the whole Scarlatti family, and Domenico apparently found no opportunity at Venice to further the operatic career he had embarked on in Naples. In fact, the only work of his that can definitely be dated to his Venetian sojourn is the chamber cantata *Ah sei troppo infelice* (July 1705). Its title is perhaps only too appropriate to Scarlatti's fortunes at this time.

ROME (1708–19)

The answer to Alessandro's prayers (although not the one he would most have wished for) came on 5 June 1707, less than two months after his despairing letter to Prince Ferdinando. Antonio Foggia, *maestro di cappella* at the basilica of Santa Maria Maggiore, had died a few days earlier, and once again Scarlatti was invited to step into that musician's shoes. He had, of course, been titular vice-*maestro* for some three and a half years, but had spent very little of his time at the basilica; in offering him the senior post the church authorities were presumably following the wishes of Cardinal Ottoboni. Their offer was conveyed by letter to Scarlatti in Urbino. He accepted somewhat reluctantly, it seems, requesting a postponement on the grounds of ill-health and the hot summer weather. Roberto Pagano observes drily that summer must have lasted longer than usual in 1707, since Scarlatti did not take up his post until December![18] However, given his prolonged stay in Urbino and the fact that only a couple of chamber cantatas can be assigned to these months, it seems not impossible that he was in fact in poor health, or perhaps suffering from depression after his Venetian experience.

As *maestro* of the Basilica Liberiana Scarlatti had at his command an organist, Tommaso Bernardo Gaffi, and fifteen regular singers (five sopranos, two altos, four tenors and four basses). For special feasts these forces were augmented by about twenty additional singers and instrumentalists, the latter including string players and three extra organists. The Roman scholar, Eleonora Simi Bonini, has been able to show that, on some occasions at least during 1708, these super-numerary musicians included none other than Domenico Scarlatti.[19]

Domenico's return from Venice is thereby advanced to January 1708 at the latest, for on the 23rd of that month he directed the second choir in the special 'messa di Spagna' for the feast of St Ildefonso. His further involvement with music at the basilica is confirmed by Dr Simi Bonini's discovery in its archives of four pieces of church music by him. These are discussed in Chapter 6 (see pp. 115–16).

The presence of Domenico Scarlatti at Santa Maria Maggiore further illustrates how tightly Alessandro continued to control his son's activities and how solicitously he mapped out his career. He had sent him to Venice as a young eagle whose flight should not be hindered, but when that flight was temporarily halted he took to treating him again like a homing pigeon. Only the afore-mentioned meeting with Handel 'at a Masquerade' persuades us that Domenico did not leave Venice with his father after the latter's ignominious defeat at the hands of the Venetian opera public. A second encounter with Handel, if it in fact occurred, may now be presumed to have taken place in 1708 or, less probably, in the early months of 1709, before Handel left Rome for Siena. This was the famous musical contest organized by Cardinal Ottoboni at one of his Monday evening soirées. The source of all subsequent accounts is that of Mainwaring, who tells how, at the Palazzo della Cancelleria, Handel

> became known to Dominico Scarlatti, now living in Spain, and author of the celebrated lessons. As he was an exquisite player on the harpsichord, the Cardinal was resolved to bring him and Handel together for a trial of skill. The issue of the trial on the harpsichord has been differently reported. It has been said that some gave the preference to Scarlatti. However, when they came to the Organ there was not the least pretence for doubting to which of them it belonged. Scarlatti himself declared the superiority of his antagonist, and owned ingenuously, that till he had heard him upon this instrument, he had no conception of its powers. So greatly was he struck with his peculiar method of playing, that he followed him all over Italy, and was never so happy as when he was with him.[20]

Contests such as this one were a feature of eighteenth-century musical society, but they did not always reach such an amicable conclusion. Only a few years after the contest between Handel and Scarlatti, their famous contemporary, J. S. Bach, was engaged at Dresden in a similar 'trial of skill' with the French organist and harpsichord player, Louis Marchand, which resulted in the igno-minious retreat of the Frenchman before the contest had even started. According to Mainwaring, Handel and Scarlatti formed a lifelong respect for each other:

Handel often used to speak of this person [Scarlatti] with great satisfaction; and indeed there was reason for it; for besides his great talents as an artist, he had the sweetest temper and the genteelest behaviour. On the other hand, it was mentioned but lately by the two Plas [José Pla and his brother Juan Baptist] (the famous Haut-bois) who came from Madrid, that Scarlatti, as oft as he was admired for his great execution, would mention Handel, and cross himself in token of veneration.[21]

Handel was by no means the only composer with whom Domenico would come into contact at Ottoboni's palace during these years. The cardinal's munificence and his great love of music attracted numerous players, singers and composers to his household, and he kept a permanent *cappella* at the head of which Arcangelo Corelli served as violinist, composer and orchestral director from 1690 until his death in 1713. In 1706 Corelli was admitted, along with Bernardo Pasquini and Alessandro Scarlatti, to membership of the literary society founded by Queen Christina of Sweden and continued in her memory as the Arcadian Academy. The relevance of Pasquini to the formation of Domenico Scarlatti's keyboard style has often been explored, though the tradition that would have Scarlatti as a formal pupil of Pasquini is not verifiable. Corelli would seem to be a much less likely influence on the young composer, and yet there are few more Corellian pages, outside Corelli's own music, than the instrumental introduction to Scarlatti's cantata *Care pupille belle* (written, however, on an earlier Roman visit).

Alessandro Scarlatti seems to have found the duties of a church musician less congenial than composing cantatas for Arcadian patrons. On 4 November 1708 the chapter of Santa Maria Maggiore met to consider a request from him for four months' leave of absence in order to compose and direct operas at Naples. Whether or not Scarlatti, at the age of forty-eight, was motivated by the desire for a tranquil old age, as Roberto Pagano has suggested,[22] it seems certain that he had his eye once again on an opening for Domenico, whom he proposed as a substitute during his absence. Not surprisingly, in view of Alessandro's reputation at Santa Maria Maggiore and the forthcoming important festivals of Christmas and St Ildefonso, the request was rejected. It was only at the insistence of Cardinal Ottoboni that the chapter agreed to allow Scarlatti any period of leave, and then only for one week during the following Lent, his stipend to be withheld against his prompt return!

Meanwhile, in Naples the Austrian army had accomplished what the Macchia conspiracy had failed to achieve five years earlier and brought to an end over two hundred years of Spanish rule. The new

Austrian viceroy, Wierich Philipp Lorenz, Count of Daun, naturally made many changes, including some important ones in the musical establishment at court. Veneziano was replaced as *maestro di cappella* by the astute Mancini, who had celebrated the Austrian victory with a *Te Deum* in Aversa Cathedral. Mancini's appointment did not last long, however, for in December 1708 a new viceroy, Cardinal Vincenzo Grimani, provided Alessandro Scarlatti with the opportunity he needed to leave Rome by inviting him to resume his former post at the head of the Naples *cappella*. At the same time Mancini was demoted to first organist and vice-*maestro*, with the duty of standing in for Scarlatti during periods of absence or illness and with the prospect of succeeding him eventually. Except for another brief period in Rome (1718–21), Scarlatti was to remain at Naples for the rest of his life, and Mancini duly succeeded him as *maestro di cappella* in 1725.

It is curious to observe how consistently Alessandro failed to secure the position he would have liked for his son. It is almost as though others recognized better than he did where Domenico's real future lay. At Santa Maria Maggiore Alessandro's lack of commitment may also have weighed against the appointment of another Scarlatti, and by April 1709 a replacement had been found in Pompeo Cannicciari, who since 1694 had been *maestro di cappella* at Santo Spirito.

Domenico Scarlatti was thus left in Rome without, for the moment, any regular employment. There was no doubt the occasional commission from his father's Roman patrons, and there were soon to be more frequent ones from Queen Maria Casimira, but it seems likely that Domenico also found openings outside Rome at this time, even if he did not follow Handel all over Italy, as Mainwaring would have us believe. A note on the sole surviving copy of the cantata *Ninfe belle e voi pastori* indicates that he was in Leghorn at some time or other, and Charles Burney's well-known account of Scarlatti's first meeting with Roseingrave suggests that he returned to Venice on at least one occasion after 1708.

The English organist and composer, Thomas Roseingrave, was the son of Daniel Roseingrave, organist from 1698 at Christ Church Cathedral and St Patrick's Cathedral, Dublin. In 1709 Thomas, then aged twenty-one, was granted a sum of money by the dean and chapter of St Patrick's in order to help him to study abroad. The relevant entry in the Chapter Book reads:

14th Dec. 1709
Then also ordered by the said Dean and Chapter that (whereas Thomas Rossingrave sonn of Daniell Rossingrave the present Organist of the said

Cathedrall being minded to travel beyonnd Seas to Improve himselfe in the art of Musick and that hereafter he may be usefull and servicable to the said Cathedrall &c) tenne Guinneas be by the proctor of the said Œconomy given him as a giuft from the said Œconomy towards bearing his Charges.

Obviously Roseingrave could not have made Scarlatti's acquaintance before 1710, and yet Burney's account of their first meeting points clearly to Venice as its location:

Being arrived at Venice in his way to Rome, as he himself told me, [Thomas Roseingrave] was invited, as a stranger and a virtuoso, to an academia at the house of a nobleman, where, among others, he was requested to sit down to the harpsichord and favour the company with a toccata, as a specimen *della sua virtù*. And, says he, 'finding myself rather better in courage and finger than usual, I exerted myself, my dear friend, and fancied, by the applause I received, that my performance had made some impression on the company.' After a cantata had been sung by a scholar of Fr. Gasparini, who was there to accompany her, a grave young man dressed in black and in a black wig, who had stood in one corner of the room, very quiet and attentive while Roseingrave played, being asked to sit down to the harpsichord, when he began to play, Rosy said, he thought ten hundred d—ls had been at the instrument; he never had heard such passages of execution and effect before. The performance so far surpassed his own, and every degree of perfection to which he thought it possible he should ever arrive, that, if he had been in sight of any instrument with which to have done the deed, he should have cut off his own fingers. Upon enquiring the name of this extraordinary performer, he was told that it was Domenico Scarlatti, son of the celebrated Cavalier Alessandro Scarlatti. Roseingrave declared he did not touch an instrument himself for a month; after this rencontre, however, he became very intimate with the young Scarlatti, followed him to Rome and Naples, and hardly ever quitted him while he remained in Italy. . . .[23]

'A grave young man dressed in black and in a black wig, very quiet and attentive': this is the only physical description we have of Domenico Scarlatti at this time of his life. It accords ill with the mental picture we form of the composer from the colourful and mercurial harpsichord music of his later years, but if Domenico resembled his father at all (and there is reason to believe that he did) then some idea of his appearance may be gained from the striking portrait of Alessandro as a young man by Nicola Vaccaro, often reproduced in the Scarlatti literature. The impression that Domenico made on young Roseingrave, his junior by three years, was profound and lasting; from 1718, at least, Roseingrave was active in making Scarlatti's music known in England and Ireland.

Mention has already been made of the elder Scarlatti's membership of the Arcadian Academy at Rome. Music played an important part in the academy's activities, but it was not usual to elect musicians to membership, and Domenico Scarlatti never achieved that distinction. Neither did Handel, although he was admitted as a guest to some of the meetings. Cardinal Ottoboni was a member, of course, and so was the person who became Domenico's principal patron in Rome, Queen Maria Casimira of Poland.

Maria Casimira was born in France, the daughter of Captain Henri de la Grange d'Arquien, in 1641. At an early age she became a maid of honour to Queen Maria Luisa Gonzaga of Poland. She grew into a young lady of exquisite beauty, with regular features, a mass of black hair and, as Kazimierz Waliszewski put it, a slender figure 'adorned . . . with treasures of grace and voluptuous beauty'.[24] In March 1657, at the age of sixteen, she married the Prince of Zamosc, by whom she bore three children; none of them survived infancy. Her husband turned out to be a foul-mouthed inebriate; Waliszewski describes him as 'a boor, who had naught of the prince about him save the name, stank of wine like an innkeeper, swore like a trooper, and did not even seem capable of appreciating the charms of which he was the happy possessor'.[25] It was not long before husband and wife became estranged. The prince's death in April 1665 was hastened by an excess of drink and an almost continual round of debauchery. Shortly afterwards, probably even before he was buried, Maria was married in secret to Jan Sobieski, the Polish hero and patriot who became King of Poland in 1674.

When Sobieski died in 1696 and Maria failed to engineer the succession in a way that would have ensured her a measure of power and prestige in Poland, she went into voluntary exile in Rome. She took with her the two younger sons of her second marriage, the princes Constantine and Alexander, and also Princess Marie Casimire, the rejected daughter of her eldest son, Prince James. Already in Rome was Maria Casimira's father, who had been raised to the purple some time before. Shortly after the queen's arrival she was honoured with a 'corona' of sonnets at a meeting of the Arcadian Academy, and admitted to membership with the anagrammatical pastoral name of Amirisca Telea. Almost inevitably, she was soon being compared with the academy's founder, Queen Christina of Sweden, whose memory was still green among the Roman aristocracy and *literati*. Despite her pretensions and the extravagance of her patronage, Maria Casimira was found to lack the wit and intelligence of her predecessor, and the Roman versifiers were not slow to point the comparison:

Nacqui da un gallo semplice gallina,
Vissi tra li pollastri, e fui reggina,
Venni a Roma, éristiana e non Cristina.[26]

[A simple young hen, daughter of a Frenchman,
she lived among the cockerels and was queen;
she came to Rome, a Christian and not a Christina.]

Maria Casimira nevertheless played an important role in a great deal of the music-making that went on in Rome during the fifteen years she spent there. For the first three years she lived as a guest of Don Livio Odescalchi, and then, in 1702, she took a lease on the Zuccari palace in the Piazza della Trinità de' Monti, named after the painter Federico Zuccaro, for whom it was built in the sixteenth century. In the same year she petitioned Pope Clement XI for permission to give 'des comedies honeste par ma troupe de comediens que ie guage'[27] and in 1704 she sought approval for the addition of a small private theatre to the palace. Permission was at first refused, and it was not until 1708 that she was able to have the theatre constructed. She then sought the approval of the pope in order to employ two 'cantarines' as servants 'pour chanter apressant [à présent] dans les ceresnade [sérénades] et lhiver dans des operas que iay dessin de fayre pour divertir ma petite fille et moi ancore quelque fois des continuels chagrins dont ie suis acablée'.[28] For the running of her theatre and the overall organization of the performances given there Maria Casimira turned to the French-born Count Giacomo d'Alibert, the most experienced entrepreneur in Roman theatrical circles. D'Alibert had served Queen Christina as secretary and diplomat and had taken charge of her theatrical interests, and it was he who had instigated and supervised the building of the Teatro Tordinona. He ended his days, at the age of eighty-seven, in the service of Queen Maria Casimira. To design the sets for her operas, and possibly also to design the theatre itself, the queen employed one of the finest architects and stage designers in Italy, Filippo Juvarra, whose best-known work in Rome was done for Cardinal Ottoboni. Unlike Ottoboni, Maria Casimira harboured no literary ambitions (and in any case probably mastered no language except her highly idiosyncratic French), and her librettos were written by the poet Carlo Sigismondo Capece (or Capeci), whom she appointed as her 'segretario delle lettere italiane e latine' in 1704.

No list exists of the musicians in Queen Maria Casimira's permanent employment. Probably the most distinguished instrumentalist at the Palazzo Zuccari was the lutenist Silvius Leopold Weiss, who was in the service of Prince Alexander Sobieski from 1708 until the prince's death in 1714. Weiss would certainly have known Domenico Scarlatti at this time, and probably played in some of the works Scarlatti wrote for performance at the palace. The queen evidently turned at first to various composers in Rome, probably including Alessandro Scarlatti, to provide music for her court and theatre. During August and September 1703 several serenatas were performed on a bridge over the Strada Felice which connected the Palazzo Zuccari to her residential quarters opposite; in 1704, and again in 1707, short dramatic works by Capece, with music by unidentified composers, served as introductions to ballets put on for the entertainment of Princess Marie, the queen's granddaughter; in July 1708 a serenata by Capece, *Le corone amorose*, in honour of Prince Alexander was set by a certain Anastasio Lingua; and on 12 September an oratorio, *La vittoria della fede*, with words again by Capece, was performed at the Palazzo Zuccari in celebration of Jan Sobieski's part in the victory over the Turks near Vienna in 1683. The music for *La vittoria della fede*, which in many respects is more a serenata than an oratorio, has often been attributed to Alessandro Scarlatti, but no firm evidence for the attribution appears to exist.[29] Considerable doubt attaches also to Alessandro's authorship of the music for a revised version of Capece's earlier drama, *Il figlio delle selve*.[30] According to an entry in Valesio's diary this was performed in January 1709,[31] but neither the printed libretto nor any other source mentions Alessandro Scarlatti as the composer. A score in the library of the Paris Conservatoire (now housed in the Bibliothèque Nationale), with an added attribution to 'Sig[re] Alessandro Scarlatti', has nothing to do either with this performance or with Alessandro Scarlatti, who by 17 January was back in Naples preparing his opera *Il Teodosio* for Vincenzo Grimani. After this, responsibility for the music at the Palazzo Zuccari passed mainly to Domenico.

Some time in 1709, possibly during Lent but more probably in September as the annual act of remembrance for Jan Sobieski, the oratorio *La conversione di Clodoveo*, with music by Domenico Scarlatti, was performed at the Palazzo Zuccari. This was apparently Scarlatti's first commission for Queen Maria Casimira, and on 27 January 1710 there followed the opera *La Silvia*. The music of both works is lost. In the libretto of the opera *L'Orlando* the following year (1711) Scarlatti is named for the first time as the queen's *maestro di cappella*, and he went on to complete at least seven operas for Maria Casimira, all to librettos by Capece. Unfortunately only one of these, *Tetide in Sciro* (1712) has survived complete in its original form, though one other, *Amor d'un ombra e gelosia d'un aura*, is extant in the version produced in London in 1720 as *Narciso*.

Amor d'un ombra e gelosia d'un aura was produced on 15 January 1714 and was Scarlatti's last opera for Queen Maria Casimira. In June that year, her fortune considerably reduced by the demands of her dependants and by her own extravagances, she left Rome, accompanied by her granddaughter and possibly also by Capece. Her son Alexander was to have accompanied her, too, but affairs called him back to Rome at the last moment and he was seized by a fever and died there on 19 November. The queen had by then returned to her native France, where she ended her days as a grace-and-favour tenant of Louis XV's châteaux on the Loire. She died at Blois on 30 January 1715. In April 1713, during a period of illness, she had signed her will, and in a codicil dated 23 February 1714 she bequeathed a pension of 400 French *livres* a year to Capece and 300 a year to his daughter, who had served her as a chambermaid.[32] Scarlatti was nowhere mentioned.

Domenico Scarlatti's activities as a composer of opera and oratorio for Queen Casimira in Rome ran parallel at this time to those of his father at the viceregal court in Naples. When Alessandro visited Rome during Carnival in 1712 to supervise the production of his *Il Ciro* for Cardinal Ottoboni at the Palazzo della Cancelleria he no doubt took a fatherly interest in Domenico's *Tetide in Sciro*, which was given at the Palazzo Zuccari at about the same time. After the Polish queen's departure in 1714, however, Domenico needed to look for fresh areas of activity and new sources of income.

One of these he had already found as assistant *maestro* of the Cappella Giulia at St Peter's, to which he was appointed on 19 November 1713. The Cappella Giulia, one of the most prestigious musical establishments in Rome, took its name from Pope Julius II, who founded it in 1513. During the succeeding two centuries its *maestri di cappella* had included such famous musicians as Palestrina, Virgilio Mazzocchi and Orazio Benevoli. From 1694 to 1713 the *maestro* was Paolo Lorenzani, and he was succeeded by Tommaso Baj at the same time that Scarlatti was appointed assistant *maestro*. Baj had by then served the *cappella* for at least forty-three years, first as an alto and then as a tenor; his compositions for the choir included a *Miserere* as regularly performed and almost as famous as Allegri's. When Baj died on 22 December 1714, after only just over a year as *maestro*, Scarlatti immediately succeeded to the senior post, with a salary of 15 scudi a month. He retained the post until he left Rome in 1719, and it was during these years and those that followed in Lisbon that most of his extant church music was composed.

Scarlatti's appointment at the Vatican did not occupy all his time, and shortly after Maria Casimira's departure he found a new outlet for his talents as a composer of secular music in the service of the Portuguese ambassador to the Vatican, Rodrigo Anes de Sá e Menses, sixth Count of Penaguião and third Marques de Fontes. In the libretto of an *applauso genetliaco* to celebrate the birth of the infante of Portugal on 6 June 1714 Scarlatti is named as '*maestro di cappella* to his excellency'. He thus made his first contacts with a royal court which only a few years later he was to serve more directly. Scarlatti presumably composed other things for the Marques de Fontes, and these perhaps included operas, for the sets of which the marquis called on the services of Filippo Juvarra; but, if so, no trace of them remains.

By 1715, in which year he celebrated his thirtieth birthday, Scarlatti must have achieved a position of some eminence as an opera composer, and this was recognized when he was invited to write an opera for performance at the Teatro Capranica, the main theatre in Rome for public opera. The libretto chosen was the *Ambleto* of Zeno and Pariati that Scarlatti's teacher, Gasparini, had first set in Venice in 1705. Scarlatti may have known Gasparini's setting, although he arrived in Venice just too late to attend a performance of the opera there. A study of the two works might have thrown up some interesting points of stylistic comparison, but, while Gasparini's score survives complete in the Deutsche Staatsbibliothek in East Berlin, all that remains now of Scarlatti's is a single aria from Act 1.

The loss of such works as this is greatly to be lamented, but just as frustrating to the biographer is the paucity of archival material relevant to Scarlatti's life and career. Of the relatively few documents that have so far been located, the one to which we now turn is certainly one of the most fascinating, and at the same time the most puzzling. What little we know about Alessandro Scarlatti's personality suggests that he acted towards his offspring with both fatherly concern and all the authority of a Sicilian paterfamilias, a role which he had been forced to assume at a very early age. He forbade his daughters Flaminia and Cristina to sing on the stage – understandably, in view of the reputation as *puttane commedianti* earned by his sisters Anna Maria and Melchiorra – and his eldest son, Pietro, testified that in 1708 (when he was nearly thirty) his father had ordered him to leave Urbino, where he was *maestro di cappella* at the cathedral, and to join him in Naples. Despite the good intentions expressed in the letter of 30 May 1705 to Prince Ferdinando (see p. 11), Alessandro had continued to exert his authority over Domenico to such an extent that at the age of thirty-one the latter had to seek the support of lawyers to gain his independence. On 28 January 1717 Cavaliere Alessandro Scarlatti (he had been knighted by Pope Clement XI in 1715 or 1716) appeared before the Neapolitan notary, Giovanni Tufarelli, and reluctantly granted Domenico emancipation 'from all paternal control and obligations', so that he might have 'full and complete ability, authority and power to do each and every lawful act, to be able to contract business or cancel it, to make a will, to make gifts or bequests, to buy and sell', etc.

Ulisse Prota-Giurleo, who was the first to quote the entire document in its original legal dog-Latin,[33] suggested that Domenico may have sought his emancipation in this way in order to emigrate or to get married. Roberto Pagano has gone still further. His most recent book (1985), which combines careful scholarship with a profound knowledge of Sicilian history and culture and an unrivalled awareness of the Sicilian 'psyche', is a fascinating study of the relationship that existed between the two greatest Scarlattis. He sees Alessandro as a kind of stern puppeteer, manipulating Domenico in the steps he wants him to take and standing in the way of any inclination his Pinocchio may have to take to another stage altogether.

As far as the Tufarelli document is concerned, Pagano was able to establish that the rights of the father, the *patria potestas*, extended in law until his death. There was no 'coming of age' as we understand it today. How, therefore, Domenico was able to challenge his father's rights in law is not clear, but evidently they were considered anachronistic even in the eighteenth century. More interesting would be the reason for Domenico's 'bid for freedom', if we knew it for certain. Pagano interprets it as a wish to contract a marriage to which Alessandro was opposed. As further evidence he cites the *Historia de familia y mi última voluntad* drawn up in 1912 by Domenico's great-great-grandson, Carlos Scarlatti, and quoted by Kirkpatrick (p. 359). Carlos's account of Domenico contains the following statements: 'Casó à disgusto de su padre. . . . Nació en Nápoles y su esposa Dª Catalina Gentili Rosetti en Roma (segundas nupcias)' ('He married in opposition to his father's wishes. . . . He was born in Naples and his wife, Donna Catalina Gentili Rosetti, in Rome (second marriage)'). While other parts of Carlos's account are patently inaccurate, there seems to be no reason for his having invented a marriage to which Alessandro was opposed. (The marriage to Maria Catarina Gentili took place, as we shall see, after Alessandro's death.) On the other hand, other official documents, including Domenico's will, refer explicitly to Maria Catarina as his first wife. We must assume that any previous marriage was short-lived, and that it produced no surviving children.

Whatever lies behind the Tufarelli document, it clearly points to a period of strained relations between father and son. Whether the legal settlement improved these or made them even more embittered is impossible to say. Alessandro's application for leave to visit Rome, granted by the viceroy, Count Daun, on 21 September 1717, may be interpreted as a move to reassert his authority or as a gesture towards reconciliation. Quite possibly it was neither of these, though Domenico may well have felt himself artistically threatened when his father's new opera, *Telemaco*, to a libretto by Capece, was given at the Teatro Capranica during the following Carnival season. Domenico's *Berenice, regina d'Egitto*, on which he collaborated with Nicola Porpora, was also staged at the Capranica during Carnival. It was Domenico's last work for the stage,[34] and it may also have been the occasion of his first meeting with the castrato Farinelli, who was one of Porpora's pupils at the time. Farinelli was later to be Domenico's most important colleague at the Spanish court in Madrid.

Alessandro was due to return to Naples at the end of the Carnival season in 1718, but he probably stayed on in Rome during Lent, if that is when his oratorio *La vergine addolorata* was performed. A revival of another oratorio, *San Filippo Neri*, at the oratory of the Padri Girolamini in Naples may have required his presence in May, and the following November his comedy, *Il trionfo dell'onore*, enjoyed a spectacular success at the Teatro dei Fiorentini. But the elder Scarlatti's ties with the Eternal City remained close. Another new opera, *Marco Attilio Regolo*, was seen at the Capranica theatre during Carnival 1719, and Alessandro's activities in Rome extended also to the composition of church music. Domenico may well have felt his position threatened, or at least that he needed to distance himself from the presence and influence of his famous father.

An entry by Francesco Colignani in the diary of St Peter's records his departure for England in September 1719.

PALERMO (1719–22)

'Sig. Scarlatti, *maestro di cappella* of St Peter's, having left for England, Sig. Ottavio Pitoni, who was at St John Lateran, was appointed *maestro*.' Colignani's diary entry has given rise to a great deal of speculation concerning Scarlatti's movements after August 1719, when he resigned his post at St Peter's. Most older writers assumed that he did in fact go to England, but attempts to support this with evidence of his activities there have invariably rested on a confusion with either Francesco Scarlatti, who spent some time in London, or another relative, Giuseppe Scarlatti, whose music was performed there.

There is no reason, though, to suppose that Colignani invented the story of Scarlatti's departure for England. The motivation to get away from Italy, to complete the emancipation he had won from his father and to seek out a new environment for his work was certainly present, and the intention of going to England could well have been in his mind. Quite possibly Domenico had made plans to join his uncle Francesco, who had been living in London since at least April 1719, or he may have been invited to the English capital by his friend Thomas Roseingrave, who was promoting his music there. Handel, his friend from earlier times, had settled in London, and quite possibly the newly formed Royal Academy, of which Handel was the musical director, had already earmarked for revival the opera *Amor d'un ombra e gelosia d'un aura* that Scarlatti had composed for Queen Maria Casimira in 1714. This was produced under the title of *Narciso* at the King's Theatre in the Haymarket on 30 May 1720, but since Roseingrave composed new items for it and apparently directed the performance it might seem unlikely that Scarlatti's participation was expected.

In the absence of any firm evidence for a London sojourn, Kirkpatrick (p. 70) was of the opinion that Scarlatti proceeded straight from Rome to Lisbon, and that he was among 'the new and excellent musicians which His Majesty . . . had brought from Rome' referred to in connection with the performance of a serenata at the royal palace on 24 September 1719. This suggestion seems the more plausible when we recall that in 1719 Scarlatti's colleague Filippo Juvarra also went to Lisbon, where he worked for King John V on the recommendation of the Marques de Fontes.[35] But the most recent findings suggest that when Scarlatti resigned from St Peter's he went neither to London nor to Lisbon, but to his father's native Palermo, in Sicily. In 1975 Roberto Pagano reported his discovery of a reference to a 'Dominicus Scarlatti' among the musicians newly admitted to the Unione di Santa Cecilia in Palermo on 16 April 1720. In the absence of any other member of the Scarlatti family who might fit this appellation, Pagano could claim to have uncovered, at last, Domenico's bolthole.

The possibility of a London visit some time between September 1719 and April 1720 still remains, however, and it seems unlikely to have taken place without Scarlatti being involved in some way or other with the forthcoming production of *Narciso* at the King's Theatre. Kirkpatrick (p. 66) could find 'no record of any participation by Domenico in this performance, either in conducting or in composing new music'. Scarlatti's presence in the Sicilian capital does

effectively rule out the possibility of his participation in the performance, but perhaps the American scholar did not look far enough (or
close enough) for evidence of Scarlatti's involvement in the quite
extensive revisions made to the score.

As will be shown in the next chapter, there are at least five items
among the *Songs in the New Opera call'd Narcissus* published by Walsh
in 1720 which are not attributed to Roseingrave and which could not
have formed part of the original Roman version of the opera. If
Roseingrave had been responsible for them, he would surely have
acknowledged his authorship, as he did that of four other items in
Walsh's publication. He could, of course, have received new music by
post from Scarlatti in Italy, but there is also the possibility that
Scarlatti was himself in London working on the revisions for the
revival, and that he was forced to leave at short notice before the work
was completed. Jane Clark, accepting Colignani's diary entry at its
face value, has suggested that the composer may have left London
because he did not wish to enter into competition with Handel's
Radamisto, which was included in the same Royal Academy season.[36]
This is, of course, possible, but it seems unlikely when one considers
the cordial relations that existed between the two composers in Italy,
and also the fact that *Radamisto* was not performed until Scarlatti had
been in Palermo for ten days at least.

Another possible explanation for Scarlatti's sudden departure
(highly conjectural, as is the whole London visit) may be suggested.
Presuming that a weakness for gambling, of which we have later
evidence, was already ingrained in Scarlatti's make-up at the age of
thirty-five, he would have found ample opportunity to indulge it in
London. Gambling of all kinds was rife in every stratum of society.
Card games and dice were popular pastimes at the coffee-houses and
gentlemen's clubs, and enormous fortunes were made and lost there.
Charles James Fox is reported to have lost £140,000 by the age of
twenty-five.[37] If Scarlatti had fallen into such company with similar
ill-luck, he may well have been forced to flee the country, in which
case his uncle Francesco, who had spent some years in Palermo, might
have suggested a place where he would be unlikely to be found, and
where he might find employment.

The main argument against the likelihood of a visit to England is the
absence of any contemporary reference to it, despite the fairly
comprehensive coverage of musical events in the London press. But
although a London newspaper advertisement of 1718 had billed the
composer as 'the famous Domenico Scarlatti' there is no reason to
suppose that he was at all well known in England at the time. The

'famous Scarlatti' in 1720 was Alessandro and, after their experience of the third-rate Francesco, Londoners may well have felt cool towards any other unknown bearing that illustrious name. Even after the publication of the *Essercizi* in 1738/9, which is when the English cult of Domenico Scarlatti really begins, there would be little reason to recall a brief visit made by the composer some twenty years earlier. Possibly the place to search for evidence of Scarlatti's supposed visit is not among musical archives and newspapers, but in the ancient records (if they exist) of Boodle's and White's. . . .

Roberto Pagano's subsequent researches have established Scarlatti's continued presence in Palermo until 9 December 1722 at least. While they solve one of the mysteries surrounding the composer, they raise other questions to which it is not possible at present to suggest answers. Why, if in fact he did not go to England, should Scarlatti have resigned a prestigious post in Rome for uncertain prospects in Sicily? Was his 'flight' in some way connected with a marriage to which his father was opposed? When, exactly, did the offer of employment come from the Portuguese court? One reason for the Sicilian visit lies, perhaps, in the revival of Alessandro Scarlatti's operas at the Teatro di Santa Cecilia in Palermo, but the true extent of Domenico's involvement in this and other activities in Sicily remains to be determined. Certainly he was already writing music for the Portuguese court in Lisbon. The serenata *Contesa delle stagioni* was performed at the royal palace on 7 September 1720 in celebration of the birthday of Queen Marianna, and another serenata, or 'cantata pastorale', was given three months later on the king's nameday (27 December, the feast of St John the Evangelist). The performance of a further unidentified serenata by 'Abbade Scarlatti' on 7 September 1722 was reported in the pages of the *Gazeta de Lisboa*.

These performances have usually, and understandably, been taken as indicating Domenico Scarlatti's presence at the Lisbon court from about mid-1720. But Roberto Pagano's researches suggest that Scarlatti merely forwarded the music to Lisbon, leaving it to others (in some cases his Sicilian friend, Baron Emanuele d'Astorga) to supervise their rehearsal and performance. Possibly Scarlatti reached Lisbon by 27 December 1722, when his *Le nozze di Baco e d'Arianna* was performed,[38] but perhaps he delayed his departure from Sicily until 1723 or 1724. That he was in the Portuguese capital by the latter date is evident from a remark in J. J. Quantz's autobiography, published in F. W. Marpurg's *Historisch-kritische Beyträge*, i (Berlin, 1754), to the effect that in Rome between June 1724 and January 1725 he had met 'Mimo Scarlatti . . . who was then in the Portuguese service'.

TWO *Operas and Oratorios*

When Domenico Scarlatti left Rome in 1719 his reputation as a composer rested mainly on his operas. It must have seemed as natural a step for him to compose his first opera at Naples in 1703 as it was for J. S. Bach to take up his first organist's post at Arnstadt in the same year. Alessandro Scarlatti was by then established as the leading opera composer in Italy and, largely as a result of his efforts, Naples was beginning to rival Venice as the principal arbiter of operatic taste and the main exporter of operatic styles. The prospects for a young and talented composer with several family connections in the theatre must have seemed encouraging, and if Domenico's first operatic ventures attracted less attention than his father's had a quarter of a century earlier, they were certainly not failures. If Domenico had remained in Italy, and perhaps succeeded Alessandro as *maestro di cappella* at the Naples court in 1725, he would probably be remembered now among the generation of Neapolitan opera composers that included Leo, Vinci and Hasse. A group of chamber cantatas composed later, perhaps in Spain (see pp. 196–202), gives some indication of the way his musical style might have developed in works for the lyric stage.

As it turned out, Scarlatti's operatic career apparently came to an end in 1718, when his last work for the theatre, *Berenice, regina d'Egitto*, was produced in Rome. His operatic activity before then falls into three periods: for the 1703–4 season he composed and adapted operas for the public theatre at Naples; between 1710 and 1714 came the seven operas he wrote for Queen Maria Casimira's private theatre; and in 1715 he was once again engaged in public opera, this time in Rome. During these sixteen years he is known to have written at least a dozen operas. Of these only two full-length ones and a one-act comic piece have survived complete; the others are known only from printed librettos or, at best, from aria collections, some of them quite substantial. Until recently the existence of the three complete scores was unknown, and it is by no means impossible that further discoveries will eventually enable us to form a truer estimate of Domenico Scarlatti's achievements as an opera composer than we can with our present knowledge.

Those achievements can only be understood and appreciated in the context of the operatic traditions and conventions within which Scarlatti worked. With the opening of the first public opera house, the Teatro San Cassiano, in 1637, Venice soon became the leading centre for opera in Italy, a position it continued to enjoy throughout the seventeenth century. During this time the musical constituents of opera, which in the early part of the century had been quite fluid, crystallized into a mostly unbroken succession of recitative (in which the text dominated the music) and arias or duets (in which the reverse was the case). By the end of the century the ternary or so-called 'da capo' structure (A–B–A) had virtually supplanted all others for the arias, and stereotyped structural formulae similarly invaded the recitative and the orchestral introduction, or 'sinfonia', with which the opera began. It took a composer of exceptional musical gifts and dramatic insight to turn the rigid conventions of *opera seria* to his advantage, and few composers (perhaps only Handel and to some extent Alessandro Scarlatti) succeeded in realizing the potentialities of music for effective characterization and the making of dramatic points. Music's role in the theatre was generally regarded as a decorative one: it served as a vehicle for great singing and as a means of intensifying the emotional impact of a particular situation. On this level Domenico Scarlatti's music, to judge from what remains of it, succeeded as well as that of most other opera composers of his day.

Opera had first been introduced to Neapolitan audiences in October 1650 by a travelling troup, the Febiarmonici, who brought with them a production of *La Didone* by the Venetian composer Francesco Cavalli.[1] It was performed on a makeshift stage erected in a pavilion in the grounds of the royal palace. The new form apparently appealed to viceregal taste and to the Neapolitan temperament, and two further operas by Cavalli, *Il Giasone* and *L'Egisto*, were seen at the royal palace the following year, when Monteverdi's last opera, *L'incoronazione di Poppea*, was also performed. Notwithstanding the important contributions of Francesco Provenzale to the Neapolitan stage during the ensuing decades, Venetian works continued to form the staple diet for Neapolitan opera audiences, both at the royal palace and at the Teatro San Bartolomeo, until the 1680s. With the appointment of Nicola Serino as impresario at the San Bartolomeo in 1693 there began a move to stem the Venetian tide, but even while Serino, Alessandro Scarlatti and others were taking steps to establish a 'Neapolitan school' in opera, Venetian works continued to be revived at Naples, usually with substitute or additional arias and other *rifacimenti* by a native composer (often Alessandro Scarlatti himself) to adapt them to Neapolitan tastes.

L'OTTAVIA RISTITUITA AL TRONO

As far as we know, Domenico Scarlatti's first chance to prove himself as an opera composer came in 1703, after his father had left Naples for Rome. With his uncle, Nicola Barbapiccola, installed as impresario of the Teatro San Bartolomeo in place of Nicola Serino, Domenico was invited to compose or arrange the music for three operas during the 1703–4 season. Responsibility for the librettos was placed in the hands of the Abbate Giulio Convo, and the first result of their collaboration was *L'Ottavia ristituita al trono*, a melodrama in the usual three acts performed at the Teatro San Bartolomeo, probably in November 1703.

Convo's libretto is based on the *Agrippina minore* (Venice, 1647) of Francesco Capocio Cuccino Berardi and forms a sequel to the events recounted in Busenello's libretto for Monteverdi's *L'incoronazione di Poppea*. The dethroned empress, Octavia, comes out of exile in Campania disguised as a shepherdess and returns to Rome, where Nero has installed Poppaea in her place. After threats of revolution by the people, Nero is forced to reinstate Octavia as both empress and consort, but not until various intrigues and deceptions have been played out which involve also Florus, Prince of Epirus, and his wife Rosilda – characters invented by Convo to help spin the thread from which the frail fabric of Baroque opera plots was woven. Octavia's nurse, Belisa, and Florus's servant, Dorillo, provide the comic element present in nearly all Neapolitan operas of the period. Dacius, a tribune in love with Poppaea, is given a few lines of recitative in Act 1, but these have been cancelled in ink in the copy of the libretto in the library of the Conservatorio di Musica Santa Cecilia, Rome; the character makes no further appearance in the opera and was probably dropped before the first performance.

A manuscript volume of thirty-four vocal items from *L'Ottavia* in the library of the Naples conservatory includes most of the arias and duets for the five principal characters, but none of the comic scenes. Nero was sung by an alto, the other serious characters by sopranos (although two arias, one for Florus and the other for Octavia, are unaccountably notated in the alto clef). The first five arias in the manuscript appear in the same order as they do at the beginning of the opera, but there is no discernible pattern behind the ordering of the remaining items. Six of the thirty-four pieces are accompanied only by basso continuo. The instrumentation of the others is not indicated, but presumably string instruments are intended, with solo or unison violins (often with violas) playing most of the obbligatos. The full string band in four parts with continuo is used only half a dozen times, mostly for Nero's arias. Nowhere in the manuscript is there any indication that Scarlatti made use of the trumpets and drums which, according to the libretto, are heard at the beginning of the opera, although wind instruments may have doubled the strings in some places. Poppaea's aria 'Tra l'erbette, tra piante' in Act 2 Scene viii is provided with a staff marked 'Eco', into which are written two phrases echoing the vocal couplet:

> e dai spechi
> rispondono gli echi
> [and from the caverns the echoes reply].

Presumably the echoes were sung from behind the scenes, but there are no words in the 'eco' part.

All the surviving arias from *L'Ottavia* are in da capo form and many are undeniably 'rather conventional, and suffer from flat and square-cut rhythms and phrase structure' (Kirkpatrick, p. 17), but some of them are not without character and charm. Octavia's aria 'Così mi lasci, oh Dio' in Act 2 is noteworthy for its accompaniment of strings in octaves, and both the duets are fine pieces, especially that for Poppaea and Nero in Act 2. That the music's melodic and harmonic style is derivative is not at all surprising in a composer who had only just reached his eighteenth birthday. The influence of Domenico's father is everywhere to be found, not least in a predilection for minor inflections towards the end of a major-key aria, and Nero's continuo aria 'Mi vuoi dar pene' (Act 2 Scene iv) shows, too, how well Domenico could emulate his father's manner of expressing pathetic sentiments by means of languishing arias in 12/8 metre, with telling use of 'Neapolitan' inflections involving the flattened supertonic (example 1).

IL GIUSTINO

Although no one would suspect it on the evidence of the music that remains, Scarlatti's other two operas for Naples were on a much more lavish and ambitious scale than the first one had been. *Il Giustino* was put on at the royal palace to celebrate the twentieth birthday of King Philip V of Spain, which fell on 19 December 1703. Presumably the

Example 1

opera was first performed on that date and repeated shortly afterwards at the Teatro San Bartolomeo.

Some idea of the opera's spectacle is suggested by the list of sets and machines for which Scarlatti's brother Giuseppe was responsible. Act 1 includes a transformation scene in which a country vista, with a plough drawn by oxen, is changed into a palace and then back again, in full view of the audience and without any interruption in the action; Act 2 opens on a rocky shore from which can be seen a naval armada, almost shipwrecked; and in Act 3 the side of a hill is struck by a thunderbolt to reveal a vast sepulchral cavern lit by torches. The action also called for two monsters, a ship, and a wheel on which the goddess Fortune is seen to turn.

Il Giustino is set in Constantinople in the early sixth century. Anastasius I has been made emperor by Ariadne, the widow of Zeno, but his monophysitic religious views provoke a rebellion led by Vitalianus, and this is crushed only when Justin (later Emperor Justin I), who has advanced from humble peasant stock to a high military rank, is given command of the army to oppose him. Entangled with the fortunes of these historical characters are others invented by the librettist, and there is also the usual comic pair (the man's part sung by a woman, the woman's by a man). The unusually large cast is listed in the printed libretto as follows:

Giustino	?
Arianna	Maria Angelica Bracci
Anastasio	Angiola Magliani
Vitaliano	Nicola Sarrubbo
Andronico [brother of Vitaliano]	Giovanni Rapaccioli
Eufemia [sister of Anastasio]	Vittoria Nascimbene
Amantio [Anastasio's general]	Tommaso Scarlatti
Polimante [Anastasio's captain]	Anna Maria Catarina Visconti
Gelidia [Andronico's nurse]	?
Brillo [Eufemia's servant]	Pompilia Jozzi

Nicola Barbapiccola had obviously been at some pains to assemble as strong a team as possible for the 1703–4 season. Few of the singers named above are remembered now, but they came mainly from outside Naples. Bracci and Magliani (soprano and contralto respectively) were in the service of Cardinal de' Medici in Rome, while Jozzi and Rapaccioli, a pupil of Gasparini and Alessandro Scarlatti, were employed by the Prince of Montesarchio. Nascimbene and Visconti were from the court of Mantua. The castrato role of Justin and the part of Gelidia were both sung by unnamed members of the royal chapel at Naples, and the tenor Tommaso Scarlatti was, of course, Domenico's uncle. Not listed in the libretto are the supernatural 'characters', Fortuna and the ghost of Vitalianus's father – small parts presumably taken by supernumerary singers or by members of the main cast.

The libretto of *Il Giustino* was originally written by Nicolò Beregan in 1683 for Giovanni Legrenzi, and the opera was first performed that year at the Teatro San Salvatore in Venice. It was evidently one of Legrenzi's most successful operas. In 1684 it was repeated at the royal palace in Naples, and by 1697 it had been seen also in Milan, Genoa, Bologna, Lucca, Rome, Verona, Modena and Vicenza. During this time the libretto had undergone several revisions, and for the 1703 performances in Naples it was almost completely rewritten. The author responsible for this is not named, but it is evident from his preface that it was Giulio Convo, the librettist of *L'Ottavia ristituita al trono*:

Dear Reader,
   If you find the present melodrama to be somewhat different from what it was originally, do not take this as an affront to its first most distinguished author, but rather as an attempt by the most feeble writer of Ottavia restituita al soglio [*sic*] to adapt the drama to the circumstances of the time. *Vivi Felice.*
   Be advised, however, that the arias indicated by the sign § *are by the original author.*

This last sentence (the italics are in the original) was taken by Claudio Sartori[2] and Kirkpatrick (p. 413) to mean that the eight arias or duets marked ' § ' in the libretto were sung to music by Legrenzi. However, there is no reason to suppose that Convo's phrase, 'the original author' ('[il] primo Autore'), refers to anyone other than the first librettist, Nicolò Beregan; indeed, one of the marked items, the duet 'E un foco amore', is included as Scarlatti's in a selection of twenty-four items from the opera contained in the same Naples manuscript that transmits the arias and duets from *L'Ottavia* mentioned above. In all probability the libretto was set completely afresh by Scarlatti.

Partly as a result of the unusually large cast, the arias and duets in *Il Giustino* are considerably more numerous than in the previous opera, totalling over sixty in all. This, together with the ubiquitous use of the

Example 2   *Il Giustino*, Act 3 Scene xi

da capo structure, means that there can be little room for lyrical expansiveness within each section of an aria, and many appear therefore short-winded and inconsequential. To judge from the music that has survived, the arias of *Il Giustino* are on the whole inferior to those of the earlier opera, and once again some of the best music comes in the duets. In the last of these, 'Pietà. Son io crudele' (Act 3), Justin and Anastasius engage in one of those disputes between friends and colleagues which so often mark a change of fortune in operatic plots of the period. Scarlatti here makes a virtue out of necessity and sharpens the exchanges by breaking the music into short phrases in which even the time-signatures and accompaniment patterns are strongly contrasted (example 2).

L'IRENE

Scarlatti's last opera for Naples was *L'Irene*, produced at the Teatro San Bartolomeo during Carnival 1704. This was an extensive *rifacimento* of Carlo Francesco Pollarolo's opera written for Venice in 1695. It was probably chosen partly because of its suitability to the cast that had performed *Il Giustino*, and possibly also because some of Giuseppe Scarlatti's sets for that opera, notably the coastal scene with the naval armada, might be used again in *L'Irene*. The name of the stage designer is not mentioned in the printed libretto, which lists the cast as follows:

Memete	Angiola Magliani
Irene	Maria Angelica Bracci
Demetrio	?
Dejanira [Irene's sister]	Vittoria Nascimbene
Solimano [favourite of Memete]	Giovanni Rapaccioli
Hali [a vizir]	Tommaso Scarlatti
Alete [Dejanira's tutor]	?
Lesbia [lady-in-waiting to Irene]	Angiola Catarina Liuzzi
Dori [a young girl]	Pompilia Jozzi
Nuto [a gardener]	?

The only named singer who did not appear in *Il Giustino* was the soprano Angiola Catarina Liuzzi, known as 'La contessina'. Alete was sung by a tenor from Naples, and the roles of Demetrius (a soprano castrato) and Nuto were taken by singers from the Neapolitan royal chapel – perhaps the same who had sung Justin and Gelidia the previous year.

The original libretto of *L'Irene* was by the poet and architect

Girolamo Frigimelica Roberti. Like his other operatic texts it was written in five acts, but for the Naples revival it was recast in three acts, presumably by Giulio Convo. The plot, filled out with the customary intrigues and lightened by comic scenes in accordance with Neapolitan taste, concerns Sultan Mahomet II, who, after taking Constantinople, falls in love with Irene, the niece of the emperor Constantine and the promised wife of Demetrius. Faced with unrest in the army and among his counsellors, and finding Irene obedient but unyielding, Mahomet finally renounces his love and claims his final victory over himself.

Twenty-five arias and a duet from Pollarolo's setting were retained in the 1704 performance. Scarlatti contributed a further forty-eight arias and duets, and he presumably composed also an overture and the final *coro*, or ensemble. Altogether fifty-seven items from the opera are preserved in manuscript in the Naples conservatory library, written in the same hand that copied the arias from *L'Ottavia ristituita al trono* and *Il Giustino*. Of these fifty-seven items, thirty-two arias and one duet are by Scarlatti.

With fewer arias to compose than in *Il Giustino*, and possibly with more time at his disposal, Scarlatti was able to produce music which, as far as we can tell, is rather more interesting. Certainly the aria accompaniments are more varied than those which have survived from the two previous operas. One aria has a bright trumpet obbligato, another an agile part for solo cello. Alete's aria 'Perché sprezzar chi t'ama' in Act 1 is accompanied by strings in octaves, Demetrius's 'Per lei caro è ogni duolo' in Act 2 by cello and lute. Two continuo arias (one of them by Pollarolo) are marked 'Tutti li strom.^{ti} all'unis.^{no}', an indication perhaps that the instrumentation of these Naples operas was richer and more varied than the aria collections suggest. Scarlatti's arias in *L'Irene* are admirably varied but, as in the other two operas, there are few signs of any real and sustained inspiration. Pollarolo's setting of 'Piangete, occhi piangete' for Demetrius in Act 3 is perhaps the most memorable thing in the opera.

L'Irene was followed by a gap of six years in Scarlatti's activities as an opera composer. In the autumn of 1704 his father's place at Naples was filled by Gaetano Veneziano, and Nicola Serino took over again from Barbapiccola as impresario at the San Bartolomeo theatre. Any hopes that Domenico may have had of establishing himself as an opera composer at Naples had to be abandoned, and he seems to have taken no part either in the operatic life of Venice during his years in the republic. If he had, the xenophobic Venetian audiences might well have received him with the same hostility they showed towards his father in 1707. It was not, therefore, until he began to fulfil Queen Maria Casimira's commissions in Rome that further opportunities to engage in opera presented themselves.

The Queen of Poland's private theatre at the Palazzo Zuccari cannot have been a large one (no plans or drawings of it have survived), and it would certainly not have been equipped with the machinery that made possible the elaborate scene changes of Scarlatti's Naples operas. But with Count d'Alibert supervising the productions, Filippo Juvarra designing the sets and Carlo Sigismondo Capece providing the librettos, Maria Casimira had assembled a formidable operatic 'team', into which in 1709 she enlisted the services of Domenico Scarlatti.

LA CONVERSIONE DI CLODOVEO

Scarlatti wrote at least seven operas for Maria Casimira's domestic theatre, all of them to librettos by Capece. But the first proof he gave the queen of his abilities as a dramatic composer was in an oratorio, *La conversione di Clodoveo*, also to a libretto by Capece. This was heard at the Palazzo Zuccari in 1709, perhaps during Lent (the libretto does not specify the time of year) or perhaps as an act of homage to the queen's husband Jan Sobieski in September. Oratorios were frequently performed in the palaces of the Roman aristocracy, especially during Lent. As early as the 1650s some of Carissimi's oratorios had been given in Queen Christina's palace in Rome, and in 1708, only a year before *La conversione di Clodoveo*, Capece had written the libretto for another oratorio, Handel's *La Resurrezione*, which was given a sumptuous performance, with elaborate staging and an orchestra of about forty-five players, at the Palazzo Bonelli, the residence of the Marquis (later Prince) Ruspoli.[3] No one pretended that such occasions were anything but secular affairs, although they required papal approval. The prayers and sermons that occupied the interval between the two parts of an oratorio when it was performed in an oratory were on these occasions replaced by refreshment of a less spiritual kind: a German visitor, J. F. A. von Uffenbach, who attended one of Ruspoli's oratorio performances in 1715, mentioned 'liquors, ices, confectionery and coffee'. Sometimes oratorios were given in a manner unashamedly resembling a serenata performance. Francesco Valesio described a sumptuous open-air performance of Alessandro Scarlatti's oratorio *Il regno di Maria Vergine* which Corelli directed at Cardinal Ottoboni's palace in Rome on 23 August 1705:

Today Cardinal Ottoboni had a noble theatre, designed by Giovanni Francesco Pellegrini, erected in the courtyard of the [palace of the] Cancelleria in order to have sung there this evening an oratorio, the words of which are by the cardinal himself.

The theatre occupied the whole length of the courtyard opposite the main door. There extended from it a large platform of imitation marble on which rested a balustrade of gilded wood, at the ends of which were four statues made from similar material. Between the statues separating the two parts of this balustrade was placed a large harpsichord with finely gilt legs, and here the four singers were situated. The rest of the platform followed the line of the balustrade, which curved inwards somewhat on each side, and on it four large plinths supported four great transparent vases of imitation alabaster, from which shone numerous torches. At the level of the balustrade, from about the middle of the platform there rose, in an inward-facing semicircle, four steps, the faces of which were decorated with flower paintings. On these steps candelabras were placed at suitable intervals, each with three large torches and a stand on which the instrumentalists placed their music; they took the form of a globe with an iris and an eagle whose wings supported the said music-stands. The singers and players were seated on the same steps. In the centre, above the steps, was painted a view of twisting columns in a mossy green colour, supporting an ornamental banner on which could be seen the title of the oratorio: *Il regno di Maria Vergine*. This formed the highest extent of the theatre, there being placed there, instead of a framed painting of the Blessed Virgin [as had originally been intended], a tapestry showing Cardinal Ottoboni's coat-of-arms. Following the line of perspective in the painting, the outlines of other twisted columns were placed in the manner of a stage set. These were surmounted by heavy cornices and vases of flowers, and in the empty spaces at some distance behind them the most beautiful illuminated tapestries were hung.

From the centre of each arch in the courtyard hung a painted wooden chandelier with twelve [oil-] pans, festooned with red draperies; the arches above were similarly adorned. The parapet of the upper portico was hung with crimson velvet, and between each pair of columns were two torch-holders with lights that wonderfully illuminated the entire courtyard throughout the evening. Open carriages had been left without horses earlier in the day, and these were occupied by many ladies and notables who came to listen, the main door having been left open with free admittance to anyone, so that by the evening the courtyard held a huge throng. After the ringing of the bell at about two hours [after sunset] the music began, and this proved to be most beautiful, with the accompaniment of eighty instruments. Copious drinks were served at all the carriages, two bowls having been placed at each archway, and altogether eight casks were consumed.[4]

The distinction between an oratorio and a serenata was often a very narrow one in the early eighteenth century, and although *La conversione di Clodoveo* may not have been given such a costly and elaborate staging as *Il regno di Maria Vergine* it was obviously designed primarily to flatter the Polish queen, as is evident from Capece's fulsome dedication: 'No one could read the name of Maria Casimira without forming a perfect idea of the Christian zeal that reigned in Clotilda'. Ursula Kirkendale has detected a more specifically political message in the libretto.[5] After a treaty concluded on 15 January 1709 between Pope Clement XI and the Emperor Joseph I, the French ambassador had left Rome protesting that the Vatican was no longer the seat of the Church. Capece's francophile text may have been designed to demonstrate Maria Casimira's pro-Bourbon sympathies. This presupposes a Lenten performance, however, which is by no means certain.

Saint Clotilda (*c.* 474–545) was, like Maria Casimira, the wife of a brave warrior king, and for many years his widow. Hagiographical oratorio texts were much in vogue in the period. As Smither points out, they 'usually present the conflict between heavenly and worldly influences during the portrayal of the saint's early, sinful life; the saint at first rejects but eventually accepts the moral arguments of the representatives of heaven'.[6] This is essentially what happens in *La conversione di Clodoveo*, except that in this case it is not the saint who undergoes conversion but her husband, King Clovis of France. He is drawn to Christianity by Clotilda's example, after his belief in pagan gods has led to near-defeat on the battlefield. While the motive of self-interest in Clovis's conversion is hardly flattering to Jan Sobieski, the emphasis in the libretto is placed upon Clotilda's religious fortitude.

La conversione di Clodoveo is divided into the customary two parts, roughly equal in length (they each occupy eight pages in the printed libretto) and amounting in all to about five hundred lines of poetry. This was the upper limit for oratorio texts advised by Arcangelo Spagna in his *Discorso intorno a gl'oratori* (Rome, 1706), and Capece followed Spagna's precepts, too, in restricting the number of characters to five. Supporting Clovis is his army captain, Uberto (apparently not a historical character), while Clotilda's faith is reinforced by Remigius, Archbishop of Rheims. Towards the end of the oratorio an angel appears with the baptismal oil which, according to legend, was brought from heaven in a vase which was used at all subsequent coronations in Rheims Cathedral. The libretto at this point refers to 'celestial harmony' from 'voices in Paradise' but, as in most Italian oratorios of the period, there is no chorus.

Capece's libretto is entirely conventional in the way it treads an uneasy path between religiosity and dramatic truth. Despite its elegant verses, the main attraction of the work must have lain in the music, and it is a matter for regret that none of this survives, either from the first performance or from the revival of 1715, when the oratorio was performed at the Jesuit Seminary in Rome.

LA SILVIA

With the completion of her private theatre at the Palazzo Zuccari, Queen Maria Casimira apparently relinquished oratorio and turned to opera. The first outcome of the operatic collaboration between Capece and Domenico Scarlatti was *La Silvia*, produced at the palace on 27 January 1710, according to Cametti.[7] *La Silvia* is described in the libretto as a 'dramma pastorale', a type of opera well suited to a modest domestic theatre, since it normally called for fewer changes of scene and a smaller cast than the heroic type of opera. (Alessandro Scarlatti's early opera, *Gli equivoci nel sembiante*, also written for private performance, had been a pastoral of this type.)

The action of *La Silvia* is located in an idealized pastoral setting on the Argive plain in Greece, and, like Capece's libretto for *Il figlio delle selve* the previous year, the opera calls for no changes of scene at all. There are five characters. Silvia, the daughter of Alcone and Arezia (both dead), has been brought up as a boy (Silvio) so that she will inherit the status accorded to descendants, through the male line only, of the illustrious Alcide, whose memory is still revered among the shepherds. Her mother had instructed the nurse Garbina that when Silvia reached the age of fifteen a marriage should be arranged for her with the shepherd Mireno, Alcide's rightful heir. Silvia, however, has fallen in love with Garbina's son, Daliso, who, not realizing that Silvio is a girl, is smitten by the charms of the nymph Laurinda. Laurinda is loved also by Mireno and, to complicate matters further, is herself in love with the supposed Silvio. After numerous changes of fortune Silvia's true identity is revealed in the third act, leading to further complications which are resolved only when Mireno explains that it was he, and not Daliso, whom Garbina ransomed from pirates when they were both infants. He is in fact Daliso, while the supposed Daliso is Mireno, and therefore Alcide's lawful heir. The lovers are paired off as befits their true identities, and all join in a final *coro*: 'Love is not a cruel tyrant when he can change pain into pleasure'.

Despite its contrived dénouement Capece has produced a neat little pastoral comedy which offers the composer plenty of opportunities for the expression of varied, if stereotyped sentiments. The characters, insubstantial as they are, are well drawn, especially Silvia, torn between love and filial duty, Daliso, constant friend and worthy recipient of the shepherds' crown, and the nurse Garbina, with her strong vein of comedy. One wonders what Scarlatti made of the opportunities given him.

TOLOMEO ET ALESSANDRO

Not a note of Scarlatti's music for *La Silvia* remains, and in 1710 the opera was probably overshadowed by Cardinal Ottoboni's rival production at the Cancelleria during the same Carnival period. This was *Il Costantino pio*, with words by Ottoboni himself, music by Pallarolo and sets designed by Filippo Juvarra. The Queen of Poland and members of her court attended a performance on 21 February 1710 and were no doubt as impressed as the other spectators were by sets and machines more elaborate and astonishing than any previously seen on a private stage in Rome. The taste for simple unit sets in domestic theatres changed overnight, and Maria Casimira hastened to secure Juvarra's services for her own operatic ventures. Juvarra probably designed the sets for her next opera, *Tolomeo et Alessandro*, and he was certainly the architect for *L'Orlando* shortly afterwards.

Maria Casimira's theatre was never as well equipped with machinery as Ottoboni's at the Cancelleria. Celestial apparitions and rapid transformations are not included in Juvarra's designs for the Palazzo Zuccari, nor are they called for in Capece's librettos. *Tolomeo et Alessandro, ovvero La corona disprezzata*, produced on 19 January 1711, is set in Cyprus, and the action calls for few modifications to the outdoor landscape set specified in the prefatory pages to the printed libretto. The plot has its historical basis in events described by Justinus in the thirty-ninth book of his *Historiae Philippicae*, which Capece embroidered with the customary sub-plots and intrigues. In the *argomento* of the printed libretto he sketched the background to the action as follows:

> Banished by his mother Cleopatra, Ptolemy is living in Cyprus disguised as a simple shepherd under the name of Osmino. Seleuca, his wife, has been taken from him and sent by Cleopatra to Tryphon, the Syrian tyrant. Thought by everyone to have been drowned in a shipwreck, she has in fact survived and, knowing her husband to be in Cyprus, has gone to look for him there, disguised as a shepherdess with the name of Delia. Alexander was similarly sent by his mother to Cyprus with a powerful army to seize Ptolemy, but he secretly decides to spare his brother and restore to him the

crown. Araspe reigns in Cyprus, where he lives with his sister Elisa in a delightful villa on the coast. He has fallen in love with 'Delia' (in fact, Seleuca) and Elisa with 'Osmino' (Ptolemy). Finally, Dorisbe, daughter of Isauro, Prince of Tyre, who was once loved and then abandoned by Araspe, is also living there as a *finta giardiniera* known as Clori.

Except that Ptolemy, on the point of suicide, saves Alexander from drowning, and that Alexander then falls in love with Elisa, the first act hardly advances the plot beyond the situation presented in the *argomento* until, in the final two scenes, Seleuca discovers her husband and is about to recognize him when she is disturbed by the jealous Araspe. Eventually, of course, the various lovers' knots are disentangled and Alexander gives up his throne to his brother. Kirkpatrick, incidentally, was mistaken in suggesting that 'Capeci designed the text as a rather far-fetched compliment to Maria Casimira's son, Prince Alessandro Sobieski, who had quite naturally seen himself obliged to yield the throne of Poland to his elder brother' (pp. 50–1), since Poland did not then have a hereditary monarchy and Prince James had not become king. This is not to say that Prince Alessandro would not have been able to draw some moral from the libretto.

The overture and first act of *Tolomeo et Alessandro* survive in a manuscript copy which came to light in a bookshop in Rome in the 1940s. It was in the personal library of the Italian musicologist S. A. Luciani until his death in 1950, after which it passed into the possession of Arrigo Perrone of Milan. Apart from the racy overture, one of Scarlatti's best, what immediately strikes one on examining this score is the superior quality of the arias, especially when compared with those of the earlier Neapolitan operas. Kirkpatrick (p. 51) rightly praised the first two arias of Ptolemy, which, he said, 'are in a fine grand tragic style quite worthy of Juvarra's scenery'. He was more condescending towards the rest of the music, and yet Seleuca's 'È un grave martire' is a no less impressive aria in the tragic vein, with an unusually florid, even tortuous vocal line of an almost Bachian cast, while Ptolemy's 'Tiranni miei pensieri' is a fine example of a type of aria much associated with Scarlatti, in which sudden changes of tempo, dynamics, melodic material and accompanimental texture respond to contrasting moods and images in the text.

No less striking is the variety of expression between one aria and another, and this extends most creatively to the accompaniments as well. Seleuca's 'Non più stelle' is the only continuo aria (though it has a string ritornello), most of the others being accompanied by the full complement of strings, sometimes with flute and oboe as well. The

emphatic unison string phrases of 'Cielo ingiusto' effectively underline Ptolemy's protests against the cruel injustices of fate, and in Elisa's
'Addio direbbe il cor' the voice is doubled by an oboe and accompanied by violins in unison, the continuo instruments playing only in
the ritornellos.

It is not surprising, if the rest of the arias were as varied and
interesting as these, that *Tolomeo et Alessandro*, despite its relatively
modest staging, proved to be more successful than the other operas
staged at Rome during the Carnival season of 1711. Filippo Amadei's
Teodosio il giovane, produced at Ottoboni's theatre in early January,
was considered 'long and boring', with singers 'better suited to the
church than to the stage'; Caldara's music for *L'Anagilda, ovvero La
fede ne' tradimenti*, mounted in Prince Ruspoli's palace on 4 January,
was judged to be 'very fine', but the opera as a whole 'too
melancholy'; *L'Engelberta, o sia La forza dell'innocenza*, possibly a
revival of Francesco Mancini and Antonio Orefice's setting of 1709,
given at the Teatro Capranica on 14 January in a performance
dedicated to Maria Casimira's granddaughter, went 'very badly'
because 'the singers were no more than average and the orchestral
players worse still'. These contemporary opinions, expressed in the
avvisi di Roma now in Munich,[8] contrast with the following report
from the same source of the first performance of Scarlatti's *Tolomeo et
Alessandro*:

Rome 24 January 1711

On Monday evening [19 January] the Queen of Poland had her opera
performed for the first time at her residence at the Trinità de' Monti by
good singers, male and female; it was generally applauded as superior to all
the others.[9]

Crescimbeni described the performance of *Tolomeo et Alessandro* in
these words: 'the voices were pleasing, the acting distinguished, the
costumes most charming and worked with marvellous design, the
music very good indeed and the orchestra outstanding.'[10] Crescimbeni nowhere mentions Scarlatti by name, but it may well have been
the success of *Tolomeo et Alessandro* that persuaded Maria Casimira to
make the composer her *maestro di cappella*.

To judge by the number of documented revivals, *Tolomeo et
Alessandro* seems to have been one of the most successful of all
Scarlatti's operas, which makes the loss of Acts 2 and 3 even more
regrettable. Shortly after its performance at the Palazzo Zuccari it was
repeated for the members of the Arcadian Academy in a specially

constructed outdoor theatre. From a volume of verses issued to commemorate the occasion we learn that the part of Dorisbe was sung by Paola Alari and that of Seleuca by Maria Giusti, both of them 'cantarine' in Maria Casimira's service; the opera requires altogether four sopranos and two altos. In 1713 it was revived at Fermo, and the inclusion of the orchestral sinfonia in a volume of overtures from operas performed at Rome in 1724 indicates another revival, probably in the private theatre of the Portuguese ambassador, André de Melo e Castro.[11] Finally, a libretto exists also for a performance at Jesi, north-west of Fermo near Ancona, in 1727.

In 1728 Nicola Haym adapted Capece's libretto for Handel's *Tolomeo, Ré di Egitto*, produced at the King's Theatre in the Haymarket, London, on 30 April.

L'ORLANDO

It is evident from a report in the Munich *avvisi di Roma* that Cardinal Ottoboni and Prince Ruspoli had both planned to celebrate Carnival in 1711 with a serious opera followed a little later by a pastoral.[12] Ruspoli's second opera was *La costanza in amor vince l'inganno*, produced on 6 February with music by Antonio Caldara. The title and composer of Ottoboni's pastoral are not known. Maria Casimira followed suit with *L'Orlando ovvero La gelosa pazzia* by Capece and Scarlatti. The date of its première is likewise unknown, but a performance on Tuesday, 17 February, followed by a party at the Palazzo Zuccari, brought the Carnival season to an end. The event was reported in the *avvisi di Roma*:

> *Rome, 21 February 1711*
>
> On the final evening of Carnival operas and plays were performed in the usual theatres. After the opera at the residence of the Queen of Poland at the Trinità de' Monti festivities were held, beginning at six hours [after sunset], at which there were masquerades by sixty ladies. The princess, granddaughter of Her Majesty, danced and looked magnificent with the most beautiful jewels, and everyone danced until after thirteen hours on Wednesday morning.[13]

Ariosto's famous epic poem, *Orlando furioso* (Ferrara, 1516), served numerous Baroque composers, including Steffani, Vivaldi and Handel, as a source for opera plots, and long before that it had been plundered more frequently for madrigal texts. By 1711 it was so well known in Italy that Capece felt able to dispense with the usual *argomento* in the printed libretto of *L'Orlando* and instead merely explained to his readers that, in order to observe the Aristotelian unities of time and action, he had drawn on Matteo Maria Boiardo's earlier *Orlando innamorato* (Reggio, 1483) for one incident in the story: Orlando's wits are restored through the power of Angelica's magic ring and not, as in Ariosto, from the phial brought by Astolfo.

Capece took from Ariosto the story of the love between Zerbin, son of the King of Scotland, and Isabel, daughter of the King of Galicia, and wove into this the account of Orlando's madness on finding that the beautiful Angelica, Queen of Cathay, was enamoured of the African prince, Medoro. A sixth character, the shepherdess Dorinda, was introduced by Capece to act as a catalyst for the conventional twists and turns in the plot, which are finally resolved when Orlando, like Mahomet in *L'Irene* and innumerable heroes in other operas, renounces his love and yields the heroine to his rival. *L'Orlando* is, of course, a pastoral, and the moral of the final *coro* is identical with that of *La Silvia*: 'Who can say that love is folly, when it changes suffering to delight?'.

None of Scarlatti's music for *L'Orlando* has survived, and the only means we have now of judging the opera's effect is from Capece's libretto and some of Juvarra's sketches which were probably made for it. Mercedes Viale-Ferrero[14] has identified the following Juvarra designs as belonging to the 1711 production of *L'Orlando*:

London, Victoria and Albert Museum, Reg.4826: ff.6, 108 and 113; Turin, Biblioteca Nazionale, Riserva 59,4: f.86(3).

Handel in London received librettos of the 1711 versions of both *Tolomeo et Alessandro* and *L'Orlando*, perhaps from Thomas Roseingrave. He used them, extensively reworked, for operas produced at the King's Theatre in 1728 and 1733 respectively.

TETIDE IN SCIRO

Soon after Easter in 1711 Queen Maria Casimira was seeking permission from Pope Clement XI to put on another opera, using singers whom her eldest son James was to bring with him to Rome. Plans were still not complete at the beginning of May, as the following report in the *avvisi di Roma* at Munich makes clear:

Rome, 4 May 1711

The Queen of Poland and her son Prince Alexander Sobieski are preparing what is necessary to put on an opera in their domestic theatre at the Trinità de' Monti at the end of the present month, having engaged some fine singers, among them the famous Tilla [Maria Domenica Pini] who has already arrived, sent here by Prince James Sobieski, Her Majesty's eldest son. The prince was to have come here from Venice, but hearing of the death of the Emperor Joseph [on 17 April] he changed his mind and returned to his estates.[15]

It is not known whether this planned opera ever reached the stage in 1711, but we may presume that it had been composed by May and that the composer was Domenico Scarlatti. It may be not without significance that the libretto for the next opera at the Palazzo Zuccari that we know about, *Tetide in Sciro*, exists in two printed versions. They are identical except for the imprint on the title-page. In one version (an incomplete exemplar of which is in the Biblioteca Casanatense, Rome) this reads: 'In Roma, a spese di Antonio de' Rossi, e si vende dal medesimo alla Chiavica del Bufalo. 1712'. In the other version (British Library, shelfmark 905.l.4) we read simply: 'In Roma, Per Antonio de' Rossi alla Chiavica de Bufalo'; there is no date. Possibly the undated title-page was printed in anticipation of a performance in 1711 which did not take place.

According to Cametti,[16] *Tetide in Sciro* was first performed on 10 January 1712 (a Sunday), but Andrea Della Corte[17] dates the performance 16 January; neither writer quotes a source for his information. *Tetide in Sciro* is of particular interest as the only full-length opera by Scarlatti to have survived complete (or almost complete) in the form in which it was first heard. The full score, lacking only a few pages at the end of Act 2, was discovered in the minorite monastery of San Francesco della Vigna, Venice, by Terenzio Zardini, who prepared an edition for a concert performance given in October 1956. Zardini, a priest, had studied music in Verona and Venice, and was therefore able to recognize the importance of the Scarlatti manuscript, which would have been disposed of as waste paper were it not for his timely intervention. How the score found its way into the library of the monastery in the first place is something of a mystery. The present librarian, Padre Modesto-Giovanni Bortoli, has suggested (in correspondence with this author) that it may have been a gift to an eighteenth-century member of the order, Padre Carlo Lodoli, who enjoyed close contacts with the Venetian intelligentsia and was much in demand as a teacher among aristocratic and patrician families in the city.

The libretto of *Tetide in Sciro* is prefaced by the usual *argomento*, in which Capece summarized the Classical theme of the opera:

SYNOPSIS OF THE DRAMA

The story of how Ulysses discovered the love of Achilles for Deidameia, daughter of King Lycomedes of Scyros, is so well known that the reader needs no further assistance in following the events of this little opera, which is based on that legend. The only addition, made to enhance the attractiveness of the tale, is the character of Antiope, daughter of Theseus. According to Plutarch and other historians, Theseus was killed by Lycomedes, and so it is plausibly imagined that Antiope, formerly loved by Lycomedes and betrothed to him but angered because she believes him to be her father's murderer, has come to Scyros in the guise of a man, Filarte, to avenge herself and kill her lover. When she sees him again her anger is dissipated and her love rekindled, but in the meantime Lycomedes has fixed his affections on Arminda, one of Deidameia's handmaidens – in fact, Achilles dressed as a girl. Deidameia has been cut off from the world by Lycomedes, who fears she might be abducted by a hidden lover, as has been predicted. In order to add dignity to the character of Ulysses, it is further imagined that he comes to Scyros in search of Achilles not as a merchant, but as an ambassador from Agamemnon asking for Deidameia's hand in marriage to Orestes. This also allows more scope for the other events of the drama, which shall be enacted on stage.

The first act of the opera does not advance the plot beyond this *argomento*, although it does make it clear that Achilles has been detained on Scyros and dressed as a girl by his mother, Thetis, who knows that her son will die at Troy. In Act 2 Deidameia, coming across 'Filarte' asleep, falls in love with 'him'. Achilles chances to find them together, and then Ulysses, whose suspicions about Achilles's true identity are strengthened by 'Arminda''s demeanour. Deidameia is puzzled by 'Arminda''s strange reaction to her show of affection for 'Filarte', and Thetis attempts to explain it to her by pretending that 'Arminda' also loves 'Filarte' and is jealous of Deidameia. Deidameia innocently repeats this fiction to Lycomedes, whose discomfort at it is observed by Thetis. She assures him that she invented the story herself to divert Deidameia from 'a certain vain affection she had formed for Filarte'. Lycomedes, not convinced, asks for some sign of love from 'Arminda' as proof.

Act 3 opens in a wood within sight of the royal palace. Among the presents that Ulysses brings from Orestes to Deidameia is a sword which so arouses Achilles's interest that Ulysses is finally convinced in his suspicions. He provokes Achilles into confessing that he has disguised and hidden himself – but for reasons of love, not cowardice. Overheard by Achilles, Deidameia confesses her love to 'Filarte', but yields 'him' to 'Arminda'. Achilles, for his part, resolves to give up Deidameia to 'Filarte' and to leave for Troy, despite his mother's fears.

Thetis pleads in vain with Ulysses not to deprive her of her son. On a rocky shore Antiope confides in Deidameia. As they embrace, Lycomedes enters and, assuming the worst, orders that his daughter should be thrown to her death in the sea. Antiope protests their innocence and reveals her true identity, but by then Lycomedes's orders have been carried out and Deidameia is reported dead. The remorseful Lycomedes is about to follow his daughter to his death when (in what must have been the most impressive *coup de théâtre* devised by Juvarra for the Palazzo Zuccari) the rock opens to reveal Thetis's grotto. Inside is Deidameia, who has been saved from drowning by the goddess and united with Achilles. Antiope is then reunited with Lycomedes (whose innocence in the matter of Theseus's death is affirmed by Thetis) and the requirements of the operatic *lieto fine* are satisfied all round.

The plot of *Tetide in Sciro* has been summarized in some detail, not only because the score has survived complete but also to give an idea of the degree of artificiality and contrivance that characterizes the serious operas of the period – although this particular one, with its absence of comic characters, is more consistent and plausible than many others. Disguises and transvestism are commonplace, contributing to the entanglements and misunderstandings in the plot. In *Tetide in Sciro* the extreme is reached in Act 3 Scene v, where we have the situation of Deidameia expressing her love for a man who is in reality a woman, but relinquishing 'him' to her friend 'Arminda', whom she believes to be a woman but who is in fact a man. On the public stage in Rome a situation such as this would have been further removed from reality by the laws prohibiting women from taking part; all the roles in *Tetide in Sciro* (they require four sopranos and two altos, as in *Tolomeo et Alessandro*) would have had to be sung by men – or rather by eunuchs. In private theatres such as Maria Casimira's, however, the participation of female singers was tolerated. With dramaturgical conventions that so strained credulity, it would have been unrealistic to expect composers to provide much more than a vehicle for fine singing and the emotional and pictorial underlining of a particular situation. Scarlatti's music for *Tetide in Sciro* is superior in quality to the average operatic score of his day, and yet it cannot be said that any of his characters is given dramatic conviction by the music.

With *Tetide in Sciro* Scarlatti came once again into close rivalry with his father. Shortly before Domenico's opera was seen at the Palazzo Zuccari, Alessandro's *Il Ciro*, with a libretto by Cardinal Ottoboni and sets by Juvarra, had gone into production at the Cancelleria. Alessandro did not, apparently, come to Rome himself for the performance of what one commentator described as 'one of the finest and most accomplished spectacles that has been seen in Rome for some time',[18] but comparisons with *Tetide in Sciro* must have been made. The existence of the autograph score of *Il Ciro* in the library of the Brussels Conservatoire and of the Venice copy of *Tetide in Sciro* allows us to compare the merits and methods of the two composers at this stage in their careers: Alessandro was fifty-one, Domenico twenty-six. Setting aside the differences that result from the more sophisticated resources of Ottoboni's theatre and his employment of 'some of the best voices in Italy',[19] one notices in particular the extensive use of accompanied recitative in *Il Ciro* and its complete absence from *Tetide in Sciro*. One might have expected to find it employed in, for example, the soliloquy for Thetis in Act 3 Scene vi that culminates in her short but forcefully expressive aria 'O numi tiranni' (in the unusual key of B♭ minor); and it would have been appropriate, too, for expressing Lycomedes's self-reproach later in the same act. Domenico Scarlatti's failure to draw on what was a potent means of intensifying the drama or pathos of a particular situation may have had something to do with the length of what Capece described as an 'operetta': accompanied recitative necessarily slows down the pace of the action. But he did show true dramatic instinct when he set Antiope's 'Crudel, che più tardi' (Act 3 Scene ix) in a manner closely approaching *recitativo stromentato* (and without the da capo repeat indicated in the libretto).

Much of the other music in *Tetide in Sciro* suffers little in comparison with Alessandro's *Il Ciro*, and the score certainly demonstrates a remarkable advance over Domenico's Neapolitan operas. The first three numbers set a very high standard indeed. Thetis's 'Vi lascio tranquille', its string phrases suggesting the calm motion of the waves from which the goddess has just stepped, and Achilles's 'Gusto il nettare bramato', in which the voice sings mostly in counterpoint with a unison string line, are both fine examples of very different kinds of aria. These two characters are then joined by Deidameia in a trio, 'Vorrebbe dal tuo cor', in which the vocal phrases mingle in a most natural and conversational manner. The promise of Scarlatti's earlier ensembles is here fulfilled. Nothing is either forced or constrained, and the composer's decision not to observe the da capo indication again means that nothing is needlessly repeated either. It is not surprising that Scarlatti did not quite succeed in maintaining the quality of these opening scenes, but the general level of interest in the rest of the opera is nevertheless exceptionally high. Kirkpatrick (p. 52) rightly praised another ensemble, 'Amando, tacendo', in which the same three characters join at the end of Act 1; here again Scarlatti ignores the da capo convention. Kirkpatrick knew this 'delicious terzet' only from the condensed score in the Naples Conservatory library, otherwise he would certainly have commented on the way that Scarlatti associates each character with a particular instrument: Thetis's part is doubled by an oboe, Achilles's by a flute and Deidameia's by violins playing pizzicato an octave higher.

These instruments, together with the usual string band and continuo, make up the complete orchestral resources of *Tetide in Sciro*, at least in so far as they are indicated in the Venice score. The opera is not noteworthy for its orchestral palette, and there is a good deal of doubling of voice parts with instruments. On the other hand, Scarlatti writes only two continuo arias (*Il Ciro* has only one), and he varies his string textures quite admirably. He could evidently count on the services of an exceptionally gifted violinist at this time, and two of Thetis's arias are notable for their virtuoso violin obbligatos. In 'E lontano il mio tormento' (Act 3) the direction 'capriccio' is twice used to indicate improvised cadenzas for the solo violin, while 'Non è il ciel, non son le stelle' (substituted for 'Sarebbe men forte' in Act 2 Scene xi) is a brilliant showpiece for both voice and violin, with the performers sometimes contending with each other (example 3a) and sometimes allowing each other to shine (example 3b).

Scarlatti's operatic music has often been dismissed as a pale reflection of his father's in a genre for which he showed no special aptitude and in which he had no genuine interest. Much of the music surveyed in earlier pages tends to confirm this, but an examination of *Tetide in Sciro* shows that even in this relatively unimportant part of his output the composer developed real individuality and a surprisingly sympathetic feeling for the voice.

In addition to the recently discovered full score, ten items from *Tetide in Sciro* (including the two trios) exist in manuscript short score in the library of the Naples Conservatory. Viale-Ferrero[20] has identified the following sketches by Juvarra as representing sets intended for *Tetide in Sciro*:

London, Victoria and Albert Museum, Reg.4826: ff.109, 112 and 114 (and possibly ff.106 and 107);
Turin, Biblioteca Nazionale, Riserva 59,4: f.119r (2).

IFIGENIA IN AULIDE, IFIGENIA IN TAURI

For the customary Carnival productions in 1713 Maria Casimira (or, more probably, Capece) formed the idea of presenting the Iphigenia myth in two operas based on the two plays of Euripides. Unlike Gluck's two famous operas on this subject, Scarlatti's were evidently planned from the start as a pair. Capece makes this clear in the *argomento* of *Ifigenia in Aulide*, where he speaks of 'the material for this opera and for the other which may perhaps be performed during the

Example 3

present Carnival'. These were not the first operas based on the Iphigenia legend: the *Iphigénie en Tauride* of Desmarets and Campra (1704, libretto by Danchet) and Coletti's *Ifiginia* (1707, libretto by Riva) are among their predecessors. But Capece and Scarlatti were among the very few before Wagner to plan an opera and its sequel from the start as a single project. The first such cycle was probably the two Sejanus operas of Antonio Sartorio (1667).

Like Gluck's operas (but in contrast to the Euripides plays) Scarlatti's were written and performed in the 'correct' chrono- logical order – that is, so that the events of the second follow those of the first. According to Alberto Cametti, *Ifigenia in Aulide* was given at the Palazzo Zuccari on 11 January 1713 and *Ifigenia in Tauride* about 15 February.[21] The libretto of the first is based on P. Ortensio Scamacca's Italian translation of Euripides. Iphigenia is summoned to Aulis by her father Agamemnon on the pretext that she is to be married to Achilles, but in fact so that she can be sacrificed to the goddess Calchas in return for favourable winds for Agamemnon's expedition against Troy. Iphigenia is saved from death on the altar by the goddess Diana, who transports her to Tauris, leaving a white hind in her place.

Capece claimed that his only embellishment of the original was to suppose that Pylades was in love with Iphigenia. This he did to secure continuity with the sequel, *Ifigenia in Tauri*, based on the Italian translation of Euripides by Capece's fellow Arcadian, the poet Pier Jacopo Martello. For the second opera he made more alterations to the original, inventing new characters and intrigues and changing the ending so that Pylades turns out to be Elisauro, the long-lost son of King Thoas, carried off by pirates when he was a child. (Capece had engineered a similar dénouement in *La Silvia* three years earlier.)

As far as is known, the only musical items remaining from the two Iphigenia operas are four alto arias in the Sächsische Landesbibliothek, Dresden. One of these is Clytemnestra's 'Se tu sarai fedel' in Act 1 of *Ifigenia in Aulide*, a da capo aria in which Scarlatti characteristically underlines the contrast of ideas in the verse by a change of key, tempo, metre and string texture in the middle section. The other three Dresden arias are all sung by Dorifile in *Ifigenia in Tauri*; possibly the singer who took this part also sang Clytemnestra in the earlier opera. The arias are 'Se pensi mai, se speri' (Act 1), 'Se vuoi che t'ami costante' and 'Consolati e spera' (both in Act 3). The second of these is an attractive love song in 12/8 metre with accompaniment of two flutes and strings. 'Consolati e spera' uses a texture frequently found in the Palazzo Zuccari operas, although not unique to Scarlatti, in which the voice is doubled almost throughout by violins, either at the unison or at the octave, without any harmonic support at all. The other instruments play only in the ritornellos.

Filippo Juvarra's collaboration in the two Iphigenia operas is attested by sketches for stage designs in London and Turin. Viale-Ferrero[22] has identified the following as relevant sketches:

London, Victoria and Albert Museum, Reg.4826: ff.105 and 114
   (*Ifigenia in Aulide*); f.107 (? *Ifigenia in Tauri*);
Turin, Biblioteca Nazionale, Riserva 59,4: ff.59v, 69(1), 69(3), and
   possibly ff.71(1), 71(3) and 84(4) (*Ifigenia in Aulide*); ff.26(6), 27(5),
   30(4), 85(1), 101(4), 123(1), 123(3) and possibly f.84(4) (*Ifigenia in
   Tauri*).

No later performances of *Ifigenia in Aulide* are known, but *Ifigenia in
Tauri* was revived in Turin during Carnival 1719. As the principal
theatre, the Teatro Ducale, was then being rebuilt (it opened in 1722 as
the Teatro Regio), the opera was given at the private theatre of the
Prince of Corignano. The cast was as follows:

Ifigenia	Diana Vico
Oreste	Andrea Pacini
Toante	Giovanni Paita
Pilade	Antonio Pasi
Dorifile	Rosa Ambreville
Ismeno	Giacomo Marchesini

For once a mature Scarlatti opera had the advantage of a highly
talented and experienced cast. Diana Vico was a Venetian contralto
much in demand all over Italy, especially in the north. Between 1714
and 1716 she was in London and sang in some of Handel's operas. She
specialized in male roles, Iphigenia being one of her comparatively
few female parts. Andrea Pacini, an alto castrato from Lucca
sometimes known as 'il Lucchesino', also sang for Handel in London,
including the title role in *Tamerlano* (1724). The tenor Giovanni Paita
was from Genoa. He sang frequently in Parma and Venice, and had
already appeared in at least one opera by Domenico Scarlatti when he
took the part of Gedone in *Ambleto* (Rome, 1715). Rosa d'Ambreville,
a soprano, was born at Modena and sang in Venice, Turin and Milan
before being employed, along with her sister Anna Maria Lodovica, at
the Viennese court from 1721 to 1740; she married the tenor Francesco
Borosini, probably in 1722. Antonio Pasi appeared in several of
Gasparini's operas in Rome. Information about the other principal
singer, Giacomo Marchesini, is difficult to come by.

The Turin performance included also intermezzi, although these
were not printed in the 1719 libretto and were presumably not
composed by Scarlatti. They were sung by Giovanni Benvenuti and
Santa Marchesini, the Bolognese alto who was later to appear in
Madrid during the period of Scarlatti's sojourn there. The libretto
specifies also sixteen guards and four pages, and names Giacomo

Antonio Gioannini of Varese as the stage designer. Mention is made of 'some minor changes in the drama . . . which have been necessary to suit the singers who will interpret it', but in fact the alterations were quite extensive. Twenty-two of the original arias were omitted and eighteen new ones added. Did Scarlatti himself compose these, and if so did he travel to Turin to supervise the music, as was customary? The answers to these questions are not known, but no other composer's name appears in the libretto.

AMOR D'UN OMBRA E GELOSIA D'UN AURA/NARCISO

Scarlatti's last opera for Queen Maria Casimira was *Amor d'un ombra e gelosia d'un aura* – one of those hendecasyllabic titles of which the Italians were so fond. (As in Mozart's *Così fan tutte*, the title is sung by the cast towards the end of the opera.) *Amor d'un ombra* was produced at the Palazzo Zuccari on 15 January 1714.[23] The two operas staged at the Teatro Capranica during Carnival that year were Caldara's *Tito e Berenice* and Gasparini's *Lucio Papirio*. From letters to the Marquis de Torcy in France it appears that Scarlatti's opera was again the most successful:

> *29 January 1714*
>
> The Queen of Poland is recovering from a violent cold which caused concern for Her Majesty's life. The little opera which the prince has had prepared for her theatre is nevertheless being performed at her residence. Donna Maria Bernardina Albani was at the première; Princess Sobieski acted as hostess. Cardinal Ottoboni and Don Carlos were also present.

> *13 February 1714*
>
> The Carnival entertainments are over at last. They have not been as lavish or as numerous as in previous years. . . . The Queen of Poland's opera was considered the best.[24]

The title-page of the printed libretto describes *Amor d'un ombra* simply as a 'dramma per musica', but a later libretto (London, 1720) categorizes it more precisely as a 'drama boschereccio'; it represents, therefore, a return to the pastoral traditions of Scarlatti's first opera for Maria Casimira. Capece's libretto is based on two myths recounted by Ovid in Books 3 and 7 of the *Metamorphoses*. There the two stories are quite independent of each other, but Capece draws them together in the opera by having the breeze (*aura*) of which Procris is jealous impersonated by Echo. He excuses his other modifications of Ovid with the following explanation: 'In making Narcissus in love not with himself but with Echo, and in having Procris only slightly wounded rather than killed by Cephalus, I have contrived to end the opera happily, rather than sadly [*funesto*], in accordance with modern custom and taste.' To Ovid's characters Capece added Aristeus, Prince of Thessaly, and the shepherd Nicandro, custodian of the Temple of Pan and Cupid.

No score or fragment of the music relating directly to the Roman production of 1714 has yet come to light, and the opera is known to us now only in the version prepared for London under the title *Narciso*. In the winter of 1718–19 a Royal Academy was founded and a subscription raised to put opera in London on a securer footing than had previously been the case. Johann Jakob Heidegger, the Swiss impresario, was appointed manager and Paolo Rolli was made Italian secretary, with responsibility for librettos. Handel, as musical director, was empowered to visit the Continent and 'make Contracts with such Singer or Singers as you shall judge fit to perform on the English Stage'. He left London in May 1719 and visited Düsseldorf, Halle (his birthplace) and Dresden, where he engaged the castratos Matteo Berselli and Senesino, the bass Giuseppe Maria Boschi and the soprano Margarita Durastanti.

Only the last named had arrived in London by 2 April 1720, when the Royal Academy opened its first season – not, as might be expected, with a Handel opera, but with Giovanni Porta's *Numitore*. Handel's *Radamisto* followed on 27 April, and the third and last production of this short first season was Domenico Scarlatti's *Narciso*. This, the only opera by the composer performed to date in Britain, opened on 30 May. It was repeated four times before the season ended, on 2, 11, 15 and 30 June. The singers, all of whom had appeared also in *Numitore* and *Radamisto*, are listed in the printed libretto as follows:

Narciso	Signora Durastanti
Cefalo	Signor Benedetto Baldassari
Aristeo	Mr Gordon
Eco	Mrs Anastasia Robinson
Procri	Mrs Turner Robinson

Durastanti had sung in Handel's *Agrippina* in Venice in 1709, and then in operas at Parma and Naples. Her considerable salary (5,225 Thaler) at Dresden when Handel engaged her for London is an indication of the high esteem in which her singing was held (Rolli compared her physical appearance to that of an elephant). Baldassari was perhaps already familiar with Scarlatti's *Narciso* before he joined the Royal Academy company, since he had sung in Gasparini's *Lucio Papirio* in Rome in the same month that *Amor d'un ombra* was first performed. Alexander Gordon (Aristeus) was a Scottish tenor who began his singing career in Italy but abandoned it in 1723 to devote himself to antiquarian studies and writings. Anastasia Robinson was born in Italy but seems never to have sung there; she took several soprano roles (including some by Handel) between 1714 and 1717, but by the time she sang in *Narciso* her voice had deepened to a contralto. Many of the arias in *Narciso* show signs of having been transposed or altered to suit her range, although others are unaccountably notated in soprano clef and retain notes which would seem to have been too high for her. The soprano Ann Turner Robinson, daughter of the singer and composer William Turner, had not sung in opera before 1720, and possibly the strain of the first Royal Academy season was too much for her. At the last performance of *Narciso* her part was taken by Margherita de L'Epine, the Italian soprano who had come to London early in the century and was married to the composer Johann Christoph Pepusch.

Thomas Roseingrave seems to have had no official connection with the Royal Academy, but it was probably on his initiative that Scarlatti's *Narciso* was included in their first opera season. Roseingrave left Italy in 1714 or 1715, and instead of returning to Dublin he proceeded to London, where he soon became active in promoting Scarlatti's music. On 26 March 1718 he took part in a benefit concert in Hickford's Rooms at which a certain 'Mademoiselle Coraill' (probably the French singer and dancer Mlle Cerail, who died of smallpox in 1723) sang 'several New Songs by the famous Domenico Scarlatti, never perform'd before in this Kingdom' (*Daily Courant*, 25 March 1718). According to Burney, Roseingrave brought the score of *Amor d'un ombra* with him from Italy and directed the performances at the King's Theatre. Burney also mentions 'several additional songs' by Roseingrave himself:

> Roseingrave's additional songs were composed in the style of his friend Mimo [Domenico] Scarlatti, in whose Music of Narcissus, though there were many new and pleasing passages and effects, yet those acquainted with the original and happy freaks of this composer in his harpsichord pieces, would be surprised at the sobriety and almost dulness of his songs. His genius was not yet expanded, and he was not so much used to write for the voice as his father, who was the greatest vocal composer of his time, as the son afterwards became the most original and wonderful performer on the harpsichord, as well as composer for that instrument. But it seems

impossible for any individual to be equally *great* in any two things of difficult attainment![25]

Burney's evaluation of *Narciso*, and of Scarlatti's vocal music in general, has too often been echoed by others with little or no experience of it.

Capece's libretto (often erroneously attributed to Apostolo Zeno) was adapted for London by Paolo Rolli and published, with a parallel English translation, by John Pickard. Rolli prefaced it with a dedication (in Italian only) to the Princess of Wales, Princess Caroline of Anspach:

Your Royal Highness
This *drama boschereccio*, which has already been given in a private theatre to comfort an unfortunate queen, now comes to the King's Theatre as a noble diversion for the most, and most justly, fortunate princess in the world. The kindness with which Your Royal Highness, through innate generosity and acquired judgment, welcomes tributes paid to you in the fine arts and in letters, emboldens me to dedicate to your royal name this opera which, while losing nothing of its former harmonious beauties, now appears adorned with new attractions as a worthy spectacle for royal entertainment. I do not offer Your Royal Highness only the work of others, since in altering the scenario, removing what is not wanted and making the necessary additions I may claim about half of the work as my own. In doing all this I hope I shall not have lessened the pleasure which, I flatter myself, your refined taste will find in both the harmony and the expression of the present opera, since Your Royal Highness possesses such a wide, learned and perfect knowledge of the Italian language and of good music. I therefore crave your gracious royal kindness in not refusing an offering which might be numbered among those 'small offerings, to be sure, and yet such that when the heart makes them in pure affection even Heaven does not refuse them'.[26]

Your Royal Highness's
most humble and devout servant
Paolo Rolli.

Rolli's claim to a half share in the version of *Narciso* that went on stage at the King's Theatre in 1720 was quite justified. The part of Nicandro was cut completely; many of the arias were revised or replaced; and the scenario of Act 3 was extensively remodelled. English audiences found Italian recitative dry and tedious (they still do) and Rolli cut that in *Narciso* to a minimum. The libretto of *Narciso* is shorter than that of *Amor d'un ombra* by about half a dozen arias and numerous lines of recitative. For the benefit of London audiences, who were hearing the opera in a foreign tongue, Rolli also printed the following synopsis of the action:

ARGUMENT

A Monstrous Boar wasting the Territory of *Athens*; *Procris* Princess of that Country proclaims a general Meeting of the most renowned Heroes and Hunters to kill the Monster; at the same time publishing her Assent to the People's Voice which had decreed to the happy Performer of that exploit the possession of her Person and Kingdom. Induc'd by the hopes of such a reward, several Neighb'ring Princes and Others repair to that remarkable Congress. The most Noted among these were *Aristeus* Prince of *Thessaly*, *Cephalus* the *Aeolian*, and *Narcissus* of *Beotia*, no less famous for his Beauty than his Disdain of the fair Sex and Contempt of *Cupid*'s Power: Is follow'd from *Beotia* (without his Knowledge) by *Echo* a Nymph who long had lov'd him, but despairing of success had always convey'd her Complaints without ever appearing, which gave occasion to the report of her being wasted to a Meer Voice. *Echo* the better to conceal her self, passes for *Aura*, and under that feign'd Name Occasions *Procris*'s Jealousie. *Cephalus* kills the Boar and overcomes all Obsticles but his Mistresses Suspicions, who watching him too Narrowly, is wounded with the same fatal Spear she gave him: But his Sorrow for the Accident convincing her both of his, and her own Mistake, She forgives him. In the Mean time *Cupid* (to punish the proud despiser of his Divinity) Makes *Narcissus*, as he stoops to Drink, fall in Love with a Shadow he sees in the Fountain. *Ovid* supposes it his own Image, and for that vain Object, makes him pine away to the Flower which bears his Name. Our Poet does not push *Cupid*'s Revenge so far; and if he have not mended the Fable, has at least made it more Agreeable to *British* Ears, by feigning that the Shadow *Narcissus* saw, was *Echo*'s from behind some bushes near the brink of the Fountain where she was conceal'd (as usual) to talk with and gaze on her Lov'd Swain. After a good deal of distress and reciprocal Jealousies the several Lovers happiness is compleated in *Cupid*'s Temple, according to the *Delphian* Oracle's Promise.

Roseingrave's share in the enterprise is more difficult to determine than Rolli's, since we do not possess a score of the original version for comparison. The musical sources at our disposal are: (i) a manuscript full score in the hand of J. C. Smith the elder (Handel's secretary and principal copyist); (ii) the *Songs in the New Opera call'd Narcissus . . . compos'd by Sig:ʳ Dom:ᶜᵒ Scarlatti*, published by Walsh soon after the first London performance; and (iii) a manuscript copy of the overture only in the Bibliothèque Nationale, Paris (formerly in the collection of the Paris Conservatoire). The Smith score is a fair copy, lacking the title-page. It once belonged to Lord Fitzwilliam and passed eventually into the collection of Friedrich Chrysander acquired by the Staats- und Universitätsbibliothek, Hamburg, in 1956. The Walsh print contains the overture, in score, and all the arias and ensembles, mostly in a short score which omits much of the orchestral detail.

In Walsh's publication Roseingrave is named as the composer of four items in Act 2: an aria for Narcissus, 'L'ozio vil di giovinezza', another for Procris, 'Perfido, traditore', a duet for Echo and Procris, 'Lascia a me sol la pena' (the text of which appears in neither the Rome nor the London libretto), and an accompanied recitative, 'Rivolgo il passo altrove' for Narcissus and Echo. Roseingrave's contribution must have gone far beyond this, however. In the first place, there would have been several transpositions and minor adjustments to be made to Scarlatti's arias in order to accommodate them to the new cast. Then, the considerable changes to the libretto made by Rolli, not to mention the new distribution of keys for the arias, must have necessitated extensive rewriting of the secco recitative. It is possible, too, that some at least of the accompanied recitative in Act 3 is by Roseingrave, especially since accompanied recitative is not present in *Tetide in Sciro*, the other serious opera by Scarlatti of which we possess a score. Roseingrave is not, of course, credited with this in the Walsh publication, which includes only one recitative, that by Roseingrave mentioned above.

It seems likely that Scarlatti's original scoring was for the most part retained in the London version, since both the style and the instrumental resources match those of *Tetide in Sciro*. As far as the overture is concerned, the evidence of the Paris score supports this. Only one Scarlatti aria, Aristeus's 'Sento che il cor mi dice', specifies instruments (flute and oboe) other than strings, and there are no continuo arias. But Roseingrave's aria 'L'ozio vil di giovinezza' calls for trumpets, horns, oboes and bassoons (two of each) as well as strings and continuo, and perhaps Roseingrave was responsible also for introducing these into the final *coro*, since most of the wind instruments seem not to have been available to Scarlatti in Rome. Indeed, Roseingrave may actually have composed the final *coro* himself: the text differs from that of the Rome libretto, and the new text would almost certainly not have fitted the original music.

Similar problems of attribution are raised by certain aria texts in *Narciso* which resemble none of those in the original Capece libretto. In many cases Rolli has paraphrased or parodied the original. Aristeus's 'Al varco, il nume arcier' in Act 1 of *Amor d'un ombra*, for example, has become 'Ma forse porterà' in Act 3 of *Narciso*. But in the following five cases it is not possible to relate the metre, rhyme scheme or phraseology to any of the arias in *Amor d'un ombra*:

> Penosi torrenti [?tormenti], con piena d'affanni (Echo, Act 2)
> Perfida, t'avvedrai (Aristeus, Act 2)
> Morirò, ma questa morte (Procris, Act 3)
> Al fin potrò morire (Echo, Act 3)
> Men volo contento (Cephalus, Act 3)

and doubts exist, too, about at least three other arias. Presumably Scarlatti set these new texts specifically for the London production, since no other composer is named in the extant sources. It is, of course, possible that arias were changed or new ones added to the original score after the Rome libretto had gone to the printer, but it seems unlikely that there would have been as many as half a dozen or more.

While these and other uncertainties remain, it would be premature to attempt an evaluation of Scarlatti's achievements in *Amor d'un ombra*, but many of the items that can be attributed to him are undoubtedly of great interest and superb quality. The first number after the overture is a trio in which Cephalus and Aristeus compare Procris's beauty to that of the sun at dawn. As in the trios of *Tetide in Sciro*, their phrases mingle and overlap in the most natural way possible, and there is no da capo (although the original libretto indicates one). Aristeus's aria 'Sento che a poco a poco' is remarkable as much for the rich scoring of the string accompaniment as for the expressive melismas of the vocal line. No fewer than twenty arias in *Narciso* are accompanied by the full strings in four parts, and Scarlatti scores them most effectively. Kirkpatrick (p. 53) drew attention to Narcissus's serenade, 'Vieni o cara a consolarmi', in Act 3, with its pizzicato accompaniment imitating the sound of a mandolin, and possibly he would not have dismissed the rest of the music so summarily if he had known it all in full score. Vigorous string scales and semiquaver reiterations contribute immensely to the urgency of Cephalus's 'suicide' aria, 'Dentro quel cupo rio', in Act 2 (it belonged originally to Narcissus in Act 1) and legato string phrases no less effectively set the mood for Cephalus's lovely 'sleep' aria later in the same act. The effect is heightened by breaking up the aria with passages of recitative (omitted from the Walsh version). There is no strict da capo, and the aria breaks off in the dominant key as Cephalus falls asleep. One wonders if Handel found something to learn from in this aria.

Among the other arias Narcissus's 'Dammi tregua se non pace' (robbed of its second section and da capo in the Hamburg manuscript) is a good imitation of Alessandro Scarlatti's 'siciliana' style in 12/8 metre. There is also the usual 'alla francese' aria, in this case 'Non è fiero ne crudele', a particularly attractive sarabande originally sung in Act 1 by Procris but in the London version given to Echo in Act 3.

The return of Queen Maria Casimira to France in June 1714 might easily have brought Domenico Scarlatti's career as a composer of opera and oratorios to an abrupt end. He soon, however, found new opportunities to exercise his talents in both genres.

CANTATA DA RECITARSI . . . LA NOTTE DI NATALE

It was customary at the Vatican on Christmas Eve for the pope to entertain the cardinals who had assisted at vespers with a musical performance in the Apostolic Palace, followed by a lavish meal there. String concertos fitted out with appropriate pastoral movements (for example the famous eighth concerto of Corelli's op. 6 set) and Christmas cantatas in the vernacular for one or two solo voices were commonly heard on these occasions, but many of the works performed in the early decades of the eighteenth century assumed the dimensions of an oratorio, and were often referred to as such. Francesco Valesio, for example, writing in his diary on Christmas Day 1705, recorded how on the previous evening there were 'eleven cardinals in the [Apostolic] Palace who were given the usual sumptuous feast and entertained with a musical oratorio [*oratorio in musica*], after which the sacred offices were observed, Cardinal Colloredo intoning the first mass'.

The 'oratorio' performed on that occasion was Alessandro Scarlatti's *Abramo il tuo sembiante*. The *Cantata da recitarsi nel Palazzo Apostolico la notte del Ss.mo. Natale* (to quote from the title-page of the original libretto), set to music by Domenico Scarlatti for performance at the Vatican on Christmas Eve 1714, is also an oratorio in all but name. The sacred subject-matter (it deals, of course, with the Nativity) and the division of the work into two sections link it firmly to the oratorio tradition, but the way the subject is treated and the literary style (if it can be so dignified) have much in common with the typical 'homage' serenata, for example with Scarlatti's *Contesa delle stagioni* (see pp. 108–11). Love, Faith and Virginity contest the importance of their respective contributions to the birth of the Saviour. The archangel Gabriel awards the palm to Love, since it was for love of suffering mankind that the Saviour came into the world in the first place; Faith and Virginity played their part afterwards. A chorus of angels is heard during Part 1 and again at the end of the piece.

The text of Scarlatti's Christmas oratorio is by Francesco Maria Gasparri, a lawyer and member of the Arcadian Academy; the music has not survived.

AMBLETO

Scarlatti's first opportunity to engage in an operatic venture after the departure of Queen Maria Casimira in 1714 came the following year, when he was invited to compose a work for the Teatro Capranica, Rome's principal theatre for public opera. The Capranica had begun as a private theatre in the palace of Pompeo and Federico Capranica, and opened its doors to the public in 1690. After extensive renovations it reopened on 18 January 1695, but a few years later Pope Innocent XII closed it, and it was not until 1711 that operatic performances were resumed. Further modifications to the stage and the lighting were made by Juvarra in 1713, and the Capranica became one of the most important theatres for serious opera in Italy outside Venice and Naples. Many of Alessandro Scarlatti's most important operas were first given there.

For his first opera at the Capranica Domenico Scarlatti used a libretto originally written in 1705 for Gasparini, whose setting Scarlatti probably knew. The libretto has often been ascribed to Apostolo Zeno, the Venetian poet and scholar who from 1718 served the Emperor Charles VI in Vienna as poet and historian and was succeeded by Pietro Metastasio in 1729. In fact, *Ambleto* was one of several texts on which Zeno collaborated with another librettist, Pietro Pariati, who also worked in Venice and Vienna. In their collaborations Zeno was normally responsible for the scenario and Pariati for the versification. *Ambleto* was one of the first librettos they wrote together. Scarlatti's setting was the first opera produced at the Capranica during the 1715 Carnival season; the text was set a third time by Giuseppe Carcani in 1742.

In the *argomento* of the 1715 libretto the source of the scenario is claimed to be the *Gesta danorum* (1150) of the Danish historian Saxo Grammaticus; also cited are the histories of Denmark by Giovanni Pontano and Joannes Meursius. Despite obvious similarities to Shakespeare's *Hamlet*, the English playwright is not mentioned in the *argomento*, and the libretto gives no indication that Zeno and Pariati were familiar with the play. Their libretto does not, of course, begin to approach Shakespeare in psychological penetration or in richness of language, although there are several dramatic situations which are common to both opera and play. In the former the usurper Gedone has murdered Prince Ambleto's father and married his mother, Gerilda, against her will. Fearing for his own life, and in order to cover his plans for revenge, Ambleto has feigned madness. The plot revolves around Gedone's three attempts to discover the true nature of Ambleto's mental state. In the first act he arranges a meeting between the prince and Princess Veremonda, whom Ambleto loves, but Veremonda is able to warn Ambleto that Gedone is eavesdropping on their conversation. In Act 2 one of Gedone's trusted followers, Iroldo, is sent to spy on Ambleto and his mother, but Ambleto, forewarned of the plot by Gedone's traitorous confidant, Sifrido, finds Iroldo in an antechamber and kills him. Finally, Gedone tries to put Ambleto to the test by getting him drunk, but (in an elaborate final scene which includes choral singing and dancing) the tyrant is slain by Sifrido and the relationships between the other characters are mended to make for the usual happy ending.

There are obvious equations to be made between the characters of *Ambleto* and those of *Hamlet*, and not only that of the prince himself. Zeno's Gedone is Shakespeare's Claudius, but a much more ruthless and promiscuous tyrant. Gerilda is, of course, the counterpart to Shakespeare's Gertrude and Veremonda to Ophelia, although Veremonda is a more straightforward character than Shakespeare's and her love for the prince is overt and unambiguous. Iroldo shares the fate of Polonius, but his is a non-singing role, without substance. Zeno's other characters, the general Valdemano and the Danish princess, Ildegarde, serve mainly to complicate the usual amatory imbroglio.

Six of the thirty-eight arias in *Ambleto* are marked with an asterisk, presumably to indicate that they were the work of another composer (possibly Gasparini), although the libretto omits any mention of this. In addition, an unusually large number of lines (well over a hundred) are virgolated – that is, marked with commas to show that they were not set to music – and this might suggest that Scarlatti's arias were on the whole more extended than those which Gasparini had written in 1705. The only surviving vocal piece from the opera, however, is the aria 'Nella mia sfortunata prigionia' (Act 1 Scene viii), in which Veremonda pleads with Gedone not to allow Valdemaro to 'exert his authority as her captor over her affections'. It is an expressive Adagio in B minor, in which the violin phrases add eloquent support to Veremonda's pleas.

The stage designs for *Ambleto* were by Pompeo Aldrovandini, and the all-male cast is set out in the 1715 libretto as follows:

Ambleto	Domenico Tempesti
Veremonda	Domenico Genovesi
Gedone	Giovanni Paita
Gerilda	Innocenzo Baldini
Ildegarde	Antonio Natilii
Valdemaro	Giovanni Antonio Archi
Sifrido	Francesco Vitali

As well as these singers the libretto lists also the cast of the comic intermezzo, *La Dirindina*, the two parts of which were to be performed between the acts of the main opera. The decision to withdraw *La Dirindina* from performance (the reasons for which are discussed below) must therefore have been taken at a late stage, after the text of the libretto had gone to the printer. In its place the Capranica audience was given a pair of *intermedi pastorali* in which the part of Elpina was sung by Domenico Fontana and that of Silvano by Michele Selvatici. Both singers were to have appeared in *La Dirindina*.

The pastoral intermezzi together make an inconsequential little piece in which the ardent but simple Silvano woos and marries the coquettish Elpina. After their marriage she arouses his jealousy by demanding a new bonnet with ribbons to wear in town, but when Silvano finds this painful she asks his forgiveness and the two express their contentment in a final duet. The music of these *intermedi pastorali* seems not to have survived, but since they were a late substitute for *La Dirindina* it is unlikely, in any case, to have been by Scarlatti. No composer is named in the printed libretto.

LA DIRINDINA/IL MAESTRO DI CAPPELLA

The comic intermezzo *La Dirindina*, or *Il maestro di cappella* as it is called in a contemporary manuscript libretto now in the Cini Foundation in Venice, was originally scheduled for performance between the acts of *Ambleto* (see above), and the cast is in fact listed in the libretto of *Ambleto* below that of the main opera:

Dirindina	Domenico Fontana
Don Carissimo	Michele Selvatici
Liscione	Tommaso Bizzarri

La Dirindina was withdrawn from performance at the last moment when the libretto fell foul of the ecclesiastical censor. It was the work of the author, playwright and satirist Girolamo Gigli, whose writings more than once got him into trouble with authority. One of Gigli's best-known comedies, *Don Pilone*, led to his dismissal from a teaching post at the University of Siena (the town where he was born) and his *Vocabolario cateriniano* later resulted in his expulsion from the Arcadian Academy in Rome and a period of imprisonment in Viterbo.

Gigli's satire in *La Dirindina* is directed mainly towards opera singers and to some extent towards opera itself. The work anticipated by about five years Benedetto Marcello's famous *Il teatro alla moda*, which deals at greater length with similar matters. Gigli's tone is crueller, if not sharper, than Marcello's, and of course his satire is directed at the very entertainment of which the intermezzo forms a part. An old singing teacher, Don Carissimo, is giving a lesson to his young pupil, Dirindina. He chides her for paying attention to the castrato Liscione, who 'sings with little grace', and points out the contrast between her indifference and the kindnesses shown him by his other female pupils. Much to the jealous Carissimo's annoyance, Liscione interrupts the lesson with the news that Dirindina has been invited to sing in the opera *Coriolano* in Milan. She rewards Liscione with just those kindnesses she has denied Don Carissimo and, despite her lack of musical skill (which has been made all too obvious during the course of the lesson), she resolves to go to Milan without her teacher.

In Part 2 Dirindina learns from Liscione how to behave like a prima donna, and in particular how to provide herself with the fine clothes and jewellery she will need for her operatic appearances. She must first distribute her favours among the rich Milanese, and then ('like La Calandrina at Pavia') pretend that she has lost the bracelet she was to have worn at the opera. 'Within an hour your admirers and the impresario himself will bring you a hundred strings of pearls so that you can appear on stage.' The farcical climax is reached when Dirindina gives Liscione a sample of her acting ability in the role of the ravished Dido. Don Carissimo, returning at this point, mistakes pretence for reality and is persuaded that 'either nature or the castrator's knife has erred'. Thinking this, he tries to prevent Dirindina from taking her life (as he imagines) and that of her unborn child with a sword. His entrance recalls dozens of similar ones in the serious operas of the time.

> *Carissimo*: Sta ferma, anima mia,
> lo manderem piuttosto all'ospedale.

Liscione: L'accidente è pur bello.
Carissimo: Piuttosto nel cervello
              ficcargli uno spillone allor che nasce,
              se d'allattarlo hai tedio.
Dirindina: È caso d'intermedio.
Carissimo: Oppure in su le fasce
              fa una notte affogar dalla nutrice
              il muletto infelice.
[*Car*: Hold, my dear; we'll place him in the orphanage instead. *Lis*: What a fine state of affairs! *Car*: Or if you find it tedious to suckle him, we'll drive a spike through his brain when he's born. *Dir*: This is just like an intermezzo! *Car*: Or we'll get the nurse to smother the poor little mule one night with his swaddling clothes.]

As Don Carissimo tries to join their hands, as though to legitimize the union, Dirindina and Liscione draw away, overcome with mirth.

Liscione: Ferma, ch'io son cappone.
Dirindina: Ferma, son pollastrina.
a 2:   Tal coppia non combina,
              e l'uovo mai non fa.
[*Lis*: Stop, I'm a capon. *Dir*: Stop, I'm a young chick. *Both*: Such a pair can never mate and produce an egg.]

It was probably the coarseness and crassness of these final exchanges that led to the intermezzo being banned from the stage of the Capranica. The first of the two passages just quoted (the language is even coarser in the manuscript libretto) was omitted from the version printed at Lucca in 1715. Kirkpatrick (p. 64) wondered 'whether *Dirindina* was actually prohibited or only withdrawn out of discretion'. The true circumstances, brought to light by Francesco Degrada,[27] are revealed in a letter dated 3 December 1715 from Gigli to Anton Francesco Marmi in Florence:

But I can imagine you saying that I have already filled a whole page without mentioning *Dirindina*, the famous scandal of the scrupulous Roman censors and the celebrated diversion of all the more discreet circles. Let's say a little about it then. But don't expect to hear some 'Musico-politico' or Father C . . ., the declared enemy of Don Pilone and of his Little Sister,[28] who have so much in common with Dirindina.

    Let me tell you, then, that when I was asked to write an intermezzo for the theatre here last Carnival I produced that trifle with no particular aim except to depict in a general way something that had never been shown on stage before. The idea was found pleasing enough to win some applause even before the piece was put into production. But the singers, afraid of making themselves look ridiculous, got Francesco de' Castris and his patrons to oppose the performance, with help from an influential lady in love with one of the cast. In short, the affair aroused so much controversy that the Governor judged it best to prohibit it; also the Master of the Sacred Palace [whose imprimatur was needed for all dramatic scripts] was persuaded by the singers to forbid publication. The theatre public, however, showed their displeasure at the ban with frequent shouts of 'We want Liscione, we want Dirindina'.

Now, finding myself a little put out by this act of censorship, I decided, with the approval of many people, to have *La Dirindina* printed and five hundred copies sent to Rome in wrappers. I did this partly to save myself money, since it was costing me too much to satisfy all those who had asked for copies [in manuscript].

It was, then, the singers who initiated the opposition to *La Dirindina* – not surprisingly in view of the nature of the satire and the fact that Domenico Fontana and presumably Tommaso Bizzarri were castratos. (In the surviving score Liscione's music is unaccountably notated in tenor clef for the first part of the intermezzo and in soprano clef for the second.) But Degrada has suggested that personal animosity towards Scarlatti on the part of the castrato Francesco de Castris (known as 'Cecchino') may also have influenced the move to have the performance banned.[29]

The five hundred copies of the libretto mentioned by Gigli in his letter to Marmi were no doubt of the 'second edition' published at Lucca by Leonardo Venturini in 1715. This was not prepared for a particular performance in Lucca, or anywhere else. No theatre or cast is mentioned, but the following note is printed at the end of the text: 'The excellent music of this *farsetta* is by Signor Domenico Scarlatti, who will be pleased to make it available to anyone'. The libretto was reprinted in a two-volume collection entitled *Raccolta copiosa d'inter-medi* (Amsterdam or Milan, 1723), and this may have stimulated performances at the Teatro San Samuele, Venice, in 1725 and 1729, although it is not clear whether or not these were with Scarlatti's music. At least one other composer, Padre Giovanni Battista Martini, made use of the libretto in the eighteenth century; his setting was composed at Bologna in 1731.

It is surprising to observe Scarlatti, whose whole life was spent in the service of monarchs, viceroys and princes, aligning himself with one of the most subversive writers of the time in a work explicitly designed to call into question the values of an art form which, more than any other, served to flatter and support the established order. It is fascinating, too, to observe Scarlatti's impressive mastery of the *buffo* style in *La Dirindina*. Degrada's rediscovery of the complete score in the collection of Ugo Levi in Venice brought to light an important contribution to the repertory of the intermezzo, and at the same time restored a dimension to Scarlatti's stature as a composer which had previously been unrecognized.

The vivacity of Scarlatti's music for *La Dirindina* suggests a whole-hearted commitment to the author's aims. His recitatives effectively point up the wit, as well as the coarse humour, of Gigli's dialogue, for example in the solmization jokes of the singing lesson (example 4); the arias are nicely suited to the characters who sing them, especially the burlesque minuet for Liscione and Don Carissimo's 'Sola voi? Mi meraviglio!', with its grotesque extensions into the bass's falsetto

Example 4

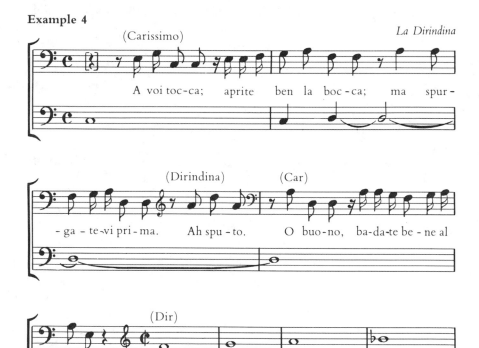

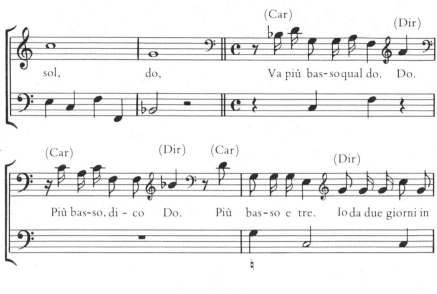

register (example 5); and the *buffo* repartee of the ensembles provides convincing evidence of the composer's real feeling for the theatre (example 6). Of all Scarlatti's theatrical works, *La Dirindina* is the one that might most easily be revived today – perhaps in a double bill with Pergolesi's *La serva padrona*, whose style it in many ways anticipates. Unfortunately (or in some ways perhaps not) the main point of Gigli's satire would be lost on a modern audience.

Example 5

so - la   e di espor-si a tal ci-men-to, a tal ci-men-to a tal ci - men-to,

Example 6

Allegro   (Dirindina)   *La Dirindina*

Fer - ma,   fer - ma,

(Carissimo)

Dam - mi la man,   dam-me -la,   dam - mi la

(vns, vas)

(bc)

6

(Liscione)
Fer - ma,   fer - ma,   fer-ma, ch'io son cap-

man Li - scio - ne,   dammela,   dammela,   che

6
5   #   #   #

BERENICE, REGINA D'EGITTO

One of the operas produced at the Teatro Capranica in Rome during Carnival 1717 was *Il Trace in catena*, in the printed libretto of which the music was said to be the work of 'Sig. Francesco Gasparini, e di due suoi Allievi'. One of these two pupils is thought to have been Giovanni Porta, and it has been suggested that the other was Domenico Scarlatti. The possibility remains, though it seems unlikely that a composer as well known in Italy as Scarlatti would have contributed anonymously to the venture.

Another opera sometimes attributed to Domenico (and sometimes to Alessandro) Scarlatti is a setting of Metastasio's first original opera libretto, *Didone abbandonata*. This was originally written for Domenico Sarro and produced with music by him at the Teatro San Bartolomeo, Naples, on 1 February 1724. The attribution to Domenico Scarlatti may have arisen from a simple confusion of the two composers' names, but it is not impossible, as Roberto Pagano has suggested, that Scarlatti undertook to revise the score for a revival in Rome during the 1724 Carnival season.[30]

Until such a hypothesis is confirmed, it must be assumed that Scarlatti's final stage work was *Berenice, regina di Egitto, ovvero Le gare di amore e di politica*, on which he collaborated with his fellow Neapolitan, Nicola Porpora, in 1718. Porpora had written some operas for Naples and one for the Viennese court, but this was his first venture on the Roman stage. The opera was produced at the Teatro Capranica during Carnival 1718 with sets designed by Antonio Canavari and painted by Giovanni Battista Bernabo; the machines were the work of Cavalier Lorenzo Mariani.

'The contest between love and politics' is a sub-title which might have been applied to practically any heroic opera of the period. In this case the contest is fought out in the heart of Berenice, who must choose between Alexander, the husband proposed for her by the Roman senate, and Demetrius whom she loves but who is politically unacceptable. The plot has its historical roots in Appian's *Bella civilia* ('Civil Wars'), which account has, of course, been embellished and fitted out with the usual intrigues and sub-plots in accordance with the prevailing operatic taste. Antonio Salvi's libretto was originally set by Giacomo Perti for Prince Ferdinando de' Medici, who had it performed in his private theatre at Pratolino in September 1709. It was set again by Giovanni Maria Ruggieri and performed at the Teatro San Samuele, Venice, in autumn 1711, with the title *Le gare di politica e d'amore*. For Rome the libretto was adapted by an unidentified writer, who (as the *argomento* puts it) added the voices of Terpsichore and Thalia to those of Melpomene and Clio. This refers to the two new characters, the servants Menenio and Sibillina, who act out their comic love scenes in the shadow of, but quite separately from, the tragic events that surround them. In 1737 Salvi's libretto was adapted again for Handel, whose *Berenice* was produced at Covent Garden, London, on 18 May that year.

By 1718 Porpora was already renowned as a singing teacher as well as a composer, and his pupils included Carlo Broschi (Farinelli), Scarlatti's future colleague in Madrid. Farinelli may have been with Porpora at Rome when *Berenice* was produced, but his début as a singer was still two years away. The cast at the Capranica in 1718 (an unusually large one for Scarlatti, and once again all-male) included only one of the singers who had appeared in *Ambleto* three years earlier. This was Michele Selvatici, who apparently specialized in comic bass roles. The complete cast is set out in the printed libretto as follows:

Berenice [Queen of Egypt]	Gaetano Narici [soprano]
Selene [her sister]	Carlo Scalzi [soprano]
Demetrio [an Egyptian prince]	Carlo Bernardi
Alessandro [a royal prince]	Domenico Gizii [Gizzi, soprano]
Fabio [a Roman ambassador]	Annibale Pio Fabri [tenor]
Arsace [an Egyptian prince]	Gasparo Geri [soprano]
Aristobolo [captain of Berenice's guard]	Carlo Macciochini
Sibillina [Selene's maid]	Pietro Ricci
Menenio [Fabio's servant]	Michele Selvatici [bass]

The list includes some distinguished names, the most famous being that of Annibale Pio Fabri, a pupil of Francesco Antonio Pistocchi and one of the leading opera singers of his day. Long before the tenor voice reached its operatic heyday the historian Charles Burney was able to say of Fabri that 'the merit of this tenor was often sufficient in Italy to supply the want of it in the principal soprano'. This may well have been the case with *Berenice, regina d'Egitto,* since little is known of Gaetano Narici, who sang the title role. Scarlatti no doubt renewed his acquaintance with Fabri in 1738–9, when the tenor journeyed to Madrid to appear in seven operatic performances there. Domenico Gizzi enjoyed a considerable reputation in Italy as a male soprano, and Carlo Scalzi, another castrato, was highly esteemed by Metastasio, who bracketed him with Farinelli as 'incomparable'.[31]

Nothing apparently remains of the music that Porpora wrote for

Berenice, and of Scarlatti's contribution only five arias have survived. They are:

> Vedi l'ape che ingegnosa (Fabio, Act 1 Scene iii)
> Che sarà quando amante (Alessandro, Act 1 Scene iv)
> Gelo, avvampo, considero (Selene, Act 1 Scene vi)
> Dice amor quel bel vermiglio (Berenice, Act 1 Scene x)
> Ruscelletto ch'è lungi dal mare (Arsace, Act 1 Scene xi)

All five arias are from Act 1, which seems to indicate, as Reinhard Strohm has pointed out, that Scarlatti's share in the composition was the first act and perhaps the first half of the second.[32] Four of these aria texts were also set by Handel in his *Berenice*. It would be foolish to draw any general conclusions from a comparison between them, especially considering the very different ages and circumstances of the two composers when they wrote them. Suffice it to say that in these particular arias Scarlatti shows as strong a dramatic sense as Handel and a melodic gift scarcely inferior. His 'Gelo, avvampo, considero', especially, yields nothing to Handel's in its vivid portrayal of the jealous fury of a woman who has just heard that the man she loves is about to marry another. Arsace's 'Ruscelletto ch'è lungi dal mare' is another very fine aria, as fresh and limpid as the waters of the brook it describes.

Remo Giazotto suggested that an opera with the title *Le gare d'amore* produced at the Teatro Falcone, Genoa, during Carnival 1724 may have been a revival of the *Berenice* of Salvi and Scarlatti.[33] Confirmation of this suggestion is still awaited, however.

THE OVERTURES

At least two-thirds of Scarlatti's music for the stage remains lost, but a study of that portion which has been recovered is enough to suggest that the secular music he composed at Rome in the ten years between 1709 and 1718 has been seriously underrated. It is evident, too, that whatever the merits or otherwise of his operas they are far from being the pale reflections of his father's which they are often taken for. Alessandro Scarlatti's vocal music has a sensuous quality, a degree of melodic originality and a close empathy with both text and singer which are rarely matched in Domenico's arias, but the younger composer makes his mark with bold strokes (frequent sudden changes of tempo and dynamics, for example, or long stretches of single-line texture) which the elder Scarlatti never attempted and perhaps would not have approved of. And Alessandro never engaged in anything as outrageous and novel as *La Dirindina*.

This is not to suggest that a fully professional revival of the two serious operas by Domenico Scarlatti that have survived complete is overdue. While a modern performance of one of these would certainly attract considerable interest, not only from Scarlatti enthusiasts, there are other neglected operas of the period (those of Handel, for example) which are even more worthy of a regular place in the repertory. But those who promote concerts of Baroque music could profitably explore Scarlatti's scores for individual vocal items and for the overtures, several of which do merit frequent performance.

In the library of the Paris Conservatoire, now housed in the Bibliothèque Nationale, there exists a manuscript volume of seventeen sinfonias, the first sixteen of which are individually and reliably attributed to Domenico Scarlatti. The source does not, unfortunately, name the works from which they are taken, but three of them can be identified as overtures to operas composed for performance at the Palazzo Zuccari in Rome: no. 12 is from *Amor d'un ombra e gelosia d'un aura* (1714), no. 13 from *Tolomeo et Alessandro* (1711) and no. 16 from *Tetide in Sciro* (1712). (The last of these is incomplete, lacking bars 15–124 in the first movement.) Almost certainly the other thirteen sinfonias are also from operas, oratorios or serenatas by Scarlatti, and since most of them are scored for oboe, strings and continuo (in two cases with flute as well) it is possible that these, too, originated in works composed for Queen Maria Casimira. In the case of nos 2 and 6 this suggestion is supported by the directions 'senza cimbalo, e senza leuto' and 'senza leuti' in the slow movements, since we know that the queen's musicians at this time included the lutenist S. L. Weiss. The final sinfonia in the manuscript, no. 17, is in a different hand from the others and bears no attribution. It cannot be considered with equal certainty to be the work of Scarlatti.

The sixteen authenticated sinfonias are all in the three-movement form (fast–slow–fast) of the so-called 'Italian' overture, or *sinfonia avanti l'opera*, established by Domenico's father in the last decade of the seventeenth century. The first sinfonia is introduced by a six-bar Grave section and the fourth is prefaced by a brief 'tempo di marciata' obviously designed to suggest a trumpet fanfare, but the only significant departure from the basic 'Italian' structure occurs in no. 9, which lacks a slow movement; possibly the sign ⌒ separating the two quick movements indicates an improvisation of the kind that was presumably inserted between the two corresponding movements of Bach's Brandenburg Concerto no. 3. In the Paris source Sinfonia no. 5 in A minor has also only two movements, an Allegro and an Adagio which comes to rest on the dominant. Since the slow movement ends on the recto side of a folio and is followed by the word 'Fine' it is obvious that in this case the opening aria, ensemble or chorus of the main work served also as the final movement of the overture.

The musical substance of these sinfonias tends to be concentrated in the opening movement. The slow movements are mostly quite short (that of no. 8 is only three bars long) and in the main tonality, cadencing on the dominant in preparation for the finale. This is in most cases a short, lightly scored movement in the binary form of a dance, with each section marked for repeat. A better balance with the rest of the work may sometimes be achieved by repeating the whole movement; the finale of Sinfonia no. 6, for example, ends with the direction: 'si replica da capo tutti assiemo'.

Despite their overall similarity of structure and instrumentation, the sinfonias are remarkably varied in style and content – a quality they share with the later harpsichord sonatas. No. 2 is particularly interesting for its antiphonal scoring, with flute and oboe or two solo violins and cello projected against the full string band. Solo and tutti contrasts are found in several other sinfonias as well, particularly in final movements, and the concertante element is taken even further in the first Allegro of no. 16 (the overture to *Tetide in Sciro*), which features a virtuoso solo violin part extending up to *a'''* in rapid semiquaver figuration.[34] The overture to *Tolomeo et Alessandro* (no. 13) is a spirited *moto perpetuo* broken only by a brief central Grave; sudden reductions from *forte* to *piano* serve to intensify the music's excitement. As in some of his arias, Scarlatti delights in bold contrasts of all kinds, and in Sinfonias 9 and 14 these extend to sudden changes of tempo, metre and texture, as well as of dynamics. The fluctuations between 4/4 and 3/4 in the first movement of no. 9 are particularly effective. In several of the sinfonias the oboe does little more than double one of the violin parts, but in others it is given important solos, and in no. 10 it is so prominent that the work almost takes on the character of an oboe concerto. The chromatically embellished solo line of the central Grave (example 7) is only one of the many striking passages in these slight but fascinating works.

Example 7

THREE *Chamber Cantatas*

The *cantata da camera*, or chamber cantata, was the favourite and most important genre of vocal chamber music in Italy during most of the seventeenth and eighteenth centuries. Practically every opera composer of the period also wrote cantatas, and some composers, including Carissimi, Benedetto Marcello and Emanuele d'Astorga, who wrote few operas or none at all, nevertheless made a speciality of cantata writing. Alessandro Scarlatti was both the greatest and the most prolific composer of chamber cantatas, his extant examples of the genre (not including those of doubtful authenticity) numbering well over six hundred. Domenico's contribution of a mere fifty firmly authenticated works, as well as over a dozen others of less certain authorship, is nugatory in comparison, but his cantatas nevertheless constitute an interesting and rewarding corpus of vocal music, and their neglect by modern publishers and performers is much to be regretted.

In its literal sense the word 'cantata' indicated a piece to be sung, as distinct from one to be played ('suonata', or 'sonata'). The earliest known use of the term on a title-page (though with a slightly different spelling) is in the first volume of *Cantade et arie* by Alessandro Grandi, which dates from 1620 or a little earlier. Grandi worked as a church musician, first at St Mark's, Venice, and later at Santa Maria Maggiore, Bergamo, where he died of plague in 1630. He wrote almost exclusively sacred music, except for the four volumes of *Cantade et arie* published at Venice between about 1620 and 1629. In the first of these Grandi applied the term 'cantada' to pieces using a strophic-bass structure – that is, one in which the same bass (with possibly minor alterations in the pitch and duration of some notes) is used to support a different vocal line for each stanza (strophe) of the text. The structure itself was not new (it was used, for example, by Monteverdi in his opera *Orfeo* (1607) and by other north Italian composers of monodies before that) but its association with the new cantata was something which caught the imagination of composers at Venice during the first three or four decades of the seventeenth century, as may be seen, for example, in the two volumes of *Cantade et arie* (1624 and 1627) by Giovanni Pietro Berti and the *Cantade* (1733) by Giovanni Felice Sances.

To a considerable extent these and similar works (not always called cantatas) by Benedetto Ferrari, Giovanni Rovetta, Carlo Milanuzzi and others may be considered as successors of the continuo madrigal developed by Monteverdi earlier in the century. But Sances was forward-looking in applying the term 'cantata' also to extended works in which recitative, arioso and aria-like sections alternate freely in response to the narrative and lyrical elements in the text. While the strophic bass continued to appear up to about 1670 in the cantatas of Carissimi, and possibly also in some of the earliest ones of Alessandro Scarlatti,[1] the hallmark of the true cantata from the mid-seventeenth century onwards was its drawing together of narrative (recitative) and lyrical (arioso or aria) styles. Among the most important composers to establish this kind of chamber cantata were Luigi Rossi, Marco Marazzoli (most of whose 379 extant cantatas have only recently come to light), Antonio Cesti and Alessandro Stradella.

In the works of these and other mid-seventeenth-century composers the stylistic development of the cantata increasingly paralleled that of opera and oratorio, and long before the end of the century the two main constituents of all three genres, recitative and aria, had become sharply differentiated. Recitative was standardized into an evenly measured *parlando* with stereotyped cadential formulae, although it was far from being as *secco* as Mozart's operatic recitative and could be relieved by occasional and sometimes quite extended passages of arioso. By 1700 the ternary da capo form (A–B–A) had superseded all others as the main, indeed the almost invariable, structure for the aria, and the overall layout of the cantata likewise became standardized in the form of two arias preceded, or separated, by recitative (R–A–R–A or A–R–A, sometimes extended to A–R–A–R–A, R–A–R–A–R–A etc.). This kind of structure is found in all but a few of Alessandro Scarlatti's mature cantatas, and in nearly all of Domenico's, too. Of the latter's fifty authenticated solo cantatas, at least twenty-four use the R–A–R–A layout and fifteen the A–R–A; only two end with recitative.

A structural feature almost ubiquitous among Italian cantatas throughout the seventeenth and eighteenth centuries is tonal unity: like sonatas and concertos they begin and end in the same key. In view of this, the relative prominence of the A–R–A layout among Domenico Scarlatti's cantatas may seem surprising, since in such works tonal unity is achieved only by writing both arias in the same key. Cantatas that begin with recitative allow for greater tonal variety.[2] The overall structure of a cantata is, of course, determined by the poet rather than the composer, and Scarlatti's frequent use of the A–R–A scheme merely reflects the increasing emphasis on the lyrical rather than the narrative or dramatic elements in cantata verse of the eighteenth century. One other tonal feature of Domenico Scarlatti's cantatas is worth mentioning, and this again is one that reflects a general trend. While adopting by and large the structures found in his father's cantatas, Scarlatti placed himself among the younger generation of composers in showing great preference for major keys. Domenico's cantatas are divided roughly equally between major and minor keys; in the cantatas of Scarlatti *père* minor keys outnumber major by almost five to one.

The cantata was principally a work for solo voice, less commonly for two voices, and only exceptionally for more than two. The vast majority of seventeenth- and eighteenth-century cantatas are for soprano and continuo, the soprano voice (whether female or castrato) being the one most in demand for leading operatic roles. Second in popularity was the alto voice, and there are also numerous cantatas for bass. Only rarely do we find cantatas for tenor, but the prefaces to a number of printed collections make it clear that soprano cantatas were often sung an octave lower by tenors. None of Domenico Scarlatti's cantatas specifies the tenor voice; forty-one of them are for soprano, eight for alto, one for bass, and there are two duet cantatas for two sopranos. These totals probably reflect quite accurately the vocal distribution among Italian cantatas in general during the first two decades of the eighteenth century. Scarlatti's preference for continuo accompaniment is also typical of the period. Only ten cantatas are scored for other instruments as well (in each case two violins) and all but two of these date from after 1725, when composers were coming more and more to prefer full string accompaniment and the cantata was beginning to lose its intimate, chamber-music character.

The chamber cantata was, of course, a literary as well as a musical genre. A specific type of cantata poetry was recognized at the end of the seventeenth century by Giovanni Mario Crescimbeni, a founder member and chronicler of the Arcadian Academy:

> Certain other types of poetry were introduced for music, which are today commonly known as cantatas. They are made up of long and short lines without any regular rhyme scheme [*versi, e versetti rimati senza legge*], mixed with arias. Some are for a single voice, some for more than one, and they were and still are written with an admixture of dramatic and narrative

elements. This kind of poetry was an invention of the seventeenth century; previously madrigals and other regular verse forms served for music.[3]

Crescimbeni clearly recognized the cantata as a verse form specifically designed for musical setting, and although cantata texts were sometimes printed separately as poetry it may be assumed that in most cases they originally served a specific composer, and often a particular occasion as well. The collaboration between poet and composer must frequently have been even closer than that between an opera composer and his librettist, and this is illustrated by Crescimbeni's well-known account of a meeting of the Arcadian Academy at which Alessandro Scarlatti set impromptu verses by a fellow Arcadian, the lawyer Gian Battista Felice Zappi: 'Meanwhile everyone was amazed to see how two such excellent *maestri*, one of poetry and the other of music, contended; and their contention reached such a degree that the first had no sooner finished repeating the last line of a new aria than the other completed the final bars of his music.'[4]

Only rarely are poets named in musical sources, especially manuscripts. Often they were members of the Arcadian or some other literary academy, or they were court poets employed primarily to provide and adapt opera librettos. In some cases a composer's patron might fancy himself as a poet. Cardinal Pamphili, for example, wrote several cantata texts for both Handel and Alessandro Scarlatti, and the words of *Dorme la rosa, aurette grate*, a cantata attributed sometimes to Domenico and sometimes to Mancini, are also by Pamphili. Only two other poets have so far been identified as authors of cantata texts set by Domenico Scarlatti. One is Pietro Metastasio, whose *Pur nel sonno almen tal'ora* Scarlatti may have set during his years in Spain; the other is Ignazio de Bonis, whose text for a particular Roman ceremony will be mentioned later. A thorough search among the poets of Scarlatti's immediate circle might eventually reveal more names, and it is worth bearing in mind that the elder Scarlatti was recognized as a poet as well as a composer.

The 'dramatic and narrative elements' mentioned by Crescimbeni take second place to lyrical expression in the eighteenth-century cantata. Previously – that is, up to and including the early cantatas of Alessandro Scarlatti – the subject-matter had been quite varied. Pastoral settings abounded, but episodes from Classical mythology and from Greek, Roman and even modern history were quite frequently encountered. There were numerous laments and, by contrast, a fair number also of humorous and satirical works, for which Carissimi and Cesti are particularly remembered. But the widespread influence of the Arcadian Academy during the last decade of the seventeenth century led to a vogue for amatory subjects in an idealized pastoral setting, and these soon outnumbered all others. Some semblance of a dramatic situation is usually preserved, but only as an excuse for Filli and Clori, Eurillo and Daliso to tell us, with unrelieved self-pity, of the heartlessness or the inconstancy of their beloved. It would be a mistake to give the impression that every text is one of auto-commiseration, however. There are some which embody lighter sentiments and several which express a love of Nature, usually as a solace for the pains of Love. This last type is well represented in Domenico Scarlatti's bass cantata *Amenissimi prati, fiorite piagge*, which begins with the following lines, set as a recitative:

> Most pleasant fields, flowery banks and limpid brooks,
> Lonely caverns, dark woods and you, melodious warblers,
> I return to see you once more.
> And during this peaceful sojourn
> I desire that Love will not disturb
> The precious freedom of my heart.

The texts that Scarlatti chose (or was given) for his other cantatas are no less conventional in subject and language.

Although the cantata developed alongside opera and was strongly influenced by it, the milieu in which it was performed was rather different. Opera was to some extent a public entertainment, even if it was financially supported by wealthy princes and cardinals. In the cantata the composer addressed himself more intimately to an audience of cognoscenti and was therefore free to express himself in an 'advanced' and even experimental style which might have puzzled or perhaps bored an opera audience. Harmonic audacities are more a feature of Alessandro's later cantatas than of Domenico's; a passage such as that at example 8, from *Onde della mia Nera* (which might be by either composer) shows a degree of harmonic sophistication rarely if ever to be found in an operatic recitative. As the elder Scarlatti had found, Rome provided a particularly favourable environment for cantata writing, and such works were in constant demand at meetings of the Arcadian Academy and at the soirées of the social élite. We have documentary evidence of cantatas composed at Rome by Alessandro Scarlatti for the cardinals Pamphili and Ottoboni and for Prince Ruspoli. Similar evidence is so far lacking in the case of Domenico's chamber cantatas, but a considerable proportion of these must have been written for the music-loving aristocracy of Rome, including of course Queen Maria Casimira, during the years 1708–19.

Example 8

Cantata: *Onde della mia Nera*

Scarlatti's earliest cantatas, however, pre-date this period. Perhaps the earliest of all to survive is *V'adoro o luci belle*, which exists in a copy in the Library of Congress, Washington. The date, in the upper left-hand corner of the manuscript, has unfortunately been partly clipped off, but the year appears to be 1699.[5] If this is so, Domenico must have been about fourteen when he wrote it, possibly with some guidance from his father. The style is certainly consistent with a date before 1700. The work as a whole is harmonically and tonally unadventurous; it ends with recitative (a retrospective feature) and the arias (both in C minor!) are short-winded, with exact repetition employed in an obvious attempt to gain some length. It nevertheless has great melodic charm.

A considerable advance on this very early work is shown in the next two dated cantatas that can with certainty be attributed to Domenico Scarlatti. These are *Care pupille belle* and *Dopo lungo servire*, both of which survive in unique copies, dated July 1702, in the Santini collection at Münster. They must have been written at Rome, where the Scarlatti family stopped on their way from Naples to visit Prince Ferdinando de' Medici in Florence. Thomas Griffin suggested they may have been among the items performed by one of Domenico's sisters (either Flaminia or the slightly younger Cristina) at a soirée in Ruspoli's palace.[6] Possibly both sisters (or a third singer) were involved, since one of the cantatas is for a soprano, the other for an alto. The soirée is mentioned in the *avvisi di Roma* at Munich:

Rome, 18 July 1702

Recently the said Marchese Ruspoli held a polite soirée for ladies and gentlemen of rank at his residence, at which were heard several noted singers, among them the daughter of the eminent Scarlatti. Scarlatti is said to be on his way to Florence, along with the singer Mignatta [Maria Maddalena Musi], to assist with the operas now being prepared for performance in the autumn in the theatre at Pratolino, the villa of the Most Serene Prince of Tuscany.[7]

In the case of the cantata *Care pupille belle*, at least, Griffin's suggestion of a performance at Ruspoli's palace is supported by the fact that the Münster copy is in the hand of Francesco Antonio Lanciani (brother of the composer Flavio Lanciani), who was often employed by Ruspoli and also by Ottoboni and Pamphili. Both cantatas are accompanied by two violins and continuo, which in *Care pupille belle* provide a Corelli-like introduction; only a single violin plays in the two arias. Kirkpatrick (p. 15) was, of course, right when he wrote that these two cantatas 'give little intimation of [Scarlatti's] later style', but such a judgment seems a trifle severe, if not actually patronizing. These cantatas are in fact exceedingly accomplished works for a youth not yet seventeen. *Dopo lungo servire*, especially, is a fluent, expressive piece which shows how well the young composer had already profited from his father's tuition and example in writing vocal chamber music. Its three arias are far in advance of most of those he was to write for the Naples opera during the next eighteen months. Whether or not Domenico at this tender age had yet experienced for himself the pangs of love here ascribed to Fileno, he certainly knew how to give them eloquent musical expression, and the cantata ends with a mature siciliana-type aria to which Alessandro himself would surely not have been ashamed to put his name (example 9).

Of the other authenticated cantatas only two can be dated accurately. One is *Ah, sei troppo infelice*, which in both the extant sources is dated July 1705 (the Bologna source specifies 30 July). It must therefore have been written shortly after Scarlatti's arrival in Venice that year, perhaps for his travelling companion, Nicolo Grimaldi. A connection with Alessandro Scarlatti's setting of Benedetto Pamphili's text, *Sarei troppo felice* (?1701), is suggested by the use of an initial arioso refrain which returns at the end of the first recitative. The same feature occurs in another (undated) cantata, *A chi nacque infelice*, also in the library of the Basilica of San Petronio in Bologna. Both these are good, if not outstanding, examples of Scarlatti's solo cantatas with continuo, and they are among the few so far available in modern editions.[8]

Example 9

Alla siciliana

Cantata: *Dopo lungo servire*

(vns)

(bc)

Ca - ra,   ca - ra se vuoi ch'io

spe - ri,

ca - ra se vuoi ch'io spe — ri   spe - rar an-cor sap-rò

No doubt Scarlatti composed other cantatas at Venice but, for reasons already stated, it is likely that most of those we possess belong to his years at Rome. A Roman provenance is certain for the copy of *Tu mi chiedi o mio ben* (in the hand of F. A. Lanciani) in the Santini collection at Münster, and probable also for those of *Al fin diviene amante* and *Che si peni in amore* in the same library. A special and at first puzzling feature of *Al fin diviene amante* is the unusually high compass of the continuo part, which in the arias is notated mostly in the tenor clef and leaves little space below the vocal line for filling in the continuo harmonies. The explanation for this is that the Münster version, in G minor for alto, has apparently been transposed from the original, in D minor for soprano, two copies of which exist in the Bibliothèque Nationale, Paris. The inexpert arranger has in several places transposed the continuo part up a 4th while at the same time transposing the voice part down a 5th. Particular interest attaches to *Al fin diviene amante* for another reason as well. It is one of only two cantata texts set by both Domenico and Alessandro Scarlatti (if, that is, the anonymous setting in the Library of Congress, Washington, is in fact the work of Alessandro).[9] Despite a striking similarity at the beginning of the central recitative (example 10), the two works are quite different in style, and Domenico's setting is certainly not inferior to the other. In fact, it may be judged to score over it in its lively but unexaggerated response to words such as 'scherza' and 'ride' in a text which warns of the danger in joking about love.

Example 10

Another cantata which probably originated in Rome is *Dorme la rosa, aurette grate*, to words by Cardinal Pamphili. Cantatas in which the singer compares his beloved to a rose or in which, as here, he addresses the flower as the emissary of his affections, were quite common in Arcadian circles. The music of *Dorme la rosa* falls somewhat short of Scarlatti's best efforts (as already mentioned, it might in fact be by Francesco Mancini), but another 'rose' cantata, *Bella rosa adorata*, is noteworthy for the first of its two arias, 'Bella rosa che fastosa' – the only example in Scarlatti's extant works of a ground bass structure. Like many of the grounds in Alessandro Scarlatti's early arias (up to about 1695), Domenico's is contained within a da capo structure. Seven statements of the bass in C minor are followed by an eighth which neatly effects a modulation to G minor for the four statements in that key that make up the middle section; a repeat of the first seven statements then completes the design. The bass theme itself is a version of the descending chromatic 4th (the *passus duriusculus*) that was the common property of all Baroque composers and a favourite expressive device in laments. It would be idle to pretend that Scarlatti uses it with the same mastery as Purcell in *The Fairy Queen* or *Dido and Aeneas*, but his realization of the harmony is very assured, and he avoids too rigid a phrase structure by sometimes omitting the final tonic note and by ensuring that the lines of verse do not always coincide with the same part of the bass theme (example 11):

Example 11

Allegro   Cantata: *Bella rosa adorata*

bel - la, van - to sei di pri - ma - ve - ra (etc)

Roman, or at any rate Umbrian, connections are suggested again by the text of *Onde della mia Nera*. The Nera is a tributary of the Tiber, and the poet looks into its waters to find the image of his distant beloved. To judge from the number of eighteenth-century sources this would seem to have been one of the best-known of Domenico Scarlatti's cantatas, but in fact the work is attributed to Alessandro Scarlatti in two manuscripts (including one in which the attribution has been altered from 'Alessandro' to 'Domenico'), and stylistic considerations alone do not make it possible in this case to judge between them. Among other cantatas whose authorship must for the moment remain undecided is one, *Selve, caverne e monti*, which has been published in a modern edition as Domenico Scarlatti's, but which appears in one source anonymously and in another as a work by Handel. This and other problems of attribution may eventually be solved when the papers, watermarks and handwriting in Scarlatti (and Handel) sources have received the same close study that has been given since about 1945 to the Bach sources. Inevitably, however, the paucity of Scarlatti's autographs will leave many questions unanswered.

Among Scarlatti's other cantatas, the three works in the Biblioteca Antoniana at Padua are more remarkable for the beauty of their calligraphy and their richly ornamented initial letters than for their intrinsic musical qualities, which rarely rise above an attractive but undistinguished competence. One of them is yet another 'rose' cantata, *Rimirai la rosa un dì*. More mature and rewarding, with adventurous harmonies and modulations in the recitatives and broader spans of melody in the arias, are four or five cantatas existing alongside others by the elder Scarlatti in the Bayerische Staatsbibliothek, Munich (MS Mus. 3188). Perhaps the finest of these is *Lontan da te mio bene*, in which the conventional sentiments of the poet yearning for his absent beloved are expressed in two simile arias of unusual poise and melodic beauty. The contrapuntal fabric of the music is in the best traditions of the chamber cantata style, and the work represents the highest point of achievement reached by Scarlatti in the genre before he left Rome in 1719.

There is no particular significance in the fact that not a single one of Scarlatti's chamber cantatas was published during the composer's lifetime. Cantatas were normally printed only when a composer happened to be working in a city where there was a publisher who specialized in such work, for example at Bologna or Venice, or when an enterprising publisher like Estienne Roger of Amsterdam or John Walsh of London could attract subscribers or foresee a market for a particular edition. The vast majority of the thousands of cantatas produced by Italian Baroque composers circulated in manuscript, and except for about half a dozen works this applied even to Alessandro Scarlatti's cantatas. But it is much to be regretted that, while we have four collected editions of Domenico's keyboard sonatas, we must continue to wait for a single edition of the complete cantatas.

The Christmas cantata (*Cantata da recitarsi . . . la notte del Ss.mo natale*), often grouped in work lists with Scarlatti's other cantatas, is in fact an oratorio, and was discussed as such in Chapter 2 (pp. 67–8); other works sometimes referred to as cantatas are more properly categorized as serenatas, and these are described in Chapter 5 (pp. 104–11). A work which must have united features of both the cantata and the serenata is *Alme dilette, e care*, composed for the prize-giving ceremony of the Accademia del Disegno di San Luca at the Palazzo del Campidoglio in Rome on 24 September 1711.[10] It was sung by the castrato Francesco Finaia (known as 'Checchino' or 'Besci') with an orchestra of about twenty players directed by Matteo Fornari, Corelli's friend and pupil. Scarlatti was paid 3 scudi for the composition, the same as Finaia. Only the text, by Ignazio de Bonis, has survived.

There remain for consideration two important sets of chamber cantatas by Domenico Scarlatti, one in the Nationalbibliothek, Vienna, and the other in the British Library, London. These are later works, some at least of them dating almost certainly from the composer's years in Spain. They are therefore discussed separately in Chapter 9.

FOUR *Portugal, c. 1723–9*

Although unaware of Scarlatti's Palermo sojourn, Ralph Kirkpatrick (p. 67) was not slow to point out that in Portugal the composer would have recognized 'certain eastern strains of his Sicilian ancestry and the Saracen traces that had remained in the surroundings of his early childhood'.

In reaching Lisbon from Palermo, Scarlatti would indeed have experienced less of a contrast than if he had proceeded there straight from Rome, as Kirkpatrick imagined. Although the English enjoyed friendly relations and favourable trading terms with Portugal (English wine-merchants had already established their Factory at Oporto), even English visitors to Lisbon in the early eighteenth century described the Portuguese capital in most unflattering terms. Writing to Charles Delafaye, an under-secretary of state, in January 1730, George Hay, Earl of Kinnoull, called the city

> the most dirty and most inconvenient for strangers of any place that ever I saw. The country Barren and not at all cultivated. A monstrous race of Lazy, Ignorant, proud people in one of the finest climates of the world.
>
> Most of those misfortunes proceed from the Nature of the Government.
>
> The prospect up the River very beautiful. There is a very Beautiful old Catholic Church and Monastery two miles below the City upon the River which is the finest old Building in Portugal. The pallace in Lisbon is an irregular Building, But there are a great many handsome large rooms in it. There are no other public Buildings or Churches in Lisbon worth notice. The King is building a very fine new Church at Mafra about 25 English miles from Lisbon in which he spares no expence, and Distresses the whole nation to carry on this work. The Equipages of the Nobility are very magnificent when they come abroad, which is very seldom; But their way of living in their own houses is very mean and parsimonous. And their Conversation as bad as can be, from people of their pride, without any sort of Education or knowledge.[1]

As a servant of the crown, Scarlatti would, of course, be spared some of the rougher aspects of life in Lisbon. The Portuguese society into which he moved, it now seems, in 1723 or thereabouts was known above all for its almost fanatical attachment to Roman catholicism, but also for its love of music, an interest acquired when the eighth duke of Bragança became King John (João) IV in 1640. John IV was born at Vila Viçosa in 1604, and it was there that he began to assemble what was eventually to become one of the most famous and valuable libraries of music and musical treatises that have ever existed. The collection was partly catalogued in 1649 and wholly destroyed in the Lisbon earthquake of 1755. John IV was also a composer and a writer on music. From him the crown passed in 1656 to Alfonso VI and then to Pedro II. John V, Scarlatti's employer, became king in 1706, and his reign, which lasted until 1750, coincided with a period of peace and prosperity for Portugal (the prosperity largely supported by Brazilian gold). John V was lavish in the financial support he gave to successive popes, and secured for the archbishop of Lisbon the style and title of Patriarch. He spent enormous sums of money on maintaining and enriching the fabric of the churches and monasteries and on building new ones. In 1748 Pope Benedict XIV bestowed on him and his successors the title of 'Most Faithful King'. King John V was also a munificent patron of learning and the arts. His musical interests naturally centred on church music, and with the creation of the patriarchate of Lisbon by a papal bull of 1716 the musical adornment of the services was made more elaborate than ever.

In accordance with the king's ambitions to make Lisbon more papal than Rome, Portuguese musicians, including Antonio Teixeira and Francisco Antonio de Almeida, were sent to study in Italy and encouraged to put Italian methods into practice on their return. Like Juvarra, Domenico Scarlatti may have owed his appointment as *mestre de capela* to a recommendation from the Portuguese ambassador in Rome, whom he had served for about five years, but John V must in any case have been highly satisfied to secure the services of a Vatican musician to lead his chapel. It is unfortunate that the documents relevant to Scarlatti's employment in Lisbon were apparently destroyed in the earthquake of 1755. What little we know about the personnel of the royal chapel we owe to the German organist, composer and lexicographer Johann Gottfried Walther, who listed the musicians in 1728 (the last year of Scarlatti's employment there) as follows:

Scarlatti, from Rome – *mestre de capela*
Joseph Antoni, from Portugal – vice-*mestre*
Pietro Giorgio Avondano, from Genoa – 1st violin
Antonio Baghetti, from Rome – 1st violin
Alessandro Baghetti, from Rome – 2nd violin
Johan Peter, from Portugal (but of German parentage) – 2nd violin

Thomas, from Florence – 3rd violin
Latur [= ?Latour], from France – 4th violin and 2nd oboe
Veith, from Bohemia – 4th violin and 1st oboe
Ventur, from Catalonia – viola
Antoni, from Catalonia – viola
Ludewig, from Bohemia – bassoon
Juan, from Catalonia – cello
Laurenti, from Florence – cello
Paolo, from Rome – double bass
Antonio Joseph, from Portugal – organ.[2]

Walther lists these as the principal instrumentalists; there were undoubtedly others. As singers, he mentions the castrato Floriani and the tenor Mossi, both from Rome. In addition he tells us that there were about thirty to forty chorus singers, 'mostly Italian'.

As far as one can tell from the few extant works that can be assigned to these years, Scarlatti used his vocal forces mainly in the composition of old-style *a cappella* church music, continuing in the tradition of St Peter's, Rome, which was so much to the king's taste. Instruments were not required, as is clear from the following description, published in Paris in 1730:

> The patriarchal seat is in the chapel of the king's palace. Its architecture and paintings are no more than ordinary, but its dimensions are vast. As well as the altar in the choir, there are twelve private altars, richly decorated, and a large two-storey gallery with screens, from which the king and queen usually hear Mass. The patriarch normally officiates there on Sundays and feastdays. Eighteen canons wearing mitres accompany him to the altar and serve there. The choir, made up of some thirty or forty beneficiaries, sings music in the Roman style, that is to say without instruments; but among the many voices there are several excellent ones.[3]

The instrumentalists listed by Walther were probably employed mainly in serenatas and other court music for special occasions. Among the serenatas *Contesa delle stagioni* has already been mentioned as the one performed at the royal palace on 7 September 1720. Another serenata by Scarlatti was the *festeggio armonico* written to celebrate the signing of the marriage contract between the infanta Maria Barbara and the crown prince Fernando of Spain. From newspaper announcements it is known that Scarlatti composed other serenatas for royal birthdays and namedays in 1722, but he must also have written the music for numerous other similar works during the Portuguese years of which all trace has now been lost.

Almost unrecognizable in Walther's list of instrumentalists at Lisbon is the young organist and composer Carlos de Seixas, identifiable from his other names, José Antonio. Seixas was the most important of Scarlatti's contemporaries at Lisbon. He arrived there shortly before Scarlatti did, and, although only sixteen, was soon appointed organist of the patriarchal chapel, where he remained for the rest of his life. Don Antonio, the king's younger brother, arranged for him to take some lessons in keyboard playing from Scarlatti, but as soon as Scarlatti heard Seixas play he recognized the younger man's talent with the words, 'It is you who should give me lessons'. Scarlatti reported back to Don Antonio: 'Your Highness commanded me to examine him. But I must tell you that he is one of the best musicians I have ever heard.'[4]

It was said by a contemporary a few years after Seixas's early death (he died in 1742 at the age of thirty-eight) that he had composed as many as seven hundred keyboard sonatas. Most of these were no doubt casualties of the earthquake; only about eighty have survived, together with a few others of doubtful authenticity. Since Seixas and Scarlatti were both exceptionally gifted keyboard players and prolific composers for their instrument, they must each have found in the other a stimulating colleague, but the impossibility of arriving at a reliable chronology for either composer's keyboard music (Seixas's autographs, like Scarlatti's, have disappeared completely) makes it difficult to determine the extent or the direction of their influence on each other. Roberto Pagano has, however, argued persuasively for Seixas as an important influence in determining the course and character of Scarlatti's later development in Portugal and Spain.[5]

In addition to his duties as court composer and *mestre de capela*, Scarlatti was responsible for the musical instruction of Don Antonio and of the king's daughter, Princess Maria Barbara. The king's son, Don José (later King José I of Portugal) seems not to have inherited the Braganças' musical talent. His sister Maria Barbara, on the other hand, showed an early inclination towards music, and particularly towards keyboard playing. If, as is reputed, most of Scarlatti's 550 harpsichord sonatas were written for her, she must have attained a quite exceptional technique on the instrument. In his *Memoirs of the Kings of Spain* William Coxe included a thumbnail sketch of Maria Barbara's character:

She was born in 1711, and in 1729 espoused Ferdinand, who was two years older than herself. By her meek and insinuating manners, she conciliated the good will of Philip and the queen her step-mother [i.e. mother-in-law];

while she gained the entire affection of her husband by her amiable deportment, and conformity to his inclinations and temper. She was homely in her features, and the original elegance of her shape was lost in corpulence.

Barbara was a woman of agreeable address, sprightly wit, and uncommon gentleness of manners. She was cheerful in public, and extravagantly fond of dancing and music; but she partook of the constitutional melancholy of her husband. Her solitary hours were haunted by two contrary apprehensions; the dread of want, the customary fate of the Spanish queens, if she survived him; and the fear of sudden death, which her asthmatic complaint, and plethoric habit, rendered not unlikely. From the first of these motives, she was greedy of amassing money, and debased her dignity by accepting presents from the ministers, and even from foreign ambassadors. Hence, notwithstanding her engaging qualities, she was never beloved nor respected in Spain.[6]

As far as Coxe's final remarks are concerned, it would not be difficult to find examples of Maria Barbara's generosity as well as of her acquisitiveness, and if she was neither 'beloved nor respected' by the Spanish populace as a whole, she certainly earned the affection and respect of her immediate circle, including Scarlatti and Farinelli. Coxe was, in any case, writing about Maria Barbara as Queen of Spain. As infanta of Portugal she seems already to have been 'homely in appearance' (Coxe elsewhere quoted a description of her 'large mouth, thick lips, high cheekbones and small eyes'), though she had not yet begun to develop the corpulence of her later years.

On at least two or three occasions Scarlatti obtained leave of absence from the Portuguese court to revisit Italy. The renowned German flautist, Johann Joachim Quantz, recalled in his autobiography (1754) that between June 1724 and January 1725 he was in Rome. 'Mimo [Domenico] Scarlatti, a *galant* clavier player in the manner of the time, also was in Rome. He was in the Portuguese service, but later went into the Spanish service, where he is still employed.' Quantz was in Rome to take lessons from Francesco Gasparini, and no doubt Scarlatti also renewed his friendship with his former teacher. But the main reason for his visit may have been to superintend a revival of his opera *Tolomeo et Alessandro*, perhaps at the palace of André de Melo e Castro. Melo e Castro, the fourth Count of Galveias, had been sent to Rome by John V in 1707 as the king's special envoy to the pope, and was so successful in pursuing Portuguese interests at the Vatican that in 1718 he was promoted to the rank of Ambassador Extraordinary. He lived extravagantly at Rome on a princely income, and commissioned a number of stage works for his private theatre, among them

Alessandro Scarlatti's pastoral serenata *La virtù negli amori*, performed in November 1721, and Gasparini's last opera, *Tigrane*, in January 1724. There is no known score or libretto relevant to a Roman revival of Domenico Scarlatti's *Tolomeo* at this time, but the overture, dated 1724, is included in a manuscript collection of overtures to operas performed at Rome in 1722–4,[7] and this strongly suggests that such a revival did in fact take place. Possibly it was during this visit to Rome that Scarlatti became acquainted with the family of his future wife.

The death of Alessandro Scarlatti at Naples on 22 October 1725 marks the close of a chapter in Domenico's life and career. He travelled to Naples to see his father before he died, and it is pleasant to think that any remaining differences between them were resolved before the moment of final parting came. At Naples Domenico met also the German composer Johann Adolf Hasse, then aged twenty-six, who had been taking lessons from Alessandro. Burney tells us that Hasse later claimed that 'the first time [Alessandro] Scarlatti saw him, he luckily conceived such an affection for him, that he ever after treated him with the kindness of a father'.[8] When Burney met Hasse in Vienna in September 1772 he asked the aged composer if he had heard Domenico play. Hasse recalled that 'he had, at the time he came from Portugal to Naples, on a visit to his father, while he [Hasse] studied under him; and he allowed him to have been possessed of a wonderful hand, as well as fecundity of invention'.[9]

At the Teatro San Bartolomeo in 1725 Domenico could have heard operas by Leonardo Leo and Leonardo Vinci – leading representatives of a new generation of opera composers at Naples. If he had been a guest in September at the country estate of Carlo Carmignano, a Neapolitan courtier, he could have listened to his future colleague Farinelli singing in Hasse's serenata *Antonio e Cleopatra*, a work which earned its composer a commission to write an opera for the San Bartolomeo theatre the following year. Perhaps even before then Domenico Scarlatti had come to accept that the future of opera was to be in the hands of composers working in, or trained in, the place from which he himself had severed all ties. Perhaps he now recognized, as the strongest of all family ties was also severed, that it was Hasse and not himself who was to inherit his father's artistic legacy. And perhaps he realized, too, that his own way ahead lay in developing the 'wonderful hand' and the 'fecundity of invention' that Hasse had marvelled at in his keyboard playing.

This may have been the last time that Scarlatti saw his native city, but it was not his last visit to Italy. He may not have been at Jesi for another revival of *Tolomeo et Alessandro* in 1727, but he was certainly in

Rome in 1728 to marry Maria Catarina Gentili, the daughter of a well-to-do Roman couple, Francisco Maria and Margarita Rossetti Gentili. The marriage took place on 15 May in the church of San Pancrazio and was registered in the *Liber matrimonium* of the parish of Santa Maria in Publicolis.

> In the church of San Pancrazio, and before the altar of the Assumption of the Blessed Virgin Mary, I questioned Domenico Scarlatti, son of the late Cavaliere Alessandro and a Roman of the parish of Santa Maria in Monterone, and Maria Catarina Gentili, daughter of Francisco Maria Gentili and a Roman of this parish, and with their full accord I joined them in matrimony . . . in the presence of Canon Joanne Monterio Brano, son of the late Antonio Freitas of Guimarães, from the parish of Santa Maria in Aquiro, Lusitania, and Jacobo Cavalli, son of Federico Jacobo of Verona, from the parish of Santa Maria in Monterone, who were witnesses to the aforesaid marriage.[10]

The ceremony was performed by the rector of Santa Maria in Publicolis, who identifies himself as 'Sextilius de Caolis'. The bride was sixteen years old, the groom forty-two. There cannot have been any romantic attachment between them before Scarlatti left Rome in 1719, or even by 1724–5 when he last visited the city, although he was quite possibly on friendly terms with the family by then. Kirkpatrick (p. 77) suggested that Scarlatti may have waited a long time before marrying because he had taken minor orders in the church. He is twice referred to in the pages of the *Gazeta de Lisboa* as 'Abbade Scarlatti'. There is, however, nothing in the marriage register to rule out the possibility of an earlier marriage on Scarlatti's part.

Only a few months after Scarlatti's marriage another wedding ceremony took place which was to be hardly less important to his future life. In January 1729 the royal families of Spain and Portugal were united by the double marriage of Crown Prince Fernando of Spain to Maria Barbara of Bragança, and of the Spanish infanta Maria Vitoria to Don José of Portugal. This 'Exchange of Princesses' took place in a pavilion built at enormous expense over the River Caia on the border between Elvas in Portugal and Badajoz in Spain. The site had no doubt been chosen partly because of its vicinity to Vila Viçosa, the ancient seat of the Braganças which, since the accession of King John IV in 1640, had served the royal family as a retreat and a hunting-lodge. At the time of the double wedding the Portuguese court spent about three weeks there, and Scarlatti's services must surely have been required for such a splendid and historic occasion, which was celebrated with 'a fine Consort of Music perform'd by the

Musick of both the King's Chappels'.[11] It was perhaps for these celebrations that Scarlatti composed the motet and *Te Deum* that are today to be found in the library of the ducal palace at Vila Viçosa. Presumably he would have made contact at this time with his opposite number from the Spanish court, Joseph de Torres y Martinez Bravo, who had been appointed *maestro de capilla* in about 1718 and was to retain the title until his death in 1738.

What Maria Barbara may have lacked in physical beauty she made up for in the strength and amiability of her personality. She soon won the lifelong devotion of her husband and earned good reports from all who came into contact with her. When she entered Spain as Princess of the Asturias she took with her the music master who was to serve her uncomplainingly for the rest of his life. As far as is known, Domenico Scarlatti never again looked for employment elsewhere.

FIVE *Serenatas*

The serenata may be thought of as a genre mid-way between the chamber cantata and the opera, being a secular vocal work longer than the first but shorter than the second. Like both of these, it consisted mainly of recitative and arias, with the occasional ensemble; sometimes a chorus was also used, and the instrumentation was more elaborate than that of most cantatas (more elaborate even than that of most operas), with brass and woodwind instruments in addition to the usual string band. In Naples and Rome serenatas were a favourite type of summer music, performed out of doors in the evening with an orchestra of usually fifty to a hundred players, sometimes even more. When conditions did not permit open-air performance serenatas were frequently given in a theatre or large salon, with elaborate staging and perhaps even costumes, but without action or gesture. Despite its secular text, the resemblance to the Italian *oratorio volgare* was very marked, especially as the serenata was frequently performed in two parts, with an interval between them during which refreshments were served.

Like the secular cantatas of J. S. Bach, by which the genre is best known today, Italian serenatas were above all occasional pieces, written for particular celebrations such as a royal birthday, nameday or wedding festivity, to greet a distinguished visitor or to commemorate an important political or social event. The earliest serenata known to have been composed by Domenico Scarlatti was *Il concilio degli dei*, performed at Naples or in Sicily in 1704. It was one of two serenatas to words by a certain Pietro Riccio celebrating the birth of a daughter to the Prince and Princess of Villafranca; the other, *L'Oreto festivo*, was composed by Domenico Sarro. The libretto of *Il concilio degli dei* was discovered by the Polish scholar Michael Bristiger;[1] the music has not so far come to light.

As *maestro di cappella* to Queen Maria Casimira in Rome, Scarlatti must have been called upon to provide music for several serenatas, since the queen and her son, Alexander, were evidently fond of such entertainments. Thomas Griffin gives details of serenata performances at the Palazzo Zuccari from 1703 onwards, drawing his information mainly from accounts in Francesco Valesio's diary, in the *avvisi di Roma* at Munich and in the *avvisi giornalieri* in the Vatican. These include the following, for which it is reasonable to suppose that Scarlatti may have supplied the music:

Saturday, 7 September 1709

The Queen of Poland had a noble serenata performed this evening at her palace at the Trinità de' Monti, at which there was a great crowd of people.[2]

Thursday, 12 September 1709

To commemorate the liberation of Vienna from the siege by the Turkish army, in which her husband King John IV [Jan Sobieski] of Poland played such a large part, the dowager queen of Poland had her residence at the Trinità de' Monti beautifully illuminated this evening. A fine musical cantata was given at the usual place where the bridge crosses the Strada Felice.[3]

8 August 1711

On Monday night [3 August] Prince Alexander, son of the Queen [of Poland], had her [the singer Maria Domenica Pini] perform a serenata with two other singers from the household on the ample balcony of his apartment opposite the Church of the Trinità de' Monti, where there was a great crowd . . .[4]

19 September 1711

On the same Saturday evening [12 September], from the balcony which Her Majesty [Queen Maria Casimira] has had built above the main entrance to her residence at the Trinità de' Monti in order to have cantatas and serenatas performed there, a serenata was sung by her two female singers [*cantarine*] and two of her male singers [*musici*], with a large band of instruments. It did not receive much applause, especially since a north wind was blowing which forced many of the ladies and gentlemen to leave in their carriages before the performance had ended. On hearing the noise this made, Her Majesty declared that if this weather persisted it would be advisable to give up serenatas and start making plans for the operas to be performed during the forthcoming Carnival.[5]

The serenatas referred to in these reports cannot now be identified, unless the 'cantata' performed on 12 September 1709 was Scarlatti's oratorio *La conversione di Clodoveo* (see p. 41). Scarlatti was certainly the composer of a serenata (or *applauso devoto*) performed at the Palazzo Zuccari on 12 September 1712 to commemorate again the role of Jan Sobieski in the liberation of Vienna. The text, a flowery tribute to the Virgin (at the same time flattering Maria Casimira herself), was by C. S. Capece; the music has not survived.

Maria Casimira was not Scarlatti's only patron in Rome, and he may have been the composer, too, of what was evidently a serenata for the nameday of King Louis XIV of France, performed before the palace of Prince Guido Vaini, a supporter of the Bourbon cause in Rome. Griffin quotes the following description from a letter written by Charles-François Poerson, director of the French Academy in Rome:

27 August 1712

On the Feast of St Louis [25 August] Prince Vaini arranged a celebration in front of his palace which was enthusiastically applauded. The words, in praise of the king, are by the lawyer Sapi [Gian Battista Felice Zappi], son-in-law of Cavaliere Maratto [Carlo Maratti] and the music by the famous Scarlati. The façade of the building was richly decorated and refreshments were served there and to those in carriages in the square.

Monsignore Molinés [Joseph Molinés, another member of the Bourbon faction], who lives opposite Vaini, had his palace illuminated and provided copious refreshments, and all about the square could be heard shouts of 'Long live great Louis'.[6]

After the departure from Rome of Queen Maria Casimira in 1714, Scarlatti must have composed several similar serenatas in his capacity as *maestro di cappella* to the Marques de Fontes. The libretto of one of these has survived; it is an *applauso genetliaco* ('birthday greeting') in honour of the Infante Don José of Portugal, brother of Scarlatti's future pupil and patron, Maria Barbara de Bragança, and later King José I (his elder brother having died in infancy). Don José was born on 6 June 1714, and the serenata composed by Scarlatti was presumably the one described in the following report from the *Gazette de France* of 8 September 1714:

11 August 1714

Yesterday the Portuguese ambassador had a *Te Deum* sung in the national church [S. Antonio dei Portoghesi] as an act of thanksgiving for the birth of a second son to his master the king. In the evening he presented a magnificent serenata on a stage erected in front of his palace in the Piazza Colonna, which was completely illuminated; there was a large gathering of the nobility and commoners.[7]

The three singers in the serenata were named in the printed libretto as follows:

Circe	Caterina Lelli Mossi
Aurora	Paola Alari
Ulisse	Vittorio Chiccheri

Paola Alari was one of the singers who had taken part in the Arcadian performance of *Tolomeo et Alessandro* in 1711. Possibly she, like Scarlatti, had found employment with the Marques de Fontes after Maria Casimira's departure for France. As Aurora ('Dawn') it is she who announces the birth of the Portuguese crown prince, the involvement of Ulysses and Circe amounting to nothing more than a long and elaborate diversion.

This *applauso genetliaco* was the first of several serenatas in which Scarlatti and his librettists (all anonymous) were to pay homage to the Portuguese court. The other serenatas were composed for Lisbon after, or (as we now know) in some cases before, Scarlatti took up his post there as *mestre de capela* to the Portuguese monarch. The style and language, however, remain Italian. On 7 September 1720 a serenata with the title *Contesa delle stagioni* was performed at the royal palace to celebrate the birthday of the queen, Marianna. On 27 December in the same year the king's nameday (or, at any rate, one of them: the feast of St John the Evangelist) was observed with a serenata (or 'cantata pastorale'). A 'serenata composta em musica pelo Abbade Scarlatti' for the queen's birthday on 7 September 1722, reported in the *Gazeta de Lisboa*, has not yet been identified, but Manuel da Costa Brito was able to identify the serenata composed for the king's nameday in December that year as *Le nozze di Baco e d'Arianna*.[8] Finally, on 11 January 1728 a *festeggio armonico* ('harmonious celebration') at the royal palace marked the betrothal of the infanta Maria Barbara to Don Fernando of Spain. This last was perhaps the most elaborate of all Scarlatti's Portuguese serenatas; there were six vocal soloists, and each of the work's two parts began and ended with a chorus.

In addition to these serenatas known to have been composed by Scarlatti, Manuel da Costa Brito listed the following anonymous ones performed at the Lisbon court between September 1719 and October 1728.[9] It is likely that some (perhaps most) were the work of Scarlatti.

24 September 1719	unidentified serenata
22 October 1719	*Triunfos de Ulysses & Glorias de Portugal*
4 November 1719	unidentified serenata
19 November 1719	unidentified serenata
26 July 1720	unidentified serenata
22 October 1720	*Trionfo delle virtù*
24 June 1721	*Componimento musicale*
7 September 1721	*Serenata pastorale*
24 June 1722	*Gl'amorosi avvenimenti*

22 October 1722	*Gli amori di Cefilo e d'Endimione*
26 July 1723	unidentified serenata
27 December 1723	*Le ninfe del Tago*
24 June 1724	*Aci, e Galatea* [? by Astorga]
26 July 1724	unidentified serenata
27 December 1724	unidentified serenata
24 June 1725	unidentified serenata
9 October 1725	unidentified serenata (to mark the matrimonial contracts of the princes of Spain and Portugal)
22 October 1725	*La costanza gradita*
25 October 1725	unidentified serenata
4 November 1725	unidentified serenata
18 December 1725	unidentified serenata
27 December 1725	*Amor nasce da un'sguardo*
31 March 1726	*Dramma pastorale*
6 June 1726	*Il doppio amore vilipeso*
24 June 1726	unidentified serenata
26 July 1726	*Andromeda*
27 December 1726	unidentified serenata
7 September 1727	unidentified serenata
4 November 1727	unidentified serenata
27 December 1727	*L'aurora*
6 June 1728	unidentified serenata
28 August 1728	unidentified serenata
22 October 1728	*Gli sogni amorosi*

Because of the occasional nature of the serenata, proportionately more examples have been lost than is the case with most other genres, and it is not altogether surprising to find that not a single serenata by Scarlatti has survived complete. Once an event had been commemorated there was no particular incentive to preserve the score and parts, except perhaps in order to adapt the music to new texts later on – a practice for which Scarlatti, unlike Bach, can have found few opportunities. The only work we have by which to judge Scarlatti's abilities as a composer of official, functional music is the first part only of a two-part serenata with the title *Contesa delle stagioni*, written to celebrate the birthday of Queen Marianna on 7 September 1720. The solo singers are not named in the printed libretto, but they are listed on a fly-leaf in the score, as follows:

Primavera	Floriano [soprano]
Estate	Cristini [soprano]
Autunno	Mossi [tenor]
Inverno	D. Luiggi [alto]

Floriano, a castrato, and Mossi, both of them from Rome, were mentioned by J. G. Walther as belonging to the Lisbon *capela* in 1728 (see p. 98). The other singers, too, were perhaps among the 'new and excellent musicians which His Majesty . . . had brought from Rome'.[10]

The contest into which the four seasons enter is one to determine which of them has contributed most to the happiness of mankind. Autumn is unanimously (and predictably) agreed to be the victor, since that was the season in which Queen Marianna came into the world. The contest having been decided in Part 1, the second part is given over to applauding Autumn as the victor and, of course, to expressing the joy and devotion of the queen's subjects on her birthday.

The music of the *Contesa delle stagioni* may not be the greatest, but it is certainly the grandest we have by Scarlatti. The orchestra includes two trumpets, two 'trombe da caccia', flute, full strings in four parts and continuo (the missing score of Part 2 may have indicated further instruments). The trombe da caccia were presumably horns; their music is notated in F, using the bass clef, and they were probably played by the two trumpeters. They are heard in Autumn's 'In simile arringo', an unusually florid aria obviously designed so that Mossi's superior vocal technique could be seen (or heard) to win the day. As might be expected, Autumn is given more arias than the other seasons, and his 'Sia dolce e caro e grato' (substituted for the 'Nel mondo giocondo' of the printed libretto), although less virtuoso, is one of the best things in Part 1, with some attractive writing for the solo flute.

Framing these and the other three arias of Part 1 are two substantial choruses. The first begins with fanfares, shared between violins and trumpets, which for the modern listener inevitably recall the openings of several of the later harpsichord sonatas. With its broad antiphonal contrasts between solo voices and the full four-part choir, which might have numbered as many as thirty or forty singers, this opening chorus must have made an imposing effect at the palace in Lisbon, whether in the royal apartments or in the open air (see example 12 overleaf).

If the *Contesa delle stagioni* is anything to go by, Scarlatti never came closer than in these Portuguese serenatas to the majestic, 'public' style of Handel's ceremonial music. Their loss has perhaps robbed Scarlatti's œuvre of an important dimension, possibly an even more important one than the church music which is the subject of the next chapter.

Example 12

Serenata: *Contesa delle stagioni*

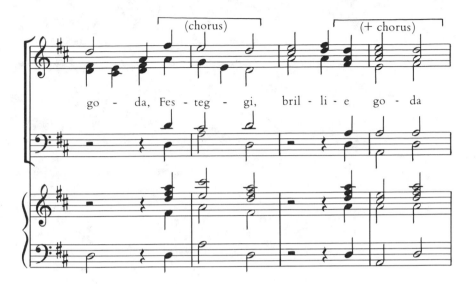

go – da, Fes – teg – gi, bril – li – e go – da

SIX *Church Music*

It would be difficult to name another composer of Domenico Scarlatti's stature who adopted and mastered, as he did, three quite different and contrasting musical styles. There are, of course, composers such as Beethoven whose development seems to proceed through three recognizably distinct phases, but whose music as a whole nevertheless shows a compelling stylistic unity. There are others such as Stravinsky who have turned fairly abruptly and with some degree of conscious intention from one style to another. But in Scarlatti's case the three musical styles encompassed are so very different from each other that it might seem almost unbelievable that they could belong to the same century, let alone to a single composer at one time. First there is the predominantly vocal style of the fashionable opera, oratorio, cantata and serenata which we have encountered in earlier chapters. Then there is the strikingly original and essentially instrumental style of the later harpsichord sonatas (see Chapter 8). The present chapter brings forward the third style, the unaccompanied (or continuo-accompanied) polyphony 'alla Palestrina' in which most of Scarlatti's extant church music is written.

While Scarlatti's simultaneous command of three different styles was exceptional, and perhaps unique, it was not uncommon for composers to be musically bilingual in the seventeenth and eighteenth centuries. Any composer employed in the Catholic church, especially at Rome, might be expected to write masses and motets in a style which had virtually ceased to exist outside the church. Scarlatti's own father had composed numerous works in what he once referred to as the 'stile sodo del Palestrina',[1] and he continued to do so right up to the year of his death (1725). The style-conscious Baroque recognized the propriety of the *stile antico* for church music, even if it overestimated its potential for creating new masterpieces.

Before turning to Domenico Scarlatti's church music it is perhaps necessary to correct one or two possible misconceptions concerning the 'stile sodo del Palestrina' in which most of it is written. The first thing to be said is that, while Scarlatti and his contemporaries would certainly have regarded the style of the *a cappella* church music they wrote as deliberately archaic, they would not have felt that in using it they were resurrecting an outworn and discarded idiom. The *stile antico* was not, admittedly, a vernacular language among musicians of the early eighteenth century, but neither was it any more dead a language than the Latin which it clothed. Latin was the daily language of church services; it was often the literary language, too, of educated men, and it had not completely died out as a means of ordinary conversation in certain contexts. Even in Lutheran Germany it survived in educational establishments such as the Thomasschule at Leipzig, where it was laid down in the school regulations that foundation scholars in the three upper classes should 'converse in Latin among themselves and with their teachers' (including J. S. Bach).[2] In Italy, too, both spoken and written Latin was widely used in schools and universities. The musical language of the *stile antico* had similarly survived in an unbroken, although not unchanging, tradition throughout the seventeenth century, and it was a language which the late Baroque musician could experience directly in the church and not merely through studying textbooks about it.

The *stile antico* should not, therefore, be thought of as a *stile usato*, a misconception which has been fostered by the term 'alla Palestrina' often used to describe it. In Domenico Scarlatti's *stile antico* works there is scarcely a single passage of more than a few bars which could conceivably be mistaken for the work of Palestrina or of any other sixteenth-century composer. The contrapuntal texture, relieved by passages of straightforward homophony, does give the music a superficial resemblance to Palestrina's, as does the *a cappella* texture, with only a simple organ continuo (if that) to accompany the voices. But the grammar and syntax of the music, and even to some extent its vocabulary, are quite different from Palestrina's. The melodic material is more regularly structured, especially in its rhythm, and there is frequent use of repetition and sequence; melodic leaps – for example, of major 6ths and diminished 7ths – proscribed in the strict Palestrina style are not infrequently found; minims are freely used as passing-notes in a 4/2 metre; and suspensions may be resolved on to crotchets. While lip-service may be paid to the modal system as far as key-signatures and the range of modulations are concerned, the strong tonal bias of the harmony is reinforced by the unfettered employment of dominant 7th chords.

Originality is probably the last thing one should expect to find in Baroque works employing the *stile antico*. By the early eighteenth century the main preoccupation for composers working in the style was to find new contexts and fresh developments for well-tried, even stereotyped contrapuntal formulae. Scarlatti's church music is certainly not free from contrapuntal clichés, but the composer organizes and develops these with considerable skill, and in at least one work succeeds in making something quite moving out of them.

It is impossible to determine an exact chronology for Scarlatti's sacred works and, given their largely impersonal physiognomy, stylistic considerations are of little help in arriving at even an approximate one. Only a single work, the A major setting of *Salve regina*, is dated in the sources, and this is an exceptional piece in every way: it was written during the last year of Scarlatti's life, long after he had ceased composing regularly for the church; it is his only sacred work for solo voice and one of only two with instrumental accompaniment other than continuo; and it is composed in a style which owes as much to secular as to ecclesiastical traditions. More detailed consideration of it will therefore be reserved for a later chapter (see pp. 202–4). Most if not all of the other sacred compositions were written, one may presume, during those periods between 1708 and 1728 when Scarlatti was employed as a church composer, first at the basilica of Santa Maria Maggiore, then at the Vatican and finally at the patriarchal chapel in Lisbon. It is not impossible, however, that he had previously been called upon to write some church music during the short time in 1701–4 when he was employed as 'organista e compositore di musica' at the royal chapel in Naples.

The present survey of Scarlatti's sacred works may conveniently begin with another *Salve regina* setting, the one in A minor for two solo voices (soprano and alto) and continuo. Loek Hautus, in his edition of the motet (Kassel, 1971), suggested that this may be the work to which Hermann Mendel and August Reissmann referred when they wrote that 'In Rome Scarlatti composed several pieces of church music [of which] a four-part mass (1712) and a *Salve regina* are known'.[3] Certainly the A minor *Salve regina* shows affinities with much Italian church music of the period, and also with the secular chamber duet in which the singers share the same text throughout. It is an intimate, devotional piece which would serve better for a small private chapel than for a church such as St Peter's, Rome. Can it be that Scarlatti's two settings of this antiphon to the Queen of Heaven were each written for one of the earthly queens he served, both of whom were called Maria?

The score of the A minor *Salve regina* in the Civico Museo Bibliografico Musicale, Bologna, is the only one known to survive. It has been transcribed from an older incomplete score and vocal parts which exist alongside it. Neither score throws any light on when or for whom the piece was composed. The present locations of manuscript sources of other sacred works do, however, offer some clues which may help towards establishing a tentative chronology for this part of Scarlatti's output. Possibly the earliest extant church pieces are those which have remained, ever since Scarlatti wrote them, in the archives of the Basilica Liberiana (Santa Maria Maggiore) in Rome. In the preface to his edition of Scarlatti's *Stabat mater* (Rome, 1941) Alfredo Casella mentioned a mass and a psalm, *Nisi quia Dominus*, as existing in the library of this church, but it was not until 1985 that, thanks to the researches of Eleonora Simi Bonini, they were restored to the Scarlatti canon. In addition, Dr Simi Bonini was able to report the discovery of two other church pieces, a *Pange lingua* and a *Cibavit nos Dominus*, in the same precious archive.

St Thomas Aquinas's hymn, *Pange lingua gloriosi*, receives from Scarlatti a simple four-part setting in a Dorian D minor, with only a little rhythmic independence between the parts. Its sixteen bars are repeated for each of the five stanzas and the doxology. The tenor part has, unfortunately, not survived, but may be reconstructed from the other three.

The antiphon *Cibavit nos Dominus* is also set for soprano, alto, tenor and bass, without organ. It was possibly intended, along with the *Pange lingua*, as part of the music sung on the feast of Corpus Christi in 1708, in the composition of which Scarlatti may have collaborated with his father. Possibly they also shared the copying of the parts, since the two hands responsible for *Cibavit nos Dominus* in the unique source show some striking similarities. Domenico's setting of the antiphon, in F major (or Ionian mode transposed, but decidedly not Lydian despite its lack of a key-signature), is one of his most successful *stile antico* pieces, with a particularly attractive, rhythmically supple 'Alleluia'. *Nisi quia Dominus*, a setting of Psalm 124 (123 in the Vulgate) uses a more modern homophonic style, with a strongly tonal (D minor) outline and regular rhythmic patterns notated in short note-values. The descending D minor arpeggio at the opening recurs often as a structural feature, especially in the bass. The usual four voice parts are accompanied by organ continuo.

The most substantial of Scarlatti's compositions for the Basilica Liberiana is a setting in A minor of the ordinary of the mass for soprano, alto, tenor and bass 'con R[ipien]o' (that is, with solo and choral sections in alternation). There is also an organ continuo part which bears the designation 'Messa a 4° breve' and the title *La stella*, evidently added later. The setting shows some unusual features: the first section of the *Agnus Dei* reuses material from the *Sanctus*, and Scarlatti sets neither the *Benedictus* nor 'Dona nobis pacem'. These omissions, curious in themselves, do not, however, account for the designation 'breve', which, as in the similar case of Palestrina's *Missa brevis*, is used to indicate a setting of relatively short duration, with a minimum of textual repetition and florid counterpoint, and with a larger proportion than usual of homophonic texture.

Perhaps the most puzzling feature of this mass is its stylistic dichotomy. The *Kyrie* and *Gloria* employ a kind of *stile misto* rather like that of the later *Stabat mater*, combining an antiquated harmonic vocabulary with post-Renaissance rhythms and periods. From the beginning of the Credo, and for the remainder of the mass, the music and its notation adopt an altogether different, more strictly *antico* physiognomy. Triple metre, which had occupied a large proportion of the first two sections, is now confined to the five bars of 'Resurrexit tertia die' (notated in 3/1 metre) and the separation of the last three sections from the first two is further emphasized by the recapitulation of material within them: not only of the *Sanctus* at 'Agnus Dei', already mentioned, but also, for example, of 'Patrem omnipotentem' at 'Confiteor unum baptisma'. It seems unlikely that Domenico Scarlatti, one of the most style-conscious of all composers, would have made this dichotomy without some reason.

In his capacity as *maestro* of the Cappella Giulia, Scarlatti must have composed a great deal more than the three pieces of his that remain today in the Vatican library: an *Iste confessor* and two *Miserere* settings. The hymn *Iste confessor* is given a strophic setting even simpler in style than that of *Pange lingua*, discussed above. Verses 1, 3 and 5 are directed to be sung by a solo treble, verses 2 and 4 by the full choir (SATB). The piece, in G major, ends with a plagal 'amen'. Kirkpatrick (p. 58) suggested that it was this setting that was performed in procession through the streets of Rome on 11 April, the feast of St Leo the Great, in 1715. If so, perhaps all the verses were sung chorally on that occasion, since it is difficult otherwise to understand how the solo treble could have been heard to much effect, or how the organ accompaniment would have been accommodated.

Scarlatti's two unaccompanied settings of the penitential psalm *Miserere mei Deus* (no. 50 in the Vulgate, no. 51 in the Authorized Version and the *Book of Common Prayer*) are both *alternatim* settings. Only the odd-numbered verses and the final verse are set polyphonically, the others being sung in unison to the traditional psalm tones. Neither setting includes the doxology (*Gloria Patri*) – a strong indication, as Magda Marx-Weber has pointed out,[4] of the occasion for which they were composed. At the Vatican it was the custom to omit the doxology when the *Miserere* concluded the service of Tenebrae on the Thursday, Friday and Saturday of Holy Week. Dr Marx-Weber draws attention to the tradition of Holy Week *Miserere* settings for the Sistine Chapel, in particular those of Gregorio Allegri, Alessandro Scarlatti and Tommaso Baj. Domenico Scarlatti's G minor *Miserere* continues that tradition in many ways: it is in the same key as the others, it recalls their *falsobordone* practice in the chordal repetitions at the beginning of several verses (or half-verses) and it makes use of the first psalm tone (at verse 1 in the tenor, at verse 11 in the soprano and at verse 15 in the bass). Particular interest attaches to the G minor setting, too, since its source is the only example so far identified of the composer's musical hand.

The *Miserere* in E minor is somewhat longer and more contrapuntal in texture. The *falsobordone* traces of the G minor setting are here set aside, leaving room for a more imitative and expressive texture which is fairly representative of Scarlatti's usual *stile antico* manner (example 13). As Magda Marx-Weber has shown, the E minor *Miserere* stands at the beginning of an entirely new tradition in Rome, and one that the Cappella Giulia was slow to accept. In the Vatican source Scarlatti's original ending, which recapitulated the opening material at the beginning of the last verse, has been struck out and replaced in a different hand by another one which restores the older traditions

Example 13

Miserere

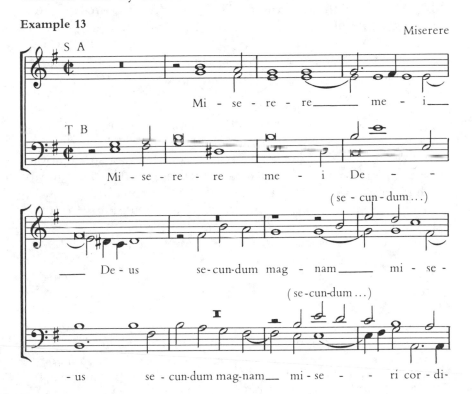

(including that of *falsobordone*). Fortunately, Scarlatti's original ending – original in more senses than one – can still be read.

For all their historical interest and importance, the compositions in the Vatican sources represent a somewhat disappointing return for the years that Domenico Scarlatti spent at St Peter's. More substantial and rewarding are four works assigned consecutive numbers in the catalogue of the Santini collection at Münster; at least two of these are also probably of Roman origin. The *Magnificat* is scored for four voices (SATB) without either divisions or instrumental support, the basso continuo part in the unique Münster source being the work of Fortunato Santini. It is an accomplished, if not exactly gripping, piece of sustained counterpoint in motet style, with a fresh point of imitation for each phrase of the text. Its predominantly seamless texture is broken occasionally by well-defined cadences in keys closely related to the basic D minor and by reductions in texture, sometimes to a single voice. Passages of homophony are few and mostly quite short. The long melismatic 'amen' reaches an effective climax, not by the more obvious and well-tried means of intensifying the sonority (by high pitch, divisi etc.) but by having the 'amen' theme itself, which recalls the opening of the work, return as a cantus firmus in measured breves, in a way which suggests a plainchant origin. The *Magnificat* commands respect for its contrapuntal skill, but it is on too even a level to engage the interest for its entire length.

The second Münster work, the motet *Memento Domine David*, a setting of Psalm 132 (no. 131 in the Vulgate), raises problems of authenticity. In the Santini copy the attribution has been altered to 'Alessandro' Scarlatti, apparently from 'Domenico', to whom the work is attributed in manuscripts at Munich and in the British Library. But in one British Library manuscript (Add. 14166) and in several other sources it is claimed as Alessandro's. E. J. Dent accepted it as such and reported that it was reputedly written during a visit to Loreto in 1722.[5] He also listed an autograph in the library of the Naples conservatory, but neither of the copies at present in that library is in Alessandro Scarlatti's hand, though they are both attributed to him. The motet recalls Domenico's *Magnificat* in the way that its opening theme is adapted for the long, florid 'amen', but the probability that the composer is not Domenico is strengthened by the fact that in several sources the work is found alongside Francesco Durante's motet *Protexisti me Deus*, composed in April 1745 for the competition organized to select a successor to Leonardo Leo at the royal chapel in Naples.

Similar considerations come into play when attempting to decide the authenticity of the curious *Capriccio fugato a dodici*, or *Fuga estemporanea* as it is called in some sources. This has been attributed to Domenico Scarlatti, and even published as his in a modern edition by Paul Winter. But this, too, often appears alongside the motets by Durante and Scarlatti just mentioned, and in most cases it is attributed simply to 'Scarlatti'. In an unpublished review of the German edition of Kirkpatrick's monograph, kindly communicated to the present writer, Loek Hautus put forward the suggestion that the work may have been Pietro Scarlatti's 'entry' for the same competition as that for which Durante wrote *Protexisti me Deus*. But, as Hautus also mentions, in manuscript 3969 of the Santini collection at Münster the *Fuga estemporanea* (as it is called there) bears the inscription: 'Sig[r] Domenico Scarlatti. Fatta per il concorso al Maggistero del Conservatorio della Pietà de Torchini in Napolis', and it is worth recalling that Leonardo Leo had been *primo maestro* at the Pietà dei Turchini from 1741 until his death. The possibility that Domenico Scarlatti, at the age of sixty, was contemplating a return to his native city is intriguing, if remote. In all the known sources the *Capriccio fugato* is textless but, as Loek Hautus has pointed out elsewhere, it must have originated as a work (or part of one) for double choir, strings and continuo.[6] The alto lines (in unison) sustain a cantus firmus in long notes which Hautus identified as the gregorian hymn *Exsultet orbis gaudiis*.

The remaining Münster work, the authenticity of which seems to be beyond any doubt, is the *Stabat mater* in C minor for ten voices with basso continuo. This was 'rediscovered' and given its first modern performance at the opening concert of the 'Settimana celebrativa' organized by the Accademia Musicale Chigiana at Siena in September 1940. Introducing it, Alfredo Casella wrote: 'The greatest revelation [among the vocal music to be performed at the 'Settimana'] will doubtless be the extraordinary *Stabat mater*, a marvellous and extensive composition in which we suddenly find ourselves face to face with a Domenico whom no one would have expected, a polyphonist of unbelievable technique whose contrapuntal skill bears comparison with Bach's'.[7] In the years since Casella wrote those words the *Stabat mater* has become the best known of all Domenico Scarlatti's compositions apart from his keyboard sonatas, and has appeared in more than one modern edition and recording.

To judge from the number of eighteenth-century copies still in existence, the *Stabat mater* was widely admired and performed during Scarlatti's lifetime as well. The thirteenth-century sequence text, often ascribed to Jacopone da Todi but probably not by him, had already been given many fine settings, including one by Palestrina. A famous setting by Scarlatti's father remained in annual use at Naples during Lent until it was superseded by Pergolesi's in 1736. The two Scarlatti works, father's and son's, illustrate the stylistic dichotomy which existed in Italian church music during the Baroque period. Alessandro's, like Pergolesi's, is scored for two solo voices, two violins and continuo. It is divided into eighteen separate, self-contained movements (one to each strophe of the text, for the most part), alternating soprano and alto solos and duets and including some passages of recitative. This division of the work into several short movements enables Alessandro Scarlatti to respond musically to the meaning of the text in a way which would not be possible in a more continuous setting. The style of the music, at times suave and sweet, at others tortured and chromatic, but always intensely subjective, draws on Scarlatti's experience as a composer of chamber cantatas.

Domenico's setting, in ten parts (four sopranos and two each of altos, tenors and basses) with continuo, is more austere than Alessandro's, but by no means inexpressive. One reason for its success may be that the composer here forsakes the true *stile antico* in favour of what is sometimes termed a *stile misto* ('mixed style'), combining elements of the strict *a cappella* tradition with other more modern idioms. The difference is evident both in the notation, only two sections ('Fac me vere' and 'Inflammatus et accensus') being written in 4/2 metre, and in the greater freedom of melodic movement, such 'forbidden' intervals as diminished 4ths, 5ths and 7ths occurring in considerable numbers. But what most distinguishes the *stile misto* of the *Stabat mater* from the *stile antico* of most of Scarlatti's other church music is the strongly rhythmic character of the music, and in particular the prominence, even predominance, of triple metre in the work. The lively 3/8 'amen' chorus is only one of several sections which are much nearer in spirit to the eighteenth than to the sixteenth century.

Although the music is continuous, the work is divided into fourteen sections, separated one from the next by double bar-lines and in some cases by pause marks as well (the sources are not entirely consistent in this). The structure may be summarized schematically as follows:

Section (incipit)	Strophes	Bar nos.	Tempo[8]	Time-signature
1 (Stabat mater)	1	1–38(38)	Andante	C
2 (Cujus animam)	2–3	39–72(34)	[Andante]	[C]
3 (Quae maerebat)	4	73–91(19)	Adagio	3/4
4 (Quis est homo)	5	92–111(20)	Andante	C
5 (Quis non posset)	6	112–24(13)	Adagio	[C]
6 (Pro peccatis)	7–8	125–84(60)	Allegro	3/4
7 (Eia mater)	9–10	185–224(40)	Andante	C
8 (Sancta mater)	11–12	225–94(70)	Adagio	3/4
9 (Fac me vere)	13	295–333(39)	Tempo giusto	¢
10 (Juxta crucem)	14–17	334–405(72)	Andantino	3/4
11 (Inflammatus)	18–19	406–59(54)	Allegro	¢
12 (Quando corpus morietur)	20(line 1)	460–75(16)	Andante	3/4
13 (Fac ut animae)	20(lines 2 and 3)	476–584(109)	Allegro	2/4
14 (Amen)	—	585–670(86)	Allegro	3/8

Most sections, it will be seen, comprise one, sometimes two, of the poem's twenty strophes, and a new section usually brings a change of metre or tempo (or both). Exceptionally, section 10 embraces four strophes of the poem, while the final strophe is divided (as in several settings by other composers) between two different sections (nos 12 and 13). The key-signature of two flats remains unchanged throughout, and so, basically, does the ten-part vocal texture.

Scarlatti does not deploy his voices antiphonally, as in some of his other sacred pieces, but instead mixes the various vocal timbres in a continually fluctuating kaleidoscope of sound. Some sources contain 'solo' and 'tutti' markings, but in the absence of an autograph it is impossible to say whether or not these are part of Scarlatti's original conception. At 'Eia mater, fons amoris' and again in the final 'amen', doubling of the voice parts reduces the texture to five parts (and in one or two very brief passages to four parts), at the same time enhancing the incisiveness of each line. For the rest, the parts remain independent, but the full ten-part choir is employed only sparingly – in fact, for fewer than seventy of the work's 670 bars. Scarlatti was obviously aware that, except where antiphony is involved, *a cappella* writing in more than five or six real parts is always in danger of stagnating because of the difficulties involved in keeping individual lines active and interesting without transgressing the rules of good part-writing, and without allowing the harmony to become static.

The *Stabat mater* is not a masterpiece, and Casella was mistaken in comparing its fragmented counterpoint to Bach's. Possibly the work's unique position in Scarlatti's output (or that part of it which is known to most musicians) has resulted in its receiving more critical attention than it might otherwise have done. But although there are some dull passages in it, there is also enough genuine inspiration and solid craftsmanship to ensure it a place in the choral repertory. It is undoubtedly the finest piece of church music by Scarlatti we have.

Most of the church compositions that survive in Portuguese archives are written in a *stile antico* even purer than that of the two Roman *Miserere* settings, perhaps reflecting King John V's ambition to emulate the oldest traditions of the papal choirs at Lisbon. *Te gloriosus*, an antiphon for All Saints' Day (1 November), is one of three sacred pieces in the library of the Fabrica da Sé Patriarcal in Lisbon; the text is related to the *Te Deum*. The music is in four parts and has a bright, open quality well suited to the words, with an appropriate contrast of expression at 'te Martyrum candidatus'; but the final fugato ('Beata Trinitas, unus Deus') is worked out rather dryly and at disproportionate length without reaching a convincing climax. There is also some clumsiness in the part-writing and not a few grammatical solecisms, including consecutive 5ths and octaves, which seems to indicate a much earlier date of composition, or possibly a corrupt copy.

More technically accomplished, and a more impressive composition altogether, is the eight-part *Laudate pueri Dominum*, a setting of Psalm 113 (no. 112 in the Vulgate). This is probably the same 'Psalmo (Laudate) ad 8' that Kirkpatrick (p. 423) reported as being a work by Alessandro Scarlatti in the opinion of Sampayo Ribeiro. The composer is named only once in the source (on the title-page of the first organ part), and then simply as 'Sig.ʳ Scarlatti'; the work's authorship must therefore remain in doubt. The location of the manuscript parts may seem to point to Domenico rather than Alessandro, but sacred works by Alessandro did, in fact, circulate in Lisbon in the 1720s, as we know from a note at the end of a copy of his four-part motet *Miserere mei Deus* in the library of the Royal Academy of Music, London (MS 12): 'Copiato dall'originale del Cav.ᶜ Alless.ᵒ Scarlatti in Lisbona Die 20 Marti 1723'. The other contents of MS 12 suggest that this copy of *Miserere mei Deus* was not, despite the inscription, made from Scarlatti's autograph, but presumably it derives indirectly from it. In any case, the presence of Alessandro's autograph in Lisbon in March 1723 might suggest that Domenico had arrived in the Portuguese capital by then, but the picture is confused by the existence of another copy of the same motet in the library of the University of California, Berkeley.[9] This bears a similar inscription, but with the date 1721.

To return to *Laudate pueri Dominum*, Alessandro Scarlatti did, in fact, make a setting of this text, perhaps in 1722, and Dent considered it the best of his psalm compositions, although he was puzzled by its 'oppressive melancholy'.[10] Domenico's *Laudate pueri* (if it is indeed his) is a very different kind of work. It is one of the purest and most correct of all his *stile antico* pieces, both in its part-writing and in its modal harmony. It has an imposing, ceremonial quality, which is enhanced by the antiphonal writing. The voices are divided into two choirs, each of SATB and each with its own organ continuo. For the most part the choirs alternate throughout the psalm, but their phrases do not always coincide with the beginning and end of a verse, and sometimes the voices join together, both in the psalm and in the doxology. The opening phrase, 'Laudate pueri Dominum', is set to the beginning of the seventh Gregorian psalm tone, and was presumably sung by a soloist or by the priest; it appears only in the organ parts. The plainchant continues in the cantus (soprano) part of the first chorus's response (*x* in example 14), after which the rest of the psalm is set freely. Plainsong cantus firmi are a feature, and an archaic one, of several of Alessandro Scarlatti's motets, but this cannot be taken to indicate his authorship in this particular case.

Also in the archives of the Fabrica da Sé Patriarcal is the score of a *Te Deum* in C major for eight voices and organ continuo. Kirkpatrick

Example 14

Laudate pueri Dominum

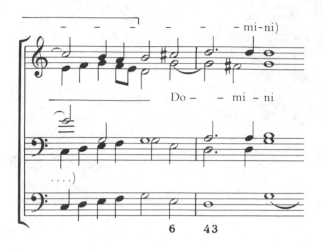

(p. 423) described this as being for 'S.A.T.B., concertino, doubling ripieno', but neither in the score nor in the parts that exist in other sources are there any solo/tutti indications, and the eight parts are independent throughout. While there is a certain amount of anti-phonal writing, the voices sound together for the most part, and for bars on end the music rarely manages to get beyond root-position primary triads in C major and the immediately related keys. This is not one of Scarlatti's most skilful or inspired choral pieces, but it might have sounded impressive in a large church or cathedral with the two choirs placed at either side of the nave and accompanied with all the colourful resources (including reeds *en chamade*) of Spanish Baroque organs. It must have been in just such a setting that the *Te Deum* was in fact designed to be heard, if this is the work of which a performance was described in the *Gazeta de Lisboa* on 1 January 1722:

> On the last day of the year 1721 there was sung in the Church of St Roch in this city in celebration of thanks for all the benefits accorded by God our Lord during the year to this realm and its inhabitants, the hymn *Te Deum Laudamus*, elegantly composed to music and distributed among various choirs of musicians by the famous Domingos Scarlatti. . . . The entire Church was magnificently decorated and filled with an infinite number of lights, and the musicians arranged in triangular tribunes especially constructed and adorned with rich hatchments, all at the order and expense of the Senhor Patriarch. . . . All the nobility of the Court was present and the concourse of the people was innumerable.[11]

It is also possible that the *Te Deum* we have was composed for, or at least performed at, the ceremonies accompanying the 'Exchange of Princesses' in 1729 (see pp. 102–3). This is suggested by the existence of a set of parts in the library of the Ducal Palace in Vila Viçosa, which Scarlatti and the Portuguese court can rarely have visited except on this occasion. In 1708 King John V had commissioned a *Te Deum* for his marriage to Maria Anna of Austria, and quite possibly he commanded his *mestro de capela* to supply a similar work for his daughter's wedding. Also in the music archive of the Ducal Palace is a motet, *Laetatus sum*, which might also have been composed for this occasion. This setting of Psalm 122 (no. 121 in the Vulgate) is scored for soprano and alto soloists and four-part choir with organ continuo. It uses a more modern style than most of Scarlatti's other sacred choral works, and might easily have been one of the best of them. There is a strong sense of thematic unity in the piece; the antiphony between soloists and chorus diverts the ear; and the counterpoint flows effortlessly in the brisk Allegro tempo. But there is also a great deal of textual repetition, so that long before verse 8 ('Propter fratres meos') brings a change of metre and tempo the listener has tired of so much music on one expressive level and mostly in the same key. Occupying in all 581 bars, the work simply outlasts its musical interest.

Scarlatti's most extended and impressive essay in *stile antico* polyphony is the *Missa quatuor vocum* copied into a choirbook of the Madrid royal chapel in 1754 – until recently the only music of any kind by Scarlatti known to have survived in Spanish archives. A rather inaccurate manuscript score in the monastery at Montserrat was apparently prepared from the Madrid choirbook, or from another set of parts now lost. The composition date is, as usual, a matter for conjecture. This is certainly not the mass referred to by Alfredo Casella in the preface to his edition of the *Stabat mater*; that work, as we have seen, has been located in the library of the Basilica Liberiana in Rome. Nor is it possible to say whether or not it is identical to the four-part mass, supposedly composed at Rome in 1712, which Mendel and Reissmann mentioned (see p. 114). Neither the Madrid choirbook nor the Montserrat score offers any clue to the date of composition. As well as Scarlatti's mass, the Madrid source contains a mass by Victoria and works by Antonio Literes and Joseph Torres.

Whenever it was composed, the *Missa quatuor vocum* is a mature work of its kind. Scarlatti sets the five sections of the ordinary – *Kyrie*, *Gloria*, *Credo*, *Sanctus* (with *Benedictus*) and *Agnus Dei* – with consummate skill and restraint. He does not make use of a plainchant cantus firmus nor (as far as one can tell) of any polyphonic model, but he does achieve a degree of musical unity through the use of recurrent melodic motifs. The opening theme of the first 'Kyrie eleison', for example, is recalled several times, in some cases in inversion. Example 15 shows some of its transformations. The *stile antico*, when it is deployed as convincingly as it is here, guarantees an impersonal and contemplative 'tone' appropriate to liturgical music. One may regret the absence of a distinct musical personality from this and other pieces like it, but the mass nevertheless represents a high point in Scarlatti's mastery of the *a cappella* style.

As far as sheer sound is concerned, however, the most imposing of all Scarlatti's church pieces is a mass in D major for voices and

Example 15

Missa quatuor vocum

instruments which has been almost entirely overlooked until recently. It survives in an incomplete set of parts at the Franciscan Santuario de Aránzazu in northern Spain, not far from Vitoria, and its existence was first reported by a monk of that order, Juan R. de Larrìnaga, at the fourth National Congress of Sacred Music held at Vitoria on 19–22 November 1928. The work was listed in the printed catalogue of the Aránzazu archive by Ion Bagües, published in 1979, but it was not until it received its first modern performance in the cathedral at Vitoria during Scarlatti's tercentenary year, on 29 November 1985, that it attracted wider attention.

The surviving parts of the mass, catalogued by Bagües as MS 389, were acquired by the Aránzazu community during Scarlatti's lifetime. Copied by a single scribe, evidently Italian, they consist of the following vocal and instrumental parts:

Soprano P:^{mo} choro	Violino 2:^{o} concertino
Alto P:^{mo} choro	Violino 2:^{o} Rip:^{no} [incomplete]
Tenore P:^{mo} choro	Obuè 2:^{o}
Basso P:^{mo} choro	Corno P:^{mo}
Soprano 2:^{o} choro	Tromba 2:^{a}
Alto 2:^{o} choro	Timpani
Basso 2:^{o} choro	Organo 2:^{o} choro.

The title-page of the second organ part reads: 'Messa, à quattro voci, con violini, trombe, obuè, timpani, corni dà caccia e ripieni', from which it may be inferred that the missing parts are those for tenor (second chorus), first violin (both concertino and ripieno), first oboe, second horn, first trumpet and first organ. It is not impossible that the original scoring may have included also a part for viola, since this instrument was frequently subsumed under the designation 'violini'.

Despite the unusually large forces employed, the D major mass is not a lengthy work. The *stile antico* is nowhere in evidence, counterpoint is at a premium, and there are no fugal 'amen' choruses such as are found in other Scarlatti works. Indeed, the setting as a whole is quite concise, with a minimum of textual repetition. As in the A minor mass for the Basilica Liberiana, Scarlatti here omits the *Benedictus* and its 'Osanna', and a good deal of the music moves along at a lively tempo. 'Qui tollis peccata mundi' in the *Gloria* and 'Et incarnatus est' in the *Credo* are set to a suitably reverential Adagio in 3/2 metre, but Allegros and sprightly rhythms prevail. Even 'Crucifixus' is without much hint of pain, and the *Agnus Dei* is among the jolliest by any composer. Every section of the mass is centred on the bright key of D major, which makes possible extensive and exultant use of the trumpets; excursions to other keys, mostly major and always closely related, serve mainly to bolster the main tonality. In fact, the insistence on D major, the lack of harmonic variety and the prevalence of dactylic rhythms (♩♫) would no doubt produce a tedious effect in a concert performance, but, of course, this would be less apparent when the various sections of the ordinary were heard in their liturgical contexts.

Why Scarlatti composed this mass, and how the parts found their way into the Santuario de Aránzazu remain matters for investigation. The mass differs from all his other sacred works not only in the use it makes of wind and string instruments, but also because the music seems to owe more to Neapolitan than to Roman traditions. It could hardly have been composed for the Basilica Liberiana or St Peter's, nor for the patriarchal chapel at Lisbon, although its scoring is similar to that of the Lisbon serenata, *Contesa delle stagioni*. A festive occasion in some other locality seems more likely, but there is nothing to indicate that this was necessarily in Spain. The loss of the first organ part is to be regretted in this connection, since it might have furnished more information about the work's origins.

The missing organ part is also a major stumbling-block for anyone trying to construct a putative original of Scarlatti's score from the surviving parts. It did not, however, prevent an unknown monk at the Santuario de Aránzazu from preparing a full score (MS 388) from these same parts in 1754. As stated on the title-page, this was 'reducida por uno de los menores del Seraphin Llagado; poniendo el violin 1.º oboe 1. clarin 2. corno 2. y acomp.^{to} p.^{s} [organ part] estos 5. papeles faltavan a dha Misa', but it is evident from the score itself that it was the first and not the second trumpet part that was missing in 1754, as now. The title-page also tells us that the score was prepared 'en el termino de 35 dias'. One might wish that the holy man had taken a little more time and made a better job of it! His work distorts Scarlatti's intentions in several important respects.

The most substantial of the monk's revisions is found in the *Sanctus*. The last five bars of this section have been brought forward to serve for 'Pleni sunt coeli et terra, osanna in excelsis', which they fit rather badly, and the music that Scarlatti originally wrote for these words (nineteen bars of 3/2 metre) has been adapted for 'Benedictus qui venit in nomine Domini' and the second 'Osanna' which, as stated earlier, Scarlatti did not set. Other revisions include the muting of the violins and the substitution of recorders for oboes at 'Qui tollis peccata mundi', the wholesale redistribution of the brass parts, some of which are incorporated into a spurious obbligato organ part, the transcribing of all 3/2 passages into 3/4 metre and the shortening of final chords (except the very last one) from a semibreve with pause to a quaver. There are in addition numerous alterations to the actual notes. The vocal parts are interfered with rather less, but bass solos are sometimes transferred to the tenor and the textual underlay is radically altered, rarely for the better.

It is difficult to understand why these revisions should have been made, unless it was with a performance in view. No parts exist, however, to confirm that such a performance took place, either at the Santuario de Aránzazu or elsewhere, and the monk's score could certainly not have been used in conjunction with the existing parts. It would not be difficult to reconstruct a full score which would convey more accurately Scarlatti's intentions, but even in its incomplete state the Aránzazu mass is a unique and important discovery. It may not be the greatest Mass in D ever composed, nor even the best of Scarlatti's sacred works, but without it our awareness and understanding of the composer has been in an important respect deficient.

SEVEN *Spain, 1729–57*

In 1713 the Treaty of Utrecht had brought to an end the War of the Spanish Succession, and with it the Habsburgs' claim on the Spanish throne they had occupied for two centuries. Philip (Felipe) V, to whom the crown had been willed by the unfortunate Charles II in 1700, was recognized as the first Bourbon king of Spain and reigned until his death in 1746. It was to his court in Seville that Maria Barbara de Bragança, now Princess of the Asturias, proceeded in 1729, and with her her master of music, Domenico Scarlatti.

SEVILLE (1729–33)

Philip V was an example of what in popular psychiatric terms might be called a manic depressive. When roused from his melancholy he could devote himself vigorously to his favourite pastime of hunting, but long periods of his life were spent in a state of complete lethargy, during which he would take to his bed and lose interest in everything, neglecting not only affairs of state but even his personal cleanliness and grooming. The government of his realm and the conduct of its foreign interests would have come to a complete halt were it not for the intervention and decision-making of his Italian-born queen, Elisabetta Farnese (his second wife), and of ambitious ministers such as Don José Patiños and the Marquis Scotti.

The king was apparently indifferent to music, as he was to most other things, until (as we shall see later) its charms began to work therapeutically on him in 1737. He did nevertheless maintain a sizeable musical establishment at court, with the Spaniard Joseph de Torres y Martinez Bravo at its head. As in Portugal, there was a strong bias towards Italian musicians in the royal *capilla*, and in 1738 Torres was succeeded by Francesco Corselli, who had served the Farnese family in Parma before Queen Elisabetta (Isabel) used her influence to bring him to Madrid in 1734. The constitution of the royal *capilla* in 1729, when Scarlatti arrived in Spain, is not known, but under Corselli in 1756 it included fifteen singers (four sopranos, four altos, four tenors and three basses) and thirty-five instrumentalists: players of oboes, flutes, horns, trumpets, bassoons and *fagotes* (?tenor bassoons), as well as a full complement of string players. In addition there were three organists: José Nebra, Antonio Literes and Miguel Rabassa (or Rabaxa, Ravassa etc.).

Italian opera in Spain had to compete with the native *zarzuela*, in which singing and dancing alternated with spoken dialogue. The *zarzuela* took its name from the royal hunting-lodge near the Pardo where the entertainments were put on. The term did not come into general use until the last decade of the seventeenth century, but the origins of the genre can be recognized in the works of Pedro Calderón de la Barca (1600–81). Some notable examples were composed in the early eighteenth century by Sebastián Durón and Antonio Literes but, with the support of an Italophile court, Italian *opera seria* soon came to occupy a more prestigious position and to attract greater financial backing, while the *zarzuela* itself was increasingly infiltrated by Italianate musical styles. The Italian faction was strengthened in 1721 by the appointment of the Parmesan envoy, Annibale Scotti, as director of the Italian opera. Scotti in his turn brought to Madrid Italian opera composers such as Francesco Corradini and Giovanni Battista Mele, both from Naples.

There is no evidence that Domenico Scarlatti took any part in the musical activities of the senior Spanish court, either in the opera house or in the royal chapel, despite the experience he had had as a composer of operas, serenatas and church music in Rome and Lisbon. It was as Maria Barbara's personal musician that he had come to Spain, and it was that princess and her husband whom he served there. Elisabettta Farnese had opposed the marriage of the Prince and Princess of the Asturias and she was jealous of the popularity they enjoyed. It is unlikely that she would have permitted their music master to display his talents among her own musicians. It is clear, however, from a report in the *Gaceta de Madrid* for 19 May 1719, quoted by Kirkpatrick (p. 87n), that 'musica de vozes', as well as instrumental music, was included in the evening concerts that Maria Barbara organized in her apartments. Despite the small quantity that has survived, it can hardly be doubted that vocal pieces by Scarlatti were performed on these occasions. The composer's main task as Maria Barbara's *maestro di musica* was nevertheless to instruct and coach her in keyboard playing, and it was in this connection that he continued to compose the remarkable series of about 550 harpsichord sonatas for which he is universally remembered.

When the royal wedding festivities on the Spanish and Portuguese border had ended in January 1729, Scarlatti and his bride Catarina followed Princess Maria Barbara and her new husband to Seville, where the Spanish court took up residence until the spring of 1733. It was there that the Scarlattis' first child, a boy, was born some time in 1729; he was christened Juan Antonio. It is impossible to say whether these names were chosen in honour of Scarlatti's Portuguese patrons, King John V and Don Antonio, as Kirkpatrick (p. 83) suggested, or whether they were given him by his godparents, since no record of his birth or baptism has yet been found. The baptism of the Scarlattis' second child, Fernando, was recorded in the register of the church of Santa Cruz in Seville on 9 March 1731:

On 9 March 1731 I, D.ʳ Don Cristobal Romero, officiating under licence from D.ʳ Don Cristobal Alvarez de Palma, priest of this parish church of Santa Cruz in Seville, confirmed and fully baptized with holy oil and holy water, at his home and as a matter of need, Fernando Nicola José Alexandro Julian, son of Don Domingo Escarlati, a native of the city of Naples, and Donna Catalina Gentili, a native of Rome, his legal wife; the godmother at the confirmation was Donna Ana Manteli, whom I notified of her duties. We signed, as above,

D.ʳ Don Cristobal Alvarez y Palma
Don Cristobal Romero[1]

It is clear from the fact that the baptism was done at home and 'as a matter of need' that Fernando was a sickly child at birth, but he survived the difficult days and years of infancy and went on to live to the age of sixty-three. There are other interesting details to note in this baptismal entry. One is that Scarlatti has now became Domingo Escarlati, and this is the way his name usually appears in Spanish sources; 'Domingo Scarlatti' is also found, for example on his will (see Appendix II). At the same time Scarlatti's wife Catarina has become Catalina. Don Cristobal Romero (de Torres), who performed the ceremony, was evidently a friend of the family. He baptized at least one more of Scarlatti's children (Domingo, in July 1747) and was named as an executor in the composer's will. As well as Juan Antonio and Fernando, another child, who died in infancy, may have been born in Seville, and it is possible that a daughter, Maria Ana Margarita (Mariana), was also born there, unless she came into the world shortly after the family moved with the Spanish court to Madrid.

Before 1729 the court had resided at Madrid or in the several palaces in the vicinity. It seems to have been in an attempt to divert King Philip V that the move to Seville was made, and it was as a means of rousing him from a particularly acute attack of melancholia that a return to Madrid was first proposed in August 1732. He had taken to his bed, refused to see anyone, and would not even allow his hair to be cut or his bed linen to be changed. But it was the prospect of war over the Polish succession in 1733 that finally revived his spirits and brought about a return to Castile. By the middle of June the court, travelling in the greatest possible secrecy, had reached Aranjuez. From there they moved in July to the palace of San Ildefonso at La Granja, and in October to the Escorial. They spent Christmas at the palace of Buen Retiro on the outskirts of Madrid, and in January 1734 moved to the royal hunting lodge at the Pardo. It was intended that the winter of 1734–5 should be spent in the royal palace, the Alcazar, in Madrid, which the court had not used since 1728, but while the building was being warmed in readiness it was burnt down, and many of its important archives and art treasures were lost.

CASTILE (1733–46)

The rebuilding of the royal palace in Madrid was immediately set in hand, and the architect Filippo Juvarra, Scarlatti's former colleague in Rome, was called in to prepare plans. He did not live to complete them. Juvarra's first published work had been a series of engravings for a volume by N. M. Sclavo, *Amore ed ossequio di Messina*, published at Messina in 1701 in honour of the young Philip V, who had just begun his reign. Now Juvarra ended his life serving that same unfortunate monarch. He died in Madrid on 31 January 1736, leaving the designs for the new palace to be revised and completed by his pupil, Giovanni Battista Sacchetti.

Domenico Scarlatti probably never saw the interior of the old Alcazar in Madrid, and the new building was not completed until about seven years after his death. But he would certainly have been familiar with the other royal residences in Castile. From notices in the Madrid press, Kirkpatrick (p. 91) was able to trace the annual round of the Spanish court during Philip V's reign. It observed the following itinerary:

January–mid-March	the hunting lodge of the Pardo
Easter	the Buen Retiro, Madrid
April–June	Aranjuez
late June	the Buen Retiro
July–October	La Granja
October–early December	the Escorial
Christmas	the Buen Retiro

Philip disliked Madrid itself and spent only short periods there. The extensive palace gardens of the Buen Retiro are now a public park; what little remains of the palace itself serves today as a military museum and as an annexe to the nearby Prado museum. The latter is the Cason which in the eighteenth century served as an antechamber to the royal theatre. In it the colourful frescoed ceiling painted at the end of the seventeenth century by the Neapolitan Luca Giordano now looks down in ironic contrast on the tortured lines and blood-drained tones of Picasso's famous *Guernica*.

Giordano's paintings adorn several rooms and chapels in other Castilian royal residences which still survive, though with several alterations. The nearby town and palace of El Pardo, built by Philip III, is set amid woodland which once furnished the Spanish kings with game for their hunting parties. To the northwest is the vast, chilly palace and monastery of El Escorial, built by Philip II in 1563–84 as an act of thanksgiving for his victory over the French at St Quentin in 1557. Scarlatti probably felt at home in the church that dominates the building, since it is built on a plan similar to that of St Peter's, Rome, with four massive pillars supporting a central cupola over three hundred feet high. Facing each other in elevated positions on the north and south walls are two organs, their reeds *en chamade* pointing across the nave.

The Bourbons did not find Philip II's sober palace much to their taste. They enlivened the austere rooms they occupied with brightly painted ceilings, tapestries and pictures, but they preferred the more congenial smaller palaces at Aranjuez and La Granja. The modern visitor is likely to share their preferences. The palace at Aranjuez is a Classical structure of brick and stone, flanked by gardens with fountains and shady walks through which the River Tagus wends its circuitous course. Both the building and its furnishings were new in the early eighteenth century and reflect the taste of Philip V, Fernando VI and their consorts. The apartments included a music room, and many of Scarlatti's harpsichord sonatas must have been composed and first performed there. It appears from a manuscript in the Santini collection at Münster that the six sonatas numbered 374–9 in Kirkpatrick's catalogue were all composed at Aranjuez in 1754. It was in that same year that the theatre at Aranjuez was rebuilt, enabling the court to enjoy the operas and other entertainments that Farinelli organized for them.

At La Granja de San Ildefonso, a few miles from Segovia, was situated the most northerly and perhaps the most attractive of all the royal palaces. In the cool mountain air of this miniature Versailles, built for Philip V himself, the Spanish court were able to escape from the discomforts of Madrid during the hottest summer months. We know from an inventory drawn up in the 1750s that Maria Barbara kept keyboard instruments (mainly harpsichords) in Madrid, Aranjuez and El Escorial, and these three locations were perhaps the most important as far as royal music-making was concerned. No instrument is listed as being at La Granja, which Fernando and Maria Barbara ceased to use as a residence when they became king and queen in 1746, but there were presumably instruments there before then.

During the reign of Philip V the Prince and Princess of the Asturias, together with their *maestro de musica*, presumably followed the rest of the court in their annual round from one palace to the next. Obviously Scarlatti would need a permanent home for himself and his growing family, and this he found in the Calle Ancha de San Bernardo in Madrid. Unless their first daughter, Mariana, was born there, the first addition to the Scarlatti family in Castile was a third son, Alexandro, who was born in 1736 or 1737. Kirkpatrick could find no record of his baptism in the registers of St Martin's Church in Madrid, which is where the baptisms of all the subsequent Scarlatti children took place. Possibly Alexandro was born and baptized at a time when Catarina was with her husband at one of the royal sites outside Madrid.

Little, if anything, is known about Scarlatti's activities at court during his years in Castile. Presumably he continued to give harpsichord lessons to Maria Barbara and also to Prince Fernando, who achieved sufficient competence on the instrument to be able to accompany soloists at the royal soirées. Presumably, too, he found ample time to compose keyboard sonatas for his royal pupils and himself to play. But what other court duties, if any, he was called upon to perform, whether he found employment as a teacher or in any other capacity outside the court, and what kind of family and social life he led – these are all matters on which the surviving documents are almost completely silent.

The king's mental and physical condition, on the other hand, was constantly observed and reported on. In an attempt to divert his recreational pursuits from the hunting field to the salon, the queen began to interest him in balls and theatricals. Her own increasing obesity and consequent ill-health made outdoor pursuits difficult for her. On 18 February 1737 Sir Benjamin Keene, the British ambassador, wrote: 'The queen is endeavouring to look out for diversion for the king, who has a natural aversion for music. If she can change his temper so far as to amuse him with it, it may keep them both from thinking of more turbulent matter.'[2] The success of the queen's course of music therapy for her husband was realized during the annual retreat to La Granja. To the summer palace of San Ildefonso she invited the Italian castrato Carlo Broschi. Broschi, universally known as Farinelli, was the most famous and highly paid singer of his day. His appearances in operas by almost all the principal composers in every important European city had earned him a reputation unsurpassed in later times by any but the most fawned-on prima donnas. Between 1734 and 1737 he reached the pinnacle of his career in London, where his performances for the Opera of the Nobility were so enthusiastically applauded that during his singing of Arbace in Hasse's *Artaserse* someone in the audience was reported to have stood up and cried out, 'One God – one Farinelli!'

Farinelli responded to the adulation of his public with a lack of conceit exceptional among opera singers of any century or country. Perhaps no other performing artist of his eminence would have given up the limelight of a public career to devote himself to alleviating a king's depressions in the comparative obscurity of a foreign court. The circumstances of Farinelli's introduction to that court are told in an oft-quoted anecdote in Burney's *History*:

> Upon the arrival of Farinelli, of whose extraordinary performance an account had been transmitted to Madrid from several parts of Europe, but particularly from Paris, her Majesty [Queen Elisabetta] contrived that there should be a concert in a room adjoining to the King's apartment, in which this singer performed one of his most captivating songs. Philip appeared at first surprised, then moved; and at the end of the second air, made the virtuoso enter the royal apartment, loading him with compliments and caresses; asked him how he could sufficiently reward such talents; assuring him that he could refuse him nothing. Farinelli, previously instructed, only begged that his Majesty would permit his attendants to shave and dress him, and that he would endeavour to appear in council as usual. From this time the King's disease gave way to medicine: and the singer had all the honour of the cure.[3]

While this anecdote may be, as Burney puts it, 'below the dignity of history', the fact remains that Farinelli spent the next twenty years of his life within the narrow confines of the Spanish court, and for as long as Philip V continued as king he repeated each evening a restricted repertory of favourite songs to ease the monarch's melancholy. In a letter to the Duke of Newcastle, dated 2 August 1738, Sir Benjamin Keene wrote:

> When he [King Philip] retires to dinner, he sets up such frightful howlings

as astonished every one at the beginning, and have obliged the *confidants* to clear all the apartments as soon as he sat down to table; and as the queen cannot be sure of his behaviour for the rest of the day, she does not fail to keep him within doors, insomuch that they do not take the air in their favourite garden of S. Ildefonso as they used to do heretofore. His diversion at night is to hear Farinelli sing the same five Italian airs that he sung the first time that he performed before him, and has continued to sing every night for near twelve months together. But your Grace will smile when I inform you that the king himself imitates Farinelli, sometimes air after air, and sometimes after the music is over, and throws himself into such freaks and howlings that all possible means are taken to prevent people from being witness to his follies. He had one of these fits this week, which lasted from twelve till past two in the morning.[4]

Keene mentions that Farinelli sang 'five Italian airs' each night to the king, and this early report may well be the most accurate we have. Much later Farinelli himself told Burney how 'for the first ten years of his residence at the court of Spain, during the life of Philip Vth, he sung every night to that monarch the same four airs, of which two were composed by Hasse, *Pallido il sole*, and *Per questo dolce amplesso*. I forget the others, but one was a minuet which he used to vary at his pleasure.'[5] Burney later recalled a third aria, *Ah non lasciarmi, no, bell'idol mio*, probably by Leonardo Vinci.[6] It has been argued that Farinelli's repertory for Philip V was much less restricted than this. In 1753 he dedicated to the Empress Maria Theresa a manuscript volume containing six arias which he described as 'a small selection of those songs which for many years I have sung for the private solace of these adorable sovereigns, my most gracious benefactors'. However, it seems likely that the 'adorable sovereigns' referred to by Farinelli were not Philip V and Elisabetta Farnese, but Fernando VI and Maria Barbara, in whose service Farinelli continued after Philip V's death in 1746. Included in the volume for Maria Theresa are the following six arias:

1. 'Quell'usignolo che innamorato' [by Geminiano Giacomelli]
2. 'Al dolor che vo sfogando' (preceded by recitative, 'In van ti chiamo')
3. 'Son qual nave ch'agitata' [by Giovanni Antonio Giai]
4. 'Io sperai del porto insano'
5. 'Vuoi per sempre abbandonarmi'
6. 'Non sperar non lusingarti' (preceded by recitative, 'Ogni dì più molesto dunque')[7]

The first three of these were specially written or adapted for Farinelli, and he included them in his London opera seasons. No. 3 is often attributed to his elder brother Riccardo Broschi, who joined him in Madrid during the 1740s and died there in 1756.

In return for his nightly recitals and for the lustre his presence added to the Spanish court, Farinelli was paid a handsome salary equivalent at the contemporary rate of exchange to about £1,500 – roughly the same as he had received for an opera season in London. It was understood that he would no longer perform in public and, like Scarlatti, he seems to have taken no part in operas staged at court. He was presumably accompanied on the harpsichord by Scarlatti on the occasions when he sang for Prince Fernando and Maria Barbara in their apartments. The jealous Queen Elisabetta, who looked upon Farinelli as her own discovery and property, attempted to put a stop to this and sent a message to the castrato commanding him never again to sing for the Prince and Princess of the Asturias. Farinelli's reply, as reported by Edward Clarke,[8] was both just and fearless: 'Go, says he, and tell the Queen, that I owe the greatest obligations to the Prince and Princess of Asturias; and unless I receive such an order from her Majesty's own mouth, or the King's, I will never obey it'.

Domenico Scarlatti's reputation in Madrid must inevitably have been eclipsed by that of Farinelli from 1737 onwards, but there is nothing to suggest that he in any way resented this. On the contrary, their friendship and esteem for each other seem to have lasted throughout their lives. Farinelli was a careful custodian of the Scarlatti manuscripts that Maria Barbara bequeathed him.

According to Burney, Farinelli 'was honoured with the order of *St. Iago* by his first royal master, Philip V, and with that of *Calatrava* by his successor, Ferdinand VI'.[9] Burney gave no date for the first of these ennoblements, and it is possible that he confused it with the knighthood conferred on Domenico Scarlatti in 1738 by his former patron, King John V of Portugal. This might well have been sought, as Kirkpatrick suggested, by Maria Barbara to compensate her music master for the honours and riches being heaped on Farinelli by the ruling monarchs. After the necessary preliminaries were completed,[10] Scarlatti was made a knight of the order of Santiago in a ceremony which took place on the afternoon of 21 April 1738 before the altar of the Capuchin monastery of San Antonio del Prado, Madrid.

It is as a 'Cavallero del Orn. de Santiago' that Scarlatti is referred to in the register recording the baptism the following November of his second daughter, Maria:

In the parish church of San Martin, Madrid, on 13 November 1738 I, Friar Mauro Plaza, Lieutenant [?] Priest of the said church, baptized Maria del

Patrocinio Juana, the legitimate daughter of Don Domingo Escarlati, Knight of the Order of Santiago and a native of the city of Naples, and of Donna Cathalina Gentili Escarlatti, native of the city and court capital of Rome; born on the 9th of the said month and year in the Calle Ancha de San Bernardo, Convent of the Novitiate of the Company of Jesus. Her godfather was Don Gaspar Gentili, Abbot and Knight Commander of San Felize de Ettalauto, whom I advised about his spiritual parenthood. Witnesses were Francesco Herrera and Manuel Bayon. Signed,

Father Mauro Plaza[11]

Gaspar Gentili, named as godfather, was Scarlatti's brother-in-law. He was godfather again to Maria Barbara, Scarlatti's sixth child, in 1743 (when he was named in the baptismal register as Commander of the Abbey of San Felix Aelauto), and he witnessed the baptism also of Scarlatti's last child, Antonio, in 1749. Domenico's parents-in-law also followed their daughter to Spain and remained there.

Within two months of Maria's birth Scarlatti's first published music, a volume of *Essercizi per gravicembalo*, was issued in London. This was a handsomely produced collection of thirty harpsichord sonatas, evidently designed as a tribute to King John of Portugal in gratitude for the knighthood he had conferred on Scarlatti. The volume bears no imprint, but the publication seems to have been supervised by members of Farinelli's circle in London. The Frenchman B. Fortier did most of the engraving and the volume was sold by the Italian Adamo Scola, 'Musick Master in Vine Street, near Swallow Street, Piccadilly, over against the Brewhouse, London', as he described himself in an advertisement in the *Country Journal or The Craftsman*, 27 January 1739. Amigoni contributed an ornate frontispiece incorporating the Portuguese royal arms and Scarlatti prefaced the work with a fulsome dedication in Italian:

To the Sacred Royal Majesty of John V, the true King of Portugal, The Algarve, Brazil, &c. &c. &c., the most humble servant Domenico Scarlatti

Sire

The magnanimity of Your Majesty in works of virtue, your generosity in others, your knowledge of the sciences and the arts and your munificence in rewarding them are well-known attributes of your great nature. Your even greater modesty tries in vain to hide them: in every language in the world they are retold, present history records them, the future will admire them, not knowing whether to call you the Most Powerful Sovereign of Kingdoms or the Affectionate Father of His People. But these are but a few of the parts belonging to that whole which, like a new shining star, attracts the gaze of every connoisseur towards you. By universal acclamation you are known as The Just: a title which embraces all other glorious ones, since good works serve no useful purpose unless they are acts of justice to oneself and others. Now, who among the least of your servants can be called vain if he makes himself known as such? Music, the solace of noble minds, granted me this enviable good fortune, and made me happy in pleasing with it the most refined taste of Your Majesty and in teaching it to your Royal Progeny, who now have knowledge and mastery of it. Gratitude and honest pride require that I make my good fortune public with this volume. Do not despise, most clement King, this trifling tribute from a humble servant. They are compositions born under Your Majesty's highest auspices and in the service of your deservedly fortunate daughter the Princess of the Asturias and of your most worthy royal brother the Infante Don Antonio. But how could I possibly express my gratitude for the immortal honour done to me by your royal command to follow this incomparable Princess? The splendour of her perfections, through her royal lineage and queenly upbringing, reflects that of the great monarch her father; but a humble servant plays his part, too, through the mastery of singing, playing and composing with which she, to the astonishment and admiration of the most excellent masters, delights princes and monarchs.

At the conclusion of this obsequious tribute (which nevertheless conveys a genuine respect for the king and, more especially, for Maria Barbara) Scarlatti turns to the purchaser of the volume and addresses him in terms more intimate and colloquial:

Reader
Don't expect, whether you are an amateur or a professional, to find any profound intention in these compositions, but rather an ingenious jesting with art [lo scherzo ingegnoso dell'Arte] by means of which you may attain freedom in harpsichord playing. It was not self-interest or ambition which led me to publish them, but obedience. Perhaps they may please you, in which case I may more willingly obey further commands to gratify you in a simpler and more varied style. Be therefore kind rather than critical, and your pleasure will be the greater. To understand the disposition of the hands, be advised that the right [Dritta] is indicated with a D, and the left [Manca] with an M. Vivi felice.[12]

The success of the Essercizi seems not to have led to the publication of a second volume, as promised, but it did encourage Thomas Roseingrave to bring out a two-volume pirated edition, published by Benjamin Cooke under the misleading title XLII Suites de pieces pour le clavecin. This included not forty-two suites, but forty-five single-movement pieces: the thirty sonatas of the Essercizi, a second version of no. 8, twelve other Scarlatti sonatas (no doubt from manuscripts in

Roseingrave's possession), a fugue by Alessandro Scarlatti and an introductory piece in the style of an allemande by Roseingrave himself. The volumes appeared in 1739 and attracted no fewer than ninety-five subscribers, including Arne, Avison, Boyce, Greene, Pepusch and Stanley, all of them leading musicians in London at the time. Possibly the terms of Scarlatti's employment in Madrid did not allow him to publish further sonatas, or perhaps the piratical nature of the music-publishing trade in the eighteenth century dissuaded him from doing so. Another edition of the original thirty *Essercizi* was brought out in 1742 by the Amsterdam publisher Gerhard Fredrik Witvogel and later reissued by his successor Jan Covens. Between 1754 and 1756 Roseingrave's collection was reissued from the original plates by John Johnson, and selections from it appeared in various volumes of *Pièces pour le clavecin* published in Paris (see p. 158).

With the granting of a knighthood and the publication of the *Essercizi*, Domenico Scarlatti was by 1739 at the very height of his fame. A sense of confidence and mastery seems to issue from the noble portrait of the composer painted at about this time by Domingo Antonio de Velasco (reproduced on the dust-jacket), and yet it is possible to detect also the hint of a smile playing about his lips. The portrait remained in the Scarlatti family for several generations before it was sold in 1912 to a Madrid dealer and then to José Relvas, the Portuguese ambassador to Spain; it was rediscovered in 1956 by Reynaldo dos Santos, and now hangs in the Instituiçao José Relvas, Alpiarça, Portugal. A portrait of Catarina Scarlatti was also sold by the family in 1912; this has not so far come to light again.

If Catarina's portrait was painted at about the same time as Domenico's, it must have shown her as she was only a year or two before her death, which came on 6 May 1739. She was only twenty-seven, exactly half as old as her husband. The reason for her early demise is not recorded, but it occurred at Aranjuez, where the court was in residence, and we may presume that Domenico was with her. She was buried at the Church of Good Hope (Buena Esperanza) in the nearby town of Ocaña (the present writer was unable to find a church of that name when he visited Ocaña in 1984). Catarina's five children, the eldest aged ten and the youngest six months, were entrusted to the care of their grandmother, Margarita Gentili.

Like J. S. Bach after the death of his first wife, Maria Barbara, in 1720, Scarlatti did not wait long before re-marrying. By 1742 he had taken as his second wife Anastasia Maxarti Ximenes, a native of Cadiz, and in doing so he had also taken, as Kirkpatrick (p. 116) pointed out, the final step in the process of his hispanization. Beyond her name and birthplace (which, however, is given as Seville in one document), nothing whatever is known about Anastasia – not even her age. She was young enough, however, to bear Domenico another four children, the first of whom, a daughter, was christened in the parish church of San Martin on 13 January 1743 with the aristo-cratic-sounding names of Maria Barbara Xaviera Vitoria de la Concepcion. The baptismal entry, transcribed by Kirkpatrick (p. 339), tells us also that the Scarlatti family had by then moved to a house in the Calle de Leganitos, where in all probability they continued to live until Domenico's death.[13] The fact that Scarlatti's brother-in-law, Gaspar Gentili, once again acted as godfather indicates that there was no estrangement from the Gentili family after Maria Catarina's death. Francesco Maria Gentili, Scarlatti's father-in-law, was named as godparent to Anastasia's second child, christened Rosa Christina Anasthasia Ramona on 30 May 1745, and Margarita Gentili seems to have been as attached to Anastasia's children as she was to her own daughter's.

Farinelli, meanwhile, continued to give his nightly recitals for King Philip V. It has been calculated that he must have sung the same four or five songs about 3,600 times each during his stay in Spain. In July 1746 he sang them for the last time. On the 9th day of that month, in the early hours of the morning, the king was seized with an attack of apoplexy and died almost immediately in his wife's arms.

THE LAST YEARS (1746–57)

The history books tell us that Philip V of Spain was succeeded in 1746 by his son Fernando VI, but it would be nearer reality to say that Elisabetta Farnese was succeeded by Maria Barbara de Bragança. The two ladies were by temperament very different, but each was the dominant personality behind the throne. As far as Scarlatti and his fellow musicians at the Spanish court were concerned, however, it might be more to the point to say that in 1746 Melancholia was succeeded by Melomania (although the new king did, unfortunately, inherit some of his father's proneness to depression). An early consequence of the new accession was the departure of Queen Elisabetta, whose intrigues in Portugal soon made her presence intolerable. She was offered a place of retirement in Segovia, Burgos or Valladolid, but chose instead her favourite palace of San Ildefonso at La Granja, where her husband was buried. La Granja was thereafter dropped from the Spanish court's annual itinerary.

Other changes included the replacement of the Marquis Scotti by

Farinelli as director of the court operas. No doubt relieved at not having to perform again the same few songs that he had sung so many times for Philip V, Farinelli undertook with enthusiasm the staging of sumptuous operas at the Coliseo Theatre of the Buen Retiro palace in Madrid. He engaged the best singers from Italy, and brought over from England his old friend, the painter Jacopo Amigoni, to design the sets. Another friend, Pietro Metastasio, provided librettos for him and discussed details of their staging in a lively and historically important exchange of letters (of which only Metastasio's remain). The resident composers were Corradini, Corselli and Mele (all Italians), who collaborated in 1747 to set *La clemencia de Tito*, based on Metastasio's libretto, and in 1748 *El Polifemo*. Corselli continued as titular *maestro de capilla*, but after 1750 most of the new operas were composed by Nicola Conforto, a Neapolitan who enjoyed a privileged position at court from 1755.

Scarlatti seems once again to have played no part in all this musical activity, and to judge from a remark in his letter to the Duke of Huescar (see below) he may even have felt unsympathetic towards the new, mainly Neapolitan style of opera in vogue at the Spanish court. The new régime apparently brought him no material advancement, and he seems to have been entirely content to continue as 'musico de clavicordio y compositor de S.M.' for the rest of his life. He is thus referred to on the reverse of a letter he wrote in 1752 to Don Fernando de Silva y Alvarez de Toledo, Duke of Huescar and later twelfth Duke of Alba. The letter is the only one in Scarlatti's hand to have survived, and it contains the only reference we have to his activities other than those of composer and harpsichordist. Scarlatti had been asked by the duke to put into score two hymns written in 1569 by the Flemish composer Pierre du Hotz for an earlier duke of Alba. The letter accompanied the requested score and the return of the original parts.

Most excellent Signore
I have been awaiting your happy return in order to pledge my obedience to you, not only in sending the enclosed manuscripts, but also in any other command Your Excellency may care to make. The underlaying of the text, which is in Latin but written in an abbreviated Gothic script, has caused me more trouble than anything else.

Your Excellency should make use of the old separate parts as well as the extract I have taken from them and put into score, not only for the sake of their own merits but also in order that many modern theatre composers may observe and (if they will) profit from the correct way and the true laws of writing counterpoint – things which I observe in few of them today, though I hear them praised.

I cannot leave my house. Your Excellency is great, strong, mag-
nanimous and in good health. Why, then, don't you come and console me
with a visit? Perhaps because I am unworthy? That is true, but where do
the virtues reside, if not in the hearts of the great?

I shall not say more. I pray that God may assist and bless you in
accordance with your desires and mine. Amen.

Scarlatti[14]

The phrase 'I cannot leave my house' suggests that Scarlatti was ill
when he wrote this letter, which would not be at all surprising at that
time for someone in his sixty-seventh year. Another interpretation
has been suggested, however, by Roberto Pagano,[15] who sees the
possibility that Scarlatti may have been kept at home not by illness,
but by Queen Maria Barbara or by Farinelli, so that he could get on
with the task of supervising the fair copying of his keyboard sonatas in
return for their help in settling his gambling debts. Scarlatti's love of
the gambling tables was commented on more than once, as we shall
see, but even Pagano admits his hypothesis to be 'fantasiosissima'!

Apart from what the letter to the Duke of Huescar tells us, the only
glimpses we are allowed into Scarlatti's domestic life in Spain are those
provided by the registers recording the baptisms of his children. His
eighth child, Domingo Pio Narciso Christoval Ramon Alexandro
Genaro, was baptized on 12 July 1747, and on 8 May 1749 Scarlatti
became a father for the last time when Antonio Manuel Miguel
Ramon was born. The baby's eldest half-brother, Juan Antonio, now
about twenty years old, stood as godfather, and Gaspar Gentili was
again present at the christening. An unusual and remarkable thing,
considering the high rate of infant mortality in the eighteenth century,
is that all the other children that had been born to Scarlatti were at that
time still living. All nine children are named as his heirs in the will he
made in October 1749 (see Appendix II).

None of Scarlatti's children seems to have shown any particular
aptitude for music; possibly the composer's memories of a domin-
ating father tended to dissuade him from encouraging too strongly a
musical career for his own offspring. His musical patrimony was
inherited rather by pupils and imitators. Among the former the most
important was Antonio Soler (1729–83), who joined the Jeronymite
monastery at the Escorial in 1752. Soler studied with Scarlatti at the
Escorial during the autumn periods when the Spanish court resided
there, and also in Madrid where the Jeronymites had an annexe.
Soler's writings, particularly his treatise *Llave de la modulacion*
(Madrid, 1762), throw interesting light on the relationship of
Scarlatti's music to that of his Spanish contemporaries.

During the last year of his life Scarlatti turned from the harpsichord sonatas to which he had devoted his main energies for so long and composed as his swan-song a lovely setting of *Salve regina* for soprano (Farinelli perhaps?), strings and continuo. Most sources describe it as 'the last of his compositions, written in Madrid shortly before his death'. This antiphon to the Virgin may have been intended also as a 'Vale regina' – a farewell to the queen Scarlatti had served for thirty-seven years. Maria Barbara had been in poor health for some time and had only a year or so to live. In her will she left 2,000 doubloons and a ring 'to my music master who has followed me with great diligence and devotion'.[16]

It was, however, Scarlatti who died first. He breathed his last on 23 July 1757 in the house in the Calle de Leganitos which his family had occupied since about the time of his second marriage.[17] His death was entered in the parish register of San Martin:

Don Domingo Escarlati, Knight of the Order of Santiago, husband by first marriage of Donna Cathilina Gentili and by second marriage of Donna Anastasia Maxarti, a native of the city of Naples and son of Don Alessandro Escarlati and Donna Antonia Ansaloni (both deceased), a parishioner of this church [living in] Calle de Leganitos, . . . made his will before Gaspar Feliciano Garcia, signed and sealed on 9 October 1749,[18] in which he ordered fifty masses for charity at three reales de vellon and named as executors his wife, the said Donna Anastasia, and D.ʳ Don Christoval Romero de Torres, priest, Chaplain to Their Majesties in the Royal Chapel of the New Kings of Toledo. And as heirs he named Don Juan Antonio, Don Fernando, Donna Mariana, Don Alexandro, and Donna Maria Escarlatti, his legitimate children by his first wife, and Don Domingo, Don Antonio, Donna Barbara, and Donna Rosa Escarlati, also his legitimate children by his aforementioned second wife. Having received Holy Sacrament, he died on the 23rd July 1757 and was buried in secret [*de secreto*] in the Convent of San Norberto of this Court Capital, under licence from the Vicar General.[19]

By the time Scarlatti died, three of the children mentioned in his will, Juan Antonio, Mariana and Alexandro, were also dead; Maria, the second daughter, died shortly afterwards. The only child of Scarlatti's first wife to survive into adulthood was Fernando, who became an official in the Contaduria General de Salinas and lived, as his father had done, in the Calle de Leganitos. He married in 1760 and had two children, through the first of whom, Francisco, the Scarlatti line was continued into the twentieth century. All four children of the second marriage apparently died without issue. Barbara married an official in the Distribution Department of the Royal Exchequer, and Domingo was employed in the secretariat of La Nueva España before joining his younger brother, Antonio, in the Soria Infantry.

Scarlatti's death was followed by Queen Maria Barbara's in August 1758 and King Fernando's a year later. The reign of the melomanes was at an end. Conforto had composed his last opera, *La forza del genio*, produced at Aranjuez in May 1758, and 'the first act of Charles [III], as sovereign of Spain, was an order issued at the instigation of the queen dowager [Elisabetta Farnese] to Farinelli, enjoining him to quit Spain without delay'.[19] Farinelli returned to Italy with a generous pension and with the harpsichords and manuscripts bequeathed to him by Queen Maria Barbara. Among the latter was the most precious legacy of all: two sets of the collected keyboard sonatas of Domenico Scarlatti. It is to these that we now turn.

EIGHT *Keyboard Works*

Domenico Scarlatti's posthumous reputation as a composer has always rested on the keyboard sonatas he wrote in Portugal and Spain, mainly for Maria Barbara. The originality, variety and sheer invention of these works have secured for their composer a permanent place in the history books, on the concert platform and in the gramophone catalogue, while their technical innovations have placed Scarlatti alongside the English virginalists, Chopin, Liszt, Debussy and Bartók as one of the most important protagonists of keyboard style. If today only a relatively small number of sonatas are regularly heard in public recitals, while many are virtually unknown even to specialists in eighteenth-century keyboard music, this is simply because there are so many of them. Recitalists naturally want to include the best ones in their repertories, and there are enough of these to ensure that the second-best, even though they are very good indeed, are hardly ever heard. The lesser-known symphonies of Haydn and the almost completely unknown concertos of Vivaldi have suffered a similar fate, and for the same reason.

Ralph Kirkpatrick catalogued 555 sonatas,[1] but not all of these can be accepted as original keyboard works. Nine of them (K73, 77–8, 80–1 and 88–91) appear to have been conceived as pieces for a solo string or woodwind instrument with continuo. All but one (K80) are multi-movement works. K73, 77 and 78 have two movements (the second is in each case a minuet) and K89 has three. The others exemplify the four-movement design, alternating slow and fast tempos, of the Baroque *sonata da chiesa*, but without the change of tonality for the second movement which normally occurs in the sonatas of, for example, Corelli, Bach and Handel. (Because all four movements of the Scarlatti sonatas are in the same tonality, there is reason to believe that the three movements of K89 may also have been preceded originally by a slow movement.) All but two of the nine sonatas in question have basses which are at least partly figured (the exceptions are K77 and 78, the second of which might conceivably be an original keyboard work), and the final chord of K91/ii unmistakably indicates the violin as the solo instrument. The violin would seem to be the most likely solo instrument for the others, too.

The string-like qualities of these works have been appreciated for a long time. The English composer Charles Avison drew on them for some of the slow movements in the *Twelve Concerto's in Seven Parts* (1744) that he arranged from sonatas by Scarlatti,[2] and Lionel Salter restored eight of the sonatas (not including K80) to their putative original form in editions for violin and continuo published in 1940–50. At the same time, it must be said that the style of these works contains nothing inimical to keyboard performance, and their inclusion in one of the principal sources of the keyboard sonatas seems to recognize this fact. In addition, several sonatas which appear unquestionably to have been written for keyboard (for example, K208, 291–2, 322, 342 and 355) are nevertheless stylistically close to the continuo-accompanied solo sonata.

MANUSCRIPT SOURCES

Every writer on Scarlatti has lamented the fact that not a single autograph of any of his keyboard works has ever been discovered. One can only speculate on their fate, but, as Kirkpatrick (p. 140) pointed out, it is unlikely that they were dispersed during the composer's lifetime or after his death, since one would then have expected at least some of them to have come to light by now. Possibly they were destroyed *in toto* in one of the fires to which the royal palaces were subject from time to time, or perhaps they still await discovery by some diligent collector or serendipitous musicologist. If so, their potential importance to Scarlatti studies can be appreciated by considering how fundamentally our understanding of Bach has been transformed by the close study scholars have made of his autographs since about 1945. Meanwhile, the primary sources for most of Scarlatti's sonatas are contained in two valuable sets of manuscript volumes copied in Spain between 1742 and 1757, probably under the composer's supervision. One at least was compiled for Queen Maria Barbara; the other may have been copied for her as well, or possibly for Farinelli, who took both sets with him when he returned to Italy in 1759. The sets subsequently became separated (although the individual volumes were fortunately not dispersed), and they are now generally referred to by the names of the cities in which they are at present located: Venice and Parma.

The Venice set was deposited in the Biblioteca Nazionale Marciana in 1835. It consists of fifteen volumes (MSS 9770–84), of which the earliest (dated 1742) contains sixty-one pieces and the second (1749) forty-one. If, as seems likely, the manuscript volume of *Obras, para clavicordio, o piano forte, de Sebastian Alvero* in the library of the Conservatorio Superior de Música in Madrid (MS 4/1727(2)) is autograph, then Sebastian Albero may be identified as the scribe of the 1742 volume, and probably also of the 1749 volume, in the Venice set of Scarlatti's sonatas. Another copyist was responsible for the other volumes, dated 1752–7, which were obviously planned and executed as a set and are numbered 1 to 13; volume 10 contains thirty-four sonatas and the remaining twelve volumes each contain thirty, making a grand total of 496 sonatas in all the fifteen volumes of the Venice set. The external appearance of the volumes reflects the purpose for which they were copied. The pages have coloured borders and the bindings are of leather, tooled in gold with the Spanish and Portuguese coats-of-arms.

The Parma set, purchased by the Biblioteca Palatina from a Bolognese antiquarian bookshop in 1899 and now housed in the Conservatorio 'Arrigo Boito', also consists of fifteen volumes (MSS AG 31406–20). These were all copied by the main Venice scribe, who may have been Scarlatti's disciple, Antonio Soler. Unfortunately we possess no identifiable example of Soler's musical handwriting, but the initial 'S' (less often 'SA') appears several times at the end of a sonata in the last two Parma volumes. Soler's time at the Escorial coincides with the period when the copies were made, and there are other reasons for supposing that he copied some of Scarlatti's music (see Kirkpatrick, p. 140). It has also been suggested that these initials might belong to Sebastian Albero, but since Albero died on 30 March 1756 this seems unlikely. The Parma volumes are plainer in appearance and less sumptuously bound than the Venice set; like them, they contain mostly thirty sonatas each (volume 7 has thirty-one and volume 15 forty-two). They were probably copied between 1752 and 1757 (volume 1 is undated), but in no case do the date and contents of a volume correspond exactly with one in the Venice set. The fifteen Parma volumes contain in all 463 sonatas, nineteen of which (K202–4a, 204b, 205, 356–7 and 544–55) are not included in the Venice set.

Most editors and scholars have accepted the Venice set as the primary source for all the sonatas it contains. It formed the basis of Alessandro Longo's complete edition of 1906–8 and of Kenneth Gilbert's critical edition (1971–84), and the now generally accepted numbering of Kirkpatrick's catalogue is largely based on the order in which the sonatas appear in the Venice volumes. However, Venice's primacy over the Parma set derives largely from its external appearance and from the fact that it contains thirty-three more pieces. Joel Sheveloff brought forward some important evidence to support his argument that the Venice manuscripts were probably copied largely from the Parma volumes and are therefore further removed from the lost originals.[3] While retaining Kirkpatrick's numbering, his list in the *New Grove Dictionary of Music and Musicians* cites Parma as the primary source in most cases.

Of secondary importance to these Spanish manuscripts are two extensive collections of Italian origin now housed in libraries in Münster (Westphalia) and Vienna. Both stem from the library of Fortunato Santini, a Roman bibliophile who during his long life (1778–1861) amassed a collection of some four and a half thousand manuscripts and over a thousand printed volumes. Most of these eventually found their way into the Diözesan-Bibliothek in Münster, where they still remain. Santini's collection, some of which was unfortunately destroyed in the bombing of World War Two, is particularly rich in works by both Domenico and Alessandro Scarlatti. Included in it are five stout volumes, numbered I to V, containing in all 352 sonatas by Domenico. Sheveloff's detailed investigations suggest that the Parma manuscripts probably served as the main source for the Münster copies,[4] which however include three sonatas (K147 and 452–3) not to be found in either of the principal Spanish codices.

Six manuscript volumes now in the library of the Gesellschaft der Musikfreunde, Vienna (MSS VII 28011/A–F), were also once in Santini's collection. Together with a seventh volume (MS VII 28011/ G), they were later owned by the composer Johannes Brahms, who provided a thematic index to each volume and made several pencil annotations in the musical text. The copies are the work of several different scribes, among whom was probably Santini himself, and they transmit in all 319 pieces, including some duplications and a few movements by Alessandro Scarlatti and Thomas Roseingrave. According to Sheveloff, the first six Vienna volumes were copied from the Münster manuscripts; the source of Vienna G is more problematic.

In addition to the four major collections in Venice, Parma, Münster and Vienna, there exist a number of lesser eighteenth-century sources, some of which are important for the variant readings they transmit and, in some cases, because they include works otherwise unknown. Add. MS 31553 of the British Library is one of the most interesting of these. It contains forty-four 'sonatas modernas' and was once the property of the English composer and organist John Worgan, whose widow presented it to Charles Wesley. The last three sonatas in the volume are unique to this source and were accepted as genuine by Kirkpatrick, who listed them as nos 142–4 in his catalogue. Their authenticity was questioned by Gerstenberg, and Sheveloff found good reason to reject them on stylistic grounds, suggesting as a possible composer Sebastian Albero, José Nebra or Joaquín de Oxinaga.[5] That the first of these composers had originally something to do with the 'Worgan manuscript' is evident from the lower half of the title-page, where an attempt at erasure has left barely legible the words (in capitals) '. . . de D. Sebastian de Albero, organista principal de la Real Capilla de su Magestad . . .'. Could this erasure have been made in an attempt to disguise the fact that not all the contents were the work of Scarlatti?

Also of Spanish provenance are two manuscript volumes acquired in Madrid in 1772 by Lord Fitzwilliam, a keen collector of the music of both Domenico and Alessandro Scarlatti. Both volumes are now in the Fitzwilliam Museum at Cambridge, where they are catalogued as nos 147 and 148 (formerly 32–F–12/13). The first contains thirty-one sonatas, all of them familiar from other sources. The title-page of the other manuscript indicates that the twenty-four sonatas contained in it were copied for the Venetian ambassador. Nos 5 and 7 are unique to this source and were numbered 145 and 146 in Kirkpatrick's catalogue. These, too, Sheveloff regards with some suspicion, although the objections he makes on stylistic grounds seem to be in this case less well founded. There is nothing in the music that puts Scarlatti's authorship beyond question, but neither is there anything in the manuscript itself to raise doubts about the scribe's attribution.

The Parma manuscripts were unknown to Alessandro Longo when he published his complete edition of the sonatas in 1906–8, and the first scholar to examine and evaluate all the sources so far mentioned was Walter Gerstenberg in 1933. The most important source discovery since then was made in 1971, when the Austrian scholar, Eva Badura-Skoda, came across twelve previously overlooked manuscript volumes of Scarlatti sonatas in the library of the Gesellschaft der Musikfreunde. One of these is a late-nineteenth-century volume which, like the other Viennese manuscripts mentioned earlier, once formed part of Brahms's library; beyond this fact it has no particular interest or importance as a source. Most (perhaps all) of the other eleven volumes (MSS Q.15112–20, Q.11432 and Q.15126), containing in all ninety-eight sonatas, not including duplicates, were originally acquired by the Viennese diplomat Aeodat Joseph Philipp du Beyne de Malechamp, usually known as Joseph DuBeine, an amateur musician and an avid music collector whose activities after his retirement from state service in 1760 provided the substance of several marginalia in the biography of Mozart. After DuBeine's death in 1811 the volumes passed to Beethoven's patron, the Archduke Rudolph, and from him to the society of which he was a prominent supporter, the Gesellschaft der Musikfreunde.

These newly discovered manuscripts have been described and evaluated by Seunghyun Choi,[6] but since their contents have not so far been reported in the published literature on Scarlatti, it might be worthwhile summarizing them here. They are:

Q.15112:   K8, 16, 19, 9, 27 and 14
Q.15113:   K1–7, 10–13, 15, 17–18, 20–6 and 28–9
Q.15114:   K474, 476, 481–3, 468, 458, 450, 426, 428–9, 446, 134, 211, 430 and 124
Q.15115:   K490, 475, 366, 112, 215 and 115
Q.15116:   K54, 259–60, 206, 132–3, 116, 96, 135, 119, 127, 56 and 487. This volume originally contained another sonata, probably K113.
Q.15117:   K8, 31–8, 40–2, 125–6, 131, 182, 179 and 211. The volume contains also the Introduction that Roseingrave printed in his 1739 edition of Scarlatti sonatas (see p. 141) and three fugues by Alessandro Scarlatti which are found also in the final volume of the other Vienna set (MS VII 28011/G) mentioned earlier. Another piece is now missing from the manuscript (probably K127).
Q.15118:   K216, 462–3, 398, 477, 159, 469 and 446
Q.15119:   K247, 299, 95, 66, 246, 298, 120, 180, 45 and 101
Q.15120:   K113 and 246–7
Q.11432:   This 'Raccolta di tutti sonate per il clavicembalo del Signore Dominico Scarlati' is divided into twelve fascicles (numbered 'opera Ima', 'opera IIda' etc.), each with a separate title-page and each containing six sonatas:

I	K474, 476, 481–3 and 468
II	K458, 450, 426, 428–9 and 134
III	K211, 430, 124, 113, 54 and 259
IV	K260, 206, 132–3, 116 and 96
V	K135, 119, 56, 487, 490 and 475
VI	K366, 112, 215, 115, 216 and 462
VII	K463, 398, 477, 159, 469 and 446
VIII	K25–6, 5, 2 and 6–7
IX	K9, 13, 15–17 and 19
X	K4, 23, 12, 22, 21 and 27
XI	K14, 28, 13, 9, 19 and 8
XII	K125–7, 131, 182 and 179

Q.15126:   K25–6, 5, 2, 6–7, 9, 13 and 15–16

It will be noticed that fascicles I–IX and fascicle XII of Q.11432 duplicate, in roughly the same order, sonatas found in the other manuscripts. Q.11432 is bound in leather and tooled in gold with a heraldic emblem of the Hungarian monarch. It was evidently the scribe's intention to bring together all the Scarlatti sonatas available to him, a task which was obviously not completed in these twelve fascicles. Seunghyun Choi dated Q.11432 to about 1780 and, on the basis of the heraldic emblem on the cover, she suggested that the collection was made for the Emperor Joseph II in his capacity as King of Hungary. However, the division of the collection into groups of six and the designation of these as 'opera Ima', 'opera IIda' etc. suggests that the manuscript may also have been assembled with a view to eventual publication. That it has some connection with more than one early printed edition cannot be doubted. Fascicle XII reproduces exactly the contents of *VI sonate . . . del Sigre. Domenico Scarlatti . . . Opera Ima*, published by Johann Ulrich Haffner of Nuremberg in 1754. Opere I–III of Q.11432 turn up again as Cahiers 6–8 of an edition of fifty-four sonatas published by the Bureau des Arts et d'Industrie, Vienna, between 1803 and 1807 (see p. 159). Although the newly discovered Vienna manuscripts bring forward no hitherto unknown works, they do shed important new light on other manuscript sources and on the early printed editions (Czerny's, as well as those already mentioned), while their mere existence underlines the importance of the Austrian capital as a centre for the cultivation and dissemination of Scarlatti's keyboard music during the second half of the eighteenth century.

It is a strange fact, quite as remarkable as the complete disappearance of the autographs of Scarlatti's keyboard music, that when Kirkpatrick (1953) and Sheveloff (1970) compiled their exhaustive lists of Scarlatti sources neither writer was able to cite a single manuscript copy of a sonata in any Spanish library or archive. This is a situation no less singular than would have been the complete disappearance from England of all Handel's oratorios, or the loss of all trace in Germany of Bach's church cantatas, and it cannot be explained simply as the result of negligence on the part of librarians, archivists and scholars. We know that Farinelli's contract with the Spanish court did not allow him to perform elsewhere. Did Maria Barbara perhaps place a similar embargo on the copying of Scarlatti's music, hoping to reserve it exclusively for her own use? Were the copies she bequeathed to Farinelli the only ones that existed at the time?

In the case of most of the sonatas the answer to this last question would seem to be Yes. At all events, it is only in recent years and in very small numbers that copies of Scarlatti's keyboard works have begun to turn up in Spanish archives. The seven 'new' works that these finds have brought to light will be discussed later in this chapter (see pp. 190–4), but it is worth mentioning that several of the Spanish copies were intended for performance on the organ, as is apparent either from their title-page or from transpositions made by the copyists to keep the music within the organ's compass. One cannot, of course, draw firm conclusions from what is a relatively small number of sources, but it does seem from the evidence we have that in Spain Scarlatti's sonatas were kept in the repertory during the late eighteenth century largely as organ pieces.

In the following list of Spanish sources the sonatas not included in Kirkpatrick's catalogue are indicated simply by keys:

Valladolid, Metropolitan Cathedral
  MS 19 : K7, (G major), (D minor), (A major), K130, 66, 65, 98 and 5

Montserrat, Monasterio de S Maria
  MS AM 484, pp. 10–11 : K533
  MS AM 484, pp. 21–2 : K19 ('Soler')
  MS AM 654, pp. 19–35 : K6, 266, 474, 437, 533 ('Soler'; incomplete)
                          and 302 ('Soler')
  MS AM 1770, pp. 74–5 : (C major)
  MS AM 2298, pp. 74–5 : K200 (?)
  MS AM 2786, pp. 42–3 : K33

Tenerife, Private collection
  Unnumbered MSS : (G major), (D minor), K298

Aránzazu, Santuario
  MS 961 : K6 and 10

Madrid, Real Conservatorio de Música
  MS D/Aut–2 : K417
  MS Roda Leg, 35/504 : (D major), (A major)
  Uncatalogued : K1–42
  MS 3/1408 :

No.	K no.	Tonality	No.	K no.	Tonality
1	183	F minor	9	126	C minor
2	158	C minor	10	319	F# major
3	316	F major	11	—	C major
4	317	F major	12	—	C major
5	331	Bb major	13	306	Eb major
6	332	Bb major	14	190	Bb major
7	160	D major	15	315	G minor
8	333	D major	16	179	G minor

17	424	G major		24	392	B♭ major
18	425	G major		25	434	D minor
19	139	C minor		26	427	G major
20	116	C minor		27	105	G major
21	432	G major		28	364	F minor
22	430	D major		29	365	F minor
23	399	C major		30	108	G minor

(These sources will be referred to hereafter by the names of the towns in which they are located.)

The Valladolid manuscript contains five keyboard sonatas by Manuel Blasco de Nebra, nephew of José Nebra and organist of Seville Cathedral in the second half of the eighteenth century. These sonatas are followed in the manuscript by nine anonymous single-movement pieces, six of which are known from other sources to be by Domenico Scarlatti; Antonio Baciero is convinced that the other three sonatas are also Scarlatti's.[7] The authenticated pieces show numerous minor differences from the versions already familiar; as is usually the case in Scarlatti sources, the more substantial variants (bars missing or added) mostly involve repeated phrases.

It was Bengt Johnsson who first drew attention to some of the Montserrat manuscripts containing works attributed to Scarlatti.[8] As in Roseingrave's edition of 1739, the Montserrat version of K33 lacks the first seventeen bars of the Venice 1742 manuscript. MS AM 654 is dated 1767 and MS AM 484 is dated 1786; they both have title-pages designating the contents as 'sonatas de organo', and several passages have been altered to keep the music within the range of that instrument. In 1985 the library reported to the present writer that the sonata K200, mentioned by Johnsson as being included in MS AM 2298, does not appear there.

The two Tenerife sonatas hitherto unknown as works by Scarlatti were published in a modern edition by Rosario Alvarez Martinez (Madrid, 1984). They were copied between 1770 and 1791 and were originally the property of a music-loving priest, Bernardo Valois y Bethencourt, who lived at Puerto de la Cruz, Tenerife, in the second half of the eighteenth century. Today they form part of the private collection of the Tenerife family, Zárate Cólogan de La Orotava. The G major sonata, attributed elsewhere to Carlos de Seixas, is on a single, unbound leaf measuring 22 × 31 cm. The D minor piece, a 'Fandango del Sig.ʳ Scarlate', occupies ff. 5–6 of a volume measuring 22 × 30.5 cm which also contains pieces by José Herrando and Agustino Massa.

K6 and 10 at Aránzazu are late copies, of no particular interest as sources. Of the four Madrid manuscripts, two were listed by Juan José Rey in an article published in 1978.[9] The version of K417, entitled 'Sonata de fuga para clavicordio del Sigr. Dn. Domingo de Scarlatti', probably dates from the late eighteenth century, like most of the other recently discovered Spanish manuscripts. Its interest lies chiefly in the intervention of a later hand, which has made several 'improvements' to the composer's textures and part-writing. The two 'new' sonatas in D and A major are found in a 'Quaderno de sonatas sin gusto para el uso de Antonio Navarro'. A note at the end of the volume states that it was copied by Indalecio Soriano Fuertes between 24 September and 22 October 1818 for his pupil Antonio Navarro. Soriano Fuertes was later appointed *maestro de capilla* at the royal chapel in Madrid, and the composer best represented in his manuscript anthology is José Lidon, who occupied the same post from 1805 until his death in 1827. Several of the Lidon works include organ registration, and possibly the whole collection was intended for practice on that instrument, since notes above c''' are studiously (if not always artistically) avoided. The first movement of Haydn's Piano Sonata in F major H.XVI:23, which occupies pages 58–61 of the *Quaderno*, has suffered considerable truncation and mangling to make it playable on an instrument of restricted compass. The two sonatas attributed to Scarlatti in this volume may also have been subject to similar revision by Soriano Fuertes, but the extent of this must remain uncertain, since they are known in no other source. They are printed for the first time as Appendix III here.

Of the two Madrid manuscripts not listed in Rey's article, one is a copy of the forty-two sonatas published in two volumes by Roseingrave in 1739 and reprinted by John Johnson between 1754 and 1756 (see p. 158). To judge from the title-pages, volume 1 was copied from the Johnson reprint and volume 2 from the original edition. They may have been bequeathed to the library of the Real Conservatorio by the Spanish pianist Santiago de Massarnau, who lived for a time in London during the first half of the nineteenth century.[10]

The remaining Madrid manuscript (3/1408) is of particular interest. Like the *Essercizi* and most of the Parma and Venice volumes, it contains thirty sonatas, and the title-page reads: 'Libro Di Sonate/Dil Sig.^{r} Domenico Scarlatti/Per la Sig.^{ra} D.ª Ygnacia Ayerbe'. Despite the rather unorthodox Italian of this title, the manuscript is very similar in appearance to others of Spanish provenance. The pages measure about 21 × 28 cm, and each sonata occupies four pages, with a single opening for each of the two sections so as to minimize the turning of pages for the player. The placing of the titles, the thickly drawn braces and the distribution of the notes between the two staves (regardless of which hand plays them) in such a way as to reduce as far as possible the need for leger lines – these are all features typical of other Spanish keyboard sources. The hand itself, however, is not recognizable from any other Scarlatti source that has so far come to light. The centring of the treble clef on the first space rather than on the second line of the staff is a distinctive and consistent feature of this scribe.

Another point of interest is that this manuscript confirms the tendency of the main Parma and Venice sources to group sonatas into pairs according to key. No less significant for the implications this has for performance is the observation that of the nine pairs in the Madrid source, only four (those with consecutive 'K' numbers in the list above) exist as pairs in other Scarlatti sources.[11] Nos 7–8, 15–16, 19–20 and 26–7 in the Madrid manuscript form pairs widely separated in other sources. The remaining pair, nos 11–12, is not found in any other Scarlatti source, but the two sonatas in question do appear together as nos 1–2 in a manuscript volume of *Sonatas para clavicordio* by Sebastian Albero in the Biblioteca Nazionale Marciana, Venice (MS 9768).[12] Their structure and to some extent their style are Scarlattian, but they lack any original feature that might link them indisputably with the Italian master. The impression they convey is rather one of an attractive but calculated imitation, and the attribution to Albero is probably the correct one.

Discussion of the relationship of MS 3/1408 to the other Scarlatti sources may be left until such time as the text, paper and handwriting have been more thoroughly investigated. Meanwhile, one would dearly like to discover the identity of Donna Ignacia Ayerbe. . . .

PRINTED EDITIONS

The only printed edition of sonatas by Scarlatti in which the composer himself participated was the *Essercizi per gravicembalo*. The circumstances of its publication have been mentioned earlier (see pp. 139–40), where it was shown that the volume must have appeared first in 1738 or 1739. An advertisement in *The Country Journal or The Craftsman* dated 27 January 1739 claims it as 'Just Publish'd', but the final paragraph of the same advertisement perhaps suggests that Roseingrave's pirated edition had by then already appeared, or at any rate was about to do so: 'Beware of incorrect printed Editions, a Scandal in this great Nation, and let not its fundamental Principles of Liberty and Property be abus'd by vile Worms that gnaw the Fruit of others ingenious Labour and Expence.' If these remarks were intended to

TABLE I *Editions of Scarlatti sonatas published during the composer's lifetime*

Title	Publisher (place, date)	Contents
1. *Essercizi per gravicembalo*	(London, [1738/9]); reprinted Witvogel (Amsterdam, 1742)	K1–30
2. *XLII Suites de pieces pour le clavecin* [includes Introduction by Roseingrave and Fugue by A. Scarlatti]	Cooke (London, [1739]); reprinted Johnson (London, [?1754–6])	K1–42
3. *Pièces pour le clavecin . . . Ir volume*	Boivin *et al*. (Paris, n.d.)	K1–10, 12–14, 19–20, 22, 29–35
4. *Pièces pour le clavecin . . . deuxsieme volume*	Boivin *et al*. (Paris, n.d.)	K11, 15–18, 21, 23–8, 36–42
5. *Pièces pour le clavecin . . . troisieme volume*	Boivin *et al*. (Paris, n.d.)	K33, 48–9, 55, 96–7 (+4 spurious)
6. *Pièces pour le clavecin*	Boivin *et al*. (Paris, n.d.)	K1, 3, 5–7, 10, 12–14, 19–20, 22, 29, 34–5, 66, 95
7. *Pièces choisies pour le clavecin . . . opera prima*	Boivin *et al*. (Paris, n.d.)	K2, 4, 8–9, 30–3, 36–9
8. *Six Double Fugues . . . by Mr Roseingrave. To which is added Sigr Dominico Scarlatti's Celebrated Lesson*	Walsh (London, [1750])	K37
9. *Libro de XII sonatas modernas*	Johnson (London, [1752])	K44, 53, 55, 100–1, 104–7, 116–17, 140
10. *VI sonate per il cembalo*	Haffner (Nuremberg, [1754])	K125–7, 131, 179, 182
11. *XX sonate per cembalo di varii autorri*	Vernadez *et al*. (Paris, [1754/5])	K125, 180
12. *Six Sonatas . . . vol. III*	Johnson (London, [1757])	K113, 120, 246–7, 298–9

refer to Roseingrave's edition, then the *Essercizi* must have been published some time before this, possibly in 1738.

The thirty sonatas of the *Essercizi* are mostly of very high quality and extraordinarily inspired; they have remained among the best-known and most frequently performed of all Scarlatti's sonatas. It can hardly be doubted that by 1738 the composer must have had a considerable number of such works from which to make his selection. The *Essercizi* served as the basis for most of the subsequent printed editions issued during Scarlatti's lifetime. These are summarized in Table 1; for more details of individual publications the reader is referred to the studies of Hopkinson, Kirkpatrick, Newton and Sheveloff.[13]

It will be seen from this table that only seventy-three of Scarlatti's 550 or so sonatas were published during his lifetime; most were printed in London and Paris, and none in his native Italy or adopted Spain. Publishers tended to reissue the same sonatas, particularly K1–30, over and over again, and since in doing so they were presumably satisfying a keen public demand, one can only infer that manuscripts of the other sonatas were not available to them. Indeed, as has already been noted, the dissemination of Scarlatti manuscripts during the composer's lifetime seems to have been unusually restricted, whether by design or accident it is impossible to say. Little wonder that a number of spurious or doubtful sonatas crept into the early editions.[14]

By the end of the eighteenth century the number of authentic sonatas available in print had almost doubled to about 125, thanks largely to editions brought out in London by Muzio Clementi (*c.* 1791) and Robert Birchall (1800; thirty sonatas from manuscripts owned by Lord Fitzwilliam). In the early nineteenth century the initiative passed from London and Paris to Vienna, where between 1803 and 1807 a consortium of Austrian publishers known as the Kunst- und Industrie-Comptoir (or Bureau des Arts et d'Industrie) issued eight *cahiers* containing in all fifty-four sonatas selected from the *Essercizi* and manuscripts now in the library of the Gesellschaft der Musikfreunde. This edition, together with other Vienna manuscripts and possibly items from Santini's collection, was used in turn by Carl Czerny for his 'collected' edition of 200 sonatas, published in two volumes by Tobias Haslinger of Vienna in 1839.

Czerny's edition remained throughout the nineteenth century the most comprehensive available, and it served as the basis for many others, some of which were quite unscrupulous in presenting a heavily edited and even bowdlerized text. Meanwhile the important Spanish manuscripts prepared for Queen Maria Barbara remained unnoticed in Parma and Venice until Alessandro Longo drew on the latter source for his complete edition of 545 sonatas, published in ten volumes and a supplement by Ricordi of Milan in 1906–8. Longo's edition was reasonably accurate in its essentials, but many of Scarlatti's harmonic asperities were smoothed out, the text was heavily encrusted with editorial phrasing, dynamic markings and modern fingerings, and the sonatas were arbitrarily grouped by key into suites of mainly four or five pieces.

Ralph Kirkpatrick's facsimile edition of 555 sonatas (New York, 1971), reproduced mainly from the Parma manuscripts, exposed the need for a new complete edition prepared under modern and rigorous editorial guidelines. To a considerable extent this need was met by the eleven-volume edition of Kenneth Gilbert (Paris, 1971–84) which, however, relies heavily on a single source – the Venice manuscripts – and is less than comprehensive in its critical notes and variant readings. A new edition by Emilia Fadini, which at the time of writing is in progress from Ricordi of Milan, promises to go further in remedying the deficiencies of earlier editions, especially with its fuller and more detailed *apparatus criticus*. Unfortunately the order in which the sonatas are printed in this edition involves yet another numbering system to add to the already conflicting ones of Longo, Kirkpatrick and Pestelli.

CHRONOLOGY AND PAIRING

A secure chronology for Scarlatti's sonatas, without which it is impossible to form a clear picture of his development as a keyboard composer, has so far eluded all investigation and will probably continue to do so unless a substantial number of manuscripts one day comes to light. Publication dates of the early editions and the dates appended to the main manuscript sources are, of course, helpful in determining a *terminus ante quem* for those sonatas to which they refer, but attempts to go beyond these have not so far proved fruitful or convincing.

Kirkpatrick was the first to argue that the order in which the sonatas were copied into the Venice and Parma volumes corresponds in general with the order in which they were composed. More than that, the close identity between the contents of the last eleven volumes in each set led him to conclude that 'most of the sonatas [all but about 200] date from the very last years of Scarlatti's life, for the most part from 1752 onwards'.[15] There is ample evidence to support what might be called Kirkpatrick's 'general theory' of a direct relationship between the order of composition and the order of copying into the two main sources. It is not unreasonable to see the enlargement of the binary structure, the clearer separation of primary and secondary themes and the general expansion of the instrumental compass as indicating a progression from an earlier to a later period. The same kind of development can be observed in pre-Classical sonatas for which an incontrovertible chronology can be established. Scarlatti's concentration on highly distinctive stylistic features, such as hand-crossing and note-clusters, within a particular span of sonatas (as suggested by the sources) supports the proposition of a general correlation between the order of composition and the order of copying, and this is not seriously challenged by the inclusion in a later volume of the occasional sonata using a narrower compass or showing retrospective stylistic features. It is much more difficult, when faced with such sonatas as K393 or 431, to accept Kirkpatrick's 'special theory', as we may call it: that the sonatas were copied into the Venice and Parma sets more or less at the time that Scarlatti completed them. Stylistic judgments inevitably play a part in testing the validity of theories such as this, even though style on its own is a notoriously uncertain criterion on which to base an exact chronology, as the work of practically any of the great composers will demonstrate.

Stylistic analysis nevertheless served Giorgio Pestelli for his 'pro-posal of a chronological order' for Scarlatti's sonatas.[16] Pestelli divided the sonatas into three broad categories which he called 'the archaic Scarlatti', 'the period of the *Esercizi* [*sic*]' and 'the great flourishing after the *Esercizi*' (the last subdivided into two periods, 1738–46 and 1746–57). Within these categories sonatas are grouped together according to certain stylistic features which they have in common. Pestelli's book is valuable for several reasons: it contains an interesting and provocative survey of twentieth-century writings on Scarlatti; it establishes the relevance of Alessandro Scarlatti's keyboard music to that of his son; and it explores relationships between Domenico's keyboard music and that of his Italian and Spanish contemporaries (including Sebastian Albero, who is for the first time accorded the attention he merits). But Pestelli's central thesis, his 'chronological' listing, must in the end be rejected. Not only does it contain inconsistencies within itself, its very premises are question-able, and particularly so, as Joel Sheveloff pointed out, when applied to music 'so diverse in form, rich in material and intricate in tonality'.[17]

Until more reliable evidence is forthcoming it seems advisable to confine our notions about the chronology of Scarlatti's sonatas to what can be inferred from the dated sources we have. If, as Scarlatti claimed in his dedication, the *Essercizi* were 'born under the highest auspices' of King John V of Portugal, then they must have been composed between 1723 and 1728. The twelve sonatas that Rosein-grave added to the *Essercizi* for his 1739 publication were presumably among those he brought back with him from Italy in 1714 or 1715; they are patently inferior in quality and anterior in composition to the *Essercizi* themselves. Kirkpatrick (p. 144) considered about forty of the extant sonatas to antedate the *Essercizi*, and Pestelli fifty-six, but there is no reason why, on stylistic grounds alone, many others should not be assigned to Scarlatti's years in Italy and Portugal. Kirkpatrick's chronology for the higher numbered sonatas forces us to draw one of two conclusions: either a large number of sonatas have been lost, or Scarlatti virtually gave up composing keyboard music for a period of over twenty years. The first of these conclusions seems unlikely in view of the evident intention behind the compilation of the Venice and Parma volumes of preserving a complete repertory. The second seems equally implausible because of the nature of the sonatas themselves: these are not the philosophical or visionary musings of an old man, and it seems incredible that Scarlatti should have 'bottled them up' for so long. It is not impossible, in fact, that by 1752, when he would have passed what would now (and perhaps even then) be thought of as retirement age, Scarlatti had virtually given up composing harpsi-chord music, and that between 1752 and 1757 the sonatas were copied from the autographs (which would presumably embody a rough chronology) by a scribe whose other duties meant that he had to take five years over the job of writing out 857 copies – more, if there was a third set which has been lost. Even if we accept the dates on the Parma and Venice manuscripts as composition rather than copying dates, they could still refer to a final revised version of pieces written many years earlier. But, once again, we enter the realms of conjecture.

What is needed, it seems, is more of the kind of hard (though, unfortunately, not conclusive) evidence provided by, for example, one of the Spanish manuscripts: MS 3/1408 of the Madrid conserv-atory. The copyist of this manuscript usually adopts the modern practice of cancelling sharps by naturals, but in three sonatas (nos 7, 8 and 27) he has followed a more archaic usage and cancelled sharps by flats. Since he has used each method consistently within a sonata, it is obvious that he was transcribing exactly what he saw, and one is therefore led to infer that the pairing of sonatas 7 and 8 (in fact, K160 and 333) may well be earlier than the pairing of K160 with K161 in the Venice and Parma sources, where K333 is a singleton. The chrono-logical implications are obvious. The pair to no. 27 (K105) in the

Madrid source is no. 26 (K427), but this cannot be shown with the same degree of confidence to be an early pairing since the sharps in K427 are never cancelled, either by flats or by naturals.

Another source with possible implications for chronology is MS FF 232 of the Civico Museo Bibliografico Musicale in Bologna. Joel Sheveloff[18] listed the contents and noted the inscription on the title-page: 'Per studio di Francesco Gasparini', but it was left to Roberto Pagano[19] to remind us that if this inscription refers to Scarlatti's teacher the contents of the volume (twelve sonatas, including K426 and 430, as well as works by Handel) must have been written by 1727, the year of Gasparini's death.[20]

As we have seen, the problem of chronology in Scarlatti's sonatas is closely bound up with that of pairing. It was Kirkpatrick (pp. 141ff.) who first drew attention to what he called the 'pairwise arrangement' of most of the sonatas in the two main sources (excluding the 1742 Venice volume, in which it is scarcely apparent). Although numbered independently, the sonatas are grouped into pairs, and occasionally into threes, according to key. The incidence of pairs, especially, is so striking that it seems inexplicable that Gerstenberg could list the entire contents of the Venice and Parma sets, complete with keys and time-signatures, without remarking on it at all.[21]

Two questions, above all, have been hotly debated by Scarlatti scholars. Was it the composer himself who arranged the sonatas in pairs, or did the pairs originate with his copyist? And was it intended that the paired sonatas should actually be performed as pairs? There are several pieces of evidence to suggest that the pairing did in fact originate with Scarlatti (who, after all, probably supervised the copying and must have been aware of numerous precedents for pairing in the sonatas of other composers). Time and again it happens that the two sonatas forming a pair employ the same compass, or, more significant still, that the restricted compass of one sonata is not exceeded in the other. To take just one example, K374 in G major employs a range of $D-d'''$; bars 29–34 in the first section were obviously recast in the second section because the instrument for which the work was written lacked both the low B' and the high g''' that would have enabled the passage to be recapitulated exactly in bars 63–8 (example 16). The sonata's companion piece, K375, also remains within the range $D-d'''$.[22] Similar instances exist in significant numbers, but it should be mentioned also that there are some examples of restricted compass that point towards the opposite conclusion. K360, 369 and 485, for example, may have been written for instruments with a wider compass than those for which their companion pieces (K361, 368 and 486–7 respectively) were designed,[23] but in the absence of autograph sources it is impossible to be certain about this.

Example 16

Evidence of various kinds can be adduced to show that sonatas were paired not only to make a neatly ordered collection but also with the intention that the two sonatas of a pair should be performed consecutively. At the end of K99 in C minor in the Venice source the instruction 'volti subito' ('turn the page immediately') can only mean that the player should proceed straight away to the C major sonata

(K100) that follows. K347 and 348, in G minor and G major respectively, are even more closely linked, with the last note of the first serving also as the first note of the second. K527 in C major is prefaced by a 'key-signature' of two naturals, cancelling the flats of its companion piece, K526 in C minor; the naturals make sense only if the player is proceeding straight from the first of the pair to the second. A similar 'key-signature' is found in the Parma version of K510 in D minor, where two naturals (repeated for every system to which they apply) cancel the two sharps of K509 in D major. Kirkpatrick (p. 142) mentions most of these instances without, however, suggesting that the lack of indications for consecutive performance in other pairs might be taken as indicating a *laissez-faire* attitude on the composer's part.

While the problem of whether or not Scarlatti intended the paired sonatas to be performed as pairs has often been discussed, the further questions it raises are rarely asked. Performed by whom? Where? On what occasions? We tend to approach the problem of pairing from the viewpoint of the modern harpsichord player (or pianist) preparing a recital programme or a recording, and it is easy to overlook the fact that concert-giving as we know it today hardly existed in Scarlatti's time, and certainly not in the social circles in which he moved. As far as we know, Scarlatti wrote most of his sonatas for his royal patron and pupil Queen Maria Barbara, or for himself to play. One can imagine the queen performing a selection of them to the assembled Spanish court and distinguished visitors, but Scarlatti would hardly be in a position to dictate to her how many sonatas should be played, and in what order, on such an occasion. If, on the other hand, he had intended to publish the sonatas, then the question of a particular order would have been more pressing. It may be that in having them copied for the queen Scarlatti did also have in mind their eventual publication, and the fact that they were mostly grouped in volumes of thirty might be seen to support this. The *Essercizi*, it is true, contain only one pair and one triptych (twelve pairs would have been possible), but there may have been special reasons for this. At all events, the ordering of the sonatas in the *Essercizi* cannot be taken as proof that the later pairs did not originate with the composer.

This, nevertheless, has been the view taken by some distinguished Scarlatti scholars. Herman Keller rejected the possibility that the pairs originated with the composer, although he recognized the appropriateness of observing them in performance.[24] Pestelli also rejected the pairs as part of Scarlatti's original conception, and argued that the inclusion of single sonatas among the larger groups supported his proposed chronology.[25] The most powerful arguments against performance in pairs are, first, that the sonatas each have a separate title and number in the sources and, second, that many of them are differently paired in different sources (for example in the recently discovered Madrid manuscripts; see p. 157). Neither of these arguments, however, really affects the priority of the pairwise arrangement, although both can be taken to indicate an option for the player. As with the problem of chronology, it is only the discovery of new evidence (especially Scarlatti's autographs) that is likely to advance the argument at all.

Meanwhile, there is much to be said for observing the pairs of the two main sources in modern performances. Attempts to trace thematic connections between paired sonatas have not been very convincing,[26] but it is possible in several pairs to sense some kind of unity at a more subliminal level. Kirkpatrick (p. 143) pointed to the similar harmonic colouring of K106 and 107 in F major. The stylistic kinship between K528 and 529 in B♭ major extends not only to the fact, but also to the manner, of their hand-crossings and wide leaps – features the more striking since they are found hardly at all in the sonatas that surround them in the main sources (Venice, volume 13, and Parma, volume 15). It is difficult to believe these two works did not always belong together, and the same goes for many other pairs in which an *alla breve* Allegro or Andante is followed by a brisk movement in triple time (3/8 or 3/4). One is led to the conclusion that even if the pairing was not part of the original conception it was nevertheless done creatively when the works were brought to their final form.

STRUCTURE

It is perhaps unfortunate that Scarlatti chose the term 'sonata' for the single-movement binary pieces that make up the bulk of his keyboard works. Obviously these have nothing to do with either the multi-movement structures for melody instrument and continuo that we normally associate with the Baroque sonata (the violin and flute sonatas of Bach, Handel and Telemann, for example) or the solo sonatas of Haydn, Mozart, Beethoven and other Classical masters. For solo keyboard pieces like Scarlatti's, English composers used the term 'lesson', and English publishers so described Scarlatti's sonatas when they reissued them in the eighteenth century. The title *Essercizi* was perhaps chosen for Scarlatti's first published collection as an Italian equivalent of this; the term seems not to have been current in

Italy itself for such pieces. Even so, the individual items in the *Essercizi* (including the final fugue) were all called 'sonata'. As a result, Scarlatti's binary structures have often been described, and even evaluated, by reference to late-eighteenth-century (worse still, late-Classical) norms of sonata form. The developed sonata structure of late Haydn and Mozart has been seen as a goal towards which Scarlatti's binary forms in some mysterious way aspire (or fail to aspire[27]); approval has been reserved for those sonatas in which a first and second subject can be clearly identified in the first section, and to which the labels 'development' and 'recapitulation' can be attached in the second; and particular importance has often been attached to those rarities in which the initial theme is restated in the tonic.

It is worth recalling in this connection that Joseph Haydn, whose music may be said to encompass Classical sonata form from its infancy to its fullest maturity, was only six years old when the *Essercizi* were published. He may not have even been born when they were written. Scarlatti's sonata structure – for which we really require a quite different label – is best understood, therefore, as a highly original, even idiosyncratic extension of a basically simple form, in the cultivation and development of which an individual gift for improvisation was guided by an unerring, if unorthodox, instinct for proportion. Although his earliest keyboard works were undoubtedly influenced by the toccatas of his father and other Italian composers such as Domenico Zipoli and Bernardo Pasquini, the starting-point for their binary structure was the dance movement familiar today from the suites of Bach and Handel, and much used by both Scarlattis in their operatic overtures. In its simplest form this consisted of two sections, each repeated, the first modulating from the tonic to a related key and the second proceeding back to the tonic. The second section may modulate more widely and even introduce new material, but its ending usually 'rhymes' with that of the first section. The form may be expressed diagrammatically as:

$$A1 \ (a^1 - b^2) :\|: A2 \ (a^2 - b^1)$$

where 'a' and 'b' represent clauses (not themes) and the superscript numbers represent keys. The scheme is to be found in many of the low-numbered sonatas of Scarlatti, but it is seen at its simplest in the sixteen bars (8 + 8) of K431.

Except for the allemande-like opening of K4, there is little in the rhythms and phrase structures of the *Essercizi* to betray their dance origins. The tendency here is towards asymmetry, with each section of the sonata made up of a different and uneven number of bars. In the suites of Bach and most other contemporaries the second section of a dance is never shorter than the first, and the relative length of the two sections can usually be expressed in simple ratios. In six of the *Essercizi* (K4, 16, 20, 24–5 and 29), however, the first section is longer than the second, and in later sonatas this becomes the norm rather than the exception.

Some of the *Essercizi* (especially K1 and 4) retain links with the dances of the late Baroque suite in their seamless continuity and lack of rhythmic, textural or thematic contrast. In others the parallelism of the 'b' clause is pushed back, often to a point which makes it possible to talk of recapitulating a section rather than of 'rhyming' a clause. When the point where the parallelism begins (what Kirkpatrick called the 'Crux') is marked by a distinctive melodic idea, one can hardly avoid, with the vocabulary available, describing the structure in sonata rather than in simple binary terms. This 'B' theme (for which the term 'second subject' seems inappropriate, since the theme rarely engenders the degree of textural or expressive duality one finds in the mature Classical sonata) may be new, or it may be a restatement of previous material. What is important to the articulation of the structure is not so much the theme itself as the manner in which it is introduced. In the *Essercizi* this may be after a well-defined perfect cadence in the related key (K5, 13, 16 and 21) or it may be *on* the dominant of the related key, the new tonic being established by the 'B' theme itself (K6–7, 9, 17 and 29). In the light of Scarlatti's later sonatas (or those presumed to be later), not to mention those of the Viennese Classical composers, the second of these alternatives must be recognized as the more progressive.

When the parallelism between the two sections begins in advance of the 'B' theme it might, in theory, be possible to recognize the presence of a transition passage; but such a conception, stemming as it does from an awareness of Classical procedures, is rarely helpful to an understanding of the Scarlatti design. A codetta (more rarely, a coda), on the other hand, often functions with just the same effect as in the Classical sonata: its harmony is static, reinforcing the closing tonality of the section, and its thematic material (often particularly attractive) is repetitive. The effect is frequently, as Kirkpatrick (p. 255) put it, 'like an airplane coasting along a landing strip'; but sometimes it is at just this point that Scarlatti introduces hemiolas, syncopations and other devices to maintain the rhythmic thrust, so that it might seem as if the aeroplane has a rather bumpy landing, or even that it is about to become airborne again. None of the codettas in the *Essercizi* is of this dynamic kind – often they merely prolong the final tonic chord of the section with right-hand figuration – but the codetta of K21 uses a bass figure (*x*) which Scarlatti was often to decorate with amazing variety and resource (example 17).

Example 17   Sonata K21

K21 shows the binary structure of Scarlatti's mature sonatas in all its essentials. It may be represented diagrammatically as:

themes : A —— B —— (codetta) :||: (C) —— B —— (codetta)

keys : T ⤳ R —————————— :||: ? ⤳ T ————————

(T = tonic key; R = related key)

The tonal structure is very straightforward, and still basically that of the late Baroque dance movement. The first half begins in the tonic and closes in a related key: the dominant if the main tonality is major, the dominant minor (or, less often, the relative major) if it is minor. The second half then restores the tonal balance, usually visiting several keys in the course of the 'C' section after the double bar, and then recapitulating the 'B' material in the tonic. The commonest alternative to the dominant for the central cadence in major keys is the mediant minor, which is found in at least fifteen cases (K130, 229, 241, 249, 256, 289, 296, 317, 366, 392, 439, 442, 457, 503, and 518; most of these are in F or B♭ major). The function of the mediant minor as a closely related key in other Baroque forms (for example, in the da capo aria) might have led one to expect it to occur more frequently in Scarlatti's sonatas; the fact that it does not may perhaps be taken as a progressive feature of his music. No. 10 in the *Essercizi*, on the other hand, is decidedly not progressive in this respect; its first half closes in the tonic (D minor), with the result that the last fourteen bars of each half are identical, a few unimportant details apart. This unpromising key scheme is found elsewhere only in a few short dance movements, mainly minuets (K32, 40, 73/ii, 77/ii and 440). There are a few other departures from the tonal norms outlined above (including K266, 280, 508 and 545, all of which begin in the major and cadence centrally in the relative minor), but on the whole the basic tonal scheme is the most predictable feature (perhaps the only one) of Scarlatti's mature sonatas.

Contrasting with the stability of the 'B' section in each half of the sonata is the tonal activity, even volatility, of the remainder of the movement (indicated in the diagram above by a wavy line). In the *Essercizi* the progress of the 'A' theme from its initial tonic to the related key of 'B' is not as a rule halted by digressions to outlying keys, although a characteristic switch from major to minor can sometimes deflect the music from its most direct course. For example, K26 begins in A major but passes through A minor and G major before reaching the dominant (minor!) for the 'B' theme. The area of greatest tonal instability is the 'C' section after the double bar-line. Even in the *Essercizi* the music can at this point wander into quite distant tonal areas. The 'C' section of K25, for example, passes through B minor, D# minor, G# minor and C# minor before regaining F# minor for the return of the 'B' theme. This progression through 5th-related keys is effected quite smoothly with the help of melodic sequences. In later sonatas modulations in the 'C' section, and often in the 'A' section too, can be much more abrupt, even startlingly so. The chasm separating D major from F minor is symbolized in K124 by the pause and (in the Parma source, at least) the double bar-lines placed between them (example 18). Tonal 'faults' (to borrow a geological term) such as this occur typically on either side of the central double bar-line (K107, 212, 499 etc.). The very late (i.e. highest-numbered) sonatas tend to be in this respect, as in certain others, somewhat less adventurous.

Scarlatti's sonata structure does not fundamentally change after the *Essercizi*, but it does undergo considerable expansion. Each section becomes longer, and there is a tendency for the 'B' theme to be more strongly characterized and often separated by a pause or a rest from the preceding material, which might be rounded off by some compositional gesture (a descending arpeggio at this point is highly

Example 18

Sonata K124

characteristic). The expanded form can also accommodate a greater degree of contrast, and this is to be observed particularly in the 'C' section after the double bar. In most of the *Essercizi* the second half begins like the first (except, of course, for the new tonality) and adapts the same basic material to a new tonal scheme until the 'B' theme is reached. This is what Kirkpatrick (pp. 266–7) described as the 'closed sonata', and it recalls the standard procedure in the Baroque suite. In those sonatas in the *Essercizi* where the second half begins differently from the first (Kirkpatrick's 'open sonata') the material immediately after the double bar-line is still as a rule derived either from later in the 'A' section (K9–10, 17 and 20) or from the 'B' theme (K18–19). Even in those sonatas (K27–8 and possibly 29) in which the second half begins with what seems to be entirely new material, the impression that this 'belongs' to the piece is very strong. In the post-*Essercizi* works the incidence of 'open' sonatas greatly increases, while the thematic relevance of the 'C' section to the rest of the sonata is sometimes minimal. This section can even take on a completely improvisatory character, perhaps involving a change of tempo and metre. A well-known instance is K394, where a tightly knit first half is followed by bravura, cadenza-like arpeggios and a curious sequence of third-related triads, taking the music far away from its home key of E minor (example 19). It was almost certainly this sonata to which Elisabeth von Herzogenberg referred in a letter to Brahms dated 11 January 1885:

How I envy you your Scarlatti, if there are many such excellent specimens! What an ingenious fellow he is, with his arpeggio figures in the unexpected A major part, and the long modulation, which has no reference to the piece itself, and his sudden recollection of the subject and prompt return to it! Ah yes, a robust talent may take liberties which become preposterous in weaker hands.[28]

Example 19

K202, 235 and 273 are all examples of sonatas in which the initial 3/8 metre changes after the double bar-line to 6/8 for a substantial section in what Scarlatti's contemporaries would immediately recognize as a pastoral vein. These works recall those 'Christmas' concertos and cantatas which include a pastoral movement in a lilting 6/8 or 12/8 metre, with drones and parallel movement in 3rds, in imitation of the *pifferari* – the Abruzzi peasant musicians who played their shawms and bagpipes in the streets of Italian cities at Christmastide. Corelli's 'Christmas' concerto op. 6 no. 8 is a well-known but by no means isolated example of the type, and Scarlatti must have heard (and probably composed) many similar works during his years in Rome. Two of the sonatas to which he himself (or his main copyist) gave the title 'Pastorale' (K446 and 513) may also be thought of as Christmas pieces.[29] The tempo markings assigned to them ('Allegrissimo' and 'Moderato') suggest a livelier pace than that usually adopted today in performances of similar movements by Corelli, Handel, Bach and others.

The Pastorale K513 (the central theme of which Longo identified as a Neapolitan Christmas song) is another example of a sonata with a totally irrelevant 'C' section (Presto, 3/8). In this case, however, there is no return to the 'Christmas' style of the first half; the new, faster material is continued to the end of the sonata, with the result that the two halves give the impression of belonging to completely different works.[30] This juxtaposing of unrelated material is by no means confined to pastorales, and K170, 227 and 333 are other examples of sonatas in which the two halves are totally contrasted in style and material. Their curious structure seems to be unparalleled in the sonatas of other composers.

The fundamental difference between Classical sonata form and the binary structure of Scarlatti's sonatas is underlined if we try to imagine an Allegro by Haydn or Mozart in which a normal exposition is followed by totally different music after the double bar-line. But there is no need to choose such extreme examples by Scarlatti in order to make the point; the structure of even the more typical binary sonatas may be distinguished from Classical sonata form in two important respects. In the first place, its proportions are quite different. As has already been pointed out, in those sonatas where the two halves are not of equal length, the section before the double bar-line is likely to be longer than the other; in Classical sonata form the reverse is the case. Secondly, in the Scarlatti scheme there is hardly ever any recapitulation of the 'A' theme in the tonic after the double bar-line. The expansion of the binary form into the three sections of the Classical sonata form – exposition, development (or episode) and recapitulation – simply does not take place in Scarlatti's sonatas, or does so so rarely and in so embryonic a fashion as to be of no real significance.

This last point, which is crucial to an understanding of Scarlatti's aesthetic, has frequently been discussed in writings on the composer, but misunderstandings about it persist. Kirkpatrick (p. 266) mentions K132, 159, 256 and 481 as sonatas in which the opening material is recapitulated in the tonic. In the first case, however, the restatement occupies only three bars and is disguised by a change of inflection from major to minor (compare also K162), while in K256 it is not the opening material but the 'B' theme derived from it that is restated in the tonic (compare bars 15ff. with bars 56ff.); K533 presents a similar case. Instances in which a part of the first theme (but not the opening) is restated in the tonic include K1, 65 and 271, and K409 is an unusual, perhaps unique, example of a sonata in which *only* the first theme, and not the second, is recapitulated in the tonic. In most of these cases the tonic restatement of the opening material seems casual and even fortuitous, but in K481, and still more in the well-known K159, one is left with the impression that Scarlatti was fully conscious of the effect created by regaining the tonic key and recapitulating the 'A' theme simultaneously. How far he was aware of the emerging sonata form in the works of his central European contemporaries is difficult to say, and in any case the lack of a certain chronology would make it impossible to draw many conclusions from it. But it does seem that he regarded the potentialities of K159, in so far as he considered them, to be irrelevant to the kind of sonata he wanted to write.

It is perhaps inevitable that sonatas such as K159, as well as those which are made up of strongly contrasting sections (like K394), should be analyzed in terms of statement, counter-statement and restatement. It is inevitable, too, that such sonatas should seize the imagination of the listener and colour his view of the composer simply because the compositional gestures are so striking, even puzzling. But a better idea of Scarlatti's individuality and mastery of musical form is to be gained from analyzing not the statement and restatement of themes, but rather the balance and imbalance of phrases, and the manipulation of motifs. Scarlatti's position on the border-line between two stylistic eras is nowhere more evident than in the phrase structure of his mature sonatas. The four-bar phrase serves as a kind of norm, but it is not used, as in Classical music, to construct sixteen-bar melodies of a symmetrical cast. Repetition or sequence (usually in one- or two-bar units) may emphasize the periodicity of the phrasing within a particular passage, but the contraction, expansion and interlocking of phrases frequently results in a seamless continuity which has more in common with Baroque than with Classical methods. This sense of continuity derives also from Scarlatti's resourcefulness in building quite long stretches of music (sometimes the whole of a section) from one or two motifs. These may be purely rhythmic (that is, the melodic direction of the motif may vary), but more characteristic are motifs in which a melodic cell is fastened to a rhythm and then woven into the fabric of the music, rather as threads might be woven into a cloth to give it a distinctive texture and colour. A few examples will show how concise and simple are the motifs from which Scarlatti constructs some of his best and most characteristic sonatas (example 20). In some sonatas, especially in the passage between the double bar-line and the restatement of the 'B' theme, the repetition of a short motif can become quite obsessive. Scarlatti often plays with an idea like a cat with a mouse, teasing it with different harmonic ploys and not letting it go until its possibilities have been completely exhausted (example 21).

Example 20

Example 21

Sonata K180

The binary structure outlined above is used in all but about a dozen of Scarlatti's extant keyboard sonatas, and few of the exceptions are of a quality to make one regret they are not more numerous. K61 is the only example in all Scarlatti's music of variation form. It probably belongs among the composer's earliest keyboard pieces and, as in most other Baroque variation sets (including Bach's infinitely finer 'Goldberg' Variations), it is not so much the theme as its accompanying harmonies that serve as the basis for the variations. The left hand is not neglected in the semiquaver figuration that most of the variations exploit (sometimes in triplets), but the only original feature in what is a derivative piece is that the two six-bar phrases of the theme and its first four variations are contracted to 5 + 5 bars for variations 5–12, and then expanded to 8 + 8 bars for the final variation, which serves also as a coda.

Four sonatas show some kind of rondo structure. K85 is the first movement of a four-movement 'Tocata' found in a Portuguese manuscript in the University Library, Coimbra. (Until recently this was the only known manuscript containing keyboard music by Scarlatti in the whole of the Iberian peninsula.) K85 begins rather in the manner of a Venetian string concerto, but its ritornello structure is based on the return in various keys not of the opening phrase, but of bars 4–5. K265, 284 and 351 are more straightforward rondos, all of them dance-like in character; K265, in particular, probably derives from some kind of dance-song of folk origin, with its octave refrain in common time and its lively contrasted episodes in 3/8.

Seven of the sonatas are fugues: K30, 41, 58, 82, 93, 287 and 417. There would be little point in using Bach's '48' as a yardstick in assessing Scarlatti's achievements as a contrapuntist. The tradition to which Scarlatti's fugues belong is quite different. Compared with Bach's their structure is much looser and the balance between resource and invention seems to be determined more by fancy than by precedent – more even than by the nature of the fugue subject itself.

Curiously enough, there are at the same time several passages that seem merely to retail contrapuntal clichés that might have been picked up from any textbook on fugue. K41, in particular, presents a decidedly 'textbook' image despite its unorthodox real answer, although its last eight bars make up for this with a majestic descent through three octaves of the first four notes of the subject. In most of the fugues it is possible to recognize a division into exposition, middle entries and final entries, and there is often a dominant pedal towards the end, but the integrity of the part-writing is frequently sacrificed to other considerations. In the exposition of K93, for example, the subject (or answer) is announced at four different pitches, but there are never more than two voices sounding together, and throughout the rest of the piece there is very little four-part texture. Probably the most successful of the fugues is also the best-known: the so-called 'Cat's Fugue' (K30), placed at the end of the *Essercizi*.[31] The legend that the bizarre and seemingly arbitrary sequence of notes that forms the subject of this fugue was suggested to Scarlatti by his cat walking up the keyboard is, of course, apocryphal (as anyone who possesses both a piano and a cat will immediately realize), but the unpredictable steps of the subject and the springy rhythms and jauntiness of the counter-subject that accompanies it do lend the piece a character which might be construed as feline. Like Scarlatti's other fugues, however, it is too long.

The D major fugue K287 is for a two-manual organ without pedals. In the Parma manuscript it is designated 'per organo da camera con due tastatura flautato e trombone' and has as a companion piece the through-composed, single-section K288, also in D major. Changes of manual are indicated in both these sonatas by drawings of a hand with its index finger pointing upwards or downwards as the case may be. Unfortunately there is no indication of which manual has the Flautado stop (presumably Principals or Diapasons) and which the Trombone, and caution is needed, therefore, in drawing any general conclusions about interpreting the harpsichord sonatas on a two-manual instrument. It does seem, however, that some degree of contrast was often called for in the playing of repeated phrases, and the evidence (particularly of K287) suggests that in such cases the repetition may have served to reinforce rather than to echo the initial phrase. This is to some extent borne out by Charles Avison's string arrangements of some of the sonatas (see Appendix I), but it should not be taken to mean that sonatas with repeated phrases necessarily require a two-manual instrument or that every repeated phrase automatically calls for contrast.

Organ registration is found also in K328, and quite possibly several other sonatas were designed for, or at least played on, chamber organs; but it seems very unlikely that the words 'oytabado' and 'tortorilla', which appear at bars 37 and 64 respectively in K255, refer to organ stops, as has often been supposed (example 22). 'Tortorilla' must surely refer to the turtle-dove, whose cooing is imitated by the three-note figure in the right hand, and one might expect 'oytabado' also to be the name of a bird (a quail, perhaps?). In the absence of any such word from Spanish and Portuguese dictionaries, Luigi Ferdinando Tagliavini has suggested that it might be a corruption of the Portuguese 'oitavado', a popular eighteenth-century dance.[32] If so, it is difficult to understand why the word should appear where it does in the music.

Example 22

STYLE

Style, in so far as it can be separated from structure, has been one of the most discussed aspects of Scarlatti's keyboard sonatas, and yet so original and 'modern' is this music that its stylistic origins and the influences that helped to form it remain largely elusive. It goes without saying that the keyboard music of Scarlatti's Italian contemporaries and immediate predecessors (including his own father) must have played a part in this, but an examination of the toccatas and sonatas by such composers as Alessandro Scarlatti, Bernardo Pasquini and Domenico Zipoli suggests that he derived from these composers only the commonplace elements of his style: a preference for two-part textures, predominantly violinistic figuration and (from Alessandro's toccatas especially) the imitative opening, usually with left hand answering the right. As William S. Newman has shown, the influence of Benedetto Marcello in this area may have been even more important. 'The two men must have known each other well during about four years that Scarlatti was in Venice (1705–8), especially as both were close to Gasparini.'[33] The length of Scarlatti's stay in Venice must now be revised to two and a half years at the most, but sonatas by Marcello that Scarlatti could have known there include wide leaps, repeated notes and hand-crossings – all features normally associated with Scarlatti only at a later date.

In this connection the possible importance of Francesco Durante, and in particular of the six *Sonate per cembalo divisi in studii e divertimenti* which he published at Naples in about 1732, is also worth investigation. Durante was an important teacher and composer, particularly of church music, at Naples. He was Scarlatti's senior by about eighteen months, and the two musicians could have known each other either at Naples or perhaps in Rome, where Durante is thought to have spent some years. In the preface to his edition of Durante's sonatas, Francesco Degrada drew attention to the 'chains of trills, hand-crossings, leaps from one part of the keyboard to another, virtuoso passages in 3rds and 6ths, repeated notes and chords, and rapid scales and arpeggios passed between the hands "con bravura" which characterize these pieces'. 'At times', Degrada continued, 'they throw light on the enigmatic origins of Scarlatti's style.' The origins nevertheless remain enigmatic, and indeed the early formation of any great composer's style will always remain something of a mystery, because we can never be sure – and the composer himself may not even be aware of it – which particular works among the music he heard in his childhood and youth most fired his creative imagination.

The individuality of Scarlatti's mature style undoubtedly owes a great deal to the interaction between his Italian background and his Iberian environment, but here again, a few guitar idioms apart, it is often difficult to isolate and identify the specifically Spanish or Portuguese elements in the music. A casual acquaintance with Spanish folk-music as transmitted by modern *flamenco* artists or through the arrangements of Ravel and Manuel de Falla is sufficient to convince the non-Spaniard of the truth of Kirkpatrick's remarks (pp. 114–15), when he states that:

there is hardly an aspect of Spanish life, of Spanish popular music and dance, that has not found itself a place in the microcosm that Scarlatti created with his sonatas. No Spanish composer, not even Manuel de Falla, has expressed the essence of his native land as completely as did the foreigner Scarlatti. He has captured the click of castanets, the strumming of guitars, the thud of muffled drums, the harsh bitter wail of gypsy lament, the overwhelming gaiety of the village band, and above all the wiry tension of the Spanish dance.

In his discussion of particular sonatas Kirkpatrick makes frequent reference to the sound of castanets, the stamping of heels and so on, but except for calling K209 a *jota* he understandably makes few attempts to relate the sonatas more precisely to specific types of Spanish folk-song and dance music. Burney tells us that Scarlatti 'imitated the melody of tunes sung by carriers, muleteers, and common people',[34] but there has so far been little success in identifying the tunes to which Burney referred. Kirkpatrick (p. 167) was able to point to only one sonata (K238) which, he said, bore some resemblance to a particular folk-song – in this case to a tune from the Estremadura. But he did not quote the folk-song, and the style of the sonata as a whole seems to derive more from French court music than from what we would normally recognize as Spanish folk style.

Specialist work in this field is still urgently needed, and a start has been made by Jane Clark, who has brought forward evidence to suggest that the Spanish quality of Scarlatti's harpsichord music derives above all from the Andalusian folk-music which he would have heard during the years he spent with the Spanish court in Seville and the surrounding district. Clark has drawn parallels between K490 and the *saeta* (a category of *cante hondo* associated with Holy Week processions in Seville), between K492 and the *baleria* and between K502 and the *petenera* (both *flamenco* forms of Andalusian origin), and she believes that 'a very large proportion of the sonatas are based on *fandangos* of one kind and another'.[35] The recent discovery in Tenerife of a fandango attributed to Domenico Scarlatti adds further substance to her theories (see p. 191).

A thorough study of Scarlatti's indebtedness to Andalusian folk-music might tell us as much about his harmony as about the rhythms and melodic inflections of his music. It is, however, possible to exaggerate the relevance of the Spanish experience to this aspect of Scarlatti's music. For example, the frequent 'Phrygian' progressions (involving the chords IVb–V) in the sonatas are often said to derive from the modes and cadences of Spanish folk-song, but they also occur prominently in *a cappella* church music and as cadences in slow movements of Italian concertos and sonatas. The oscillation of these two chords, associated particularly with the 'B' themes of the sonatas,[36] is a not infrequent feature of Scarlatti's earlier vocal music, too; a good example is provided by the aria 'Torna sol per un momento' in Act 1 of *Tolomeo et Alessandro* (1711). Similarly, the harmonies of Spanish folk-music have been cited to account for the frequent sudden switches from major to minor and vice versa in the sonatas, but this, too, is something frequently encountered in the vocal music of Scarlatti's Italian years, and it is a feature also of Alessandro Scarlatti's harmony, especially in the approach to the final cadence of an aria. Possibly Neapolitan as well as Spanish popular music should be examined in this connection.

The most distinctive stylistic fingerprint in Domenico Scarlatti's harmony is the overlaying of an ordinary diatonic chord with unessential notes, notated not as appoggiaturas or 'grace notes' but as part of the chord itself. Often the unessential notes, if they can be called that, are so numerous that the chord consists of nothing but a succession of adjacent tones and semitones, taking on the appearance of what a modern theorist might describe as a 'note-cluster'. Alessandro Longo expunged these from the main text of his complete edition, either because he distrusted the sources or because he regarded the strange conglomerations of pitches as the barbaric crudities of an earlier age. More recent research and more accurate editions have focused attention on them as a distinctive ingredient of Scarlatti's musical style. The dissonances have usually been explained as acciaccaturas, and there must certainly be some significance in the fact that the first theorist to describe dissonances of this kind in print was Scarlatti's own teacher, Francesco Gasparini, whose *L'armonico pratico al cimbalo*, published in 1708, Scarlatti would certainly have known. In the section of the treatise that deals with the accompaniment of recitative Gasparini describes the *mordente* as a non-harmonic note struck together with, or slightly before, the principal note and then immediately released. He distinguished this from the true acciaccatura, which he showed as a note a tone below the principal note, and which he implied might be held on longer than the *mordente*. Among the music examples that serve to illustrate his remarks is an elaboration of the progression V⁷d–Ib in the key of A minor (example 23); the black note in the first bar denotes an acciaccatura and that in the second bar a *mordente*.

Some of the note-clusters in Scarlatti's harpsichord music may well have their origin in the composer's experience of accompanying recitative in operas and cantatas during his years at Rome. The

Example 23

simplest and most common dissonance is a 5-4 chord (possibly in combination with a 7th), the 4th of which does not resolve downwards by step, as it would do if it obeyed the normal rules of harmonic progression and good part-writing. There are precedents for the use of this chord in Alessandro Scarlatti's harpsichord music (see example 24*a*), but not for the boldness and frequency with which Domenico employs the dissonance (example 24*b*) or for the distinctive cadence he makes with it (example 24*c*; the final unison is as idiosyncratic as the 5-4 chord itself).

Example 24

(a)   Toccata (A. Scarlatti)

(b)   Andante   Sonata K215

(c)   Adagio e cantabile   Sonata K208

While in these contexts the 5-4 harmonies might possibly be understood as including acciaccaturas to be struck in advance of the main note and released immediately, it is obvious that a passage such as that shown in example 25 cannot lend itself to this kind of interpretation. While there might just be time for the player to arpeggiate the chords very rapidly, he would certainly not be able to release the dissonant notes of one chord before sounding the next. In passages like this Scarlatti is clearly relishing the discords for their percussive effect, and the note-clusters are best explained, perhaps, by analogy with guitar music, and in particular with the technique, common among folk-musicians, of advancing the left hand up the fingerboard on certain strings while leaving the others open, thereby producing exotic and largely unpremeditated combinations of notes. Certainly the *rasgueado* of the guitar player is being imitated by the 5-4 chords of the left hand at the opening of K141, while the right hand suggests the rapid alternation of fingers on the *chanterelle* (the instrument's highest string) which is another favourite device of guitar technique (example 26; for another instance of this combination of guitar effects see K261, bars 39–66).

It is interesting that occurrences of 5-4 harmonies and note-clusters in Scarlatti's keyboard works are concentrated in a particular section of the repertory as it has come down to us. They are present in some of the *Essercizi* (for example, K24 and 26), but they are much more numerous among sonatas in the K120–220 range. After K215

Example 25

Sonata K175

Example 26

Allegro

Sonata K141

(something of a *locus classicus* for both note-clusters and 5-4 chords) they are relatively infrequent. This observation, which extends to other stylistic features as well (notably hand-crossing) though with a different spread of occurrences, tends to support Kirkpatrick's 'general theory' that the main sources reflect the chronology of the works' composition (see pp. 160–61).

Scarlatti has always been regarded as one of the most important protagonists of keyboard technique. More than any other composer during the two centuries after the English virginalists – more than Frescobaldi in Italy, Froberger in Germany or Couperin in France – Scarlatti extended the technical vocabulary of the instrument and raised keyboard playing to a new level of virtuosity. Scales and arpeggios employing the whole range of the instrument, prolonged trills (sometimes in an inner voice), frequent octave passages (including some in both hands simultaneously), glissandos[37] and rapidly repeated notes (in pairs or larger groups) all contribute to the brilliant effect and immediately recognizable individuality of the harpsichord sonatas. Two things for which Scarlatti is particularly famous, or notorious, are hand-crossings and wide leaps (the former usually, but not always, entail the latter). He was by no means the first composer to instruct his players to cross the left hand over the right, or vice versa; John Bull had anticipated him in this, and also in the writing of wide leaps and rapidly repeated notes, in his 'Walsingham' Variations over a century earlier. But Scarlatti employed hand-crossing with greater resource and daring than any other composer before or since. In many instances it is used in a perfectly natural way, in order to maintain a particular running figure (usually in semiquavers) in one hand while the other 'duets' above and below it; the C minor sonata K11 from the *Essercizi* furnishes a well-known example. Certain other cases seem to imply that the music was conceived for a two-manual instrument, with each hand on a different manual; to register K109 in this way, for example, produces an effective kaleidoscope of timbres in passages where the hand-crossing seems otherwise to have no purpose at all. There remain, however, several instances of hand-crossing which appear to have been introduced for the sole purpose of testing the mental and digital dexterity of the executant. Does the crossing of hands in bars 5–21 and bars 54–68 of Sonata no. 5 in the *Essercizi*, for example, serve any other purpose than that of a mind-bending and finger-twisting exercise (example 27)? Is this what Scarlatti had in mind when he referred in the *Essercizi* to 'an ingenious jesting with art'?

Example 27

[L = left hand; R = right hand]

Many of the technical difficulties in Scarlatti's keyboard works are not intrinsic to the substance of the music, and not even apparent to the listener except when wrong notes betray their presence. Numerous passages could be simplified to produce the same effect with few or no alterations to the actual notes. To do so, however, would be to deprive the music of two important qualities which, if they have little to do with the intended sound, have a great deal to do with Scarlatti's temperament and genius. One of them is the sheer physical engagement that the player experiences in performing the sonatas. No other keyboard music of the eighteenth century, and very little of any other century, is so 'choreographed' to employ the fingers, hands, wrists, arms, shoulders and even the waist of the performer. This is music to be played rather than listened to, and it is not surprising that Scarlatti enthusiasts tend to be themselves pianists or harpsichord players. The other quality in the music that a more severely practical approach to its keyboard layout would deprive it of is what might be called its 'tightrope' element. This is present above all in those passages where rapid hand-crossing involves wide leaps, often of more than three octaves (example 28). No amount of careful practice will guarantee absolute accuracy in passages such as this; the player must simply take his courage into one hand and trust to luck. It has been suggested that

Example 28

wide and rapid leaps should be taken as indicating a steadier tempo than might otherwise have been the case, but this cautious approach seems contrary to the spirit of Scarlatti, and it is frequently contradicted by the character of the music. K427 is directed to be played as fast as possible ('presto, quanto sia possibile'), and yet it includes leaps of two and three octaves (less one note) to be covered in the space of a semiquaver (bars 13, 15–16, 30–1 and 33).

Hand-crossing is the feature of keyboard technique with which Scarlatti's name has been most often associated, and yet instances of its use are concentrated, like the note-clusters, in a relatively small portion of his output, and presumably therefore in a particular chronological period. The crossing of hands is present in about half of the *Esercizi* and it is common also among the sonatas numbered 44–65 and 95–145 in Kirkpatrick's catalogue. Among the higher numbered sonatas it is comparatively rare: K174–5, 217, 243, 348, 352, 482, 528–9 and 554 account for most, if not all, occurrences. A possible explanation of this is contained in a much-quoted report of a conversation which Charles Burney had with Monsignor Alexander Ludwig L'Augier (or Laugier), a Viennese court physician and amateur musician, in 1772:

> M. L'Augier . . . has been in France, Spain, Portugal, Italy, and Constantinople, and is, in short, a living history of modern music. In Spain he was intimately acquainted with Domenico Scarlatti, who, at seventy-three, composed for him a great number of harpsichord lessons which he now possesses, and of which he favoured me with copies. The book in which they are transcribed contains forty-two pieces, among which are several slow movements, and of all these, I, who have been a collector of Scarlatti's compositions all my life, have never seen more than three or four. They were composed in 1756, when Scarlatti was too fat to cross his hands as he used to do, so that these are not so difficult, as his more juvenile works, which were made for his scholar and patroness, the late queen of Spain, when princess of Asturias.[38]

Burney was clearly mistaken about Scarlatti's age, and recent biographers have cast doubts on the veracity of his account as a whole, especially since the rediscovery in 1956 of the Velasco portrait, in which the composer's slender face and hands seem to contradict any tendency towards corpulence. Of course, a great deal could have happened to Scarlatti's physical condition during the last twenty years of his life, but it may be that Scarlatti abandoned hand-crossings in his later sonatas as much for Queen Maria Barbara's comfort as for his own. L'Augier also was of 'uncommon corpulency', as Burney put it.

It is no longer possible to identify the forty-two sonatas of L'Augier's volume. If they were in fact composed in 1756 they would presumably have been among the final hundred or so copied into the Parma and Venice sets for Queen Maria Barbara. The final volume of the Parma set does contain forty-two sonatas, but the proportion of slow movements among them (or, for that matter, among the last hundred sonatas as a whole) is not unduly high. It is nevertheless significant that Burney should have chosen to mention the slow movements in L'Augier's collection. The prominence and popularity of the more brilliant, extrovert and virtuoso pieces have always tended to deflect attention from the intimate, refined and even soul-searching expression of K208, 213, 462 and several other sonatas in a slow tempo, and yet to ignore these is to remain unaware of an important facet of Scarlatti's genius. Among other sonatas in slower tempos, K217 is noteworthy for the jerky rhythms and scalic upbeats of its opening bars, which constitute a rare but confident gesture towards the French style (example 29).

Example 29   Sonata K217

Scarlatti's rhythmic wit, one of the most vital and characteristic ingredients of his mature keyboard style, is of course present above all in the Allegros, Prestos and Vivos that make up the majority of the sonatas. The influence of Spanish and Portuguese folk-dances on the rhythms of Scarlatti's music has already been mentioned, but there is also a more urbane and sophisticated aspect to be considered. Syncopation (the displacement of the melodic accent from its established position within a bar) and hemiola (the superimposition of duple accents onto a basic triple metre) are favourite devices which Scarlatti uses to imbue his music with rhythmic vitality, but they by no means exhaust his ingenuity in this regard. One of the most rhythmically inventive of the sonatas, K233, includes examples of syncopation (bars 7–8, 27–32 etc.) and hemiola (bars 59–62 etc.), as well as passages of cross-rhythm almost worthy of Brahms (example 30; note also in this example the five-bar phrases, typical of both composers).

It would be possible to enumerate and illustrate at length various other stylistic 'fingerprints' in Scarlatti's sonatas which have not so far been mentioned here: the downward arpeggios that so frequently

Example 30

Allegro

Sonata K233

[*repeat 8ve lower*]

begin or end a sonata (or, perhaps even more characteristically, serve to introduce the 'B' theme); the imitations of bells, trumpet fanfares, horn calls and so on that contribute so much in the way of local colour to the music; and the chromatic appoggiaturas that can lend it an unmistakably *galant* air. (One might add to these a negative attribute: the almost complete absence of that otherwise ubiquitous *galant* accompanimental figure known as the 'Alberti bass'; for rare instances of its use, see K57, 461 and 517.) These and other stylistic features have been well documented in the Scarlatti literature. Like the hand-crossings, the grasshopper leaps, the bold modulations and the amazing note-clusters, they lend themselves to easy imitation, and *were* imitated by several of Scarlatti's pupils and disciples. What no epigone could hope to capture, however, was the freshness of Scarlatti's invention – the way that every device, every gesture is employed in his sonatas as if for the first time. The ability to surprise, and yet at the same time to convince, was something that Scarlatti possessed to a degree unparalleled among eighteenth-century composers, except by Haydn. His filling of a repetitive binary structure with an inexhaustible variety of ideas was an astonishing achievement, surpassing in inventiveness even that of his father's 750 or so *cantate da camera*. One need not endorse the jibe that Vivaldi composed not 450 concertos, but the same concerto 450 times, to see the point behind it. It would never occur to anyone to make a similar comment about Scarlatti's 550 sonatas, despite the fact that their structure is less susceptible to variation than that of Vivaldi's concertos. One may argue about the extent to which Scarlatti's intentions went beyond a mere 'ingenious jesting with art' in the sonatas, but it seems safe to say that in no comparable corpus of music is repetitiveness of structure allied to such diversity of expression and content.

THE 'NEW' SONATAS

Manuscript sources recently discovered in Spanish archives (see pp. 154–7) have brought to light the existence of eight hitherto unknown sonatas attributed by the copyists to Domenico Scarlatti, or for other reasons thought to be by him. They are:

G major, 3/8 ⎫
D minor, 3/8 ⎬ Valladolid, Metropolitan Cathedral, MS 19
A major, 3/8 ⎭

C major, 2/4   Montserrat, Monasterio de Santa Maria, MS 1770

D minor, 3/4 ⎫
G major, 6/8 ⎬ Tenerife, private collection [uncatalogued]

D major, 12/8 ⎫ Madrid, Real Conservatorio de Música, MS Roda Leg.
A major, C ⎬ 35/504

Five of these have appeared in modern editions, and two of the others are included as Appendix III in the present study. In view of the evident intention behind the two great Parma and Venice collections of bringing together a complete set of the Scarlatti sonatas, it is inevitable that any consideration of sonatas not contained in them will centre first on the question of their authenticity, especially when they exist only in manuscripts copied long after the composer's death.

The three new Valladolid sonatas have been published in an edition by Antonio Baciero (1978), along with K5, 65, 98 and 130; the versions of K7 and 66 in the Valladolid source have not so far appeared in print. The sonatas appear anonymously in MS 19; Baciero's conviction that the 'new' ones are authentic seems to rest, firstly, on the fact that they are grouped in the manuscript between other works known to be Scarlatti's and, secondly, on stylistic analysis of the music. The dangers in accepting the first of these criteria are obvious; who would have questioned the authorship of the two uncatalogued sonatas in MS 3/1408 of the Conservatorio de Música, Madrid, were they not attributed elsewhere to Sebastian Albero? As far as style is concerned, the three Valladolid sonatas certainly exhibit several Scarlattian traits: hand-crossings, octaves, repeated notes (in pairs) and possibly glissando scales (in the D minor sonata). The downward arpeggios introducing the 'B' theme of the D minor sonata add another characteristic touch, as do also the minor inflections of the G major sonata. Despite all this, none of the sonatas can be said indisputably to bear the stamp of Scarlatti's musical personality; since they are not specifically attributed to Scarlatti by the scribe, and since the source is a late one, it seems advisable to place them for the present among the composer's doubtful works. The nine sonatas in the Valladolid manuscript were evidently selected, and in some cases adapted, for an instrument (perhaps an organ) with a compass extending only as far as c''' in its upper range, and probably with a short octave in the bass.

The Montserrat sonata in C major, headed 'Tocata de Scarlati' in MS 1770, seems on the face of it less acceptable than the Valladolid sonatas as a work by Domenico Scarlatti. It is a short, pleasant, but rather perfunctory piece, whose only typically Scarlattian feature is its 'closed' binary structure. Bengt Johnsson's attempt to support an attribution to Domenico Scarlatti by isolating six short motifs and relating them to other Scarlatti sonatas is not, in the end, very convincing. Other motifs are decidedly un-Scarlattian, particularly the left-hand figure connecting the first four-bar phrase to its repetition (x in example 31; it occurs again after the double bar-line). Pending further investigation, this sonata, too, might best be regarded as a doubtful Scarlatti work.

Of the two Tenerife pieces edited by Rosario Alvarez Martinez (1984), the more remarkable is the Fandango in D minor, attributed in the source to 'Sigr. Scarlate'. This is quite unlike any other piece by Scarlatti, but it does resemble in many ways, including its tonality, other keyboard fandangos of roughly the same period: the *Fandango de España* attributed by Rosario Alvarez to José Blasco de Nebra and the well-known Fandango by Soler. Scarlatti's piece is much more ambitious than Nebra's but, with 109 bars (not including repeats), it is less than a quarter of the length of Soler's.

Example 31

Scarlatti employs his usual bipartite structure, with each section marked for repeat and with a characteristic change of metre and tempo (to Presto, 3/8) during the course of the second half. But the tonal structure is quite different from those of his other sonatas; like the fandangos of Nebra and Soler (as well as the famous one for string quintet by Boccherini), the piece consists of nothing more than an alternation of tonic and dominant harmonies, with the occasional subdominant chord by way of variety (example 32). A feature of the fandango as a dance is its absence of cadences, and Scarlatti's example, as it has come down to us, lacks even a final cadence, coming to an abrupt stop on the dominant chord at the very end of a bar; the source is possibly incomplete. Scarlatti's intention in the piece was obviously to convey the atmosphere and excitement of the popular dance and to suggest its traditional accompaniment of guitars and castanets. It represents one of the earliest attempts (perhaps the very first) to transfer this particular folk-dance to the aristocratic salon; possibly the composer considered it too 'raw' to be included in the queen's library of harpsichord music.

The other Tenerife piece is a more sedate sonata in G major, 6/8, without tempo indication. The attribution, 'del Gran d.ⁿ Dom.º Scarlatti', sounds suspiciously like an attempt to pass off an inferior piece as the work of a master, and indeed the same sonata is attributed to Carlos de Seixas in MS 57 of the Biblioteca Geral da Universidade, Coimbra (Portugal). This much more credible ascription was accepted by Macario Santiago Kastner, who included the work as

Example 32   'Fandango'

no. 46 in his edition of eighty sonatas by Seixas (Lisbon, 1965).

Rosario Alvarez's publication includes also a keyboard piece which throws new light on a long-standing Scarlatti mystery. Shortly before Longo's edition began to appear in 1906, the Spanish composer Enrique Granados edited a volume of *Ventiseis sonatas inéditas*, freely adapted from a manuscript discovered in Spain by the publisher Vidal Llimona. The present whereabouts of the manuscript are unknown, but the extent of Granados's 'editing' can be judged from a comparison of twenty-four of the sonatas with the versions that exist in the Parma and Venice sources.[39] As far as the other two sonatas (nos 10 and 13) are concerned, Granados's edition has been the only known source, and doubts about their authenticity have therefore remained unresolved. Rosario Alvarez's volume includes a sonata in A major by Francesco Corselli (or Francisco Courcelle), who, as already mentioned, succeeded Joseph de Torres in 1738 as *maestro de capilla* of the royal chapel in Madrid. This sonata, edited from a late and incomplete manuscript copy owned by Lothar Siemens (it stops short about mid-way through the second half), turns out to be the otherwise unidentified sonata no. 10 of Granados's edition. This discovery does not, of course, resolve the question of the work's authorship. Ironically enough, the 'Corselli' sonata is more Scarlattian in style than either of the 'Scarlatti' sonatas in Rosario Alvarez's volume.

The two Madrid sonatas (see Appendix III) also raise difficult problems of attribution. They add little to Scarlatti's reputation as a composer, and they contain certain features that argue against his authorship. For example, the last two bars of the D major sonata (and especially the repeated tonic chords of the final bar) could belong to any pre-Classical composer, but are wholly untypical of Scarlatti. Bars 63 and 124 of the A major sonata may similarly be ruled out as his, and the diminished 7th chords at bars 60 and 119 also sound unconvincing. But although the sonatas as transmitted in the nineteenth-century Madrid source must be regarded with suspicion, it is not impossible that they derive from genuine Scarlatti works. Like the Valladolid sonatas, they have been adapted for an instrument (again, probably an organ) with a limited compass, and judging from how the scribe (Soriano Fuertes) has treated the first movement of Haydn's F major sonata H.XVI:23 in the same manuscript, he may well have made other substantial alterations to these 'Scarlatti' pieces, too, in order to render them suitable for inclusion in his 'Quaderno . . . sin gusto'.

It is perhaps not surprising that the quality of these 'new' sonatas should turn out to be on the whole disappointing in comparison to the ones we already know. Their discovery may encourage hopes that the autographs of Scarlatti's sonatas may one day turn up in Spain, but not the expectation of finding new masterpieces among them.

NINE *Late Vocal Works*

It has frequently been stated, or tacitly assumed, that Domenico Scarlatti gave up composing vocal chamber music after he left Rome in 1719, and indeed the only vocal piece of any kind normally attributed to him during his years in Spain is the late *Salve regina* for soprano, strings and continuo, discussed on pp. 202–4. Kirkpatrick (p. 129) spoke of Scarlatti's deserting the harpsichord 'for what may have been the first time in years' to compose this work, and elsewhere of a 'complete split between the two halves of his existence, involving a drastic change in his way of life after the death of his father, the adoption of a new country, a late first marriage, and the abandonment of all but harpsichord music with the exception of one piece [the *Salve regina*]'.[1]

It has been further argued that Scarlatti's concentration on vocal music during the years before he went to Spain can be attributed directly, even solely, to the overbearing influence of his father, and that it was only after Alessandro's death in 1725 that Domenico felt himself free to develop his true gifts. It is a point of view expressed with particular force and eloquence by Roberto Pagano, who maintains that, even after reluctantly conceding legal emancipation to his grown-up son, Alessandro continued to exercise tight control over his artistic life.[2]

There is no evidence, though, that Domenico Scarlatti might have regarded the vocal music of his Italian years as so much time wasted. As a reluctant opera composer he was a remarkably successful one, and his only documented remarks on music (see the letter to the Duke of Huescar on pp. 143–4) reveal him as an apologist for the *stile antico* in which most of his church music was written. It may have been as much lack of opportunity as lack of interest that caused him (as far as we know) to abandon these types of composition in Spain, just as it was the presence of an exceptionally gifted patron there that stimulated him to compose his most important and original works, the keyboard sonatas.

Research so far undertaken – and much more is needed in this area –

suggests that Scarlatti took no part at all in the opera productions that the Marquis Scotti and, later, Farinelli put on at the Spanish court. But he would certainly have been called upon for the musical soirées that Fernando and Maria Barbara, as Prince and Princess of the Asturias and later as King and Queen of Spain, held in their apartments. Exactly what music was heard on such occasions we do not know. It seems from a painting of one of them by Louis-Michel Van Loo[3] that it included instrumental chamber music or concertos with keyboard, and it is evident from a remark reported by Edward Clarke (see p. 138) that Farinelli was also a regular performer, presumably singing arias and cantatas. King Philip V may have been satisfied with the same four or five arias from Farinelli every evening, but his more musical son and daughter-in-law presumably insisted on more varied and up-to-date entertainment. Should we assume that Scarlatti wrote no vocal music at all for these gatherings? The extant works suggest quite clearly that we should not.

CHAMBER CANTATAS

The chamber cantatas discussed in Chapter 3 were all almost certainly composed before Scarlatti left Italy. The remaining extant cantatas are contained in two manuscript volumes, one in the Österreichische Nationalbibliothek, Vienna, and the other in the British Library, London. Both are copied on the same paper and in the same careful, fluent hand, a feature of the script being the backward pointing hook on the downward stems of quavers and semiquavers (♪, ♪). The same peculiarity is found in other Scarlatti manuscripts of Iberian origin (for example, the *Te Deum* parts at Guimarães, the score of the serenata, *Contesa delle stagioni*, in the Biblioteca Nazionale Marciana at Venice, and the choirbook containing Scarlatti's mass in the Royal Palace, Madrid), but never in Italian copies. The Vienna manuscript seems to have been designed as a set: it contains eight cantatas, all for soprano, two violins and continuo. The twelve cantatas in the London volume are more varied in the forces they require: eight are for soprano and continuo, and two for two sopranos and continuo. The other two duplicate cantatas from the Vienna collection: *O qual meco Nice cangiata* and *Pur nel sonno almen tal'ora*. The last named is a setting of lines by Pietro Metastasio, and must therefore have been composed after Scarlatti left Rome in 1719.

Pietro Metastasio was born in 1698. He trained for the law, and it was not until the death of his guardian in 1718 that he decided on a career as a poet. His first wholly original opera libretto, *Didone abbandonata*, was performed at Naples in February 1724 with music by Domenico Sarro. Its success established Metastasio's reputation as a writer for the lyric stage, and the librettos he went on to provide for operas, oratorios, serenatas and other dramatic or semi-dramatic works were set hundreds of times by some of the outstanding composers of the eighteenth century. After working mainly in Rome and Venice, he succeeded Apostolo Zeno in 1729 as court poet to Charles VI and then to the Empress Maria Theresa at Vienna, where he died in 1782.

Metastasio stated that he wrote nearly all his cantata texts after he went to Vienna – that is, after 1729.[4] Twelve of them were set by the Neapolitan composer Nicola Porpora and published in London in 1735; possibly Scarlatti's London set was also compiled with a view to publication, or at least in imitation of published collections, which were often in twelves. *Pur nel sonno almen talora* ('Il sogno') is among the cantatas that Porpora set. The text exists in two versions, published as nos 12 and 22 in the edition of Brunelli.[5] The two arias are practically the same in both versions, but the central recitative shows many differences and is appreciably shorter in one version than in the other. It is the shorter, and presumably later, version that both Porpora and Scarlatti composed. Porpora's setting is relatively modest, and scored for soprano and continuo only. Scarlatti's is more ambitious, with a two-movement 'Introduzzione' for the violins and continuo, consisting of a binary Allegro and a Minuet. The arias are both fine examples of the Neapolitan style, with some lively interplay of motifs between the voice and the violins, and the recitative is set mostly as a *stromentato*, much of it in a vividly dramatic style (example 33).

Example 33

Cantata: *Pur nel sonno almen talora*

The close personal friendship between Metastasio and Scarlatti's colleague in Madrid, Farinelli, prompts speculation as to whether *Pur nel sonno almen tal'ora* and other late cantatas were composed at Farinelli's suggestion, and possibly for him to sing. J. J. Quantz, who heard Farinelli in Giovanni Maria Capelli's *I fratelli riconosciuti* at Parma in 1726, left the following description of the great singer:

> Farinelli had a penetrating, full, rich, bright and well-modulated soprano voice, whose range extended at that time from *a* through *d'''*,. A few years afterwards it had extended lower by a few tones, but without the loss of any high notes, so that in many operas one aria (usually an adagio) was written for him in the normal tessitura of a contralto, while his other arias were of soprano range. His intonation was pure, his trill beautiful, his breath-control extraordinary, and his throat very agile – so that he performed even the widest intervals quickly and with the greatest ease and certainty. Passagework and all variety of melismas were of no difficulty whatever for him. In the invention of free ornamentation in adagio he was very fertile.[6]

Quantz might have been describing the kind of voice needed for the

Scarlatti cantatas under discussion. The fact that they include long trills, elaborate melismas and *passaggi*, as well as several examples of wide, rapid leaps, and that they require in all a vocal range of *a to bb"* does not, of course, prove that they were composed for Farinelli, but the possibility is there. At all events, they could not have been written for the singers who performed Scarlatti's other cantatas, discussed in Chapter 3. Is it possible that the two duet cantatas were written for Farinelli to sing with one of the Italians who visited Madrid to take part in opera there – Caffarelli, perhaps, or the great Gioacchino Conti (known as 'Gizziello', or 'Egizziello', after his teacher Domenico Gizzi)?

Quite apart from the Metastasio connection and the evidence of the notation, most of the eighteen London and Vienna cantatas show stylistic features that point unmistakably to a relatively late date of composition. To begin with, about seventy-two per cent of them are in major keys, compared with only about thirty per cent in the case of the other cantatas; this confirms a trend towards major keys in music, not only cantatas, of the period after about 1725. Then, the slow rate of harmonic change in many of the arias, the often sharp differentiation in tempo, metre, key and expression between the middle and outer sections of a da capo aria, the numerous written 'grace' notes (particularly the slide) and the prominence of Lombard and other rhythms associated with the pre-Classical style are all new to Scarlatti's vocal music. They are, however, common in the music of the younger composers resident at the Spanish court and in the operas by Italian composers such as Conforto, Hasse and Jommelli that were performed there. Some of these features – the Lombard rhythms (or 'Scotch snaps'), the slides and the slow rate of chord change in a major tonality – are illustrated in the opening of the aria 'Ben crudele è chi la mira' from the cantata *Che vidi oh ciel, che vidi?* (example 34).

Example 34

Andante cantabile   Cantata: *Che vidi oh ciel?*

Ben cru - de - le è chi la   mi-ra,   e non   pian-ge,   e non sos-

2 vns
bc

6   4   3 7 6 5

Although not among the finest arias in these cantatas (it has an unusually clumsy final cadence), 'Ben crudele è chi la mira' is fairly typical in its length and proportions, the first section of the da capo structure occupying fifty-four bars and the second sixteen bars. The second of the two arias in the cantata, 'Se nube oscura ricopre il giorno', is similar in its proportions (the outer sections consisting of 108 bars in ₵ metre, Allegro moderato, the central section of thirty-eight bars, 3/8, Andante moderato), but it is much more representative of Scarlatti's late cantatas at their best. The picture of a stormy day (symbolic, of course, of the torment raging in the lover's breast) is painted in bold strokes, with long melismas on 'freme' ('rages'), wide leaps over the whole range of the voice, and some vigorous string passages (example 35; note again the slow rate of harmonic change). The eighteen later cantatas include numerous arias calculated, like this one, to leave an audience breathless (not to mention their effect on the singer!), and there are, in addition, many dramatic and intensely expressive recitatives which require singing of the highest virtuosity and insight.

Example 35

Allegro moderato

Cantata: *Che vidi oh ciel?*

Se nu-be os-cu-ra ri-co - pre il gior - - no, or - ri-do il cie - lo fre - - - - - - - - me d'in-tor - no

It is fascinating to observe certain stylistic parallels between the later cantatas and many of the keyboard sonatas, despite their profound differences. Sudden switches from major to minor and back again occur frequently in both genres, as they did also in the earlier vocal works. The oscillation in the sonatas between dominant and subdominant harmonies (especially in the 'B' themes) is also to be observed in the cantata arias, for example in the splendidly impassioned 'Quante furie ha il cieco averno' from *Dir vorrei, ah m'arrossisco*. The syncopations in the first solo aria of *Se per un sol momento*, the frequent changes of tempo in arias from *Qual pensier, quale ardire ti guida?* and *Tinte a note di sangue*, and the unexpected empty bars in the final arias of *Fille già più non parlo* and of *Piangete, occhi dolenti* are again familiar as stylistic traits of the harpsichord works as well.

But the interest and importance of these late cantatas goes far beyond their stylistic links with the harpsichord pieces. Their existence makes it more than ever difficult to understand Scarlatti's non-participation in the operatic activities of the Spanish court. Only one of the cantatas, the setting of Metastasio's *Pur nel sonno almen tal'ora*, has ever appeared in print; the others are overdue for attention on the part of both singers and scholars.

SALVE REGINA

The only other vocal work known to date from Scarlatti's years in Spain is the second of his two settings of the Marian antiphon, *Salve regina*. This is scored for solo soprano, four-part strings and continuo, and manuscript copies of it exist in libraries in Bologna, Naples, Berlin and Münster. The relatively large number of sources suggests that the work was quite well known in the eighteenth century, and this may be attributed in part to a note on the surviving scores to the effect that it was Scarlatti's 'last work, composed in Madrid shortly before he died'. From this has grown the legend that Scarlatti dictated the *Salve regina* from his deathbed, in the same way that Bach is supposed to have dictated his final organ chorale or Mozart his unfinished *Requiem*.

Although the legend has no foundation in fact, the *Salve regina* does contain several passages of poignant and even valedictory expression, despite being written in the bright key of A major. Like the A minor setting of this text (see p. 114), it falls into six sections. The division of the text is similar in both settings, but not identical, as the following summary analysis shows:

A minor setting	*A major setting*[7]
1. Salve regina, Adagio, C	Salve regina, —, 3/4
2. Ad te clamamus, Moderato, 3/4	Ad te clamamus, Andante, C
	(alternating with Grave, 3/4)
3. Ad te suspirans, Adagio, 3/4	Ad te suspirans, Adagio, C
4. Eja ergo, Moderato, C	Eja ergo, Andante, C
5. Et Jesum, Adagio, C	Nobis post hoc, Andante, ¢
6. O clemens, o pia, Adagio, 3/4	O clemens, o pia, Adagio, 3/4
7. —	Amen, Allegro, ¢

The most obvious difference between the two compositions, apart from their mode and scoring, is the addition of an 'amen' to the A major setting. This is set as a kind of 'amen chorus' for solo voice, if such a thing can be imagined, and it allows Scarlatti to end the work in a cheerful, confident vein. It could be argued that the quiet, restrained ending of the A minor setting, with its lingering repetition of the name 'Maria', is more in keeping with a prayer addressed to the Virgin from a 'vale of tears' (words, incidentally, which Scarlatti underlines with particular emphasis in both works). But in the A major *Salve regina* the anguished entreaties of 'O clemens, o pia, o dulcis Virgo Maria', to which the violins' appoggiaturas lend forceful expression, find their quietus in a silent bar followed by a passage unforgettable for its simplicity and serenity (example 36). Never did Scarlatti employ his favourite juxtaposition of major and minor to more profound effect. The 'vale of tears' has been left behind, and in the final 'amen' the composer rejoices on another shore.

Example 36

Here, at the end, there is no 'jesting with art', but rather a moving farewell to art, to life, and perhaps also to the queen whom Scarlatti had served as music master for so many years.

TEN

Scarlatti's Reputation and Influence

Thanks to the finely executed painting by Domingo Antonio de Velasco, we now have a very good idea of Domenico Scarlatti's physical appearance, at least during his mature years. But of his character and personality we still know very little indeed. Even the bare facts of his life and career are hard to come by, especially for his years in Portugal and Spain. For the period up to 1719, except for the years he spent in Venice, there are at least the librettos of operas, oratorios and serenatas to chronicle his main activities as a composer and bring us into contact with some of the patrons and colleagues among whom he worked. The awesome presence of his father and the activities of other members of the Scarlatti family also serve to fill out our picture of the composer during this period. Documents which might have thrown light on Scarlatti's duties and career at the Portuguese court were presumably destroyed in the disastrous earthquake at Lisbon in 1755, in which some of his compositions probably perished as well. Biographical data of Scarlatti's years in Spain are restricted almost entirely to the births and baptisms of his children, his second marriage and the circumstances of his knighthood. They give very little idea of his daily routine as a musician or of his activities outside the court; of his temperament, character and beliefs they tell us nothing at all.

As a result of all this we may be tempted to imagine Scarlatti as something of a recluse, but this is not an idea which easily relates to the kind of music he wrote in Spain. Perhaps the most significant thing about the composer's relationship with his adopted country is simply the fact that he remained there for the last thirty or so years of his life. It would be interesting to speculate on why so many eighteenth-century Italian musicians and artists who travelled widely – the composer Boccherini and the painter Tiepolo among them – ceased their wanderings once they reached Madrid. In the case of Scarlatti and Farinelli the main reason must surely have been that the Spanish royal family, whatever their eccentricities, valued their musicians and looked after them well. In the dedication of a manuscript volume of songs presented to the Empress Maria Theresa (now in the National-bibliothek, Vienna) Farinelli spoke of 'those adorable sovereigns, my most generous benefactors'. Scarlatti may not have enjoyed the same royal favours as Farinelli, but he was evidently well-contented with the pattern of his life in Madrid.

What we lack more than anything else in attempting to form a picture of Scarlatti's character and personality is the kind of intimate correspondence that so vividly brings to life other composers of the past, such as Mozart and Beethoven. The only one of Scarlatti's private letters to survive is that written in 1752 to the Duke of Huescar (see pp. 143–4). Beyond suggesting that Domenico moved as easily among the aristocracy of Madrid as his father had among the nobility of Rome and Naples, this tells us little about the composer; the friendliness of his nature does, however, come across with sufficient clarity to make one regret the loss of similar documents. Also frustrating is the almost complete absence of references to Scarlatti in other correspondence and memoirs emanating from the Spanish court, and it is particularly to be regretted that Farinelli left no first-hand account of his great friend and compatriot.

It is nevertheless to Farinelli's conversations with Charles Burney that we owe most of what we know about Scarlatti's life in Spain, as well as one of the few insights we have into his character – unfortunately not a very flattering one. Burney tells us that

this original composer and great performer, like many men of genius and talents, was so inattentive to common concerns, and so much addicted to play, that he was frequently distressed in his circumstances, and as often extricated by the bounty of his royal mistress; who, as Farinelli assured me, not only often paid his debts, but, at his intercession, continued a pension of four thousand crowns to his widow and three daughters, who were left destitute at his decease.[1]

Burney later amended his account (incorrectly) so that Scarlatti's widow was left with only two daughters. He also made rather more of the composer's weakness for gambling, at the same time referring to his agreeable disposition:

Farinelli informed us, that Domenico Scarlatti, an agreeable man in society, was so much addicted to play, that he was frequently ruined, and as frequently relieved in his distress by his royal patroness, the queen of

Spain, who was constant in her admiration of his original genius and incomparable talents. He died in 1758 at 76 [*sic*], in very bad circumstances, leaving a wife and two daughters totally unprovided of a subsistence; but the queen extended her liberality to the family of her old master, and settled a pension upon them, nearly equal to Scarlatti's own court appointment.[2]

Farinelli's report of Scarlatti's impoverishment is not supported by the inventories of those parts of his estate that went to his daughter Maria and his son Domingo,[3] although it is true that a royal pension was settled on the widow and children. There is no reason to suppose, on the other hand, that Farinelli invented stories about Scarlatti's gambling activities or that he lied to Burney any more than to his first biographer, Giovenale Sacchi, who reported:

> Not only did he [Farinelli] assist his friends while they were alive, but he also helped their families after their death. This he did in the case of the painter Amigoni and also of Domenico Scarlatti, the first of whom did not live long enough to provide for his dependants, while the second had unhappily gambled away the fruits of his talent and the gifts he had received from his royal patron.[4]

Anyone familiar with Scarlatti's keyboard sonatas, or at least with those that deal in wide and rapid leaps (see example 28 on p. 186), will readily believe them to be the work of someone who was prepared to allow luck to play its part in the ordering of his life, or at any rate of his finances. To indulge in further speculation about Scarlatti's character from the evidence of the music might, however, be to suspect him of intermittent schizophrenia, or at least of some kind of mental and emotional instability, for which there is not the slightest evidence. But can it be doubted that the coruscant textures of Scarlatti's harpsichord music, its unpredictable turns of phrase and its inexhaustible invention came from a composer with an unusual zest for life and with a genial disposition? It comes as no surprise to learn that his contemporaries found him 'an agreeable man in society'.

Scarlatti was born in the same year as two even greater musical giants of the late Baroque, Johann Sebastian Bach and George Frideric Handel. It is inevitable that comparisons should be made between the music of these three composers, and equally inevitable that Scarlatti should suffer most by those comparisons. If originality were the only criterion of genius, and if it were to be measured by the ability and readiness of a composer to seek out new techniques, to keep abreast of changing aesthetics and to bend accepted rules and conventions to his own ends, then Scarlatti would have to be judged a greater figure than either Bach or Handel. But the importance of a composer's achievement is measured in other ways as well, not least by the scope and breadth of his output. Merely to mention, say, the *Orgelbüchlein*, the Brandenburg Concertos and the *St Matthew Passion* of Bach, or the *Water Music*, the op. 6 concertos and the oratorio *Messiah* of Handel is to point to a universality and a command of different genres which Scarlatti's output hardly begins to match, even if his operas, cantatas and church music are included in the assessment. To argue that the nature of Scarlatti's employment in Spain did not allow him to extend his creative activities in the same way as Bach was able to do in Germany and Handel in England is perhaps to explain his stature as a composer, but it does not alter it. Scarlatti's secular vocal music has yet to find the recognition it deserves, but even when this happens his importance to posterity will always reside in his harpsichord sonatas – a narrow field, perhaps, but one in which neither Bach nor Handel had much to offer.

As far as musical style is concerned, Scarlatti stands closer to Handel than to Bach, though not very close to either. Scarlatti and Handel shared to some extent the same background and training, and as young men they each formed a lasting admiration for the other's musical gifts. The lack of an exact chronology makes any direct comparison of their early keyboard pieces impossible, but the close result of the contest between them as organists and harpsichordists in Rome in 1708/9 suggests that their styles of keyboard playing and improvisation may at that time have been very similar. Certainly, as far as vocal chamber music was concerned there was a great deal of common ground between them – so much, in fact, that it is now impossible to determine to which of the two composers the cantata *Selve, caverne e monti* properly belongs. Their musical styles soon diverged, as Scarlatti responded to his Spanish environment and Handel to his more conservative, but at the same time more cosmopolitan, English one, but even as late as 1739 Handel was able, without any hint of stylistic incongruity, to incorporate several ideas from the *Essercizi* into his Grand Concertos op. 6, as Alexander Silbiger has shown.[5] By that time Handel seems to have given up composing original keyboard music (his last publication of this kind was a volume of *Six Fugues or Voluntarys* issued in 1735) and further comparison between the two composers loses its point.

Unlike Handel, Bach never visited Italy, and Scarlatti was probably only dimly aware of the existence of his greatest contemporary, whose isolation as a schoolmaster and church musician in Lutheran

Leipzig was as complete as his own in the narrow confines of the Spanish court; possibly he never heard a note of Bach's music in his life. On the other hand, Bach, whose inquisitiveness about contemporary musicians was unparalleled, must surely have heard of Scarlatti. Although the two never met, they did have a mutual acquaintance in the lutenist Silvius Leopold Weiss, who had been in the service of Prince Alexander Sobieski, son of the Queen of Poland, at the same time that Scarlatti was employed by Maria Casimira in Rome. Weiss later served at the Saxon court in Dresden, where he was well-known to Bach. On at least one occasion, in 1739, Weiss spent some time with Bach in Leipzig, and it may be not without significance that this visit was made only a few months after the publication of Scarlatti's *Essercizi*. It has even been suggested that Bach's 'Goldberg' Variations, published in 1741 or 1742 as *Clavier Übung . . . vors Clavicimbal*, owe something to Scarlatti's example.[6] There are thirty variations, all in binary form with repeats, and many of them are virtuoso in character, with hand-crossings and wide leaps not particularly characteristic of Bach's other keyboard works.

On the whole, though, the difficulties of Bach's keyboard music are of a different order from those of Scarlatti's. The Italian presents a physical challenge to the performer, who must train his hands to move rapidly over the keyboard and his fingers to dance nimbly 'on the spot'. Bach's challenge is directed more at the intellect of the player, whose fingers must obey the logic of musical lines which are shaped by the ear and the brain, rather than by the nature of the hand or the instrument. The developments in keyboard technique and the refinement of pedagogical methods since the eighteenth century have rendered some of Scarlatti's difficulties less formidable, but Bach's keyboard music continues to challenge the performer, and especially the sight-reader.

While it is interesting and sometimes instructive to look for similarities in the music of Bach, Handel and Domenico Scarlatti, any comparison between them will inevitably show how *little* Scarlatti has in common with the other two. Indeed, it is often difficult to believe that he belonged to the same generation, let alone the same year, as they did. Charles Burney was right to find a closer resemblance between Scarlatti and Bach's second son, Carl Philipp Emanuel. Although Scarlatti's junior by almost thirty years, C. P. E. Bach was in many ways his spiritual brother. In November 1771 Burney wrote to Mynhere Ebeling:

I was no less surprised than pleased to find Mr C. P. E. Bach get out of the trammels of Fugues and crowded parts in which his father so excelled. Domenico Scarlatti did the same at a Time when a Fugue followed every passage like its Shadow. They both struck out a style of their own. Scarlatti is full of Enthusiasm fire and passion, Bach's every thing, by turns, that music can express.[7]

Burney returned to the comparison shortly afterwards:

Both were sons of great and popular composers, regarded as standards of perfection by all their contemporaries, except their own children, who dared to explore new ways to fame. Domenico Scarlatti, half a century ago, hazarded notes of taste and effect, at which other musicians have but just arrived, and to which the public ear is but lately reconciled; Emanuel Bach, in like manner, seems to have outstript his age.[8]

Burney might have pressed the comparison further. Both composers had to escape from their fathers' proximity and influence before they could find their individualities as creative artists; both were outstandingly gifted keyboard players; and both served most of their working lives as harpsichordists to European monarchs – Scarlatti, it seems, in perfect contentment, Bach with increasing dissatisfaction. As composers, however, the affinity between the two men was less a question of musical style than of artistic temperament, exemplified in their love of sharp contrasts of mood and sudden, remote modulations. Eugene Helm has written that C. P. E. Bach 'perpetuated the brilliant harpsichord idiom of Domenico Scarlatti',[9] but it is difficult to accept this judgment without some qualification. Bach's keyboard sonatas would probably have been no different if Scarlatti had never lived. Their structures are quite unlike Scarlatti's and their keyboard writing is rooted more in the clavichord than in the harpsichord. Bach's originality is manifest above all in his slow movements, where his *Empfindsamkeit* has little to do with the Italian composer. Some of the single-movement sonatinas of Bach's Berlin colleague Georg Benda (for example, the one in D minor edited by Alfred Kreutz in *Eighteenth Century Clavier Pieces*[10]) are closer to Scarlatti's sonatas in structure, if not in style.

While C. P. E. Bach enjoyed widespread renown during his lifetime, furthered by numerous publications of his keyboard works and by the wide circulation of his influential treatise, *Versuch über die wahre Art das Clavier zu spielen* ('Essay on the True Art of Playing Keyboard Instruments'), Scarlatti passed his days in comparative isolation and obscurity. The fact that he failed to follow up the successful *Essercizi* with other volumes of keyboard sonatas suggests that his royal patrons may have opposed further dissemination of his music, just as they prevented Farinelli from making public appearances as a singer. This could explain also the paucity of manuscript copies apart from those owned by the queen or made after her death. The result was that, while C. P. E. Bach exercised an important influence on more than one generation of Classical composers (including Haydn and Beethoven), Scarlatti's immediate influence was confined to a small circle of pupils and admirers.

Chief among the former was Antonio Soler, the Jeronymite monk who lived from 1752 at the Escorial and studied with Scarlatti there. Soler's extant keyboard sonatas, numbering 120, have been published in a modern edition by Samuel Rubio (Madrid, 1957–72); they include twenty-seven that were presented to Lord Fitzwilliam in 1772 and first published in London in about 1796. Many of the stylistic features in Soler's sonatas are obviously indebted to Scarlatti's example, including the numerous imitative openings, the extensive octave writing and passages of acrobatic hand-crossing. There are also examples of repeated notes (e.g. nos 1, 84 and 88 in Rubio's edition), sudden excursions into 3rd-related keys (nos 4 and 69), glissandos (no. 76) and downward arpeggios (nos 86, 103 and 107), all reminiscent of Soler's teacher. Unresolved 5-4 chords are also found (nos 14 and 86), but not the more daring note-clusters of Scarlatti. In a number of Soler's single-movement binary sonatas the 'A' material is recapitulated in the tonic (nos 41, 42, 45 etc.), but on the whole the composer adopts the typical Scarlatti structure. In certain other respects, for example in their employment of Alberti basses and in their often more regular phrase structure, Soler's sonatas are more in tune with the generation after Scarlatti. But whether following his master or escaping from his influence, Soler was amazingly fertile in inventing new and fresh-sounding ideas.

Even more Scarlattian are many of the sonatas of Sebastian Albero, who from 1749 (and possibly before) until his early death in 1756 served King Fernando VI as organist of the royal chapel in Madrid. A volume of thirty sonatas, in the hand of the scribe mainly responsible for Queen Maria Barbara's copies of Scarlatti's sonatas, exists in the Biblioteca Nazionale Marciana, Venice.[11] In addition there are six sonatas in a manuscript volume of *Obras para clavicordio* in the library of the Real Conservatorio de Música, Madrid (MS 4/1727(2)), each preceded by a 'recercata' (in effect a *prélude non mesuré* like those of the French clavecinistes) and a fugue in the same key. All the features mentioned above as common to Scarlatti and Soler are also to be found in the thirty Venice sonatas of Albero, while the Madrid works contain several examples of note-clusters quite as striking as any of Scarlatti's.

Like Soler, Albero succeeded in bringing something fresh, even individual, to the single-movement sonata, and his command of keyboard style is impressive. Genoveva Gálvez has noted an 'indescribably pre-Chopinesque melancholy' in Albero's music, which she sees as an early manifestation in Spain of the 'empfindsamer Stil'; and Macario Santiago Kastner, in a preface to Gálvez's edition, has warned against the too easy assumption that everything we think of today as a 'Scarlatti-ism' was brought to Spain by the Neapolitan. Nevertheless, it is difficult not to believe that in passages such as example 37, from the last of the Madrid sonatas, Albero was setting out to prove to King Fernando (to whom the volume is dedicated) that anything Scarlatti could do he could do, if not better, at least just as well.

Example 37

[L = left hand]

The Italians had known Scarlatti principally as an opera composer during the time he spent in his native country, and it is not surprising that he was virtually forgotten there after his departure from Rome in 1719, especially since tastes in operatic music were changing. After the death of Alessandro Scarlatti in 1725 and the revival of *Tolomeo et Alessandro* in Jesi in 1727, there can have been little talk of Domenico in

Italy, at least until the return of Farinelli in 1759. Domenico Scarlatti's name appears hardly at all in the voluminous correspondence of Padre Martini in Bologna, and there is no evidence to suggest that his keyboard sonatas were at all well-known in Italy during the eighteenth century. The two Italian composers whose keyboard music is most strongly influenced by Scarlatti's, Domenico Paradies and Muzio Clementi, both came to know his music in England. Outside Spain, Scarlatti's reputation spread first to England, where Thomas Roseingrave had been promoting his music ever since his return from Italy in 1714 or 1715. Roseingrave's work on the revival of the opera *Narciso* at the King's Theatre, London, in 1720 and his edition of forty-two Scarlatti sonatas in 1739 have already been mentioned. The sonatas (or 'lessons', as the English called them) enjoyed immense popularity in England throughout the eighteenth century. In his article on Scarlatti for Rees's *The Cyclopaedia* Burney wrote:

> The Lessons of M. Scarlatti were in a style so new and brilliant, that no great or promising player acquired notice of the public so effectually by the performance of any other music. Kelway kept them in constant practice; Worgan played no other music, except his own. In short, everyone played, or tried to play, Scarlatti's.

Roseingrave was still performing Scarlatti's sonatas in public in 1753, apparently from his own edition to judge from a report in the *Dublin Journal* for 3 February of that year, which speaks of his playing 'Scarlatti's "Lessons on the Harpsichord" . . . and his celebrated "Almand" '. Roseingrave's own compositions include *Eight Suits of Lessons for the Harpsicord or Spinnet*, published by Walsh in 1725. They show little influence of Scarlatti, except perhaps in occasional passages of syncopation; the dominant influence is Handel's.

John Worgan was a pupil of Roseingrave. He held various posts as a church organist in London and a similar appointment at Vauxhall pleasure gardens from 1751 to 1761, and again from 1770 to 1774. He owned the important *Libro de XLIV sonatas modernas*, a collection of forty-four Scarlatti sonatas, now in the British Library (Add. MS 31553), to which Burney referred in his *History*:

> In his youth, he [Worgan] was impressed with a reverence for Domenico Scarlatti by old Roseingrave's account of his wonderful performance on the harpsichord, as well as by his lessons; and afterwards he became a great collector of his pieces, some of which he had been honoured with from Madrid by the author himself. He was the editor of twelve at one time and

six at another, that are admirable, though few have now perseverance sufficient to vanquish their peculiar difficulties of execution. He is still in possession of many more, which he has always locked up as Sybil's leaves.[12]

Burney apparently confused one of Worgan's two publications of 'sonatas modernas', each of which contains twelve works, with the volume of six sonatas published by John Welcker in 1776–7. Welcker followed the style of Worgan's title-pages, but the contents (not included in Add. MS 31553) are identical with the Haffner publication of 1754 (see Table 1 on p. 158). All the sonatas in Worgan's two editions are taken from Add. MS 31553.

Worgan's own compositions include a volume of six sonatas, published in 1769. Although multi-movement works, they are more Scarlattian than Roseingrave's in structure and style. An excursion to the tonic minor is to be observed towards the end of some major-key movements, and there are several passages calling for hand-crossings. The last movement of Sonata no. 4 recalls Scarlatti in its frequent changes of tempo. Perhaps the most Scarlattian feature of the set, however, is the note placed at the head of Sonata no. 5: 'Lest the consecutive fifths at the beginning of the Theme of this movement should escape the Critic, the Author here apprizes him of them'.

The other Scarlatti enthusiast mentioned by Burney was Joseph Kelway, a pupil of the Italian composer and violinist, Francesco Geminiani. Kelway was organist at the church of St Martin-in-the-Fields and, from 1764, harpsichord master to Queen Charlotte. Burney said of him:

Mr Kelway, a scholar of Geminiani, kept Scarlatti's best lessons in constant practice, and was at the head of the Scarlatti sect. He had, in his voluntaries on the organ, a masterly wildness, and long supported the character of a great player, in a style quite his own, bold, rapid, and fanciful. With his harpsichord playing I was not acquainted, but have often been assured, that he executed the most difficult lessons of Scarlatti, in a manner peculiarly neat and delicate. As to composition, it is to be lamented that he did not exercise his pen and fancy more early in life, or that he ever attempted it at all; for on the arrival of [Johann Christian] Bach, and appointment at court, as chamber-musician to the Queen, to whom he dedicated his first publication in this country, Mr Kelway thought it necessary, as music-master to her Majesty, to publish a book of harpsichord lessons, which are, perhaps, the most crude, aukward, and unpleasant pieces of the kind that have ever been engraved. There is a manifest want of facility and experience, which proves that though he was old in practical Music, he was young in its theory and in composition.[13]

It is somewhat disappointing to find that what excited Burney's displeasure in the six sonatas that Kelway published in 1764 was not the result of any attempt to imitate the style of the Scarlatti sonatas he so much admired. In fact, there is nothing particularly Scarlattian about them. Each sonata is in three or four movements, and most of the quick movements exhibit an embryonic sonata form, with the first theme recapitulated in the tonic. The textures are on the whole much thicker than Scarlatti's. What Burney found 'crude, aukward, and unpleasant' was perhaps the ungainliness and the outworn style of such passages as the opening of Sonata no. 4 (example 38). Other movements show a much more vigorous and original style.

Joseph Kelway's patron was Lord Fitzwilliam, a keen collector of music by the Scarlattis – Alessandro's as well as Domenico's. In 1768 Lord Fitzwilliam owned the copy of Domenico's *Narciso* (*Amor d'un*

Example 38   Kelway: Sonata no. 4

ombra e gelosia d'un aura) now in the Staats- und Universitäts-bibliothek, Hamburg, and in 1772 he brought back from Madrid two volumes of Scarlatti's keyboard sonatas, one containing thirty-one works and the other, originally prepared for the Venetian ambassador to Madrid, twenty-four; both volumes are now in the Fitzwilliam Museum, Cambridge.

Admiration for Scarlatti's keyboard music in England persisted throughout the eighteenth century, as witness the new and reissued editions of his sonatas. One of these, entitled *The Beauties of Dominico Scarlatti. Selected from his Suites de Lecons . . . and Revised with a Variety of Improvements by Ambrose Pitman* and consisting of fifteen sonatas from Roseingrave's 1739 volumes, is particularly interesting for its preface:

> The Lessons of Dominico Scarlatti have ever been esteemed by Musical Theorists for their many excellencies of Taste, Genius, and Originality. – But this Acknowledgement of Merit has hitherto been confined to a very limited Circle; their reception into General Practice having been greatly retarded by the many superfluous and studied difficulties with which they abound. – In Manuscript, their obscurity was not without an intention; – as they were expressly composed for the Practice of a very brilliant Performer, the Infanta Maria, to whom Scarlatti was Master of Music; every Opportunity was taken by the Author to introduce difficult and affected Passages, for no other use or reason than merely as extraordinary excercises for the eminent ability of his Pupil.
>
> To remove these Obstacles, which have, in some measure, obscured such admirable Lessons from Public Notice, and that they may, in future, be more readily understood by the Student, has been the principal Design of the present Editor. – In the first Instance – he has selected the most beautiful movements – such as are of distinguished excellence – divested them of their pedantic difficulties, and arranged them in distinct Lessons; the frequent and unnecessary introduction of the Tenor Cleff, intended only to perplex the Sight of the Performer, he has every where rejected, and substituted in its stead that of the Treble, as being more familiar to the generality of Practitioners; – unnatural and cramp positions of the hands, he has avoided or altered, that the fingering might be rendered easy and graceful; – and he has been enabled, by the improvement of modern Instruments, to restore some passages and amend others, which the Author himself must have admitted, had the Harpsichords of his Time extended as high in Alt, as do those of the present day. – These, as some of the principal amendments, will be particularly seen in the first and fourth Lessons, especially in the Allegro movement of the former.
>
> Among the enthusiastic admirers of Scarlatti's Lessons, was the late Dr. Arne, who always considered them, with the 'Suites de Pieces' of Handel,

as the best calculated Performances to compleat the Practical Part of a Musical Education. – And the Editor of the ensuing Work, must here acknowledge himself indebted to that celebrated Master for many improvements which were advised at the time he was the Doctor's Pupil, and when these elegant Pieces of Harmony constantly made a Part of his daily studies. – The advantages of this valuable aid first induced him to a revisal of the Work, an Epitome of which is now submitted to the Amateurs of Music; under the Title of 'The Beauties of Dominico Scarlatti.'

Pitman was not the last editor to attempt to make Scarlatti's sonatas 'more readily understood by the Student'. His preface introduces the name of another late-eighteenth-century Scarlatti admirer, his teacher Thomas Augustine Arne, and to this may be added that of Kelway's pupil, Charles Wesley. But the most important figure on the English scene at the turn of the century, as far as Scarlatti's posthumous reputation is concerned, was the Italian Muzio Clementi. Clementi was born in Rome, but was brought to England by Peter Beckford at the age of fourteen and served a kind of apprenticeship for seven years at Beckford's country estate in Dorset. Clementi got to know many of Scarlatti's sonatas in England and included them in his public recitals. His own early works are deeply influenced by them, especially the op. 2 set of six sonatas published in London in 1779. Of these Clementi's most recent biographer, Leon Plantinga, has written: 'Only one keyboard composer within Clementi's ken can be urged as a convincing model for the individual devices and the overall thrust of opus 2: Domenico Scarlatti. Scarlatti's extravagant new sounds and sparkling figurations seem to have served as a ready fund of techniques from which Clementi fashioned the most prominent elements of his own keyboard style.'[14] Plantinga finds that Scarlatti continued to exert a powerful influence on Clementi's music as late as 1790, in the op. 25 sonatas.[15]

As an editor, too, Clementi contributed to the English cult of Scarlatti with a volume of Scarlatti's Chefs-d'œuvre for the Harpsichord or Piano-Forte; Selected from an Elegant collection of Manuscripts, in the Possession of Muzio Clementi (London, c. 1791). This included twelve works, of which one is by Soler and another is generally regarded as spurious, and possibly by Clementi himself. The whole volume was, in fact, reissued two years later in Paris as Douze sonates . . . composées dans le stile du celèbre Scarlati, a plagiarism which Clementi quite possibly condoned. It is, incidentally, to Clementi that we owe also the nickname of 'Cat's Fugue' for the last of the Essercizi (K30).

Except for the publication of J. U. Haffner's edition of six sonatas (Nuremberg, 1754), there is little evidence of any interest in Scarlatti's music in Germany during the eighteenth century. J. G. Walther devoted only a few lines to Domenico as part of the brief article on Alessandro Scarlatti in his *Musicalisches Lexicon*;[16] he mentions the Portuguese appointment and an allowance of 2,000 Thaler which Domenico is said to have received for the journey to Lisbon according to a Halle newspaper which cannot now be traced. J. P. Kirnberger, in his *Die Kunst des reinen Satzes in der Musik*, mentioned 'a certain Domenico Scarlatti' only to criticize a passage in one of the sonatas.[17] And E. L. Gerber's one-column entry on Scarlatti in his *Historisch-biographisches Lexicon der Tonkünstler* draws on Burney and Quantz for biographical information and includes mention of some of the published keyboard sonatas.[18]

In Vienna Scarlatti's keyboard music enjoyed a much keener following, as we know from DuBeine's important manuscript collection (see pp. 151–3) and from the eventual publication of Carl Czerny's edition of 200 sonatas in 1839. This edition did more than anything else to keep Scarlatti's name before the musical public during the nineteenth century, despite an unenthusiastic review of it from Robert Schumann in the pages of the *Neue Zeitschrift für Musik* (1839):

Haslinger of Vienna has published Domenico Scarlatti's clavier works ('Collected Works for the Pianoforte', fingered by C. Czerny), well set out in separate fascicles. The first four contain thirty-three movements, mostly fast, and give us a good idea of the composer's style. Scarlatti has many good qualities which distinguish him from his contemporaries. The so-to-speak 'armoured' [*geharnischt*] regularity and logic of Bach's music is not to be found here; Scarlatti's is lighter, more ephemeral and more rhapsodic. It is difficult sometimes to follow him, so quickly does he tie and untie the threads; in the context of his time his style is abrupt, attractive and piquant. His works now hold an important place in the keyboard repertory: they contain much that was novel in their time, they can be seen to make varied use of the instrument and, above all, they call for more independent use than was previously made of the left hand. Yet, to be frank, there is a great deal here that can no longer satisfy us – nor should it. How could any of these pieces measure up to the works of one of our more gifted composers! How awkward the structure is, how undeveloped the melody and how restricted the modulations! Especially when compared to Bach! It is, as a brilliant composer once said when comparing Emanuel with Sebastian Bach, 'as though a dwarf had come among giants'. Nevertheless, the true keyboard player should not remain ignorant of leading representatives of the various schools, and especially by Scarlatti, who obviously brought keyboard technique to a higher level. One should not, though, play too many of these pieces in succession, since they are very similar in tempo and character; but when brought forward a few at a time and in the right context they will always sound fresh to the listener. The present collection, which will eventually comprise thirty fascicles, should prove to be a worthwhile one. An older, incomplete edition [Schumann no doubt refers to the eight *cahiers* published by the Bureau des Arts et d'Industrie in 1803–7], also published in Vienna, is out of print and unreliable. Herr Czerny's contribution is the fingering. It is not clear what purpose such fingering can serve, still less in Bach's compositions.[19]

Most early-nineteenth-century pianists seem to have regarded Scarlatti's keyboard works mainly as pupil-fodder, or to have ignored them altogether. Those who could appreciate their musical qualities were often reluctant to include them in their recitals, and Chopin is even reported to have aroused censure when he gave his pupils the sonatas to work on. It seems that Scarlatti's music was seldom played in public during the early nineteenth century. Both Johann Baptist Cramer, who was no doubt introduced to it during his year of study with Clementi, and Liszt played pieces by Scarlatti in Rome in the 1830s but this was to a private audience at Santini's house. Liszt did, however, include some Scarlatti in his public recitals as well, and was perhaps the first great pianist to do so.

Stimulated by the publication of Czerny's collected edition, concert pianists gradually came to pay more attention to the virtuoso qualities of Scarlatti's piano sonatas (as they were by then thought of). Robert Schumann's wife, Clara Wieck, is reported to have almost fallen from the piano stool while negotiating some acrobatic hand-crossing in one of them. But it was her friend Johannes Brahms who, of all the great nineteenth-century composers, best understood and valued Scarlatti's keyboard music. Brahms knew the sonatas not only from Czerny's edition but also from the numerous manuscripts in his collection, which he studied, indexed and annotated. In 1885 he sent one of these (probably a copy of K394) to his friend Elisabeth von Herzogenberg (see pp. 171–2), to whom he wrote on May 6 that year:

I should, of course, send more Scarlatti if there were any others as good. I have over 300 beautiful old manuscript copies, of which 172 are unpublished. Czerny made use of them for a collection, which is as admirably selected as edited. His edition, containing 200 pieces, probably stopped short where it did by chance, or he would hardly have overlooked your specimen [K394 is not in Czerny's edition]. You should really try to get a copy (Czerny's edition, Haslinger, Vienna) through some good antiquarian. It is rare now. I had to wait a long time before I could find a complete copy.[20]

Nine years before this Brahms had paid Scarlatti the compliment of basing his setting of Goethe's humorous *Unüberwindlich* (op. 72 no. 5) on the opening of the sonata in D major K223, one of those included in Czerny's edition. Brahms transposes the music to A major and displaces the bar-lines, but otherwise his quotation is exact, even to the inclusion of Scarlatti's ornament on the fifth note (example 39). Motifs from these bars, which Eric Sams has likened to 'a dry and sparkling wine',[21] permeate the music like champagne bubbles, and the whole phrase is twice worked into the vocal line.

Example 39

It would be difficult to prove that Scarlatti's influence on Brahms went beyond this deliberate quotation from K223, or that Brahms's music would have been significantly different if he had not known Scarlatti's, but the German composer must surely have been impressed with what seems to us now the Brahmsian texture of such passages as example 40, from the sonata K299, and delighted with the irregular phrase lengths and cross-rhythms of K233 (see example 30 on p. 189; compare bars 130–7 and 333–40 in the finale of Brahms's Second Symphony). Brahms would have known both K299 and 233

Example 40

Example 41

from Czerny's edition, where he would have found also K180, containing an example of the obsessive repetitions of a short musical figure that occur so frequently in the sonatas, especially in passages after the double bar-line. Was Brahms aware, perhaps, of Scarlatti's example when he wrote bars 66–72 of the fugue from the Handel Variations op. 24 (1861) (example 41; compare the passage from K180 quoted at example 21 on p. 175)?

Three things in particular have contributed to Scarlatti's posthumous reputation in the twentieth century. One of these is the flowering of Spanish nationalism in music during the early decades of the century, stimulated in large measure by the pioneering work in various fields of the scholar and composer Felipe Pedrell. Composers such as Albéniz, Granados and, above all, Falla (all of them pupils of Pedrell) recognized and were influenced by the Spanish, and more particularly by the Andalusian, qualities they found in Scarlatti's harpsichord music, and their own piano works, in turn, served to focus greater attention on this aspect of the older master. Both Falla and the Cuban-born Joaquín Nin actually regarded Scarlatti as a Spanish composer. It is, however, possible that the hispanism of later generations has distorted our perception of the nature of Scarlatti's response to the folk-music of his adopted country. What is now urgently needed to place our understanding of this whole area on a more scientific footing is a thorough investigation into the influence of Iberian folk-music on Scarlatti by some ethnomusicologist familiar also with the art music of eighteenth-century Spain and Portugal.

Another factor affecting Scarlatti's present reputation is the twentieth-century revival of the harpsichord. Some of Scarlatti's sonatas were unquestionably written for the chamber organ, and others were probably composed with the early Florentine piano (a very different instrument from the modern concert grand) in mind. Recitalists will no doubt go on playing Scarlatti on the piano, but for most of the sonatas, and certainly for those one thinks of as most characteristic of the composer, there really is no adequate substitute for the brilliance and clarity of a period or reproduction harpsichord. Fortunately for a true understanding and appreciation of Scarlatti's keyboard music, such instruments now exist in greater numbers than at any time since the eighteenth century, and for those unable to experience them at first hand there is the compensation of gramophone recordings.

Finally, the extent to which modern scholarship has contributed to Scarlatti's reputation should be acknowledged. The biographical and critical study of Ralph Kirkpatrick (1953) remains pre-eminent among books on the composer, especially in the revised edition published only a few months before Kirkpatrick's death in 1984. Scholars such as Joel Sheveloff in the USA and Loek Hautus in the Netherlands have reviewed and built on Kirkpatrick's work, and a new landmark in Scarlatti studies was reached with the completion of Kenneth Gilbert's edition of the keyboard sonatas in 1984, just in time for the composer's tercentenary. It is gratifying, too, to observe the extent to which Scarlatti has found recognition in his native Italy since about 1900, first with the edition and monograph of Alessandro Longo, and since then with the writings of Alberto Basso, Massimo Bogianckino, Francesco Degrada, S. A. Luciani, Giorgio Pestelli, Luigi Tagliavini, Cesare Valabrega and others. Roberto Pagano's biographical study (1985) has added a new dimension to our understanding of Scarlatti the man, and his book on the keyboard sonatas will be keenly awaited. Finally, the new Ricordi edition of the sonatas, for which Emilia Fadini is responsible, promises to rival Kenneth Gilbert's as the most accurate and authoritative available.

Although at the time of writing at least three harpsichordists have embarked on the task of recording the complete sonatas, Scarlatti's reputation still rests on a comparatively small proportion of his total output, and too many recitalists continue to regard the sonatas as little more than spicy hors-d'œuvres to precede the meatier dishes in a concert programme. Scarlatti's place among the most individual and congenial of music's immortals is now assured, but his reputation will only be enhanced as all his music becomes even better-known.

APPENDIX I   *Some Scarlatti Arrangements*

Musical arrangements are made for a variety of reasons: to bring a quick return to an opportunist publisher; to respond to popular enthusiasm for a particular piece; to extend the repertory of an instrument not well provided with original compositions; to simplify music for the less advanced player (or in some cases to make it more technically demanding for the virtuoso); and to satisfy the creative urge of an arranger who sees possibilities in a piece of music which the original composer did not explore. In most arrangements more than one of these considerations will operate; but, as far as published ones are concerned, the expectation of commercial success is usually predominant, and arrangements can therefore be seen to some extent as a measure of a piece's popularity at the time they were made.

There are other things to be taken into consideration, however. If Domenico Scarlatti's music has been less subject to arrangements than, say, Bach's and Handel's, this is not necessarily because it is less popular than theirs. The majority of Scarlatti's keyboard sonatas (which is the only part of his œuvre that concerns us here) are so idiomatic to the harpsichord that they would seem almost to defy the arranger's hand. Not surprisingly, the instrument most often favoured with Scarlatti arrangements has been the guitar. It is not the purpose of this appendix, however, to survey the large and still growing repertory of guitar arrangements, since most of these involve the minimum reorganization of the original material beyond transposition to a suitable key. We are concerned here with arrangements in which some degree of creative reinterpretation is involved – arrangements in which the composer's original conception has been 'sieved' through another (and in most cases a much later) musical imagination, or in which the music has been placed in a new context. The most interesting and at the same time the most historically important of these are the twelve string concertos of Charles Avison.

CHARLES AVISON: TWELVE CONCERTOS

Charles Avison was born in Newcastle upon Tyne in 1709 and served as organist at the parish church of St Nicholas (now Newcastle Cathedral) from 1736 until his death in 1770. He is remembered as the most prolific and one of the most gifted English composers of string concertos in the tradition of Corelli and Geminiani, and he also published an important treatise on musical aesthetics and criticism, *An Essay on Musical Expression* (London, 1752). His twelve concertos based on Scarlatti appeared in 1744, and they testify to the insatiable demand among English musicians for string concertos of this kind, as well as to the popularity of the *Essercizi* and of Roseingrave's edition of forty-two Scarlatti sonatas, which had appeared only a few years earlier.

Before sending all twelve concertos to the printer, Avison tested the market early in 1743 with *I Concerto in Seven Parts done from the Lessons of Sigr. Domenico Scarlatti*, an arrangement of K29 and 21 (both in D major) printed for the author in Newcastle and sold 'at the golden Harp in New Street Covent Garden, Mr Simpson by ye Royal Exchange and Mr Wamsley in Piccadilly'. On the reverse of the title-page Avison solicited subscriptions for a complete set of twelve concertos, announcing that 'they will not be publish'd till One Hundred Setts are subscribed for'. Avison then goes on to justify his decision to make the arrangements by claiming, as so many later arrangers have, that he has done the original composer a service.

> THESE LESSONS for the HARPSICHORD being extremely difficult, and many delightful Passages entirely disguised, either with capricious Divisions, or an unnecessary Repetition in many Places, few Performers are able to execute them with that Taste and Correctness they require: Therefore, the forming them into Parts, and taking off the Mask which concealed their natural Beauty and Excellency, will not only more effectually express that pleasing Air, and sweet Succession of Harmony, so peculiar to the Compositions of this Author, but render them more easy and familiar to the Instrument for which they were first intended. To evince the Justness of this Opinion, one *Concerto* is now published, and sold at the Music Shops in *London*; which the Publick may be assured is not pitched upon as being superior to the rest, for the whole will be found to contain a Collection of the most genteel and lively Pieces.

The specimen concerto was apparently criticized for its lack of a slow movement, and when Avison reissued it later in the year he added the following 'P.S.', dated 23 May 1743:

IT is but too obvious that this Undertaking would have been liable to
Exceptions from a Want of slow Movements in the Original, which is now
sufficiently remov'd, Mr AVISON having been favour'd (since the printing
of this Specimen) with as many Pieces of the same Author's as will be an
Addition, in general, of two to each *Concerto*; and, tho' attended with an
extraordinary Expence, yet shall not impede the Prosecution of this
Design, there being all imaginable Hopes of succeeding in a Work which
has already had the Approbation of the ablest Judges.

Avison succeeded in attracting 151 subscribers, both individuals
(including 'Mr Kelway', but not Thomas Roseingrave) and orchestral
societies in Carlisle, Glasgow, Norwich, Oxford, York and 'the
Crown and Anchor in the Strand on the Wednesday nights'; he went
ahead with the publication of the complete set the following year.

Roseingrave's 1739 edition served as the main source for the
concertos, but Avison's greatest problem in assembling them was
obviously to find a sufficient number of slow movements. In order to
follow the fashionable four-movement 'da chiesa' layout used by his
teacher Geminiani, he required twenty-four slow movements in all,
and Roseingrave's edition supplied only a couple. (Strangely enough,
Avison did not use K34, a Larghetto which seems admirably suited to
the purpose.) Some of the required movements he found in sonatas for
a solo instrument (probably violin) and continuo which he managed
to obtain at 'extraordinary expence'. These presumably did not come
from Scarlatti himself, either directly or through a third party, since if
they had one would have expected to find them all included in the
Venice manuscripts, the copying of which had already begun. Ten
movements do, in fact, appear in the 1742 Venice volume, but
Avison's versions show discrepancies which indicate that Venice was
not the source for them. The first movement of concerto no. 3, for
example, contains eight bars (bars 13–20) which Scarlatti later deleted,
or which the scribe of K89/ii (possibly Sebastian Albero) inadvert-
ently omitted, bars 12 and 20 being almost identical.

After exhausting his newly acquired Scarlatti manuscripts, Avison
still found himself short of slow movements. In concertos nos 10 and
12 he evidently supplied some himself – brief movements consisting
of a few sustained chords with improvisatory flourishes for the first
soloist, quite unlike any known keyboard pieces by Scarlatti. For two
of these Avison used the unusual term 'temporeg[g]iato', probably
indicating that they should be played in a meditative manner. In seven
cases Avison was forced into the expediency of simply arranging a
quick movement as an Andante or Adagio (or Amoroso – a term
Scarlatti never used), and it is likely, too, that the Lentemente (*sic*) of

concerto no. 12 was originally a fast movement. The sources for Avison's twelve concertos, in so far as they have been identified, are summarized in Table 2.

TABLE 2 *Contents of Avison's Twelve Concertos (1744)*

Concerto/ movement no.	K.no. (etc.)	Key, new/ original	Tempo, new/ original
1/i	91/i	A/G major	Adagio/Grave
ii	24	A/A major	Allegro/Presto
iii	91/iv	A/G major	Amoroso(3/4)/Allegro(3/8)
iv	26	A/A major	Allegro/Presto
2/i	91/iii	G/G major	Largo/Grave
ii	13	G/G major	Allegro/Presto
iii	4	g/g minor	Andante/Allemanda
iv	2	G/G major	Vivace/Vivace
3/i	89/ii	d/d minor	Largo andante/Grave
ii	37	d/c minor	Allegro spiritoso/Allegro
iii	38	F/F major	Vivace/Allegro
iv	1	d/d minor	Allegro/Allegro
4/i	12	a/g minor	Andante/Presto
ii	3	a/a minor	Allegro/Presto
iii	(unknown)	C/? major	Largo/?
iv	36	a/a minor	Vivace/Allegro
5/i	(unknown)	d/? minor	Largo/?
ii	11	d/c minor	Allegro/Allegro
iii	41	d/d minor	Andante moderato/Andante moderato
iv	5	d/d minor	Allegro/Allegro
6/i	(unknown)	D/? major	Largo/?
ii	29	D/D major	Con furia/Presto
iii	89/iii	d/d minor	Adagio/Allegro
iv	21	D/D major	Vivacemente/Allegro
7/i	88/i	g/g minor	Adagio/Grave
ii	19	g/f minor	Allegro/Allegro
iii	88/iv	g/g minor	Adagio/Minuet
iv	17	G/F major	Allegro affettuoso/Presto
8/i	81/i	e/e minor	Adagio/Grave
ii	20	E/E major	Allegro/Presto
iii	81/iv	e/e minor	Amoroso/Allegro
iv	15	e/e minor	Vivace/Allegro

9/i	(unknown)	C/? major	Largo/?
ii	31	a/g minor	Con spirito/Allegro
iii	(unknown)	a/? minor	Siciliana/?
iv	7	a/a minor	Allegro/Presto
10/i	(unknown)	D/? major	Gratioso/?
ii	10	d/d minor	Allegro/Presto
iii	(?Avison)	d minor	Adagio
iv	9	d/d minor	Allegro/Presto
11/i	(unknown)	G/? major	Con affetto/?
ii	28	G/E major	Allegro/Presto
iii	25	g/f# minor	Andante moderato/Allegro
iv	6	G/F major	Vivacemente/Allegro
12/i(a)	(?Avison)	D major	Grave, temporegiato
(b)	(unknown)	D/D major	Largo/?
ii	23	D/D major	Allegro spiritoso/Allegro
iii	(unknown)	d/? minor	Lentemente/?
iv(a)	(?Avison)	D major	Temporegiato
(b)	33	D/D major	Allegro/Allegro

Avison's arrangements are on the whole skilfully done. The keyboard figuration is so convincingly adapted to the string orchestra that in most cases it might be imagined that the music had originally been conceived for that medium. As far as the actual substance of the music is concerned, in some cases this is little altered: the last movements of the third and eleventh concertos remain essentially faithful to the substance of K1 and K6 respectively, and the second movements of nos. 2, 7, 8 and 9 also remain very close to the original Scarlatti versions. Most of the other concerto movements, however, show substantial differences, including rhythmic alterations, changes to the harmony (Scarlatti's idiosyncratic 5-4 harmonies are invariably smoothed out) and the addition of inner counterpoints to fill out the texture. One of the most striking examples of recomposition occurs at the recapitulation of the 'B' theme in the last movement of concerto no. 9 (bars 106–20). In K7 the corresponding passage (bars 122–37) is in A minor; Avison alters this to A major, and then repeats the last phrase only, in A minor.

The most numerous and controversial of Avison's alterations are the cuts he makes. Some of the most extensive occur, naturally, in those cases where a quick movement has been adapted as a slow one: the ninety-four bars of K89/iii (Allegro), for example, have been reduced to only thirty-nine 3/4 bars in the third movement (Adagio) of concerto no. 6. But even where no change of tempo is involved, the excisions are often quite substantial. In the second movement of concerto no. 4 the ninety-four bars of K3 have been reduced to sixty, and the D minor fugue K41 ends up considerably less than half its original length in concerto no. 5. In this last instance, at least, Avison's version must be considered superior to Scarlatti's sprawling original, and it has the advantage, too, of a vigorous new counter-subject. Avison's excision of what he considered 'unnecessary repetition in many places' is more open to criticism, and it certainly has an injurious effect on the well-known D minor sonata K9, which suffers also from some ill-judged revision to its harmony. It would be easy to condemn wholesale Avison's general practice of cutting out phrase repetitions, and perhaps it ought to be condemned as an unwarranted tampering with another composer's work. But this is to apply the standards of modern aesthetics and scholarship to an age when priorities were very different, and, in any case, if Scarlatti's originals had been lost it is doubtful if anyone would now find Avison's concerto movements unduly cramped.

Avison did not, of course, eliminate all of Scarlatti's phrase repetitions, and those that remain in the concertos help to throw light on an important aspect of performance relevant to the sonatas. In the vast majority of cases the arranger has scored the initial statement and its repetition in identical ways, without even indicating a change of dynamic level. In only one movement, the first Allegro of concerto no. 5 (= K11), do we find a repeated phrase scored in such a way as to suggest an echo. Bar 9 (corresponding to bar 10 of the original) is scored for the full string band, its immediate repetition for solo violin and continuo only (example 42). (Note that the change of instrumentation cuts across what seems to be the natural phrasing of the melody. Is this an example of ham-fistedness or imprecision on Avison's part, or was it normal eighteenth-century practice to make

Example 42
Allegro

Avison: Concerto no.5

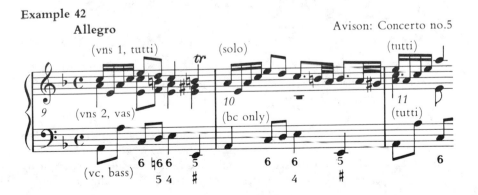

the echo coincide with the bar-line?) The corresponding passage in bars 23–4 (originally bars 24–5) in the second half of the movement is similarly treated.

The last movement of the same concerto, taken from K5, exemplifies the reverse procedure. In this case the initial phrase, bars 44–5 (equivalent to bars 54–5 in the sonata) is scored for solo violin and its repetition for the whole band (example 43). The *forte* repetition is actually more common than the echo in Avison's concertos; other examples occur in the finales of the second and fourth concertos and in the Allegro of concerto no. 8. Since Avison's arrangements are more or less contemporary with the original sonatas, their treatment of repeated phrases might be taken as a caution to the modern pianist or two-manual harpsichordist not to overdo the use of echo effects when playing Scarlatti.

Example 43

Avison: Concerto no. 5

Avison was not the only eighteenth-century musician to make concertos out of Scarlatti's keyboard sonatas. An anonymous article in the *European Magazine* (1785) includes the following paragraph:

In 1760, finding his health considerably amended, he [Burney] returned to London [from King's Lynn in Norfolk]; where, from the zeal of his former friends, and the performance of his eldest daughter, a child of 7 or 8 years old, he was instantly offered more scholars than he could undertake. The late Duke of York, to whom he had the honour of being introduced by the late Earl of Eglinton, was so captivated by some of the most wild and difficult lessons of Scarlatti, which he had heard his little daughter play, that his Royal Highness desired him to put parts to them in the way of Concertos, in which form he threw the principal movements not already turned to that account by Mr. Avison. These were frequently performed to his Royal Highness and his friends by the late Mr. [Thomas] Pinto, at the head of a select band.[1]

Burney's daughter Esther, who acquired a considerable reputation as a harpsichord player, was born in 1749, and must therefore have been eleven or twelve years old when Burney returned to London in 1760. The string concertos that her playing inspired seem not to have survived.

VINCENZO TOMMASINI: LES FEMMES DE BONNE HUMEUR

The two most important Scarlatti arrangements after Avison's are both associated with the rise of neo-classicism in Italy during the early decades of the twentieth century: Tommasini's *Les Femmes de bonne humeur* and Casella's *Scarlattiana*. Along with them may be mentioned the somewhat later *Divertimento scarlattiano* and *Le petit chat* (a gloss on K30) by another Italian composer, Goffredo Petrassi.

The ballet *Les Femmes de bonne humeur* occupies a place in Vincenzo Tommasini's works analogous to that of *Pulcinella* in Stravinsky's, marking a shift from the impressionism of his earlier music towards the neo-classical tendencies of the works he produced after about 1923 (Stravinsky's *Pulcinella*, based on music by or attributed to Pergolesi, is actually a slightly later work, composed in 1919–20.) *Les Femmes de bonne humeur* dates from 1916 and was first produced by the Ballets Russes at the Teatro Costanzi, Rome, on 12 April 1917, with choreography by Massine. The well-known orchestral suite from the ballet followed in 1920.

The scenario is based on a comedy by Goldoni – a complicated story of a love affair between Costanza and Rinaldo, and their attempts to overcome the opposition of their parents. It is as full of disguises and mistaken identities as any of Scarlatti's operas. The music consists of an overture and twenty-two other numbers, each one based on a single Scarlatti sonata. In order to preserve continuity, transpositions are made and linking passages added. Except in the overture, repeats are omitted. The other main changes are summarized in Table 3; except where indicated in the second column, Tommasini retains the original tempo marking of Longo's edition.

TABLE 3 *Contents of Tommasini's 'Les Femmes de bonne humeur'*

No. Ballet title (tempo)	Source (tempo)	Remarks
1. Overture (Allegro)	K63	accidentals altered, bars 9, 11, 53 and 59
2. Serenade of Count Rinaldo (Andante cantabile)	K474	bars 17–28 and 45–9 omitted
3. Entry of Costanza and Mariuccia, and scene with Felicita (Presto)	K2	link to next number (22 bars)
4. Entry of Dorotea and Pasquina (Allegro)	K428	introduction (Vivo) added (4 bars); link to next number (5 bars)
5. Scene of Count Rinaldo and the four women (Presto)	K461	bars 49–56 and 65–77 omitted; link to next number (2 bars)
6. Scene of Rinaldo and Silvestra (Piùttosto presto che Allegro)	K419	transposed to G; bars 34–49 and 106–15 omitted; link to next number (9 bars)
7. Entry of Mariuccia and scene with Leonardo (Allegro)	K489	bars 9–16, 29–32 and 37–73 omitted; side-drum rolls added (5 bars)
8. Entry of Battista, and preparation of the supper (Allegro)	K435	
9. Entry of Old Luca (Allegro moderato)	K391 (Allegro)	bars 22–7, 37–40 and 50–5 omitted; final bar altered; link to next number (1 bar)
10. Supper scene (Presto)	K492	bars 44–80 omitted; last 2 bars replaced by link to next number
11. Dance of Mariuccia to guitar accompaniment (Allegro moderato)	K107 (Allegro)	bars 11–14, 24–7, 45–106, 123–30 and 133–4 omitted; some harmonies altered
12. Recitative (Moderato)	K358	freely based on material from K358
13. Battista's dance (Presto)	K17	bars 56–129 omitted
14. Recitative (Moderato)	K358	as for no. 12
15. Pas de deux, Mariuccia and Leonardo (Non presto, ma a tempo di ballo)	K430	transposed to D♭; bars 20–31 and 73–84 omitted; link to next number (5 bars)
16. Pas de trois, Mariuccia, Battista and Leonardo (Allegro)	K441	transposed to A; bars 65–80 omitted

17. Battista's flight and Luca's fall (Presto)	K373	link to next number (8 bars)
18. Costanza's dance and 'passage' of the beggar (Andante)	K87	bars 9–34 omitted
19. The conspiracy against Luca (Allegretto)	K101 (Allegro)	bars 42–3, 47–54 and 99–100 omitted; bars 104–17 altered as link to next number (6 bars)
20. Dance of Leonardo and Battista, dressed as women, with Old Luca (Andante)	K279	bars 33–6, 40–3 and 45–9 omitted; link to next number (3 bars)
21. Nicolo's disguise (Allegro)	K455	bars 32–8 omitted; bars 48–74 transposed down a 4th; bars 75–91 recast as 7 bars; bars 92–108 transposed up a 5th
22. Conspiracy of the women to mock Silvestra (Moderato)	K39	bars 74–118 and final bar omitted
23. Final scene (Presto)	K445	transposed to G; last 2 bars expanded as coda (14 bars)

ALFREDO CASELLA: SCARLATTIANA

Like Tommasini's ballet, Alfredo Casella's *Scarlattiana*, a 'divertimento on music by Domenico Scarlatti for piano and small orchestra', came on the wave of the neo-classical tide. It was composed in 1926 and first performed at Carnegie Hall, New York, on 22 January 1927 by the composer, with the New York Symphony Orchestra conducted by Otto Klemperer. It is a light, attractive, loosely structured piece in five movements, distinguished chiefly by its skilful and imaginative orchestration.

Each of Casella's movements introduces several Scarlatti themes, often in only fleeting references, and treats them quite freely. The main material is as follows:

1. Sinfonia (Lento, grave – Allegro molto vivace)	: K52, 81 and 345
2. Minuetto (Allegretto ben moderato e grazioso)	: K440, 380 and 132
3. Capriccio (Allegro vivacissimo ed impetuoso)	: K31, 90, 89 and 63
4. Pastorale (Andantino dolcemente mosso)	: K513, 202 and 426
5. Finale (Lento molto e grave – Presto vivacissimo)	: K147, 11, 487, 412 and 30.

These are by no means all the Scarlatti themes heard during the course of this divertimento. Identification of the others might provide hours of harmless diversion for connoisseurs of Scarlatti sonatas.

Scarlattiana has often been compared with Stravinsky's *Pulcinella*. It is, perhaps, a measure of the relative genius of the two composers that, while Stravinsky treats his borrowed material much less freely than Casella, his own personality is much more strongly felt.

JULIUS HARRISON: SUITE FOR STRINGS

Julius Harrison's Suite for string orchestra (or string quartet) dates from about the same time as Casella's *Scarlattiana*; it was published in 1925. Each of its three movements is a straightforward arrangement of a single Scarlatti sonata. Repeats are observed, and no cuts or additions are made. The movements are:

1. Praeludium (Allegro scherzando, non presto): K430 (transposed to C)
2. Sarabande (Andante con moto)   : K8 (transposed to A minor)
3. Capriccio (Presto, brillante)   : K20 (transposed to C)

ARTHUR BENJAMIN: SUITE FOR FLUTE AND STRINGS

The Australian-born composer Arthur Benjamin wrote his Suite for flute and strings in 1946. Although the title-page states that the music is 'freely adapted from piano sonatas by Domenico Scarlatti', Benjamin is much more faithful to the substance of the originals than any of the arrangers so far mentioned, with the exception of Julius Harrison. Only in the introduction to the first movement does Benjamin make any textual omissions, and he even retains many of Scarlatti's repeats. His five movements are mostly straightforward but skilful arrangements, with Scarlatti's implied harmonies filled out in many places, a few new counterpoints added, and the original ornaments fully written out. For the most part the flute takes the original top line, but repeated phrases are usually rescored, both to vary the texture and to allow the soloist a breathing-space. The material of Benjamin's suite is summarized in Table 4.

TABLE 4 *Contents of Benjamin's Suite for Flute and Strings*

Movement	Source (tempo)	Remarks
1. Introduzione (Maestoso e non troppo lento) ed Allegro	K217 (Andante)	bars 21–65 omitted; bars 75–6 replaced by 1 bar of subdominant harmony; bars 79–100 replaced by 2 cadential bars
	K418 (Allegro)	transposed to A
2. Allegro	K188 (Allegro)	2nd repeat omitted (except *ad lib* repeat of bars 137–48); coda added (3 bars)
3. Allegretto	K181 (Allegro)	2nd repeat omitted; some accidentals altered
4. Andante	K481 (Andante e cantabile)	transposed to F# minor; 2nd repeat omitted
5. Allegro di molto	K487 (Allegro)	transposed to A; 1 bar (rest) added after bar 89; last 3 bars expanded to 7; 2nd repeat omitted

APPENDIX II *Scarlatti's Will*

Testament

19 October [1749]

Don Domingo Scarlati

In the name of the all powerful God, Amen: Know by this public document, being my last will and testament, that I, Don Domingo Scarlati, Knight of the Order of St James, resident in this court, legitimate son of the legitimate marriage of Don Alexandro Scarlati and Doña Antonia Ansaloni his wife, now deceased, formerly residents of the city of Naples, in which city I was born, husband during my first marriage of Doña Cathalina Gentil, and at present in my second marriage of Doña Anastasia Maxarti: Being in sound health, by the infinite grace of our Lord God, and having the full judgment and natural understanding which his Divine majesty has granted me, believing steadfastly in the mysterious holy sacrament of the Blessed Trinity, Father, Son and Holy Ghost, three distinct persons in one true God, and in the Incarnation and Resurrection of our Lord Jesus Christ, true God and Man, and in all else believed and confessed by the Holy Mother Church, Catholic, Roman and Apostolic, under whose faith and beliefs I have lived and intend to live and to die as her son, albeit unworthy, and being fearfully aware that death might snatch away my life at any time, and desiring in the final parting from that life to have no temporal concern that might hinder my asking God, our true Lord, for forgiveness of my sins: Do authorize that my will should be drawn up in the following manner –

Firstly, commending my soul to our Lord God, who created it and redeemed it with the infinitely precious blood of His Son, our Lord Jesus Christ, that my body should be restored to the earth from which it was formed –

It is my wish that when it should serve the will of our Lord God to take me from this present life, my body should be clothed in or shrouded with the capitular cloak of the aforementioned Order of St James, as befits my being a Knight of that Order, and buried in the church, place and site chosen by my executors (or where I shall specify in a separate memorial), to whom I leave it to choose the form of my funeral and burial and to make arrangements for the same: On which day, if time allows (and if not on the day following), a Requiem Mass should be sung for me, with deacon[s], a vigil and responses, and fifty more said masses, each one paid for by a charitable payment of three reales de vellon,[1] one fourth of them celebrated by the Parish Church, and the remainder where and by whom my executors may specify –

In accordance with the customary requirements I leave to the Holy Places of Jerusalem an ex gratia payment for each of six reales de vellon, by means of which I discharge once and for all all obligations on my goods and chattels –

I declare that I shall leave a memorial signed in my own hand,[2] or in that of Dr Don Cristoval Romero de Torres, priest, chaplain to His Majesty in the royal chapel of the New Monarchs of Toledo, resident in this court and one of my executors nominated below, in my power or in his, in which I shall take action to foresee, command and declare the other matters that I desire, and those that might occur to me, and I desire that the clauses covered in this memorial should be discharged and carried out at all times inviolably, as part and portion of this my will and according to and in the manner in which it is to the letter here expressed, and this will take effect immediately after my death and be dealt with according to the usual protocol –

I allow and nominate as my executors the aforementioned Dr Don Cristoval Romero de Torres, priest, chaplain to His Majesty in the royal chapel of the New Monarchs of Toledo, and Doña Anastasia Maxarti, my wife, to whom and each acting individually and in their own right I give such power and authority as they may require, without any limitation whatsoever, to enter and take possession of all goods, property and effects remaining to me after my death, and to sell and dispose of them, according to what is necessary, either by public auction or otherwise, and from the proceeds to discharge and pay for what is contained in this my will, and in the other aforementioned document which remains as part and portion of it, even though the year of legal custody of my temporal affairs may have passed, because I naturally extend that time by whatever may be necessary –

And after all that I have here requested in my will, together with that contained in the memorial which I will leave, has been discharged and paid for, as the sole and universal heirs to all that remains from all my goods, property and assets, houses and furniture, credits, rights and shares, present and future, and that which for whatever reasons or cause I might receive or inherit, I allow and nominate Don Juan Antonio: Don Fernando: Doña Mariana: Don Alexandro: and Doña Maria Scarlati, my five legitimate children by the aforementioned Cathalina Gentil, my first wife, and Doña Barbara: Doña Rosa: Don Domingo: and Don Antonio Scarlati, also my legitimate children by my present and second wife, and any other children that it may be God's will to grant me by my present wife, so that all nine may inherit it with God's blessing and my own: And with respect to the aforementioned Doña Barbara, Doña Rosa, Don Domingo and Don Antonio Scarlati, my children not yet come of age, and naturally availing myself of the laws and rights of these kingdoms, I elect and nominate as tutor and guardian of their persons and belongings the aforementioned Doña Anastasia Maxarti, my wife and their mother, who is freed from the obligation of giving any sureties whatsoever due to the great satisfaction I have in her good wisdom and Christian behaviour, and without obligation I pray and beseech that the judge to whom this formal clause will be presented should grant her this said duty, for such is my wish –

I hereby revoke, annul and renounce as having no further validity or effect all other wills, codicils, authorizations to draw up a will, and other last stipulations, which may have been drawn up or authorized before this will, in writing, by word of mouth, or in any other form, that they should have neither validity nor credence either within the law or outside it, and that as my last wishes and bequests only this, the will I now make and the aforementioned memorial which I shall leave as part and portion of it, should survive and be valid: In witness whereof I thus authorize it, before the present notary in the city of Madrid, on the 19th day of the month of October 1749, being called and sworn as witnesses Don Juan Joseph Ciordia Mirafuentes, priest, Joseph de la Rera, Andres Pasqual, Juan Antonio Alvarez and Miguel [?]Mexía, citizens and residents in this court,

the person authorizing it being known to me, the

[signed]   notary
Don Domingo Scarlatti

before me,
Gaspar Feliciano Garcia[3]

APPENDIX III *Two Unpublished Sonatas*

Source: Madrid, Real Conservatorio Superior de Música, MS Sign. Roda Leg. 35/504, pp. 51–6.

Editorial notes: The two keyboard sonatas in this appendix are here published for the first time by kind permission of the Real Conservatorio de Música, Madrid. They are attributed in the source to 'Scarlati'. The manuscript contains no tempo, dynamic or phrase markings. In the present edition the notation of accidentals has been brought into line with modern practice and bar numbers have been added. Other editorial markings are enclosed within square brackets, with the exception of the following:

Sonata I (D major)
bar 25 : right hand (r.h.), last 4 notes octave lower in MS
bar 25 : left hand (l.h.), 10th note *a'* in MS
bar 27 : r.h., 7th note *g#''*, 8th note *a''* in MS
bar 28 : r.h., 2nd note octave lower in MS
bar 57 : r.h., 9th note *c#''*, 11th note *a''*, 12th note *c#''* in MS
bar 58 : r.h., 1st note *c#''*, 2nd note *g''*, 3rd note *e''* in MS
bar 63 : l.h., last note *b* in MS
bar 68 : r.h., notes 2–5 octave lower in MS
bar 68 : l.h., notes 2–4 octave lower in MS

Sonata II (A major)
bars 71, 73, 74 : r.h., *f×'* notated *g'* in MS
bar 79 : r.h., 1st note *a#* in MS
bar 81 : l.h., 1st note *c#'* in MS
bars 100, 103 : r.h., 2nd and 3rd notes octave lower, 6th note *d''*, 7th note *e''* in MS.

The Madrid manuscript was evidently copied for use on an instrument of restricted compass, and most of the above editorial changes have been made to restore the music to its putative original. Possibly other passages, too, were originally notated at a higher pitch.

Sonata I (D major)

Sonata II (A major)

APPENDIX IV   *List of Compositions*

This catalogue lists Domenico Scarlatti's compositions in broadly the same order in which they are discussed in the foregoing pages. It is divided into six sections, as follows:

Operas	Serenatas
Oratorios	Sacred Music
Chamber Cantatas	Keyboard Works

Within the sections for operas, oratorios and serenatas the arrangement is chronological, and within those for chamber cantatas and sacred music it is alphabetical by incipit or title. The keyboard works follow the now standard numbering of Kirkpatrick's facsimile edition (New York, 1971) and of the catalogue in his monograph on Scarlatti (1953). Since Longo's edition (and the literature based on it) is still widely used, a cross-index from Longo to Kirkpatrick is also provided.

Except in the case of the published keyboard works, the sources of which are fully discussed in the text, the present locations of known manuscript sources are indicated. Library sigla are those used in *RISM (Répertoire Internationale des Sources Musicales)*, series A. They are as follows:

A–Wgm	Vienna, Gesellschaft der Musikfreunde		Preussischer Kultur-besitz
A–Wn	Vienna, Österreichische Nationalbibliothek	D–Bds	Berlin (East), Deutsche Staatsbibliothek
B–Bc	Brussels, Conservatoire Royal de Musique	D–Dlb	Dresden, Sächsische Landesbibliothek
		D–Hs	Hamburg, Staats–und Universitätsbibliothek
D–B	Berlin (West), Staatsbibliothek	D–Mbs	Munich, Bayerische Staatsbibliothek

D–MÜs Münster, Diözesan-Bibliothek (Santini MSS)

D–SWl Schwerin, Wissenschaftliche Allgemeinbibliothek

E–Mc Madrid, Real Conservatorio de Música

E–Mn Madrid, Biblioteca Nacional

E–Mp Madrid, Palacio Real

E–MO Montserrat, Monasterio de Santa Maria

E–V Valladolid, Cathedral

F–Pc Paris, Conservatoire Nationale de Musique [in F–Pn]

F–Pn Paris, Bibliothèque Nationale

GB–Lam London, Royal Academy of Music

GB–Lbl London, British Library

GB–Lcm London, Royal College of Music

GB–Mp Manchester, Central Public Library

I–Bc Bologna, Civico Museo Bibliografico Musicale

I–Bsp Bologna, Basilica di San Petronio

I–Fc Florence, Conservatorio di Musica Luigi Cherubini

I–Gi(l) Genoa, Conservatorio di Musica Nicolò Paganini

I–Mc Milan, Conservatorio di Musica Giuseppe Verdi

I–Nc Naples, Conservatorio di Musica San Pietro a Majella

I–Pca Padua, Biblioteca Antoniana

I–PAc Parma, Conservatorio di Musica Arrigo Boito

I–Rsc Rome, Conservatorio di Musica Santa Cecilia

I–Rvat Rome, Biblioteca Apostolica Vaticana

I–Vc Venice, Conservatorio di Musica Benedetto Marcello

I–Vlevi Venice, Fondazione Ugo e Olga Levi

I–Vnm Venice, Biblioteca Nazionale Marciana

I–Vsf Venice, Convento San Francesco della Vigna

P–Em Elvas, Biblioteca Pública Horténsia

P–G Guimarães, Arquivo Municipal Alfredo Pimenta

P–Lf Lisbon, Fábrica da Sé Patriarcal

P–VV Vila Viçosa, Paço Ducal

US–NH Yale, University, School of Music

US–Wc Washington, Library of Congress

In addition to standard abbreviations and contractions, the following are used:

A	alto, contralto	org	organ
B	bass	S	soprano
bc	basso continuo	str	strings
fl(s)	flute(s)	T	tenor
hn(s)	horn(s)	tr(s)	trumpet(s)
inst(s)	instruments	va	viola
movt	movement	vc	violoncello
ob(s)	oboe(s)	vn(s)	violin(s)

Works of doubtful authenticity are indicated by an asterisk (★).

OPERAS

Cap – Rome, Teatro Capranica
PR – Naples, Palazzo Regio

PZ – Rome, Palazzo Zuccari
SB – Naples, Teatro San Bartolomeo

Title, genre	Librettist	Sources	First performance; remarks
L'Ottavia ristituita al trono, melodramma	G. Convo	I–Nc Rari 7.1.21 (32 arias, 2 duets, score)	SB, ?Nov. 1703
Il Giustino, dramma per musica	Convo, after Beregan	F–Pn Rés. Vmc. ms. 71 (10 arias); I–Nc Rari 7.1.21 (21 arias, 3 duets, score)	PR, 19 Dec. 1703
L'Irene, dramma per musica	?Convo, after G. F. Roberti	F–Pn Rés. Vmc. ms. 71 (10 arias); I–Nc Rari 7.1.20 (32 arias, 1 duet, score)	SB, Carnival 1704; revision of Pollarolo's setting, 1695
La Silvia, dramma pastorale	Capece	—	PZ, 27 Jan. 1710

Tolomeo et Alessandro, ovvero La corona disprezzata, dramma per musica	Capece	Arrigo Perrone (Act 1, score)	PZ, 19 Jan. 1711
L'Orlando, ovvero La gelosa pazzia, dramma	Capece	—	PZ, Feb. 1711
Tetide in Sciro, dramma per musica	Capece	_I–Vsf_ (score); _I–Nc_ (8 arias, 2 trios, short score)	PZ, ?10 Jan. 1712; extracts ed. T. Ochlewski (Kraków, n.d.)
Ifigenia in Aulide, dramma per musica	Capece	_D–Dlb_ 1–F–30 (1 aria, score)	PZ, 11 Jan. 1713
Ifigenia in Tauri, dramma per musica	Capece	_D–Dlb_ 1–F–30 (3 arias, score)	PZ, ?15 Feb. 1713
Amor d'un ombra e gelosia d'un aura, dramma per musica	Capece	_D–Hs_ M/A 708 (score); overture and arias pubd. London, 1720	PZ, 15 Jan. 1714; as _Narciso_, London, King's Theatre, 30 May 1720 (rev. P. A. Rolli and T. Rosein-grave); _D–Hs_ score is of London version.
Ambleto, dramma per musica	A. Zeno and P. Pariati	_I–Bc_ DD.47 (1 aria, score)	Cap, Carnival 1715
Intermedi pastorali, inter-mezzo [Elpina e Silvano]	?	—	Cap, Carnival 1715; probably not by Scarlatti
La Dirindina, farsetta	G. Gigli	_I–Vlevi_ (score)	?; ed. F. Degrada (Milan, 1985)
Berenice, regina d' Egitto, ovvero Le gare d'amore e di politica, dramma per musica	A. Salvi (adapted)	_D–MÜs_ 185 (5 arias, score)	Cap, Carnival 1718; collaboration with N. Porpora

Sinfonias (*F–Pc, Rés. 2364*)

No.	Key	Movements	Scoring	Remarks
1.	A major	Grave–Presto Adagio Allegrissimo presto	str (3 vns), bc	
2.	G major	Allegro Grave Minuet (Allegro)	fl, ob, str (3 vns, vc), bc	
3.	G major	Allegrissimo Grave Allegrissimo	str (3 vns), bc	
4.	D major	Tempo di marciata– Presto Adagio Prestissimo	ob, str, bc	
5.	a minor	Allegro Adagio	str (2 vns), bc	
6.	D major	Allegro Grave e staccato Allegro	ob, str (2 vns), bc	
7.	C major	Presto Adagio e staccato Allegrissimo	str, bc	
8.	Bb major	Allegro Grave Minuet (Allegro)	ob, str, bc	
9.	d minor	Presto–Allegro Minuet	ob, str, bc	
10.	G major	Allegro Grave Allegro	ob, str (3 vns), bc	
11.	C major	Allegro Adagio Minuet (Allegro)	ob, str, bc	
12.	G major	Allegro Grave Presto	ob, str, bc	Overture to *Amor d'un ombra/Narciso*

13. Bb major	Presto Grave Presto	ob, str, bc	Overture to *Tolomeo et* *Alessandro* ; F–Pc D.12741(7)
14. G major	Allegro–Presto Adagio Minuet (Allegro)	fl, ob, str, bc	
15. Bb major	Allegro Grave Allegro	ob, str, bc	
16. A major	Allegro Grave Allegro	ob, str, bc	Overture to *Tetide in Sciro*; 1st movt incomplete
★17. C major	Allegro e presto Largo e staccato Presto	2 obs, str, bc	anonymous

ORATORIOS

Title	Librettist	Source	First performance
La conversione di Clodoveo	C. S. Capece	—	Rome, Palazzo Zuccari, 1709

Cantata da recitarsi
  . . . la notte del
  Ss.mo Natale
	F. M. Gasparri	—	Rome, Vatican, 24 Dec 1714

CHAMBER CANTATAS

Incipit [Title] (Author), date	Scoring	Sources; remarks
A chi nacque infelice	A, bc	I–Bsp L.1.S; ed. L. Bianchi (Milan, 1958)
Ah, sei troppo infelice, 30 July 1705	S, bc	GB–Lam 93, I–Bsp L.1.S; ed. L. Bianchi (Milan, 1958)
Al fin diviene amante	S/A, bc	D–MÜs 866, F–Pc X.118B, F–Pn Vm7.58, F–Pn Rés. Vmc. ms. 70

Alla caccia di tiranna beltà	A, bc	*I–Rsc* G.Ms. 380
Alme dilette, e care [La virtù in trionfo] (Ignazio de Bonis), 24 Sept. 1711	S, insts, bc	music lost, text in G. Ghezzi: *Le belle arti* . . . (Rome, 1711) (see Piperno, 1982, pp. 196–7)
Amare e tacere, temere e sperar	S, bc	*F–Pn* Rés. Vmc. ms. 70
Amenissimi prati, fiorite piagge	B, bc	*GB–Lbl* Add. 14166; ed. L. Hautus (Cologne, 1971)
Avrei ben folle il core	S, bc	*F–Pn* Rés. Vmc. ms. 81
Bella rosa adorata, cara pompa di Flora	S, bc	*I–Gi(l)* B.2b.46 (*olim* A.1.11), *I–Nc*
★ *Belle pupille care*, 1697	S, bc	*D–MÜs* 864, *F–Pn* Vm7.55, *GB–Mp* Q544/ 51; probably by Francesco Scarlatti
Cara qualhor lontano	S, bc	*D–Mbs* 3188
Care pupille belle, July 1702	S, 2 vns, bc	*D–MÜs* 3963
★ *Che pretendi, o tiranna*	S, bc	*D–MÜs* 864, *F–Pn* Rés. Vmc. ms. 70 ['Alessandro Scarlatti'], *F–Pn* Rés. Vmc. ms. 79 ['Aless.o Scarlatti']
Che si peni in amore	A, bc	*D–MÜs* 866
Che vidi, o ciel	S, 2 vns, bc	*A–Wn* 17664, *I–Rsc* 491 (modern copy by V. Argenti)
Chi in catene ha il mio core	S, bc	*F–Pc* X.638, *F–Pn* Rés. Vmc. ms. 70
Con qual cor mi chiede pace	S, bc	*GB–Lbl* R.M.23.b.27
★ *Dal bel volto d'Irene*	S, bc	*F–Pc* D11858
Deh che fate o mie pupille	S, bc	*I–Pca*
Di Fille vendicarmi vorrei	S, bc	*GB–Lbl* R.M.23.b.27
Dir vorrei, ah m'arrossisco	S, 2 vns, bc	*A–Wn* 17664, *I–Rsc* 491 (modern copy by V. Argenti)
Dopo lungo servire, 2 July 1702	A, 2 vns, bc	*D–MÜs* 3962
★ *Dorme la rosa, aurette grate* (B. Pamphili)	S/A, bc	*B–Bc* 15.173, *D–B* 30226, *D–MÜs* 2459 ['Fran.co Mancini'], *F–Pn* Rés. Vmc. ms. 69 ['Mancini'],

		GB–Ouf 18.d.1 ['Mancini'], *I–Nc* 28 (*olim* 33.3.33) ['Francesco Mancini'], *I–Nc* 183 (*olim* 33.3.32) ['Fran.co Mancini'], *I–Rc* 2248 ['Mancini'], *I–Rvat* Vat.lat. 10206 (text only)
E pur per mia sventura	S, bc	*US–Wc* M.1621.A2.S
E temerario ardire	S, bc	*D–Mbs* 3188
Fille già più non parlo	S, bc	*GB–Lbl* R.M.23.b.27
Già che al partir t'astringe	S, bc	*F–Pn* Rés. Vmc. ms. 81
★ *In questa lacrimosa orrida valle* [Tantalo sitibondo]	S, bc	*F–Pc* D11856, *US–Bp*, 360.10.v.4 (A. Scarlatti)
★ *La cagion delle mie pene*	S, bc	*F–Pn* Rés. Vmc. ms. 73, *GB–Lbl* Add. 29249 (A. Scarlatti)
Lontan da te mio bene	S, bc	*D–Mbs* 3188
Mio ben mi fido, ma pur sento	S, bc	*F–Pc* D11856 (incomplete), *F–Pn* Rés. Vmc. ms. 75
★ *Mi tormenta il pensiero*, 10 March 1701	S, bc	*D–MÜs* 864, *F–Pn* Vm7.58, *F–Pn* Rés. Vmc. ms. 81 ['Alessandro Scarlatti']
Ninfe belle e voi pastori	S, bc	*I–PAc* CF.VI.44(34477)
No, non fuggire o Nice	S, bc	*GB–Lbl* R.M.23.b.27
Ogni core innamorato, Sept. 1724	S, bc	*F–Pc* D11856
★ *Onde della mia Nera*	A/S, bc	*A–Wgm* VI 6793, *B–Bc* 15.172, *D–B* 19653, *D–SWl* 4820, *I–Fc* B.2428
O qual meco Nice cangiata	S, 2 vns, bc	*A–Wn* 17664, *GB–Lbl* R.M.23.b.27, *I–Rsc* 491 (modern copy by V. Argenti)
Pende la vita mia	S, bc	*D–SWl* 4819
Perché vedi ch'io t'amo, Feb. 1703 (or 1705)	S, bc	*F–Pn* Rés. Vmc. ms. 73
Piangete, occhi dolenti	S, 2 vns, bc	*A–Wn* 17664, *I–Rsc* 491 (modern copy by V. Argenti)

★ *Piango ogn'ora del mio core*, 19 May 1703	S, bc	F–*Pn* Rés. Vmc. ms. 73, GB–*Lbl* Add. 31511 (A. Scarlatti)
Povero cor fedele	S, bc	F–*Pn* Rés. Vmc. ms. 70
Pur nel sonno almen tal'ora (P. Metastasio)	S, 2 vns, bc	A–*Wn* 17664, GB–*Lbl* R.M.23.b.27, I–*Rsc* 491 (modern copy by V. Argenti); ed. L. Bianchi (Rome, 1963)
★ *Qui dove a pie' d'un colle*	S, bc	D–*MÜs* 3902, F–*Pc* F.G. 10503 [A. Scarlatti], F–*Pn* Rés. Vmc. ms. 73, I–*Nc* 34.5.12
Qual pensier, quale ardire ti guida?	S, bc	GB–*Lbl* R.M.23.b.27
Quando miro il vostro foco	A, bc	I–*Pca*
★ *Quando penso a Daliso*	S, bc	GB–*Lcm* 580, I–*Rvat* Chigi Q VI 79 [D. Fregiotti]
Rimirai la rosa un dì	A, bc	I–*Pca*
Scritte con falso inganno	S, 2 vns, bc	A–*Wn* 17664
Se dicessi ch'io t'amo	S, bc	D–*Mbs* 3188
Se fedele tu m'adori	S, 2 vns, bc	A–*Wn* 17664, I–*Rsc* 491 (modern copy by V. Argenti)
Se la sorte crudele mi divise	S, bc	F–*Pn* Rés. Vmc. ms. 70
★ *Selve, caverne e monti*	S, bc	D–*MÜs* 1901 ['Handel'], GB–*Lbl* Add. 14165, GB–*Lbl* Add. 14182 [anon]; ed. L. Hautus (Kassel, 1973)
Se per un sol momento	S, S, bc	GB–*Lbl* R.M.23.b.27
Se sai qual sia la pena	S, bc	I–*PAc* CF.VI.44(34478)
Se ti dicesse un core	S, bc	GB–*Lbl* R.M.23.b.27
★ *Sono un'alma tormentata*	S, bc	I–*Nc* Q.5.2, I–*Nc* 34.5.4; by ? Alessandro Scarlatti
Sospendi o man per poco	S, bc	GB–*Lbl* R.M.23.b.27
Sovra l'egizia arena [La Cleopatra]	A, bc	F–*Pc* D 11841
★ *Su la sponda fiorita di limpido ruscello*, 20 Aug.?1718	S, bc	GB–*Lbl* Add. 14215, I–*Nc* 9.7.10 (?lost)
★ *T'amai Clori t'amai*	S, bc	D–*B* 30226 [anon]
Tinte a note di sangue	S, 2 vns, bc	A–*Wn* 17664, I–*Rsc* 491 (modern copy by V. Argenti)

Ti ricorda o bella Irene	S, bc	*GB–Lbl* R.M.23.b.27
Tirsi caro–Amata Fille	S, S, bc	*GB–Lbl* R.M.23.b.27
* *Tirsi, mentr'io dormiva*	S, bc	*D–Mbs* 3188
Tu mi chiedi o mio ben	S, bc	*D–MÜs* 864
V'adoro o luci belle, ?1699	S, bc	*US–Wc* M.1621.A2.S
* *Vago il ciel non saria*	S, bc	*E–Mn* M2244, *D–MÜs* 3907, *GB–Lcm* 685
* *Vuoi ch'io spiri tra i sospiri* [Amante desideroso di morire per libberarsi dall'amore]	S, bc	*A–Wn* 17683 (19th-century copy), *D–MÜs* 3909, *D–SWl* 4824, *F–Pc* D11858; by ? Alessandro Scarlatti

SERENATAS

Title (librettist)	Performance	Sources; remarks
Il concilio degli dei (P. Riccio)	Naples or Sicily, 1704	music lost
* [Unidentified serenata for Prince Vaini (G. B. F. Zappi)]	Palazzo Vaini, Rome; 25 Aug. 1712	music and text lost
Applauso devoto [Il Tempo, Il Sonno, L'Eternità] (C. S. Capece)	Rome, Palazzo Zuccari, 12 Sept. 1712	music lost
Applauso genetliaco [Circe, Aurora, Ulisse]	Palazzo del Marques de Fontes, 1714	music lost
Contesa delle stagioni [Primavera, Estate, Autunno, Inverno]	Lisbon, Royal Palace, 7 Sept. 1720	*I–Vnm* 9769 (Part I only, score): S, S, A, T, chorus, fl, 2 trs, 2 hns, str, bc
Cantata pastorale [Tirsi, Olindo, Rosalba, Delmira, Damone, Polidora]	Lisbon, Royal Palace, 27 Dec. 1720	music lost
[Unidentified serenata]	Lisbon, Royal Palace, 7 Sept. 1722	music and text lost
Le nozze di Baco e d'Arianna	Lisbon, Royal Palace, 27 Dec. 1722	music lost
Festeggio armonico [Fama, Venere, Cleride, Dori, Ibero, Tago, Coro di Nereidi]	Lisbon, Royal Palace, 11 Jan. 1728	music lost

SACRED MUSIC

Work (date)	Scoring	Sources (scores unless otherwise indicated); remarks
* [Capriccio fugato a dodici (Fuga estemporanea)]	[SATB, SATB, str, bc]	D–Mbs Coll. Mus. Max. 129, D–MÜs 3960, D–MÜs 3969, GB–Lbl Egerton 2451; no text, ed. P. Winter (Cologne, 1969), see Hautus (1971)
Cibavit nos Dominus (c. 1708)	SATB	I–Rlib (parts)
* Dixit Dominus	?	lost, see A. Soler: Llave de la modulacion (Madrid, 1762), p. 115
Iste confessor	S, SATB, org	I–Rvat Bas. Giulia V–32 (score and parts); ed. in Musica sacra, iii (Milan, 1879)
Laetatus sum	S, A, SATB, org	P–VV Maço CXIII/7 (parts)
* Lauda Jerusalem	?	lost, see A. Soler: op. cit., p. 115
* Laudate pueri	SATB, SATB, bc	P–Lf 198–2 (parts); probably by D. Scarlatti
Magnificat	SATB	D–MÜs 3959
* Memento Domine David	SATB	D–Bds, D–Dlb, D–Mbs Coll. Mus. Max. 129, D–MÜs 3960, F–Pc, GB–Lbl Add. 14166, GB–Lbl Egerton 2451, I–Bc, I–Mc, I–Nc 22–4–11; by ? Alessandro Scarlatti
Miserere, e minor	SATB, SATB	I–Rvat Bas. Giulia V–31 (parts)
Miserere, g minor	SATB, SATB	I–Rvat Bas. Giulia V–31 (autograph parts), P–Em
Missa, D major	SATB, SATB, 2 obs, 2 hns, 2 trs, timpani, 2 vns, org	Aránzazu, Santuario (score and incomplete parts)

Missa 'La stella', a minor (*c.* 1708)	SATB, org	*I–Rlib* (parts)
Missa quatuor vocum	SATB	*E–Mp* Capilla 102 (choir-book), *E–MO* AM 2716; ed. L. Bianchi (Rome, 1961)
Nisi quia Dominus (?1708)	SATB, org	*I–Rlib* (parts)
Pange lingua (*c.* 1708)	SATB	*I–Rlib* (parts); incomplete, lacks T
Salve regina, A major (1756–7)	S, str, bc	*D–B* Winterfeld 13, *D–MÜs* 3514, *I–Bc* KK95, *I–Nc* 22–4–2; ed. R. Ewerhart (Cologne, 1960), ed. R. Leppard (London, 1979)
Salve regina, a minor	S, A, org	*I–Bc* KK93 (score and parts); ed. L. Hautus (Kassel, 1971)
Stabat mater	SSSSAATTBB, bc	*A–Wn* 16739, *D–B* Mb.o.605 [lost], *D–Mbs* Coll. Mus. Max. 66, *D–MÜs* 3961, *I–Bc* KK92, *I–Vc* 152, *US–G.* B. Weston, private collection; ed. A. Casella (Rome, 1941), ed. J. Jürgens (Mainz, 1973)
Te Deum (?1721)	SSAATTBB, org	*P–G* 92, *P–Lf* 198/3, *P–VV* Maço CXIII/6 (parts)
Te gloriosus	SATB, bc	*P–Lf* 198/1

KEYBOARD WORKS

K – ed. R. Kirkpatrick: *D. Scarlatti: Complete Keyboard Works in Facsimile* (New York, 1971); also, ed. K. Gilbert: *D. Scarlatti: Sonates* (Paris, 1971–84)

L – ed. A. Longo: *Opere complete per clavicembalo di Domenico Scarlatti* (Milan, 1906–8); s = supplement

F – ed. Emilia Fadini: *D. Scarlatti: Sonate per clavicembalo* (Milan, 1978–)

P – catalogue in G. Pestelli: *Le sonate di Domenico Scarlatti* (Turin, 1967)

K	Key	L	F	P	K	Key	L	F	P
1	d minor	366	517	57	42	Bb major	s36	553	120
2	G major	388	518	58	43	g minor	40	1	133
3	a minor	378	519	59	44	F major	432	2	116
4	g minor	390	520	60	45	D major	265	3	230
5	d minor	367	521	61	46	E major	25	4	179
6	F major	479	522	62	47	Bb major	46	5	115
7	a minor	379	523	63	48	c minor	157	6	87
8	g minor	488	524	64	49	C major	301	7	178
9	d minor	413	525	65	50	f minor	440	8	144
10	d minor	370	526	66	51	Eb major	20	9	151
11	c minor	352	527	67	52	d minor	267	10	41
12	g minor	489	528	68	53	D major	261	11	161
13	G major	486	529	69	54	a minor	241	12	147
14	G major	387	530	70	55	G major	335	13	117
15	e minor	374	531	71	56	c minor	356	14	50
16	Bb major	397	532	72	57	Bb major	s38	15	108
17	F major	384	533	73	58	c minor	158	16	39
18	d minor	416	534	74	59	F major	71	17	22
19	f minor	383	535	75	60	g minor	13	18	29
20	E major	375	536	76	61	a minor	136	19	16
21	D major	363	537	77	62	A major	45	20	49
22	c minor	360	538	78	63	G major	84	21	32
23	D major	411	539	79	64	d minor	58	22	33
24	A major	495	540	80	65	A major	195	24	142
25	f# minor	481	541	81	66	Bb major	496	26	134
26	A major	368	542	82	67	f# minor	32	27	125
27	b minor	449	543	83	68	Eb major	114	28	7
28	E major	373	544	84	69	f minor	382	29	42
29	D major	461	545	85	70	Bb major	50	30	21
30	g minor	499	546	86	71	G major	81	31	17
31	g minor	231	53	19	72	C major	401	32	1
32	d minor	423	547	14	73	c minor	217	33	30
33	D major	424	39	130	74	A major	94	34	34
34	d minor	s7	548	15	75	G major	53	35	35
35	g minor	386	549	20	76	g minor	185	36	23
36	a minor	245	23	91	77	d minor	168	38	10
37	c minor	406	37	2	78	F major	75	40	26
38	F major	478	25	97	79	G major	80	41	204
39	A major	391	550	53	80	G major	–	41	28
40	c minor	357	551	119	81	e minor	271	42	13
41	d minor	–	552	37	82	F major	30	43	25

K	Key	L	F	P	K	Key	L	F	P
83	A major	s31	44	31	124	G major	232	83	110
84	c minor	10	45	45	125	G major	487	84	152
85	F major	166	46	24	126	c minor	402	85	128
86	C major	403	47	122	127	Ab major	186	86	198
87	b minor	33	48	43	128	bb minor	296	87	199
88	g minor	36	49	8	129	c minor	460	88	148
89	d minor	211	50	12	130	Ab major	190	89	272
90	d minor	106	51	9	131	bb minor	300	90	154
91	G major	176	52	11	132	C major	457	91	295
92	d minor	362	54	44	133	C major	282	92	218
93	g minor	336	55	38	134	E major	221	93	143
94	F major	–	507	27	135	E major	224	94	234
★95	C major	358	554	–	136	E major	377	95	113
96	D major	465	62	210	137	D major	315	96	231
★97	g minor	–	555	5	138	d minor	464	97	95
98	e minor	325	56	219	139	c minor	6	138	126
99	c minor	317	57	135	140	D major	107	139	127
100	C major	355	58	232	141	d minor	422	508	271
101	A major	494	59	156	★142	f# minor	–	509	240
102	g minor	89	60	88	★143	C major	–	510	267
103	G major	233	61	233	★144	G major	–	511	316
104	G major	442	63	109	★145	D major	369	512	105
105	G major	204	64	90	★146	G major	349	513	106
106	F major	437	65	197	147	e minor	376	514	48
107	F major	474	66	98	148	a minor	64	98	291
108	g minor	249	67	92	149	a minor	93	99	241
109	a minor	138	68	290	150	F major	117	100	205
110	a minor	469	69	129	151	F major	330	101	238
111	g minor	130	70	99	152	G major	179	102	114
112	Bb major	298	71	94	153	G major	445	103	235
113	A major	345	72	160	154	Bb major	96	104	183
114	A major	344	73	141	155	Bb major	197	105	208
115	c minor	407	74	100	156	C major	101	106	248
116	c minor	452	75	111	157	C major	405	107	391
117	C major	244	76	181	158	c minor	4	108	123
118	D major	122	77	266	159	C major	104	109	418
119	D major	415	78	217	160	D major	15	110	131
120	d minor	215	79	146	161	D major	417	111	216
121	g minor	181	80	93	162	E major	21	112	162
122	D major	334	81	118	163	E major	63	113	206
123	Eb major	111	82	180	164	D major	59	114	274

K	Key	L	F	P	K	Key	L	F	P
165	C major	52	115	292	205	F major	s23	492	171
166	C major	51	116	190	206	E major	257	154	307
167	F major	329	117	200	207	E major	371	155	140
168	F major	280	118	182	208	A major	238	156	315
169	G major	331	119	247	209	A major	428	157	209
170	C major	303	120	164	210	G major	123	158	293
171	G major	77	121	153	211	A major	133	159	277
172	Bb major	s40	122	313	212	A major	135	160	155
173	b minor	447	123	51	213	d minor	108	161	288
174	c minor	410	124	149	214	D major	165	162	430
175	a minor	429	125	136	215	E major	323	163	281
176	d minor	163	126	163	216	E major	273	164	320
177	D major	364	127	184	217	a minor	42	165	287
178	D major	162	128	392	218	a minor	392	166	237
179	g minor	177	129	89	219	A major	393	167	278
180	G major	272	130	192	220	A major	342	168	309
181	A major	194	131	253	221	A major	259	169	215
182	A major	139	132	207	222	A major	309	170	236
183	f minor	473	133	150	223	D major	214	171	188
184	f minor	189	134	102	224	D major	268	172	225
185	f minor	173	135	121	225	C major	351	173	202
186	f minor	72	136	46	226	c minor	112	174	101
187	f minor	285	137	145	227	b minor	347	175	52
188	a minor	239	140	213	228	Bb major	399	176	224
189	Bb major	143	141	257	229	Bb major	199	177	139
190	Bb major	250	142	256	230	c minor	354	178	47
191	d minor	207	143	18	231	C major	409	179	393
192	Eb major	216	144	322	232	e minor	62	180	317
193	Eb major	142	145	254	233	e minor	467	181	497
194	F major	28	146	479	234	g minor	49	182	286
195	F major	s18	147	185	235	G major	154	183	172
196	g minor	38	148	244	236	D major	161	184	201
197	b minor	147	149	124	237	D major	308	185	446
198	e minor	22	150	132	238	f minor	27	186	55
199	C major	253	151	276	239	f minor	281	187	56
200	C major	54	152	242	240	G major	s29	188	368
201	G major	129	153	252	241	G major	180	189	431
202	Bb major	498	488	173	242	C major	202	190	243
203	e minor	380	489	96	243	C major	353	191	394
204a	f minor	—	490	170	244	B major	348	192	298
204b	f minor	—	491	255	245	B major	450	193	299

K	Key	L	F	P	K	Key	L	F	P
246	c# minor	260	194	296	288	D major	57	236	311
247	c# minor	256	195	297	289	G major	78	237	249
248	B♭ major	s35	196	187	290	G major	85	238	396
249	B♭ major	39	197	424	291	e minor	61	239	282
250	C major	174	198	461	292	e minor	24	240	223
251	C major	305	199	314	293	b minor	s44	241	157
252	E♭ major	159	200	203	294	d minor	67	242	470
253	E♭ major	320	201	239	295	d minor	270	243	211
254	c minor	219	202	186	296	F major	198	244	305
255	C major	439	203	226	297	F major	s19	245	448
256	F major	228	204	480	298	D major	s6	246	194
257	F major	169	205	138	299	D major	210	247	268
258	D major	178	206	494	300	A major	92	248	312
259	G major	103	207	469	301	A major	493	249	361
260	G major	124	208	304	302	c minor	7	250	279
261	B major	148	209	300	303	c minor	9	251	212
262	B major	446	210	301	304	G major	88	252	492
263	e minor	321	211	283	305	G major	322	253	397
264	E major	466	212	308	306	E♭ major	16	254	456
265	a minor	s32	213	168	307	E♭ major	115	255	449
266	B♭ major	48	214	251	308	C major	359	256	318
267	B♭ major	434	215	363	309	C major	454	257	333
268	A major	41	216	369	310	B♭ major	248	258	284
269	A major	307	217	432	311	B♭ major	144	259	227
270	C major	459	218	481	312	D major	264	260	334
271	C major	155	219	447	313	D major	192	261	398
272	B♭ major	145	220	518	314	G major	441	262	505
273	B♭ major	398	221	174	315	g minor	235	263	54
274	F major	297	222	491	316	F major	299	264	193
275	F major	328	223	330	317	F major	66	265	258
276	F major	s20	224	433	318	F# major	31	266	302
277	D major	183	225	275	319	F# major	35	267	303
278	D major	s15	226	434	320	A major	341	268	335
279	A major	468	227	306	321	A major	258	269	450
280	A major	237	228	395	322	A major	483	270	360
281	D major	56	229	289	323	A major	95	271	411
282	D major	484	230	166	324	G major	332	272	285
283	G major	318	231	482	325	G major	37	273	451
284	G major	90	232	169	326	C major	201	274	336
285	A major	91	233	321	327	C major	152	275	399
286	A major	394	234	410	328	G major	s27	276	485
287	D major	s9	235	310	329	C major	s5	277	337

K	Key	L	F	P	K	Key	L	F	P
330	C major	55	278	222	371	Eb major	17	317	264
331	Bb major	18	279	471	372	G major	302	318	402
332	Bb major	141	280	519	373	g minor	98	319	158
333	D major	269	281	338	374	G major	76	320	472
334	Bb major	100	282	412	375	G major	389	321	414
335	D major	s10	283	339	376	b minor	34	322	246
336	D major	337	284	262	377	b minor	263	323	245
337	G major	s26	285	340	378	F major	276	324	347
338	G major	87	286	400	379	F major	73	325	107
339	C major	251	287	189	380	E major	23	326	483
340	C major	105	288	420	381	E major	225	327	323
341	a minor	140	289	103	382	a minor	s33	328	508
342	A major	191	290	341	383	a minor	134	329	269
343	A major	291	291	495	384	C major	2	330	487
344	A major	295	292	221	385	C major	284	331	220
345	D major	306	293	342	386	f minor	171	332	137
346	D major	60	294	250	387	f minor	175	333	415
347	g minor	126	295	294	388	D major	414	334	370
348	G major	127	296	462	389	D major	482	335	331
349	F major	170	297	452	390	G major	234	336	348
350	F major	230	298	413	391	G major	79	337	364
351	Bb major	s34	299	165	392	Bb major	246	338	371
352	D major	s13	300	343	393	Bb major	74	339	326
353	D major	313	301	401	394	e minor	275	340	349
354	F major	68	302	486	395	E major	65	341	273
355	F major	s22	303	344	396	d minor	110	342	435
356	C major	443	493	488	397	D major	208	343	325
357	C major	s45	494	270	398	C major	218	344	493
358	D major	412	304	457	399	C major	274	345	458
359	D major	448	305	425	400	D major	213	346	228
360	Bb major	400	306	520	401	D major	365	347	436
361	Bb major	247	307	214	402	e minor	427	348	496
362	c minor	156	308	159	403	E major	470	349	437
363	c minor	160	309	104	404	A major	222	350	489
364	f minor	436	310	345	405	A major	43	351	438
365	f minor	480	311	112	406	C major	5	352	509
366	F major	119	312	263	407	C major	s4	353	521
367	F major	172	313	453	408	b minor	346	354	350
368	A major	s30	314	506	409	b minor	150	355	403
369	A major	240	315	259	410	Bb major	s43	356	372
370	Eb major	316	316	346	411	Bb major	69	357	351

K	Key	L	F	P	K	Key	L	F	P
412	G major	182	358	463	453	A major	–	516	280
413	G major	125	359	416	454	G major	184	398	423
414	D major	310	360	373	455	G major	209	399	354
415	D major	s11	361	175	456	A major	491	400	377
416	D major	149	362	454	457	A major	292	401	442
417	d minor	462	363	40	458	D major	212	402	260
418	F major	26	364	510	459	d minor	s14	403	167
419	F major	279	365	524	460	C major	324	404	378
420	C major	s2	366	352	461	C major	8	405	324
421	C major	252	367	459	462	f minor	438	406	474
422	C major	451	368	511	463	f minor	471	407	512
423	C major	102	369	455	464	C major	151	408	460
424	G major	289	370	374	465	C major	242	409	406
425	G major	333	371	426	466	f minor	118	410	501
426	g minor	128	372	500	467	f minor	476	411	513
427	G major	286	373	464	468	F major	226	412	507
428	A major	131	374	353	469	F major	431	413	514
429	A major	132	375	439	470	G major	304	414	379
430	D major	463	376	329	471	G major	82	415	327
431	G major	83	377	365	472	Bb major	99	416	475
432	G major	288	378	465	473	Bb major	229	417	355
433	G major	453	379	440	474	Eb major	203	418	502
434	d minor	343	380	498	475	Eb major	220	419	319
435	D major	361	381	466	476	g minor	340	420	427
436	D major	109	382	404	477	G major	290	421	419
437	F major	278	383	499	478	D major	12	422	503
438	F major	381	384	467	479	D major	s16	423	380
439	Bb major	47	385	473	480	D major	s8	424	381
440	Bb major	97	386	328	481	f minor	187	425	504
441	Bb major	s39	387	375	482	F major	435	426	356
442	Bb major	319	388	229	483	F major	472	427	407
443	D major	418	389	376	484	D major	419	428	428
444	d minor	420	390	441	485	C major	153	429	490
445	F major	385	391	468	486	C major	455	430	515
446	F major	433	392	177	487	C major	205	431	421
447	f# minor	294	393	191	488	Bb major	s37	432	382
448	f# minor	485	394	261	489	Bb major	s41	433	522
449	G major	444	395	405	490	D major	206	434	476
450	g minor	338	396	422	491	D major	164	435	484
451	a minor	243	397	366	492	D major	14	436	443
452	A major	–	515	195	493	G major	s24	437	383

K	Key	L	F	P	K	Key	L	F	P
494	G major	287	438	444	525	F major	188	469	529
495	E major	426	439	384	526	c minor	456	470	530
496	E major	372	440	332	527	C major	458	471	531
497	b minor	146	441	357	528	Bb major	200	472	532
498	b minor	350	442	367	529	Bb major	327	473	533
499	A major	193	443	477	530	E major	44	474	534
500	A major	492	444	358	531	E major	430	475	535
501	C major	137	445	385	532	a minor	223	476	536
502	C major	3	446	408	533	A major	395	477	537
503	Bb major	196	447	196	534	D major	11	478	538
504	Bb major	29	448	265	535	D major	262	479	539
505	F major	326	449	386	536	A major	236	480	540
506	F major	70	450	409	537	A major	293	481	541
507	Eb major	113	451	478	538	G major	254	482	542
508	Eb major	19	452	516	539	G major	121	483	543
509	D major	311	453	387	540	F major	s17	484	544
510	d minor	277	454	525	541	F major	120	485	545
511	D major	314	455	388	542	F major	167	486	546
512	D major	339	456	359	543	F major	227	487	547
513	C major	s3	457	176	544	Bb major	497	495	548
514	C major	1	458	389	545	Bb major	500	496	549
515	C major	255	459	417	546	g minor	312	497	550
516	d minor	s12	460	523	547	G major	s28	498	551
517	d minor	266	461	517	548	C major	404	499	552
518	F major	116	462	390	549	C major	s1	500	553
519	f minor	475	463	445	550	Bb major	s42	501	554
520	G major	86	464	362	551	Bb major	396	502	555
521	G major	408	465	429	552	d minor	421	503	556
522	G major	s25	466	526	553	d minor	425	504	557
523	G major	490	467	527	554	F major	s21	505	558
524	F major	283	468	528	555	f minor	477	506	559

Note: although included among the keyboard works, the following were probably originally written for vn and bc: K73, 77–8, 80–1 and 88–91.

Sonatas not included in Kirkpatrick's catalogue

Key	Tempo(s)	Source; edition
A major	Allegro	Lisbon, Instituto Português do Património Cultural
★A major	Allegro; Spiritoso	GB–Lbl Add. 14248
★A major	—	E–V 19; ed. A. Baciero (1978), pp. 47–50
★A major	—	E–Mc Roda Leg. 35/504
★C major	Presto	US–NH 18
★C major	Prestissimo	US–NH 19
★C major	Andantino	E–MO AM 1770
★D major	—	E–Mc Roda Leg. 35/504
★d minor	—	E–V 19; ed. A. Baciero (1978), pp. 41–6
d minor	—	Tenerife, private collection; ed. R. A. Martinez (1984), no. 3
★E major	—	ed. E. Granados: *D. Scarlatti: 26 sonatas ineditas* (Madrid etc., *c.* 1905), no. 13
★G major	—	E–V 19; ed. A. Baciero (1978), pp. 37–40
★g minor	—	I–Bc FF232 ('Fuga')

CROSS-INDEX FROM LONGO'S TO KIRKPATRICK'S NUMBERING

L	K	L	K	L	K	L	K
1	514	16	306	31	318	46	47
2	384	17	371	32	67	47	439
3	502	18	331	33	87	48	266
4	158	19	508	34	376	49	234
5	406	20	51	35	319	50	70
6	139	21	162	36	88	51	166
7	302	22	198	37	325	52	165
8	461	23	380	38	196	53	75
9	303	24	292	39	249	54	200
10	84	25	46	40	43	55	330
11	534	26	418	41	268	56	281
12	478	27	238	42	217	57	288
13	60	28	194	43	405	58	64
14	492	29	504	44	530	59	164
15	160	30	82	45	62	60	346

L	K	L	K	L	K	L	K
61	291	102	423	143	189	184	454
62	232	103	259	144	311	185	76
63	163	104	159	145	272	186	127
64	148	105	340	146	497	187	481
65	395	106	90	147	197	188	525
66	317	107	140	148	261	189	184
67	294	108	213	149	416	190	130
68	354	109	436	150	409	191	342
69	411	110	396	151	464	192	313
70	506	111	123	152	327	193	499
71	59	112	226	153	485	194	181
72	186	113	507	154	235	195	65
73	379	114	68	155	271	196	503
74	393	115	307	156	362	197	155
75	78	116	518	157	48	198	296
76	374	117	150	158	58	199	229
77	171	118	466	159	252	200	528
78	289	119	366	160	363	201	326
79	391	120	541	161	236	202	242
80	79	121	539	162	178	203	474
81	71	122	118	163	176	204	105
82	471	123	210	164	491	205	487
83	431	124	260	165	214	206	490
84	63	125	413	166	85	207	191
85	290	126	347	167	542	208	397
86	520	127	348	168	77	209	455
87	338	128	426	169	257	210	299
88	304	129	201	170	349	211	89
89	102	130	111	171	386	212	458
90	284	131	428	172	367	213	400
91	285	132	429	173	185	214	223
92	300	133	211	174	250	215	120
93	149	134	383	175	387	216	192
94	74	135	212	176	91	217	73
95	323	136	61	177	179	218	398
96	154	137	501	178	258	219	254
97	440	138	109	179	152	220	475
98	373	139	182	180	241	221	134
99	472	140	341	181	121	222	404
100	334	141	332	182	412	223	532
101	156	142	193	183	277	224	135

L	K	L	K	L	K	L	K
225	381	266	517	307	269	348	244
226	468	267	52	308	237	349	146
227	543	268	224	309	222	350	498
228	256	269	333	310	414	351	225
229	473	270	295	311	509	352	11
230	350	271	81	312	546	353	243
231	31	272	180	313	353	354	230
232	124	273	216	314	511	355	100
233	103	274	399	315	137	356	56
234	390	275	394	316	370	357	40
235	315	276	378	317	99	358	95
236	536	277	510	318	283	359	308
237	280	278	437	319	442	360	22
238	208	279	419	320	253	361	435
239	188	280	168	321	263	362	92
240	369	281	239	322	305	363	21
241	54	282	133	323	215	364	177
242	465	283	524	324	460	365	401
243	451	284	385	325	98	366	1
244	117	285	187	326	505	367	5
245	36	286	427	327	529	368	26
246	392	287	494	328	275	369	145
247	361	288	432	329	167	370	10
248	310	289	424	330	151	371	207
249	108	290	477	331	169	372	496
250	190	291	343	332	324	373	28
251	339	292	457	333	425	374	15
252	421	293	537	334	122	375	20
253	199	294	447	335	55	376	147
254	538	295	344	336	93	377	136
255	515	296	128	337	336	378	3
256	247	297	274	338	450	379	7
257	206	298	112	339	512	380	203
258	321	299	316	340	476	381	438
259	221	300	131	341	320	382	69
260	246	301	49	342	220	383	19
261	53	302	372	343	434	384	17
262	535	303	170	344	114	385	445
263	377	304	470	345	113	386	35
264	312	305	251	346	408	387	14
265	45	306	345	347	227	388	2

L	K	L	K	L	K	L	K
389	375	430	531	471	463	s12	516
390	4	431	469	472	483	s13	352
391	39	432	44	473	183	s14	459
392	218	433	446	474	107	s15	278
393	219	434	267	475	519	s16	479
394	286	435	482	476	467	s17	540
395	533	436	364	477	555	s18	195
396	551	437	106	478	38	s19	297
397	16	438	462	479	6	s20	276
398	273	439	255	480	365	s21	554
399	228	440	50	481	25	s22	355
400	360	441	314	482	389	s23	205
401	72	442	104	483	322	s24	493
402	126	443	356	484	282	s25	522
403	86	444	449	485	448	s26	337
404	548	445	153	486	13	s27	328
405	157	446	262	487	125	s28	547
406	37	447	173	488	8	s29	240
407	115	448	359	489	12	s30	368
408	521	449	27	490	523	s31	83
409	231	450	245	491	456	s32	265
410	174	451	422	492	500	s33	382
411	23	452	116	493	301	s34	351
412	358	453	433	494	101	s35	248
413	9	454	309	495	24	s36	42
414	388	455	486	496	66	s37	488
415	119	456	526	497	544	s38	57
416	18	457	132	498	202	s39	441
417	161	458	527	499	30	s40	172
418	443	459	270	500	545	s41	489
419	484	460	129	s1	549	s42	550
420	444	461	29	s2	420	s43	410
421	552	462	417	s3	513	s44	293
422	141	463	430	s4	407	s45	357
423	32	464	138	s5	329		
424	33	465	96	s6	298		
425	553	466	264	s7	34		
426	495	467	233	s8	480		
427	402	468	279	s9	287		
428	209	469	110	s10	335		
429	175	470	403	s11	415		

BIBLIOGRAPHY

Allorto, Riccardo: 'Clementi non ha plagiato Scarlatti', *Musica d'oggi*, new series, ii (1959), pp. 66–7

Álvarez Martinez, Maria del Rosario (ed.): *Obras inéditas para tecla* (Madrid, 1984)

—: 'Dos obras inéditas de Domenico Scarlatti', *Revista de musicologia*, viii (1985), pp. 51–6

Baciero, Antonio (ed.): *Nueva biblioteca española de música de teclado*, iii (Madrid, 1978)

Basso, Alberto: *La formazione storica ed estetica della sonata di Domenico Scarlatti* (dissertation, University of Turin, 1957)

—: 'Domenico Scarlatti', in *La musica*, iv (1966), pp. 159–77

Bauer, Luise: *Die Tätigkeit Domenico Scarlattis und der italienischen Meister in der ersten Hälfte des 18. Jahrhunderts in Spanien* (dissertation, University of Munich, 1933)

Benton, Rita: 'Form in the Sonatas of Domenico Scarlatti', *The Music Review*, xiii (1952), pp. 264–75

Bogianckino, Massimo: *L'arte clavicembalistica di Domenico Scarlatti* (Rome, 1956; English translation, Rome, 1967)

Bonucci, Rodolfo: 'Le sonate per violino e cembalo di Domenico Scarlatti', *Studi musicali*, xi (1982), pp. 249–59

Boyd, Malcolm: 'Nova Scarlattiana', *The Musical Times*, cxxvi (1985), pp. 589–93

Boydell, Brian: 'Domenico Scarlatti and his Irish Connection', in *European Music Yearbook 1985* (Dublin, 1985)

Burney, Charles: *A General History of Music* (London, 1776–89); ed. F. Mercer (London, 1935)

—: *Memoirs of the Life and Writings of the Abate Metastasio* (London, 1796)

—: *Dr Burney's Musical Tours in Europe*, ed. P. Scholes (London, 1959)

Cametti, Alberto: 'Carlo Sigismondo Capeci (1652–1728), Alessandro e Domenico Scarlatti e la Regina di Polonia in Roma', *Musica d'oggi*, xiii (1931), pp. 55–64

Casella, Alfredo: 'Le musiche vocali e strumentali', in *Gli Scarlatti . . .* (Siena, 1940), pp. 20–2

Cassingham, Jack Lee: *The Twelve Scarlatti–Avison Concertos of 1744* (dissertation, University of Missouri, Kansas City, 1968)

Choi, Seunghyun: *Newly Found Eighteenth Century Manuscripts of Domenico*

Scarlatti's Sonatas and their Relationship to other Eighteenth and Early Nineteenth Century Sources (dissertation, University of Wisconsin, 1974)

Clark, Jane: 'Domenico Scarlatti and Spanish Folk Music', *Early Music*, iv (1976), pp. 19–21

—: ' "His own worst enemy": Scarlatti: Some Unanswered Questions', *Early Music*, xiii (1985), pp. 542–7

Dale, Kathleen: 'Hours with Domenico Scarlatti', *Music and Letters*, xxii (1941), pp. 115–22

—: 'Domenico Scarlatti: his Unique Contribution to Keyboard Literature', *Proceedings of the Royal Musical Association*, lxxiv (1948), pp. 33–44

Daw, Stephen: 'Muzio Clementi as an Original Advocate, Collector and Performer, in Particular of J. S. Bach and D. Scarlatti', in *Bach, Handel, Scarlatti: Tercentenary Essays*, ed. P. Williams (Cambridge, 1985), pp. 61–74

Degrada, Francesco: 'Una sconosciuta esperienza teatrale di Domenico Scarlatti: *La Dirindina*', in *Il palazzo incantato: studi sulla tradizione del melodramma dal Barocco al Romanticismo* (Fiesole, 1979), pp. 67–97

Della Corte, Andrea: '*Tetide in Sciro*: l'opera di Domenico Scarlatti ritrovata', *La rassegna musicale*, xxvii (1957), pp. 281–9

Dent, Edward J.: *Alessandro Scarlatti: his Life and Works* (London, 1905; 2nd edition, 1960)

Fabbri, Mario: *Alessandro Scarlatti e il Principe Ferdinando de' Medici* (Florence, 1961)

Fienga, Pasquale: 'La véritable patrie et la famille d'Alessandro Scarlatti', *La revue musicale*, x (1929), pp. 227–36

Flood, W. H. Grattan: 'Domenico Scarlatti's Visit to Dublin, 1740–1', *The Musical Antiquary*, i (1910), pp. 178–81

Fuller, David: 'The "Dotted Style" in Bach, Handel, and Scarlatti', in *Bach, Handel, Scarlatti: Tercentenary Essays*, ed. P. Williams (Cambridge, 1985), pp. 99–117

Gálvez, Genoveva (ed.): *Treinta sonatas para clavicordio por Sebastian Albero* (Madrid, 1978)

Gerstenberg, Walter: *Die Klavier-Kompositionen Domenico Scarlattis* (Regensburg, 1933)

Gli Scarlatti (Alessandro – Francesco – Pietro – Domenico – Giuseppe) (Siena, 1940)

Griffin, Thomas: *The Late Baroque Serenata in Rome and Naples: a Documentary Study with Emphasis on Alessandro Scarlatti* (dissertation, University of California, Los Angeles, 1983)

Hamilton, Mary Neal: *Music in Eighteenth-Century Spain* (Urbana, 1937)

Hanley, Edwin: *Alessandro Scarlatti's Cantate da Camera: a Bibliographical Study* (dissertation, Yale University, 1963)

Hautus, Loek: 'Zu dem Domenico Scarlatti zugeschriebenen *Capriccio fugato a dodici*', *Die Musikforschung*, xxiv (1971), pp. 294–5

—: 'Beitrag zur Datierung der Klavierwerke Domenico Scarlattis', *Die Musikforschung*, xxvi (1973), pp. 59–61

Hopkinson, Cecil: 'Eighteenth-Century Editions of the Keyboard Compositions of Domenico Scarlatti', *Transactions of the Edinburgh Bibliographical Society*, iii (1948), pp. 47–71

Johnsson, Bengt: 'Eine unbekannte Sonate von Domenico Scarlatti', *Die Musikforschung*, xxxiv (1981), pp. 309–10

Kárpáti, János: *Domenico Scarlatti* (Budapest, 1959)

Keller, Hermann: *Domenico Scarlatti, ein Meister des Klaviers* (Leipzig, 1957)

Kirkpatrick, Ralph: *Domenico Scarlatti* (Princeton, 1953, and later editions)

—: 'Domenico Scarlatti's Choral Music', in *Essays on Music in Honor of Archibald Thompson Davison*, ed. R. Thompson (Cambridge, Massachusetts, 1957), pp. 243–6

—: 'Scarlatti Revisited in Parma and Venice', *Notes*, xxvii (1971), pp. 5–15

—: 'Who Wrote the Scarlatti Sonatas?', *Notes*, xxix (1973), pp. 426–31

Lang, Paul Henry: 'Scarlatti: 300 years on', *The Musical Times*, cxxvi (1985), pp. 584–9

Lindley, Mark: 'Keyboard Technique and Articulation: Evidence for the Performance Practices of Bach, Handel and Scarlatti', in *Bach, Handel, Scarlatti: Tercentenary Essays*, ed. P. Williams (Cambridge, 1985), pp. 207–43

Longo, Alessandro: *Domenico Scarlatti e sua figura nella storia della musica* (Naples, 1913)

Luciani, S. A.: 'Alla scoperta degli autografi di Domenico Scarlatti', *Archivi*, 3rd series, ii (1935), pp. 298–304

—: *Domenico Scarlatti* (Turin, 1939)

—: 'Postilla Scarlattiana', *La rassegna musicale*, xliv (1940), pp. 200–3

—: 'Un'opera inedita di Domenico Scarlatti', *Rivista musicale italiana*, xlviii (1946), pp. 433–45

Mainwaring, John: *Memoirs of the Life of the Late George Frederic Handel* (London, 1760)

Malinowski, Wladislaw: 'O teatrze Krolowei Marii Kazimiery Domenico Scarlattim i kilku innych sprawach z Michalem Bristigerem', *Ruch Muzyczny*, xx (1976), no. 13, pp. 2–6

Malipiero, Gian Francesco: 'Domenico Scarlatti', *The Musical Quarterly*, xiii (1927), pp. 476–88

Marx-Weber, Magda: 'Römische Vertonungen des Psalms *Miserere* im 18. und frühen 19. Jahrhundert', in *Geistliche Musik: Studien zu ihrer Geschichte und Funktion im 18. und 19. Jahrhundert* (*Hamburger Jahrbuch für Musikwissenschaft*, viii) (Hamburg, 1985), pp. 7–43

Mazza, José: *Dicionario biografico de musicos portugueses* ([Lisbon], 1944–5)

McCredie, Andrew: 'Domenico Scarlatti and his Opera *Narcisso*', *Acta musicologica*, xxxiii (1961), pp. 19–29

Montaiglon, Anatole de: *Correspondance des directeurs de L'Académie de France à Rome* (Paris, 1887–1908)

Morelli, Arnaldo: 'Alessandro Scarlatti maestro di cappella in Roma ed alcuni suoi oratori', *Note d'archivio*, new series, ii (1984), pp. 117–44

Newman, William S.: *The Sonata in the Classic Era* (Chapel Hill, 1963; 3rd edition, 1983)

Newton, Richard: 'The English Cult of Domenico Scarlatti', *Music and Letters*, xx (1939), pp. 138–56

Pagano, Roberto: *Alessandro Scarlatti* [with Lino Bianchi and Giancarlo Rostirolla] (Turin, 1972)

—: 'Le origini ed il primo statuto dell'Unione dei Musici intitolata a Santa Cecilia in Palermo', *Rivista italiana di musicologia*, x (1975), pp. 545–63

—: *Scarlatti, Alessandro e Domenico: due vite in una* (Milan, 1985)

Pannain, Guido: 'L'arte pianistica di Domenico Scarlatti', *Studi musicali*, i (1972), pp. 133ff.

—: 'Scarlatti junior e la sonata', in *Scritte in onore di Luigi Ronga* (Milan and Naples, 1973), pp. 511–13

Pestelli, Giorgio: *Le sonate di Domenico Scarlatti: proposta di un ordinamento cronologico* (Turin, 1967)

—: 'Bach, Handel, D. Scarlatti and the Toccata of the Late Baroque', in *Bach, Handel, Scarlatti: Tercentenary Essays*, ed. P. Williams (Cambridge, 1985), pp. 277–91

Piperno, Franco: 'Anfione in Campidoglio', in *Nuovissimi studi corelliani*, ed. S. Durante and P. Petrobelli (Florence, 1982), pp. 151–209

Prota-Giurleo, Ulisse: *Alessandro Scarlatti 'il Palermitano'* (Naples, 1926)

Rey, Juan José: 'Manuscritos de música para tecla en la Biblioteca del Conservatorio de Madrid', *Revista de musicologia*, i (1978), pp. 221–33

Sacher, Josephine Pettit: *Selected Solo Vocal Music of Domenico Scarlatti (1685–1757)* (dissertation, Columbia University, 1966)

Sartori, Claudio: 'Gli Scarlatti a Napoli: nuovi contributi', *Rivista musicale italiana*, xlvi (1942), pp. 373–90

Sheveloff, Joel: *The Keyboard Music of Domenico Scarlatti: a Reevaluation of the Present State of Knowledge in the Light of the Sources* (dissertation, Brandeis University, 1970)

—: '(Giuseppe) Domenico Scarlatti', in *The New Grove Dictionary of Music and Musicians*, ed. S. Sadie (London, 1980), xvi, pp. 568–78

Silbiger, Alexander: 'Scarlatti Borrowings in Handel's Grand Concertos', *The Musical Times*, cxxv (1984), pp. 93–5

Sitwell, Sacheverell: *A Background for Domenico Scarlatti 1685–1757* (London, 1935)

Solar Quintes, Nicolas A.: 'Documentos sobre la familia de Domenico Scarlatti', *Anuario musical*, iv (1949), pp. 137–54

Strohm, Reinhard: *Italienische Opernarien des frühen Settecento (1720–1730)*, *Analecta musicologica*, xvi (1976)

Tagliavini, Luigi Ferdinando: 'Remarks on the Compositions for Organ of Domenico Scarlatti', in *Bach, Handel, Scarlatti: Tercentenary Essays*, ed. P. Williams (Cambridge, 1985), pp. 321–5

Valabrega, Cesare: *Il clavicembalista Domenico Scarlatti: il suo secolo, la sua opera* (Modena, 1937; 2nd edition, 1955)

Valesio, Francesco: *Diario di Roma*, ed. G. Scano (Milan, 1977–9)

various authors: *Domenico Scarlatti: 13 recherches* (Nice, 1986)

Viale-Ferrero, Mercedes: *Filippo Juvarra scenografo e architetto teatrale* (Turin, 1970)

Waliszewski, Kazimierz: *Marysieńka: Marie de la Grange d'Arquien, Reine de Pologne, femme de Sobieski 1641–1716* (Paris, 1896; English translation, 1898)

Williams, Peter: '*Figurae* in the Keyboard Works of Scarlatti, Handel and Bach: an Introduction', in *Bach, Handel, Scarlatti: Tercentenary Essays*, ed. P. Williams (Cambridge, 1985), pp. 327–45

NOTES

1. ITALY, 1685–1722

1. Antonino Mongitore: *Bibliotheca sicula* (Palermo, 1714), ii, p. 274.
2. These are admirably summarized in Frank D'Accone's edition of the opera published in 1982 by the Harvard University Press. See also F. D'Accone: *The History of a Baroque Opera: Alessandro Scarlatti's 'Gli equivoci nel sembiante'* (New York, 1985).
3. Facsimile of original in R. Pagano *et al*: *Alessandro Scarlatti* (Turin, 1972), facing p. 49.
4. R. Pagano: *Scarlatti, Alessandro e Domenico* (Milan, 1985), pp. 57–8.
5. Ibid., p. 161, citing a paper by William C. Holmes read at an international conference on 'La musica a Napoli durante il seicento' at Naples, 11–14 April 1985.
6. See M. Fabbri: *Alessandro Scarlatti e il Principe Ferdinando de' Medici* (Florence, 1961), pp. 48–9.
7. Her first husband, Paolo Massonio Astrolusco, had accompanied the army of the Marquis of Flaudis to Hungary and died there; see U. Prota-Giurleo: *Alessandro Scarlatti 'il Palermitano'* (Naples 1926), p. 16.
8. Pagano *et al*: *Alessandro Scarlatti* (Turin, 1972), p. 78.
9. Original in Fabbri, op. cit., pp. 58–9.
10. Original in Fabbri, op. cit., p. 59.
11. Original in Fabbri, op. cit., p. 60.
12. Original in Fabbri, op. cit., p. 61.
13. M. Pincherle: *Vivaldi* (Paris, 1955; English translation, 1958), p. 10.
14. C. Burney: *A General History of Music* (Mercer edition, London, 1935), ii, p. 635.
15. R. Strohm: 'Händel in Italia: nuovi contributi', *Rivista italiana di musicologia*, ix (1974), pp. 152–74.
16. J. Mainwaring: *Memoirs of . . . Handel* (London, 1760), pp. 51–2.
17. Original in Fabbri, op. cit., pp. 85–6.
18. Pagano: *Scarlatti, Alessandro e Domenico* (Milan, 1985), p. 303.
19. E. Simi Bonini: 'L'attività degli Scarlatti nella Basilica Liberiana', a paper read in June 1985 at a conference on 'Haendel e gli Scarlatti a Roma' to celebrate the 400th anniversary of the Accademia Nazionale di Santa Cecilia, Rome.
20. J. Mainwaring, op. cit., pp. 59–60.

21. Ibid., p. 61.
22. Pagano, op. cit., p. 307.
23. Burney, op. cit., ii, p. 704.
24. K. Waliszewski: *Marysieńka* (Paris, 1896; English translation, 1898), p. 31.
25. Ibid., p. 35.
26. F. Valesio: *Diario di Roma*, ed. G. Scano (Milan, 1977–9), i, p. 32.
27. British Library, Add. MS 8526, f.2v.
28. Ibid., f.144r.
29. See T. Griffin: *The Late Baroque Serenata* (dissertation, University of California, Los Angeles, 1983), pp. 555–6.
30. Ibid., pp. 571–3.
31. Valesio, op. cit., iv, p. 221.
32. Both parts of the will were published in the *Bulletin de la Société Nivernaise* (second series), iii, pp. 393–403.
33. U. Prota-Giurleo: *Alessandro Scarlatti 'il Palermitano'* (Naples, 1926), pp. 34–6.
34. References to Scarlatti as the composer of a *Didone abbandonata* to a libretto by Metastasio may result from a confusion with Domenico Sarro's opera produced at the Teatro San Bartolomeo, Naples, on 1 February 1724.
35. See M. Viale-Ferrero: *Filippo Juvarra* (Turin, 1970), p. 70n.
36. J. Clark: ' "His own worst enemy" ', *Early Music*, iv (1976), p. 544.
37. R. Porter: *English Society in the Eighteenth Century* (Harmondsworth, 1982), p. 256.
38. Costa Brito, M. C. da: *Domenico Scarlatti e la musica alla corte di Giovanni V di Portogallo*, read at a conference on 'Domenico Scarlatti e il suo tempo' at the Accademia Musicale Chigiana, Siena, in September 1985.

2. OPERAS AND ORATORIOS

1. For opera performances at Naples in the seventeenth century, see especially Lorenzo Bianconi: 'Funktionen des Operntheaters in Neapel bis 1700 und die Rolle Alessandro Scarlattis', in *Colloquium Alessandro Scarlatti Würzburg 1975*, ed. W. Osthoff and J. Ruile-Dronke (Tutzing, 1979), pp. 13–111.
2. C. Sartori: 'Gli Scarlatti a Napoli', *Rivista musicale italiana*, xlvi (1942), pp. 376–7.
3. For an account of this performance, see Howard E. Smither: *A History of Oratorio*, i (Chapel Hill, 1977), pp. 264–5.
4. F. Valesio: *Diario di Roma*, ed. G. Scano (Milan, 1977–9), iii, pp. 438–9.
5. U. Kirkendale: *Antonio Caldara: sein Leben und seine venezianisch-römischen Oratorien* (Graz, 1966), pp. 163–4.
6. H. E. Smither, op. cit., p. 304.
7. A. Cametti: 'Carlo Sigismondo Capeci . . .', *Musica d'oggi*, xiii (1931), p. 60.

8. See T. Griffin: *The Late Baroque Serenata* (dissertation, University of California, Los Angeles, 1983), pp. 613–15.
9. Ibid., p. 616.
10. G. M. Crescimbeni: *L'Arcadia* (Rome, 1708; 2nd edition, 1711), p. 326.
11. See R. Strohm: *Italienische Opernarien des frühen Settecento*, *Analecta musicologica*, xvi (1976), ii, p. 226.
12. Griffin, op. cit., pp. 616–17.
13. Original in Griffin, op. cit., p. 620.
14. M. Viale-Ferrero: *Filippo Juvarra* (Turin, 1970).
15. Original in Griffin, op. cit., p. 623.
16. Cametti, op. cit., p. 60.
17. A. Della Corte: 'Tetide in Sciro . . .', *La rassegna musicale*, xxvii (1957), p. 282.
18. A. de Montaiglon: *Correspondance des directeurs de L'Académie de France à Rome* (Paris, 1887–1908), vi, p. 64.
19. They included the famous soprano castrato Senesino. See Gaynor G. Jones: 'Alessandro Scarlatti's *Il Ciro*', *Hamburger Jahrbuch für Musikwissenschaft*, iii (1978), pp. 225–37.
20. Viale-Ferrero, op. cit., p. 57n.
21. Cametti, op. cit., pp. 60–1.
22. Viale-Ferrero, op. cit.
23. Viale-Ferrero, op. cit., p. 107, from information in A. de Montaiglon, op. cit.
24. Originals in Griffin, op. cit., p. 653.
25. C. Burney: *A General History of Music* (Mercer edition, London, 1935), ii, p. 706.
26. Rolli here quotes from the prologue to Guarini's *Il pastor fido*: 'picciole offerte sì; ma però tali,/che, se con puro affetto il cor le dona;/anco il ciel non le sdegna'.
27. F. Degrada: 'Una sconosciuta esperienza teatrale di Domenico Scarlatti', in *Il palazzo incantato* (Fiesole, 1979), pp. 69–70.
28. Gigli refers here to his two satirical comedies, *Don Pilone* (?1707) and *La sorellina di Don Pilone* (1712), which had excited widespread interest and controversy.
29. Degrada, op. cit., pp. 96–7.
30. R. Pagano: *Scarlatti, Alessandro e Domenico* (Milan, 1985), pp. 371–3.
31. Winton Dean: 'Scalzi, Carlo', in *The New Grove Dictionary of Music and Musicians*, ed. Stanley Sadie (London, 1980), xvi, p. 546.
32. Strohm, op. cit., p. 226. Strohm suggests that the two arias 'Dona pace alle sue pene' and 'Nò, nò, si puo celar' that follow these in MS Sant. 185 of the Diözesan-Bibliothek, Münster, might be additional arias for the same opera. However, these two arias do not appear in the libretto and they bear no attribution in the MS, where they are copied in a different hand from the others.
33. R. Giazotto: *La musica a Genova* (Genoa, 1951), p. 331.
34. The passage is missing from the Paris source.

3. CHAMBER CANTATAS

1. At least three cantatas (nos 241, 504 and 770 in Edwin Hanley's catalogue) in a manuscript volume in the library of the Paris Conservatoire (F.G.10499; now in the Bibliothèque Nationale) employ strophic-bass technique, but their authenticity has been questioned. See E. Hanley: *Alessandro Scarlatti's Cantate da Camera* (dissertation, Yale University, 1963), p. 108.

2. In cantatas beginning with recitative the home key is often approached obliquely. For example, Scarlatti's *Lontan da te mio bene* opens with a dominant 7th (first inversion) of Bb, although the key of the cantata as a whole is C minor.

3. G. M. Crescimbeni: *L'istoria della volgar poesia* (Rome, 1698; 3rd edition, 1731), i, pp. 299–300.

4. G. M. Crescimbeni: *L'Arcadia* (Rome, 1708), p. 293.

5. Another cantata, *Vuoi ch'io spiri tra i sospiri*, is dated 20 September 1699 in a copy in the Diözesan-Bibliothek, Münster, and attributed to 'Sig. Dom. Scarlatti' in a copy in the Paris Conservatoire library (now housed in the Bibliothèque Nationale). Although the first aria shows a striking resemblance to the aria 'Io non voglio dal mio bene' in the cantata *Che si peni in amore*, the authorship of *Vuoi ch'io spiri*, which is elsewhere attributed to Alessandro Scarlatti, is uncertain. An even earlier cantata, *Belle pupille care*, has sometimes been attributed to Domenico, but copies at Paris and Münster are ascribed simply to 'Scarlatti'. Hanley (op. cit., p. 129) included it in his catalogue of Alessandro's cantatas as a work of doubtful authenticity, but he did not list the Manchester source, where it is dated 1697 and attributed to Francesco Scarlatti. (I am indebted to Michael Talbot for information about the Manchester copy.) In view of the indifferent quality of the music, this is probably the correct attribution; it is, at all events, unlikely that Domenico was composing cantatas at the age of eleven or twelve!

6. T. Griffin: *The Late Baroque Serenata* (dissertation, University of California, Los Angeles, 1983), pp. 382–3.

7. Original in Griffin, op. cit., p. 380.

8. Edited by Lino Bianchi (Milan, 1958). Bianchi transposes *Ah, sei troppo infelice* down a tone and *A chi nacque infelice* up a 4th.

9. See Hanley, op. cit., p. 91.

10. See F. Piperno: 'Anfione in Campidoglio', in *Nuovissimi studi corelliani* (Florence, 1982), pp. 196–9.

4. PORTUGAL, *c.* 1723–9

1. J. Black: 'Lisbon in 1730: the Account of a British Traveller', *Bulletin of the British Society for Eighteenth-Century Studies*, nos 7–8 (1985), pp. 11–14.

2. J. G. Walther: *Musicalisches Lexicon* (Leipzig, 1732), p. 489.

3. *Description de la ville de Lisbonne* (Paris, 1730), pp. 16–18.
4. J. Mazza: *Dicionario biografico de musicos portugueses* ([Lisbon], 1944–5), p. 30; translation in Kirkpatrick, p. 73.
5. R. Pagano: *Scarlatti, Alessandro e Domenico* (Milan, 1985), pp. 382–4.
6. W. Coxe: *Memoirs of the Kings of Spain* (London, 1813; 2nd edition, 1815), iii, pp. 18–19.
7. Paris Conservatoire, MS D.12741 (now in the Bibliothèque Nationale). See R. Strohm: *Italiensiche Opernarien des frühen Settecento, Analecta musicologica*, xvi (1976), p. 226.
8. P. Scholes (ed.): *Dr Burney's Musical Tours in Europe* (London, 1959), ii, p. 118.
9. Ibid., p. 119.
10. Latin original in Kirkpatrick, pp. 334–5.
11. *The Political State of Great Britain*, xxxvii (1729), p. 176.

5. SERENATAS

1. See Malinowski: 'O teatrze Krolowei Marii Kazimiery Domenico Scarlattim . . .', *Ruch Muzyczny*, xx (1976), no. 13, pp. 2–6.
2. Original in T. Griffin: *The Late Baroque Serenata* (dissertation, University of California, Los Angeles, 1983), p. 597, quoting from F. Valesio's diary.
3. Ibid., p. 597, quoting from Valesio's diary.
4. Ibid., p. 626, quoting from the *avvisi di Roma* in Munich.
5. Ibid., p. 630, quoting from the *avvisi di Roma* in Munich.
6. Ibid., p. 642.
7. Original in Griffin, op. cit., p. 654.
8. Costa Brito, M. C. da: *Domenico Scarlatti e la musica alla corte di Giovanni V di Portogallo*, read at a conference on 'Domenico Scarlatti e il suo tempo' at the Accademia Musicale Chigiana, Siena, in September 1985.
9. Ibid.
10. R. Kirkpatrick (p. 70), quoting from the *Gazeta de Lisboa* of 28 September 1719.

6. CHURCH MUSIC

1. The 'strict [or strong] style of Palestrina'; the phrase occurs in a letter to Prince Ferdinando de' Medici. See M. Fabbri: *Alessandro Scarlatti e il Principe Ferdinando de' Medici* (Florence, 1961), p. 106.
2. See C. S. Terry: *Bach, a Biography* (London, 1928; 2nd edition, 1933), p. 171n.
3. H. Mendel and A. Reissmann: *Musikalisches Conversations-Lexicon* (Berlin, 1878), ix, p. 72.
4. M. Marx-Weber: 'Römische Vertonungen des Psalms *Miserere* im 18.

und frühen 19. Jahrhundert', *Hamburger Jahrbuch für Musikwissenschaft*, viii (Hamburg, 1985), p. 7.

5. E. J. Dent: *Alessandro Scarlatti* (London, 1905; 2nd edition, 1960), p. 191.
6. L. Hautus: 'Zu dem Domenico Scarlatti zugeschriebenen *Capriccio fugato a dodici*', *Die Musikforschung*, xxiv (1971), pp. 294–5.
7. A. Casella: 'Le musiche vocali e strumentali', in *Gli Scarlatti . . .* (Siena, 1940), p. 21.
8. The tempo indications here follow Jürgen Jürgens's edition (Mainz, 1973); not all are present in every source.
9. MS 2038/A66/Case X.
10. Dent, op. cit., p. 139.
11. Translation from Kirkpatrick, p. 69.

7. SPAIN, 1729–57

1. Original in Kirkpatrick, p. 335.
2. Quoted in Edward Armstrong: *Elisabeth Farnese* (London, 1892), p. 338.
3. C. Burney: *A General History of Music* (Mercer edition, London, 1935), ii, p. 815.
4. Quoted in Armstrong, op. cit., p. 344.
5. P. Scholes (ed.): *Dr Burney's Musical Tours in Europe* (London, 1959), i, pp. 154–5.
6. From the opera *Didone abbandonata*. Burney (*Musical Tours*, i, p. 206) mistakenly attributed the aria to Hasse.
7. Nationalbibliothek, Vienna, MS 19111. See Emilio Cotarelo y Mori: *Origenes y establecimiento de la opera en España hasta 1800* (Madrid, 1917), p. 109; see also Robert Freeman: 'Farinello and his Repertory', in *Studies in Renaissance and Baroque Music in Honor of Arthur Mendel*, ed. R. L. Marshall (Kassel, 1974), pp. 301–30.
8. E. Clarke: *Letters Concerning the Spanish Nation* (London, 1763), p. 329.
9. C. Burney, op. cit., ii, p. 815.
10. Documents relevant to Scarlatti's ennoblement are summarized in Kirkpatrick (pp. 336–8). See also N. A. Solar Quintes: 'Documentos sobre la familia de Domenico Scarlatti', *Anuario musical*, iv (1949), pp. 144–6.
11. Original in Kirkpatrick, p. 338.
12. Literally, 'Live happily': a conventional ending to prefaces in opera librettos and other publications in the eighteenth century.
13. According to Kirkpatrick (p. 118), Scarlatti's dwelling was probably at no. 35 Calle de Leganitos. The original building was demolished and by 1967 replaced by a new one, the ground floor of which was in use in 1984 as a showroom for office furniture. In about 1978 the Calle Gaztambide, in the north-west of the city near the university, was renamed the Calle de Domenico Scarlatti. This is a modern street in which stand multi-storey flats, government buildings and the Alsace restaurant. Like the

Via Scarlatti in Palermo, it has no historical connections with the composer whose name it bears.

14   The original letter, in the Casa de Alba, Madrid, is reproduced in facsimile in Kirkpatrick, Plate 3a.

15.   R. Pagano: *Scarlatti, Alessandro e Domenico* (Milan, 1985), pp. 428–30.

16.   Maria Barbara's will is in the library of the Royal Palace, Madrid (MS VII E 4 305); see Kirkpatrick, p. 131.

17.   Luise Bauer, in her dissertation *Die Tätigkeit Domenico Scarlattis . . .* (University of Munich, 1933), quoted documents which indicate that from 1750 Scarlatti lived in the Calle de San Marcos; see Kirkpatrick, pp. 343–4.

18.   The will is in fact dated 19 October 1749; see Appendix II.

19.   Original in Kirkpatrick, p. 345.

20.   William Coxe: *Memoirs of the Kings of Spain*, iv (London, 1813, 2nd edition, 1815), pp. 232–3.

8. KEYBOARD WORKS

1.   Kirkpatrick, pp. 442–56; the standard Kirkpatrick numbering, indicated by the letter 'K', is adopted throughout this chapter.

2.   See Appendix I. Possibly the movement 'missing' from K89 survives in the first movement of Avison's fifth concerto, also in D minor.

3.   J. Sheveloff: *The Keyboard Music of Domenico Scarlatti* (dissertation, Brandeis University, 1970), pp. 232–47.

4.   Ibid., pp. 230–2.

5.   W. Gerstenberg: *Die Klavier-Kompositionen Domenico Scarlattis* (Regensburg, 1933), pp. 342–4; Sheveloff, op. cit., pp. 448–50.

6.   S. Choi: *Newly Found Eighteenth Century Manuscripts of Domenico Scarlatti's Sonatas* (dissertation, University of Wisconsin, 1974).

7.   A. Baciero (ed.): *Nueva biblioteca española de música de teclado*, iii (Madrid, 1978), p. x.

8.   B. Johnsson: 'Eine unbekannte Sonate von Domenico Scarlatti', *Die Musikforschung*, xxxiv (1981), pp. 309–10.

9.   I am grateful to Señor Rey for drawing my attention to all four manuscripts, and for supplying photocopies of them.

10.   Information from Señor Rey.

11.   What significance, if any, should be attached to the fact that nos 21 and 22 appear together in the Münster (III) and Vienna (F) manuscripts (in reverse order) is not clear.

12.   See the modern edition by Genoveva Gálvez (Madrid, 1978).

13.   C. Hopkinson: 'Eighteenth-Century Editions . . .', *Transactions of the Edinburgh Bibliographical Society*, iii (1948), pp. 47–71; Kirkpatrick, pp. 401–9; R. Newton: 'The English Cult of Domenico Scarlatti', *Music and Letters*, xx (1939), pp. 138–56; J. Sheveloff, op. cit., pp. 111–45.

14.   An edition of six *Sonates pour le clavecin par Dom.º Scarlatti . . . opera IV*, published by Boivin and Le Clerc (Paris, in the 1740s), contains arrangements of arias from Alessandro Scarlatti's opera *Pirro e Demetrio*;

see Kirkpatrick, p. 426. Sheveloff (op. cit., p. 445) has questioned the authenticity of K95 and 97, also published by Boivin (see Table 1, nos 5 and 6).

15. Kirkpatrick, p. 144.
16. G. Pestelli: *Le sonate di Domenico Scarlatti* (Turin, 1967).
17. Sheveloff, op. cit., p. 573.
18. Ibid., pp. 102–3.
19. R. Pagano: *Scarlatti, Alessandro e Domenico* (Milan, 1985), pp. 386–7.
20. The Handel pieces are all movements from his keyboard suites published in 1720.
21. Gerstenberg, op. cit., pp. 10–26.
22. These sonatas form part of a complex of six (K374–9) written at Aranjuez, according to the Münster source. All six remain within the compass $C–d'''$, except for K378, which descends to $B\flat'$.
23. K485 employs a wider range ($F'–g'''$) than any other Scarlatti sonata. It appears, therefore, to exceed the range of any of the inventoried instruments belonging to Queen Maria Barbara, unless a special tuning was adopted.
24. H. Keller: *Domenico Scarlatti, ein Meister des Klaviers* (Leipzig, 1957), p. 34.
25. Pestelli, op. cit., p. 96.
26. See W. S. Newman: *The Sonata in the Classic Era* (Chapel Hill, 1963; 3rd edition, 1983), p. 267. Newman claims the incipits of K308 and 309 and those of K490, 491 and 492 to be thematically related, but finds them 'too rare and inconclusive to be considered'. Thematic similarities between non-paired sonatas are often more striking; see, for example, the openings of K24 and 39, 310 and 332, 348 and 445, 505 and 540.
27. See Keller, op. cit., pp. 77–8.
28. Max Kalbeck (ed.): *J. Brahms: Briefwechsel*, i (Berlin, 1907; English translation, London, 1909), pp. 218–19.
29. K415, also called 'Pastoral' in both the Venice and the Parma sources, shows few of the usual Christmas features. The same title given to K9 in many modern editions has no authority.
30. K513 has a curious parallel in the Pastorale for organ BWV590 by J. S. Bach, which also breaks off the 'Christmas' movement prematurely (in this case in the mediant minor key) and never returns to it.
31. The convention of ending such collections of pieces with a fugue may have been Scarlatti's main motive for writing some of these pieces. K41 is placed at the end (no. 30) of volume 3 in the Parma manuscripts, and K417 is also the last (no. 30) in volume 9 of the Venice set. K93 in the 1742 Venice manuscript is followed only by a second copy of a sonata found earlier in the volume (K52), while volume 8 of the Venice manuscripts and volume 10 of the Parma set both end with a binary sonata (K387) marked 'Veloce e fugato', although this has no fugal characteristics. Sebastian Albero (whose fugues outdo Scarlatti's in their less than heavenly length) ended each half of his collection of thirty

'Sonatas para clavicordio' with a fugue (nos 15 and 30).

32. L. F. Tagliavini, reviewing the edition by Loek Hautus in *L'organo*, viii (1970), pp. 111–14.

33. Newman, op. cit., p. 39.

34. P. Scholes (ed.): *Dr Burney's Musical Tours* (London, 1959), ii, p. 87.

35. J. Clark: 'Domenico Scarlatti and Spanish Folk Music', *Early Music*, iv (1976), p. 21. I find unconvincing the inference about chronology that the author draws from her researches.

36. The subdominant chord may be in root position (for example, K135, 213, 290 and 292) or first inversion (for example, K216, 241 and 383).

37. Scarlatti's usual indication for a glissando is 'con dedo solo' ('with one finger'), but he gives no guidance on what to do when the glissando includes both white and black keys. Modern commentators are silent on this matter, too. Are we to assume that the B♭s in the right hand of K468, bars 84–7, are to be played as naturals?

38. Scholes (ed.), op. cit., ii, pp. 86–7.

39. See Sheveloff, op. cit., pp. 475–82.

9. LATE VOCAL WORKS

1. R. Kirkpatrick: 'Who wrote the Scarlatti Sonatas?', *Notes*, xxix (1973), pp. 427–8.

2. R. Pagano: *Scarlatti, Alessandro e Domenico* (Milan, 1985), passim.

3. In the Hermitage, Leningrad. The painting is reproduced in Curt Sachs: *The History of Musical Instruments* (New York, 1943), Plate XXIV.

4. See B. Brunelli (ed.): *Tutte le opere di Pietro Metastasio*, ii (Milan, 1947), p. 1325.

5. Brunelli, op. cit., pp. 719–20 and 736–7.

6. J. J. Quantz, autobiographical sketch in F. W. Marpurg: *Historisch-kritische Beyträge zur Aufnahme der Musik*, i (Berlin, 1754), pp. 197–250.

7. Details of tempo and metre follow the Bolognese source.

10. SCARLATTI'S REPUTATION AND INFLUENCE

1. C. Burney: *Memoirs of the Life and Writings of the Abate Metastasio* (London, 1796), ii, pp. 205–6.

2. Article on Scarlatti in A. Rees: *The Cyclopaedia*, xxxi (London, 1819).

3. See Kirkpatrick, pp. 345–56.

4. G. Sacchi: 'Vita del Cavaliere Don Carlo Broschi', *Raccolta ferrarese di opuscoli scientifici e letterari*, xv (1784), pp. 29–30.

5. A. Silbiger: 'Scarlatti Borrowings in Handel's Grand Concertos', *The Musical Times*, cxxv (1984), pp. 93–5.

6. Robert L. Marshall: 'Bach the Progressive', *The Musical Quarterly*, lxii (1976), pp. 313–57, especially pp. 347–9.

7. Quoted in Percy Scholes: *The Great Dr Burney* (London, 1948), i, p. 202.

8. P. Scholes (ed.): *Dr Burney's Musical Tours* (London, 1959), ii, p. 220.

9. E. Helm: 'Carl Philipp Emanuel Bach', in *The New Grove Dictionary of Music and Musicians*, ed. S. Sadie (London, 1980), i, p. 851.
10. Published by Schott (Mainz and London, 1935).
11. Modern edition by Genoveva Gálvez (Madrid, 1978).
12. Burney: *A General History of Music* (Mercer edition, London, 1935), ii, p. 1009.
13. Ibid., p. 1009.
14. L. Plantinga: *Clementi: his Life and Music* (London, 1977), p. 49.
15. Ibid., pp. 140–2.
16. J. G. Walther: *Musicalisches Lexicon* (Leipzig, 1732), p. 547.
17. J. P. Kirnberger: *Die Kunst des reinen Satzes in der Musik*, ii (Berlin, 1776), p. 89.
18. E. L. Gerber: *Historisch-biographisches Lexicon der Tonkünstler* (Leipzig, 1790–2), col. 402–3.
19. Original in R. Schumann: *Gesammelte Schriften über Musik und Musiker* (Leipzig, 1854; 3rd edition, 1883), ii, pp. 76–7.
20. M. Kalbeck (ed.): *J. Brahms: Briefwechsel*, i (Berlin, 1907; English translation, London, 1909), p. 225.
21. E. Sams: *Brahms Songs* (London, 1972), p. 45.

APPENDIX I. SOME SCARLATTI ARRANGEMENTS

1. 'Some Account of the Life and Writings of D.ʳ Charles Burney', *European Magazine*, vii (1785), pp. 163f.

APPENDIX II. SCARLATTI'S WILL

1. A Spanish monetary unit, equivalent to twenty-five centimos, or one quarter of a peseta.
2. The memorial referred to by Scarlatti has never been found.
3. Madrid, Archivo Histórico de Protocolos, MS 16343, ff. 754–755v; Spanish original in Kirkpatrick, pp. 341–3.

INDEX

Agostini, Pietro Simone (*c.* 1635–80) 3
Alari, Paola 48, 106–7
Alba, Duke of, *see* Silva y Alvarez de
  Toledo, Fernando de
Albani, Giovan Francesco, *see* Clement XI
Albani, Maria Bernardina 60
Albéniz, Isaac (1860–1909) 222
Albero, Sebastian (1722–56) 149, 151, 157,
  161, 191, 211–12, 226, 288: Sonata in E
  major 212, ex. 37
Albinoni, Tomaso Giovanni (1671–1751)
  14
Aldrovandini, Pompeo (1677–1735 or
  1739) 70
Alfonso VI, King of Portugal (1643–83) 97
Alibert, Giacomo d' (1626–1713) 23, 41
Allegri, Gregorio (1582–1652) 25, 117:
  Miserere 25, 117
Alliata e Bonanno, Giovanna, Princess of
  Villafranca 104
Alliata e Colonna, Giuseppe, Prince of
  Villafranca 104
Almeida, Francisco Antonio de (*c.* 1702–
  55) 97
Alpiarça 141
Alvarez, Juan Antonio 238
Alvarez Martinez, Rosario 155, 191, 193
Alvarez y Palma, Cristobal 132
Amadei, Filippo (*fl.* 1690–1730): *Teodosio
  il giovane* 47
Amati family 1
Amato, Eleonora d', *see* Scarlatti (or
  Scarlata), Eleonora
Amato, Vincenzo (1629–70) 1–2: *Il martirio
  di Santa Caterina* 2; *Isaura* 2; *St John
  Passion* 2; *St Matthew Passion* 2
Ambreville, Rosa 59
Amigoni, Jacopo (1682–1752) 139, 143,
  207
Anes de Sá e Menses, Rodrigo, Count of
  Penaguião and Marques de Fontes 26,
  29, 97, 106–7
Antonio de Bragança (1695–1757) 99, 132,
  140
Anzalone, Antonia Maria, *see* Scarlatti,
  Antonia Maria

Aquinas, Thomas (1224/5–74) 115
Aranjuez 133–4, 135, 141, 146, 288
Aránzazu: Santuario 127–9, 154–6
Arcadian Academy, *see* Rome
Archi, Giovanni Antonio 70
Ariosto, Ludovico (1474–1533) 48–9
Armstrong, Edward 286
Arne, Thomas (1710–78), 141, 216–17
Arquien, Henri de la Grange d', *see*
  Grange d'Arquien, Henri de la
Ascalona, Duke of, *see* Pacheco de Acuña,
  Francesco
Astorga, Emanuele d' (1680–?1757) 31,
  84: *Aci, e Galatea* 108
Astrolusco, Paolo Massonio 281
Avison, Charles (1709–70) 141, 148, 177,
  224–31: Concerto no. 5 229–30, 287,
  exx. 42, 43
Ayerbe, Ignacia 156–7

Bach family 1
Bach, Carl Philipp Emanuel (1714–88)
  209–11, 218
Bach, Johann Christian (1735–82) 214
Bach, Johann Sebastian (1685–1750) 9, 18,
  32, 94, 104, 108, 113, 120, 122, 141,
  147, 148, 153, 166, 167–8, 172, 202,
  207–9, 218–19, 224: Brandenburg
  Concertos 81, 208; Goldberg
  Variations 176, 209; *Orgelbüchlein* 208;
  Pastorale BWV 590 288; *St Matthew
  Passion* 208
Bach, Maria Barbara (1684–1720) 141
Baciero, Antonio 155, 190–1, 287
Badajoz 102
Badura-Skoda, Eva 151
Bagües, Ion 127
Baj, Tommaso (*c.* 1650–1714): *Miserere*
  25, 117
Baldassari, Benedetto (*fl.* 1708–29) 61–2
Baldini, Innocenzo 70
Barbapiccola, Nicola 10, 34, 37, 40
Bartók, Béla (1881–1945) 147
Basso, Alberto 223
Bauer, Luise 287

Beckford, Peter (1740–1811) 217
Beethoven, Ludwig van (1770–1827) 112, 152, 166, 206, 211
Benavides y Avila, Francesco de, Count of Santo Stefano 5
Benda family 1
Benda, Georg (1722–95) 210
Benedict XIV, Pope [Prospero Lambertini] (1675–1758) 97
Benevoli, Orazio (1605–72) 25
Benjamin, Arthur (1893–1960): Suite for flute and strings 234–5
Benvenuti, Giovanni 59
Berardi, Francesco Capocio Cuccino, see Capocio Cuccino Berardi, Francesco
Beregan, Nicolò (1627–1713) 37, 38
Bernabo, Giovanni Battista 78
Bernardi, Carlo 79
Bernardi, Francesco, see Senesino
Berselli, Matteo (fl. 1709–21) 61
Berti, Giovanni Pietro (d. 1638): Cantade et arie 85
Bianchi, Lino 284
Bianconi, Lorenzo 282
Biffi, Antonio (1666/7–1733) 13
Birchall, Robert (c. 1760–1819) 159
Bizzarri, Tommaso 70, 73
Black, Jeremy 284
Blois 25
Boccherini, Luigi (1743–1805) 192, 205
Bogianckino, Massimo 223
Boiardo, Matteo Maria (1440/1–94) 49
Boivin, publishers 158, 287, 288
Bologna 37, 73, 95, 213
Bonis, Ignazio de 87, 95
Bononcini, Giovanni (1670–1747) 14
Borosini, Francesco (b. c. 1690) 59
Bortoli, Modesto-Giovanni 50
Boschi, Giuseppe Maria (fl. 1698–1744) 61
Boyce, William (1711–79) 141
Bracci, Maria Angelica 37, 39
Brahms, Johannes (1833–97) 150, 151, 171, 188, 219–22: Handel Variations 221, ex. 41; Symphony no. 2 220; Unüberwindlich 220
Brano, Antonio Freitas 102
Brano, Joanne Monterio 102
Bristiger, Michael 104
Broschi, Carlo, see Farinelli
Broschi, Riccardo (c. 1698–1756) 138
Brunelli, Bruno 197, 289
Bull, John (?1562/3–1628): Walsingham Variations 184
Burney, Charles (1726–1814) 15, 20, 79, 101, 136–7, 138, 180, 187, 206, 209–10, 213–15, 218, 230–1, 281, 282, 283, 286, 289, 290
Burney, Esther (1749–1832) 230–1
Busenello, Giovanni Francesco (1598–1659) 34

Cadiz 141
Caffarelli [Gaetano Majorano] (1710–83) 199
Caldara, Antonio (c. 1670–1736) 14: L'Anagilda 47; La costanza in amor 48; Tito e Berenice 60
Calderón, Pedro (1600–81) 131
Cametti, Alberto 44, 50, 58, 282, 283
Campra, André (1660–1744): Iphigénie en Tauride 57
Canavari, Antonio (1681–after 1758) 78
Cannicciari, Pompeo (1670–1744) 20
cantata 3, 84–8, 104, 172
Caolis, Sextilius de 102
Capece (Capeci), Carlo Sigismondo (1652–1728) 23, 24, 25, 28, 41, 43, 44–5, 46, 48, 50–1, 53, 54–7, 58, 60–1, 63–4, 65–6, 105
Capelli, Giovanni Maria (1648–1726): I fratelli riconosciuti 198
Capocio Cuccino Berardi, Francesco 34
Cappella Giulia 25, 116, 117
Capranica, Federico 68
Capranica, Pompeo 68
Carafa, Domenico 7
Carafa, Domenico Marzio, Duke of Maddaloni 6–7
Carcani, Giuseppe (1703–79) 68
Cardines, Eleonora, Princess of Colobrano 6–7
Caresana, Cristoforo (c. 1640–1709) 10
Carissimi, Giacomo (1605–74) 2, 3, 4, 41, 84, 85, 87
Carmignano, Carlo 101
Caroline of Anspach, Princess (1683–1737) 63
Carpio, Marchese del, see Haro y Gusman, Gaspar de
Casella, Alfredo (1883–1947) 115, 119–20, 125, 286: Scarlattiana 231, 233–4
Castris, Francesco de [Cecchino] 73
'Cat's Fugue' 217
Cavalli, Federico Jacopo 102
Cavalli, Francesco (1602–76) 2, 13, 33: La Didone 33; L'Egisto 33; Il Giasone 2, 33
Cavalli, Jacobo 102
Cecchino, see Castris, Francesco de

Cerail (Coraill), Mlle (d. 1723) 62
Cerda, Luis Francisco de la, Duke of
  Medinaceli (1660–1711) 5–6, 7, 8, 10
Cesti, Antonio (1623–69) 85, 87
Charles II, King of Spain (1661–1700) 130
Charles III, King of Spain (1716–88) 60,
  146
Charles VI, Emperor (1685–1740) 68, 197
Charlotte, Queen of England (1744–1818)
  214
Chiccheri, Vittorio 106
Choi, Seunghyun 153–4, 287
Chopin, Fryderyk (1810–49) 147, 219
Christina, Queen of Sweden (1626–89) 4,
  6, 19, 22, 23, 41
Chrysander, Friedrich 65
Clark, Jane 30, 180, 282, 289
Clarke, Edward 138, 196, 286
Clement IX, Pope [Giulio Rospigliosi]
  (1600–69) 3
Clement XI, Pope [Giovan Francesco
  Albani] (1649–1721) 23, 26, 43, 49
Clementi, Muzio (1752–1832) 159, 213,
  217, 219
Coletti, Agostino Bonaventura (c. 1675–
  1752): Ifiginia 57
Colignani, Francesco 28, 29, 30
Colloredo, Cardinal 67
Colobrano, Princess of, see Cardines,
  Eleonora
concerto 3, 67, 172, 176, 181
Conforto, Nicola (1718–after 1788) 143,
  199: La forza del genio 146
Conti, Gioacchino (1714–61) 199
Contini, Domenico Filippo 4
Convo, Giulio 34, 37–8, 40
Cooke, Benjamin (1734–93) 140, 158
Corelli, Arcangelo (1653–1713) 3, 19, 67,
  90, 95, 147, 225: Concerto op. 6 no. 8
  172
Corignano, Prince of 59
Corradini, Francesco (c. 1700–after 1749)
  131: La clemencia de Tito 143; El
  Polifemo 143
Corselli, Francesco (c. 1702–78) 130, 193:
  La clemencia de Tito 143; El Polifemo
  143
Costa Brito, Manuel Carlos da 98, 107–8,
  282, 285
Cotarelo y Mori, Emilio 286
Couperin family 1
Couperin, François (1668–1733) 184
Covens, Jan 141
Coxe, William (1747–1828) 99–100, 285,
  287

Cramer, Johann Baptist (1771–1858) 219
Crescimbeni, Giovanni Mario (1663–
  1728) 47, 86–7, 283, 284
Cristini, soprano 108–9
Czerny, Carl (1791–1857) 153, 159, 218–
  19

D'Accone, Frank 281
Danchet, Antoine (1671–1748) 57
Daun, Count of, see Lorenz, Wierich
  Philipp
Dean, Winton 283
Debussy, Claude (1862–1918) 147
Degrada, Francesco 72–3, 74, 179, 223,
  283
Delafaye, Charles 96
Della Corte, Andrea 50, 283
Dent, Edward J. 118–19, 286
Desmarets, Henry (1661–1741): Iphigénie
  en Tauride 57
Dolmetsch family 1
DuBeine, Joseph (1717–1803) 151–2, 218
Durante, Francesco (1684–1755): Protexisti
  me Deus 119; Sonate per cembalo 179
Durastanti, Margarita (fl. 1700–34) 61
Durón, Sebastián (1660–1716) 131

Ebeling, Christoph Daniel (1741–1817)
  209
El Escorial 133–5, 144, 149, 211
Elisabetta (Isabel), Queen of Spain
  (1692–1766) 99, 130, 131, 135–6, 138,
  142, 146
El Pardo 133–4
Elvas 102
Euripides (c. 485–c. 406 BC) 55, 58

Fabbri, Mario 281, 285
Fabri, Annibale Pio (1697–1760) 79
Fadini, Emilia 160, 223
Falla, Manuel de (1876–1946) 179–80, 222
Farinelli [Carlo Broschi] (1705–82) 28, 79,
  100, 101, 134, 136–8, 142, 143, 144,
  145, 146, 148, 153, 196, 198–9, 205–7,
  211, 213
Farnese, Elisabetta, see Elisabetta, Queen
  of Spain
Febiarmonici 33
Fermo 48
Fernando VI, King of Spain (1713–59) 98,
  100, 102, 107, 131, 134, 135, 138, 142,
  146, 196, 211, 212
Ferrari, Benedetto (?1603/4–81) 85
Finaia, Francesco 95
Fitzwilliam, Lord Richard (1745–1816)
  65, 151, 159, 211, 215

flamenco 179–80
Flaudis, Marquis of 281
Florence 8, 9, 11, 12, 78, 89–90
Floriani (Floriano), soprano castrato 98, 108–9
Foggia, Antonio (1650–1707) 4, 17
Fontana, Domenico 70, 73
Fontes, Marques de, *see* Anes de Sá e Menses, Rodrigo
Fornari, Matteo 95
Fortier, B. 139
Fox, Charles James (1749–1806) 30
Freeman, Robert 286
Frescobaldi, Girolamo (1583–1643) 184
Frigimelica Roberti, Girolamo (1653–1732) 16, 40
Froberger, Johann Jacob (1616–67) 184

Gaffi, Tommaso Bernardo (*c.* 1667–1744) 17
Gàlvez, Genoveva 211, 287, 290
Garcia, Gaspar Feliciano 145, 238
Gasparini, Francesco (1668–1727) 14, 15, 21, 59, 69, 100, 163, 179, 181: *Ambleto* 26, 68; *Andate, o miei sospiri* 15; *Lucio Papirio* 60, 62; *Tigrane* 101; *Il Trace in catena* 78
Gasparri, Francesco Maria 68
Geminiani, Francesco (1687–1762) 214, 225, 226
Genoa 37, 59: Teatro Falcone 80
Genovesi, Domenico 70
Gentili, Francisco Maria 102, 142
Gentili, Gaspar 139, 142, 144
Gentili, Margarita 102, 141, 142
Gentili, Maria Catarina, *see* Scarlatti, Maria Catarina
Gerber, Ernst Ludwig (1746–1819) 218, 290
Geri, Gasparo 79
Gerstenberg, Walter 151, 163, 287, 288
Giacomelli, Geminiano (*c.* 1692–1740) 137
Giai, Giovanni Antonio (*c.* 1690–1764) 137
Giazotto, Remo 80, 283
Gigli, Girolamo (1660–1722) 71, 72–3, 75, 283
Gilbert, Kenneth 149, 160, 223
Gioannini, Giacomo Antonio 59–60
Giordano, Luca (1632–1705) 134
Giusti, Maria 48
Gizzi, Domenico (*c.* 1680–1758) 79
Gluck, Christoph Willibald (1714–87) 55, 58
Goethe, Johann Wolfgang von (1749–1832) 220

Goldoni, Carlo (1707–93) 231
Gordon, Alexander (*c.* 1692–1754/5) 61–2
Grammaticus, Saxo, *see* Saxo Grammaticus
Granados, Enrique (1867–1916) 193, 222
Grandi, Alessandro (?*c.* 1577–1630): *Cantade et arie* 84
Grange d'Arquien, Henri de la (1608–1705) 22
Greene, Maurice (1696–1755) 141
Griffin, Thomas 89–90, 106, 282, 283, 284, 285
Grimaldi, Nicolo [Nicolini] (1673–1732) 11, 12, 90
Grimani, Cardinal Vincenzo (1655–1710) 20, 24
Guarini, Battista (1538–1612) 283
Guarneri family 1

Haffner, Johann Ulrich (1711–67) 153, 158, 214, 217
Halle 61, 218
Handel, George Frideric (1685–1759) 9, 15–16, 18–19, 20, 22, 29, 33, 49, 62, 64, 66, 81, 87, 109, 147, 153, 163, 166, 167, 172, 207–8, 216, 224: *Agrippina* 61; *Berenice* 79, 80; *Messiah* 208; *Radamisto* 30, 61; *La Resurrezione* 41; *Selve, caverne e monti* 94; *Tamerlano* 59; *Tolomeo* 48; *Water Music* 208
Hanley, Edwin 284
Haro y Gusman, Caterina 7
Haro y Gusman, Gasparo de, Marchese del Carpio (*d.* 1687) 5
Harrison, Julius (1885–1963): Suite for strings 234
Haslinger, Tobias (1787–1842) 159, 218–19
Hasse, Johann Adolf (1699–1783) 32, 137, 199, 286: *Antonio e Cleopatra* 101; *Artaserse* 136
Hautus, Loek 114, 119, 223, 286, 289
Hay, George, Earl of Kinnoull (*d.* 1758) 96
Haydn, Joseph (1732–1809) 147, 156, 166, 167, 173, 190, 194, 211
Haym, Nicola (1678–1729) 48
Heidegger, Johann Jakob (1666–1749) 61
Helm, Eugene 210, 290
Herrando, José (*c.* 1700–*c.* 1765) 155
Herzogenberg, Elisabeth von (1847–92) 171–2, 219
Holmes, William C. 281
Hopkinson, Cecil 159, 287
Hotz, Pierre du (*fl.* 1556–86) 143–4

Huescar, Duke of, *see* Silva y Alvarez de Toledo, Fernando de

Innocent XI, Pope [Benedetto Odescalchi] (1611–89) 3, 4
Innocent XII, Pope [Antonio Pignatelli] (1615–1700) 68

Jacopone da Todi (*c.* 1232–1306) 120
Jan III Sobieski, King of Poland (1629–96) 22, 24, 41, 43, 105
Jesi 48, 101
John IV, King of Portugal (1604–56) 97, 102
John V, King of Portugal (1689–1750) 29, 97, 100, 107, 122, 125, 132, 138–40, 162
Johnson, John (*fl.* 1740–62) 141, 156, 158
Johnsson, Bengt 155, 191, 287
Jommelli, Nicolo (1714–74) 199
Jones, Gaynor G. 283
José I, King of Portugal (1714–77) 99, 102, 106
Joseph I, Emperor (1678–1711) 43, 50
Joseph II, Emperor (1741–90) 153
Jozzi, Pompilia 37, 39
Julius II, Pope [Giuliano della Rovere] (1443–1513) 25
Jürgens, Jürgen 286
Justinus, Marcus Junianus (*fl.* 3rd century) 45
Juvarra, Filippo (1676–1736) 23, 26, 29, 41, 45, 46, 49, 52, 54, 58–9, 68, 97, 133

Kalbeck, Max 288, 290
Kastner, Macario Santiago 192–3, 212
Keene, Benjamin (1697–1757) 135, 136–7
Keller, Hermann 165, 288
Kelway, Joseph (*c.* 1702–82) 213, 214–15, 226: Sonata no. 4 215, ex. 38
Kinnoull, Earl of, *see* Hay, George
Kirkendale, Ursula 43, 282
Kirkpatrick, Ralph 9, 27, 29–30, 35, 38, 46, 53–4, 66, 72, 90, 102, 116, 119, 122, 123–4, 131, 132, 133, 142, 147, 148, 149–50, 151, 153, 154, 159, 160, 162, 163, 165, 166, 168, 171, 173, 179–80, 184, 195, 223, 285, 286, 287, 288, 289, 290
Kirnberger, Johann Philipp (1721–83) 218, 290
Klemperer, Otto 233
Kreutz, Alfred 210

La Granja 133–5, 136, 142
Lanciani, Flavio (*c.* 1655–1724) 90
Lanciani, Francesco Antonio 90, 91
Larrìnaga, Juan R. de 127
L'Augier, Alexander Ludwig (*c.* 1719–74) 187
Le Clerc, Charles-Nicolas (1697–1774) 287
Leghorn 8, 20
Legrenzi, Giovanni (1626–90) 13, 37–8
Leo, Leonardo (1694–1744) 32, 101, 119
L'Epine, Margherita de (*c.* 1683–1746) 62
Levi, Ugo 74
Lidón, José (1746–1827) 156
Lingua, Anastasio 24
Lisbon 25, 29, 31, 96–9, 107–9, 114, 122–3, 128, 131, 205, 218: St Roch 124
Liszt, Franz (1811–86) 147, 219
Literes, Antonio (1673–1747) 125, 131
Liuzzi, Angiola Catarina 39
Lodoli, Carlo 50
Lodovica, Anna Maria 59
London 2, 24, 28–30, 48, 49, 54, 59, 61–7, 95, 122, 136, 137, 138, 139, 159, 196, 213, 230–1: Covent Garden 79; Hickford's Rooms 62; King's Theatre 29, 48, 49, 62, 63, 212; St Martin-in-the-Fields 214
Longo, Alessandro 149, 151, 160, 181, 193, 223
Lorenz, Wierich Philipp, Count of Daun (1668–1741) 20, 28
Lorenzani, Paolo (1640–1713) 25
Lotti, Antonio (*c.* 1667–1740) 14
Louis XIV, King of France (1638–1715) 106
Louis XV, King of France (1710–74) 25
Lucca 37, 59, 72, 73
Luciani, Sebastiano Arturo 46, 223
Luigi, alto castrato 108–9

Macchia conspiracy 8, 19
Macciochini, Carlo 79
Maddaloni, Duke of, *see* Carafa, Domenico Marzio
Madrid 59, 79, 125, 132–6, 141, 144, 149, 151, 154–7, 198, 199, 202, 205–6, 211, 213, 216, 238: Alcazar 133; Buen Retiro 133–4, 143; San Antonio del Prado 138; San Martin 135, 138, 142, 145
Magliani, Angiola 37, 39
Mainwaring, John (*c.* 1724–1807) 15, 18–19, 20, 281
Majorano, Gaetano, *see* Caffarelli

Malinowski, Wladislaw 285
Mancini, Francesco (1672–1737) 10–11:
    Ariovisto 10; *Dorme la rosa* 87, 92;
    L'Engelberta 47; *Lucio Silla* 10; *Te
    Deum* 20
Manteli, Ana 132
Marazzoli, Marco (*c.* 1605–62) 85
Marcello, Alessandro (1684–1750) 14
Marcello, Benedetto (1686–1739) 14, 71,
    84, 179
Marchand, Louis (1669–1732) 18
Marchesini, Giacomo 59
Marchesini, Santa 59
Maria Anna (Marianna) of Austria,
    Queen of Portugal (1683–1754) 31,
    107, 108, 109, 125
Maria Barbara de Bragança, Queen of
    Spain (1711–58) 98, 99–100, 102–3,
    106, 107, 114, 130–2, 135, 138, 140,
    142, 144, 145, 146, 147, 148, 153, 159,
    165, 187, 196, 204, 206–7, 211, 216,
    287, 288
Maria Casimira, Queen of Poland (1641–
    1715) 20, 22–5, 29, 32, 41, 43, 44, 45,
    46, 48, 49–50, 52, 54, 60, 67, 68, 81,
    88, 104–7, 114, 209
Maria Luisa Gonzaga, Queen of Poland
    (1612–67) 22
Mariani, Lorenzo 78
Maria Theresa, Empress (1717–80) 137,
    197, 206
Maria Ana Vitoria, Infanta of Spain, later
    Queen of Portugal (1718–81) 102
Marmi, Anton Francesco 72, 73
Marpurg, Friedrich Wilhelm (1718–95)
    31, 289
Marshall, Robert L. 286, 289
Martello, Pier Jacopo (1665–1727) 58
Martini, Giovanni Battista (1706–84) 73,
    213
Marx-Weber, Magda 116–17, 285
Massa, Agustino 155
Massarnau, Santiago de 156
Massine, Leonid (1896–1979) 231
Maxarti Ximenes, Anastasia, *see* Scarlatti,
    Anastasia
Mazza, José (*c.* 1735–1797) 285
Mazzocchi, Virgilio (1597–1646) 25
Medici, Cardinal Francesco Maria de'
    (1660–1711) 37
Medici, Grand Duke Cosimo III de'
    (1642–1723) 8, 9
Medici, Prince Ferdinando de' (1663–
    1713) 7, 8, 9, 11–13, 14, 16–17, 26, 78,
    89–90, 285

Medinaceli, Duke of, *see* Cerda, Luis
    Francisco de la
Mele, Giovanni Battista (1701–after 1752)
    131: *La clemencia de Tito* 143; *El
    Polifemo* 143
Melo e Castro, André de, Count of
    Galveias (1668–1753) 48, 100–1
Mendel, Hermann 114, 125, 285
Menuhin family 1
Metastasio, Pietro (1698–1782) 68, 78, 79,
    87, 143, 196–8, 202, 282
Meursius, Joannes (1579–1639) 68
Mexía, Miguel 238
Mignatta, *see* Musi, Maria Maddalena
Milan 37, 59
Milanuzzi, Carlo (*d. c.* 1647) 85
Mirafuentes, Juan 238
Molinés, Joseph 106
Mongitore, Antonino (1663–1743) 281
Montaiglon, Anatole de (1824–95) 283
Montesachio, Prince of 37
Monteverdi, Claudio (1567–1643) 13, 85:
    L'incoronazione di Poppea 33, 34; *Orfeo*
    84
Morelli, Arnaldo 4
Morosini, Alvise 7, 12, 14–15
Mossi, tenor 98, 108–9
Mossi, Caterina Lelli 106
Mozart, Wolfgang Amadeus (1756–91)
    85, 152, 166, 167, 173, 206: *Così fan
    tutte* 60; *Requiem* 202
Musi, Maria Maddalena [Mignatta] 8, 90

Naples 2, 5–12, 13, 17, 19, 20, 21, 24, 25,
    26, 27, 32, 35, 37, 54, 61, 89, 90, 104,
    114, 119, 120, 131, 179, 202, 206, 236,
    282: Chiesa di Montesanto 6;
    Conservatorio della Pietà dei Turchini
    119; Conservatorio di Santa Maria di
    Loreto 5; Oratorio dei Padri
    Girolamini 28; Teatro dei Fiorentini
    28; Teatro San Bartolomeo 5, 6, 10,
    33, 34, 36, 39, 40, 78, 101, 282
Narici, Gaetano 79
Nascimbene, Vittoria 37, 39
Natilii, Antonio 70
Navarro, Antonio 156
Nebra, José (1702–68) 131, 151, 155, 191,
    192
Nebra, Manuel Blasco de (*c.* 1750–84) 155
Newcastle, Duke of, *see* Pelham-Holles,
    Thomas
Newman, William S. 179, 288, 289
Newton, Richard 159, 287
Nicolini (Nicolino), *see* Grimaldi, Nicolo

Nin, Joaquín (1879–1949) 222

Ocaña 141
Odescalchi, Benedetto, see Innocent XI, Pope
Odescalchi, Livio (1652–1713) 23
opera 3, 6, 10, 14, 32–4, 44, 45, 52, 71, 88, 104
oratorio 3, 24, 41–3, 67, 104
Orefice, Antonio (fl. 1708–34): L'Engelberta 47
Osthoff, Wolfgang 282
Ottoboni, Cardinal Pietro (1667–1740) 3, 6, 17, 18, 19, 22, 23, 25, 41–2, 45, 47, 48, 52–3, 60, 88, 90
Ovid (43 BC–AD 17) 60–1
Oxinaga, Joaquín de (1719–89) 151

Pacheco de Acuña, Francesco, Duke of Ascalona and Marquis of Villena 8, 10
Pacini, Andrea (c. 1690–1764) 59
Pagano, Nicola 10
Pagano, Roberto 7, 10, 17, 19, 27, 29, 31, 78, 99, 144, 163, 195, 223, 281, 282, 283, 285, 287, 288, 289
Pagano, Tommaso 10
Paita, Giovanni 59, 70
Palermo 28–31, 96: San Antonio Magno Abate 2; Seminario dei Chierici 1; Teatro di Santa Cecilia 31
Palestrina, Giovanni Pierluigi da (1525/6–94) 3, 25, 112–13, 285: Missa brevis 115–16; Stabat mater 120
Pamphili, Benedetto (1653–1730) 3, 87, 88, 90
Paradies, Domenico (1707–91) 213
Pariati, Pietro (1665–1733) 26, 68
Paris 136, 141, 159
Parma 59, 61, 130, 148–9, 198
Pasi, Antonio 59
Pasqual, Andres 238
Pasquini, Bernardo (1637–1710) 3, 19, 167, 178
Patiños, José (1666–1736) 130
Pedrell, Felipe 222
Pedro II, King of Portugal (1648–1706) 97
Pelham-Holles, Thomas, Duke of Newcastle (1693–1768) 136
Pellegrini, Giovanni Francesco 42
Penaguião, Count of, see Anes de Sá e Menses, Rodrigo
Pepusch, Johann Christoph (1667–1752) 62, 141
Pergolesi, Giovanni Battista (1710–36) 231: La serva padrona 75; Stabat mater 120

Perrone, Arrigo 46
Perti, Giacomo (1661–1756) 78
Pestelli, Giorgio 160, 161–2, 165–6, 223, 288
Petrassi, Goffredo (b. 1904) 231
Philip II, King of Spain (1527–98) 134
Philip III, King of Spain (1578–1621) 134
Philip V, King of Spain (1683–1746) 8, 35–6, 99, 130–8, 142–3, 196
Picasso, Pablo (1881–1973) 134
Pickard, John 63
Pignatelli, Antonio, see Innocent XII, Pope
Pincherle, Marc 15, 281
Pini, Maria Domenica 50, 105
Pinto, Thomas (1714–83) 231
Piperno, Franco 284
Pistocchi, Francesco Antonio (1659–1726) 79
Pitman, Ambrose (1763–1817) 216–17
Pitoni, Giuseppe Ottavio (1657–1743) 28
Pla, José 19
Pla, Juan Baptist 19
Plantinga, Leon 217, 290
Poerson, Charles-François 106
Pollarolo, Carlo Francesco (c. 1653–1723) 10, 14, 39: Il Costantino pio 45; L'Irene 10, 39–41, 49
Pontano, Giovanni (1426–1503) 68
Porpora, Nicola (1686–1768) 7, 197: Berenice, regina d'Egitto 28, 78–80
Porta, Giovanni (?c. 1690–1755) 78: Numitore 61
Porter, Roy 282
Posillipo 6
Pozzuoli 6
Prota-Giurleo, Ulisse 27, 281, 282
Provenzale, Francesco (c. 1626–1704) 5, 9–10, 11, 23
Purcell, Henry (1659–1695): Dido and Aeneas 93; The Fairy Queen 93

Quantz, Johann Joachim (1697–1773) 31, 100, 198, 218, 289

Rabassa, Miguel 131
Rapaccioli, Giovanni 37, 39
Ravel, Maurice (1875–1937) 179
Rees, Abraham (1743–1825) 213, 289
Reissmann, August 114, 125, 285
Relvas, José 141
Rera, Joseph de la 238
Rey, Juan José 156, 287
Ribeiro, Sampayo 122
Ricci, Pietro 79

Riccio, Pietro 104
Riva, Giuseppe (?c. 1685–c. 1737) 57
Roberti, Girolamo Frigimelica, see
    Frigimelica Roberti, Girolamo
Robinson, Anastasia (c. 1692–1755) 61–2
Robinson, Ann (née Turner) (d. 1741)
    61–2
Roger, Estienne (1665/6–1722) 95
Rolli, Paolo (1687–1765) 61, 63–4, 65–6,
    283
Rome 2–4, 5, 6, 8, 10, 11, 13, 15, 16, 17–
    28, 31, 32, 34, 37, 43, 44, 46, 49, 59,
    65, 66, 78, 80, 87, 88, 89, 91, 94, 96,
    97, 100, 102, 104–6, 125, 131, 172,
    179, 181, 194, 196, 197, 206, 208, 209,
    212, 217, 219: Arcadian Academy 19,
    22, 47–8, 68, 71, 86, 87, 88, 107;
    Palazzo Bonelli 41; Palazzo del
    Campidoglio 95; Palazzo della
    Cancelleria 18, 25, 41–2, 45, 47, 52–3;
    Palazzo Zuccari 23, 24, 25, 41, 44, 45,
    47, 48, 50, 52, 58, 60, 81, 104–5; San
    Antonio dei Portoghesi 106; San
    Gerolamo della Carità 4, 9; San
    Giacomo degli Incurabili 4; San
    Giovanni Laterano 28; San Pancrazio
    102; Santa Maria Maggiore (Basilica
    Liberiana) 9, 17–18, 19, 20, 114–16,
    125, 127, 128; Santo Spirito 20; St
    Peter's 25, 28, 29, 98, 114, 118, 128,
    134; Teatro Capranica 26, 28, 47, 60,
    68, 78, 79; Teatro Costanzi 231;
    Teatro Tordinona 3, 23; Vatican 25–6,
    67, 97, 105, 114, 116, 117
Romero, Cristobal 132, 145, 237
Roseingrave, Daniel (d. 1727) 20
Roseingrave, Thomas (1688–1766) 20–1,
    29, 30, 49, 62, 64–6, 140–1, 150, 152,
    155, 156, 213–14, 216, 225, 226
Rospigliosi, Giulio, see Clement IX, Pope
Rossi, Antonio de' 50
Rossi, Luigi (c. 1597–1653) 85
Rovere, Giuliano della, see Julius II, Pope
Rovetta, Giovanni (c. 1595–1668) 85
Rubio, Samuel 211
Rudolph, Archduke of Austria 152
Ruggieri, Giovanni Maria (fl. c. 1690–
    1720): Le gare di politica e d'amore 78
Ruile-Dronke, Jutta 282
Ruspoli, Francesco Maria (1672–1731) 8,
    41, 47, 48, 88, 89–90

Sacchetti, Giovanni Battista 133
Sacchi, Giovenale (1726–89) 207, 289
Sachs, Curt 289

Sadie, Stanley 290
Salter, Lionel 148
Salvi, Antonio (d. 1742) 78, 79, 80
Sams, Eric 220, 290
Sances, Giovanni Felice (c. 1600–79):
    Cantade 85
Santini, Fortunato (1778–1861) 89, 91,
    118, 119, 134, 150, 159, 219
Santos, Reynaldo dos 141
Santo Stefano, Count of, see Benavides y
    Avila, Francesco de
Sarro, Domenico (1679–1744) 10–11:
    Didone abbandonata 78, 197, 282;
    L'Oreto festivo 104
Sarrubbo, Nicola 37
Sartori, Claudio 38, 282
Sartorio, Antonio (1630–80) 58
Savioni, Mario (1608–85) 3
Saxo Grammaticus (fl. 1200) 68
Scalzi, Carlo (fl. 1719–38) 79
Scamacca, P. Hortensio 58
Scarlata, see Scarlatti
Scarlatti family 1, 8, 89, 141
Scarlatti, Alessandro, father of Domenico
    2–12, 14–22, 24–8, 31–4, 37, 41–4,
    52–3, 68, 78, 80–1, 84–8, 90, 92, 94–5,
    101–2, 115, 117–20, 122–3, 141, 145,
    150–2, 161, 178–9, 181–2, 190, 195,
    205–6, 212, 215, 218, 236, 284
  cantatas: Al fin diviene amante 92;
    Andate, o miei sospiri 15; Sarei troppo
    felice 90; Vedi Eurilla quel fior 7
  church music: Laudate pueri 123;
    Miserere 122; Stabat mater 120
  keyboard music: Toccata 181, ex. 24a.
  operas: Il Ciro 25, 52–4; Flavio
    Cuniberto 8; Gli equivoci nel sembiante 4,
    6–7, 44; Il figlio delle selve 22, 44; Il
    trionfo dell'onore 28; L'honestà negli
    amori 4; Marco Attilio Regolo 28; Il
    Mitridate Eupatore 16; Pirro e Demetrio
    287; La serva favorita 8; Telemaco 28; Il
    Teodosio 24; Tiberio, imperatore
    d'Oriente 8; Il trionfo della libertà 16
  oratorios: Abramo il tuo sembiante 67;
    Cain, ovvero Il primo omicidio 16; Il
    regno di Maria Vergine 41–3; La vergine
    addolorata 28; La vittoria della fede 24;
    San Filippo Neri 28
  serenatas: Cari lidi, amene sponde 8; La
    virtù negli amori 101
Scarlatti, Alessandro Raimondo, uncle of
    Domenico 6
Scarlatti, Alexandro, son of Domenico
    135, 145, 238
Scarlatti, Anastasia (née Maxarti

Ximenes), second wife of
Domenico 141–2, 145, 236–8
Scarlatti, Anna Maria, aunt of Domenico
2, 10, 26
Scarlatti, Anna Maria Antonia Diana 2
Scarlatti, Antonia (née Anzalone), mother
of Domenico 4, 6, 145, 236
Scarlatti, Antonio, son of Domenico 139,
144, 145–6, 238
Scarlatti, Barbara, daughter of Domenico
139, 142, 145–6, 238
Scarlatti, Benedetto Bartolomeo, brother
of Domenico 6
Scarlatti, Carlos (1838–1914) 27
Scarlatti, Catarina (née Gentili), first wife
of Domenico 27, 101, 102, 132, 135,
139, 141, 142, 145, 236, 238
Scarlatti Cristina, sister of Domenico 6,
26, 89
Scarlatti, Domenico (1685–1757)
    cantatas 7, 8, 17, 19, 32, 67, 84–95,
    196–202, 208: A chi nacque infelice 90,
    284; Ah, sei troppo infelice 17, 90,
    284; Al fin diviene amante 91–2, ex. 10;
    Alme, dilette e care 95; Amenissimi prati
    88; Bella rosa adorata 92–4, ex. 11; Belle
    pupille care 284; Care pupille belle 19,
    89–90; Che si peni in amore 92, 284;
    Che vidi oh ciel? 199–201, exx. 34, 35;
    Dir vorrei 202; Dopo lungo servire 89–
    91, ex. 9; Dorme la rosa 87, 92; Fille già
    più non parlo 202; Lontan de te mio bene
    94–5, 284; Ninfe belle e voi pastori 8,
    20; Onde della mia Nera 88, 94, ex. 8;
    O qual meco Nice 196; Piangete, occhi
    dolenti 202; Pur nel sonno 87, 196, 197–
    8, 202, ex. 33; Qual pensier 202; Selve,
    caverne e monti 94, 208; Se per un sol
    momento 202; Tinte a note di sangue 202;
    V'adoro, o luci belle 89; Vuoi ch'io spiri
    284
    Capriccio fugato 119
    church music 18, 25, 112–29, 131, 208:
    Cibavit nos Dominus 115; Iste confessor
    117; Laetatus sum 125; Laudate pueri
    122–3, ex. 14; Magnificat 118, 119;
    Mass, A minor 115–16, 127; Mass, D
    major 126–9; Memento Domine David
    118–19; Miserere, E minor 116–17,
    122, ex. 13; Miserere, G minor 116–17,
    122; Missa quatuor vocum 125–6, 196,
    ex. 15; Nisi quia Dominus 115; Pange
    lingua 115, 116; Salve regina, A major
    114, 145, 195, 202–4, ex. 36; Salve
    regina, A minor 114, 202–3; Stabat

mater 115, 119–22; Te Deum 103,
    123–5, 196
    operas 10, 24, 32–41; 44–83, 131, 208:
    Ambleto 26, 59, 68–70; Amor d'un
    ombra/Narciso 24–5, 29–30, 60–7, 81,
    213, 215–16; Berenice, regina d'Egitto
    28, 32, 78–80; La Dirindina 70–7, 80,
    exx. 4–6; Il Giustino 10, 35–9, 40, ex.
    2; Ifigenia in Aulide 54–60; Ifigenia in
    Tauri 54–60; L'Irene 10, 39–41, 49;
    L'Orlando 24, 45, 48–9; L'Ottavia
    ristituita al trono 10, 34–6, 37, 38, 40,
    ex. 1; La Silvia 24, 44–5, 49, 58; Tetide
    in Sciro 24, 25, 49–57, 65, 66, 81, 82,
    ex. 3; Tolomeo et Alessandro 45–8, 52,
    81, 82, 100, 101, 107, 181, 212
    oratorios 24, 41–4, 67–8, 81: Cantata da
    recitarsi . . . la notte di Natale 67–8, 95;
    La conversione di Clodoveo 24, 41–4,
    105
    serenatas 26, 31, 81, 95, 98, 104–11,
    131: applauso devoto 105; applauso
    genetliaco 26, 106; Contesa delle stagioni
    31, 67, 98, 107–11, 128, 196, ex. 12;
    festeggio armonico 98, 107; Il concilio
    degli dei 104; Le nozze di Baco e
    d'Arianna 31, 107
    sinfonias 46, 48, 66, 80–3, 101, ex. 7
    sonatas 7, 31, 82, 95, 99, 109, 131, 134,
    144, 145, 146, 147–94, 195, 207, 213–
    14, 219, 222: Essercizi (K1–30) 31,
    139–41, 156, 157–9, 161, 162, 165,
    166–71, 177, 183, 185, 187, 202, 208,
    209, 210, 217, 225; K1 152, 154, 158,
    173, 227, 228; K2 152, 154, 158, 227,
    232; K3 152, 154, 158, 227, 229; K4
    152, 154, 158, 227; K5 152, 154, 158,
    168, 185, 190, 227, 230; K6 152, 154,
    158, 168, 227, 228; K7 152, 154, 158,
    168, 190, 228; K8 152, 154, 158, 234;
    K9 152, 154, 158, 168, 171, 228, 229,
    288; K10 152, 154, 158, 170, 171, 228;
    K11 152, 154, 158, 185, 227, 229, 234;
    K12 152, 154, 158, 227; K13 152, 154,
    158, 168, 227; K14 152, 154, 158; K15
    152, 154, 158, 227; K16 152, 154, 158,
    168; K17 152, 154, 158, 171, 227, 232;
    K18 152, 154, 158, 171; K19 152, 154,
    158, 171, 227; K20 152, 154, 158, 171,
    227, 234; K21 152, 154, 158, 168, 169,
    227, ex. 17; K22 152, 154, 158; K23
    152, 154, 158, 228; K24 152, 154, 158,
    183, 227, 288; K25 152, 154, 158, 170,
    227; K26 152, 154, 158, 170, 183, 227;
    K27 152, 154, 158, 171; K28 152, 154,

158, 171, 227; K29 152, 154, 158, 168, 171, 227; K30 154, 158, 176–7, 217, 231, 234; K31 152, 154, 158, 228, 234; K32 152, 154, 158, 170; K33 152, 154, 155, 158, 228; K34 152, 154, 158, 226; K35 152, 154, 158; K36–8 152, 154, 158, 227; K39 152, 154, 158, 233, 288; K40 152, 154, 158, 170; K41 152, 154, 158, 176–7, 227, 229, 288; K42 152, 154, 158; K44 158; K45 152; K48–9 158; K52 234, 288; K53 158; K54 152; K55 158; K56 152; K57 189; K58 176; K61 176; K63 232, 234; K65 152, 173, 190; K66 152, 154, 158, 190; K73 147, 170; K77 147, 170; K78 147; K80 147; K81 147, 227, 234; K82 176; K85 176; K87 233; K88 147, 227; K89 147, 226, 227, 228, 234; K90 147, 234; K91 147, 227; K93 176–7, 288; K95–6 152, 158; K97 158; K98 154, 190; K99 164; K100 158, 165; K101 152, 158, 233; K104 158; K105 155, 158, 162; K106 158, 166; K107 158, 166, 170, 232; K108 155; K109 185; K112 152; K113 152, 158; K115 152; K116 152, 154, 158; K117 158; K119 152; K120 152, 158, 186, ex. 28; K124 152, 170–1, ex. 18; K125 152, 158; K126 152, 155, 158; K127 152, 158; K130 154, 169, 190; K131 152, 158; K132 152, 173, 234; K133–4 152; K135 152, 289; K139 154; K140 158; K141 183–4, ex. 26; K142–6 151; K147 150, 234; K158 154; K159 152, 173–4; K160 154, 162; K161 162; K162 173; K170 173; K174 187; K175 183, 187, ex. 25; K179 152, 154, 158; K180 152, 158, 175, 221, ex. 21; K181 235; K182 152, 158; K183 154; K188 235; K190 155; K200 154, 155; K202 172, 234; K206 152; K208 148, 182, 187, ex. 24c; K209 180; K211 152; K212 170; K213 187, 289; K215 152, 182, 183, ex. 24b; K216 152, 289; K217 187, 188, 235, ex. 29; K223 220, ex. 39; K227 173; K229 169; K233 188–9, 220, ex. 30; K235 172; K238 180; K241 169, 289; K243 187; K246–7 152, 158; K249 169; K255 178, ex. 22; K256 169, 173, 175, ex. 20; K259–60 152; K261 183; K266 154, 170; K267 176; K271 173; K273 172; K279 233; K280 170; K284 176; K287 7, 176–7; K288 7, 177; K289 169; K290 289; K291 148; K292 148, 289; K296 169; K298 152, 158; K299 152, 158, 220–1, ex. 40; K300 154; K303 175, ex.

20; K306 155; K308–10 288; K313 175, ex. 20; K315 155; K316 154; K317 154, 169; K319 155; K322 148; K328 7, 134, 178; K331 154; K332 154, 288; K333 154, 162, 173; K338 175, ex. 20; K342 148; K345 234; K347 165; K348 165, 183, 288; K351 176; K352 187; K355 148; K358 232; K360 163; K361 164; K364–5 155; K366 152, 169; K368 164; K369 163; K373 233; K374 134, 163–4, 288, ex. 16; K375 134, 163, 175, 288, ex. 20; K376–9 134, 288; K380 234; K383 289; K387 288; K391 232; K392 155, 169; K393 161; K394 171–2, 174, 219, ex. 19; K398 152; K399 154; K405 175, ex. 20; K409 173; K412 234; K415 288; K417 154, 156, 176, 288; K418 235; K419 232; K424–5 154; K426 152, 163, 234; K427 155, 163, 186; K428 152, 232; K429 152; K430 152, 154, 163, 232, 234; K431 160; K432 154; K434 155; K435 232; K437 154; K439 169; K440 170, 234; K441 232; K442 169; K445 233, 288; K446 152, 172; K450 152; K452–3 150; K455 233; K457 169; K458 152; K461 189, 232; K462 152, 187; K463 152; K468 152, 289; K469 152; K474 152, 154, 232; K475–7 152; K481 152, 173, 235; K482 152, 187; K483 152; K485 163, 288; K486 164; K487 152, 164, 234, 235; K489 232; K490 152, 288; K491 288; K492 232, 288; K499 170; K503 169; K505 288; K508 170; K509–10 165; K513 172–3, 234, 288; K517 189; K518 169; K526–7 165; K528–9 166, 187; K533 154, 173; K540 288; K545 170; K554 187; without K numbers 154–6, 190–4, exx. 31, 32, Appendix III

Scarlatti, Domingo, son of Domenico 132, 144, 145–6, 207, 238

Scarlatti (Scarlata), Eleonora (née d'Amato), paternal grandmother of Domenico 1, 2

Scarlatti, Fernando, son of Domenico 132, 145, 238

Scarlatti, Flaminia, sister of Domenico, 6, 26, 89

Scarlatti, Francesco, uncle of Domenico 2, 28–9, 30–1, 284

Scarlatti, Giuseppe (c. 1718–77) 28

Scarlatti, Giuseppe, brother of Domenico 10, 36

Scarlatti, Juan Antonio, son of Domenico 132, 144, 145, 238

Scarlatti, Maria, daughter of Domenico
  138–9, 145, 207, 238
Scarlatti, Mariana, daughter of Domenico
  132, 135, 145, 238
Scarlatti, Melchiorra Brigida, aunt of
  Domenico 2, 5, 10, 26
Scarlatti (Scarlata), Pietro, paternal
  grandfather of Domenico 2
Scarlatti, Pietro Filippo, brother of
  Domenico 4, 6, 16, 17, 26, 119
Scarlatti, Rosa, daughter of Domenico
  142, 145, 238
Scarlatti, Tommaso, uncle of Domenico
  2, 10, 37, 39
Scholes, Percy 285, 286, 289
Schumann, Clara (née Wieck) (1819–96)
  219
Schumann, Robert (1810–56) 218–19, 290
Sclavo, Nicola Maria 133
Scola, Adamo 139
Scotti, Annibale 130, 131, 142, 196
Seixas, Carlos de (1704–42) 98–9, 155,
  192–3
Selvatici, Michele 70, 79
Senesino [Francesco Bernardi] (d. 1759)
  61, 283
serenata 6, 23, 24, 29, 41–3, 104–5
Serino, Nicola 33–4, 40
Serino, Nicola 33–4, 40
Seville 129–33, 155, 180
Shakespeare, William (1564–1616) 68–9
Sheveloff, Joel 150, 151, 153, 159, 161,
  163, 223, 287, 288, 289
Siemens, Lothar 193
Siena 18, 71, 119, 282
Silbiger, Alexander 289
Silva y Alvarez de Toledo, Fernando de,
  Duke of Huescar, later Duke of Alba
  143–4, 195, 206
Simi Bonini, Eleonora 17, 18, 115, 281
sinfonia 33, 81
Smith, John Christopher (d. 1763) 64
Smither, Howard E. 43, 282
Sobieski, Jan, see Jan III Sobieski
Sobieski, Prince Alexander (1678–1714)
  22, 23–4, 25, 46, 49–50, 105, 209
Sobieski, Prince Constantine (1684–1727)
  22
Sobieski, Prince James (1667–1737) 22,
  46, 49–50
Sobieski, Princess Marie Casimire (d.
  1723) 22, 23, 24, 25, 47, 60
Solar Quintes, Nicolas Alvarez 286
Soler, Antonio (1729–83) 144, 149, 191,
  192, 211, 217
Solimena, Francesco (1657–1747) 6

sonata 3, 8, 147–8, 181, 211
Soriano Fuertes, Indalecio (1787–1851)
  156, 194
Sorrentino, Giuseppe 6
Spagna, Arcangelo (1631/2–after 1720) 43
Spanish Succession 9, 43, 106, 130
Sportonio, Marc'Antonio (c. 1631–after
  1680) 2, 4
Stanley, John (1712–86) 141
Steffani, Agostino (1654–1728) 48
stile antico 3, 112–14, 115, 116, 120, 122,
  125–6, 195
stile misto 120
Stradella, Alessandro (1644–82) 3, 85
Stravinsky, Igor (1882–1971) 112, 231,
  234
Strohm, Reinhard 80, 281

Tagliavini, Luigi Ferdinando 178, 223,
  289
Talbot, Michael 284
Teixeira, Antonio (1707–after 1759) 97
Telemann, Georg Philipp (1681–1767) 166
Tempesti, Domenico 70
Terry, Charles Sanford 285
Thomas Aquinas, see Aquinas, Thomas
Tiepolo, Giovanni Battista (1696–1770)
  205
Tilla, see Pini, Maria Domenica
Todi, Jacopone da, see Jacopone da Todi
Tommasini, Vincenzo (1878–1950): Les
  Femmes de bonne humeur 231–3
Torcy, Marquis de 60
Torres, Joseph de (c. 1665–1738) 103, 125,
  130, 193
Tortelier family 1
Trapani 2
Tufarelli, Giovanni 27
Turner, Ann, see Robinson, Ann
Turner, William (1651–1740) 62

Uffenbach, Johann Friedrich Armand
  von (1687–1769) 41
Urbino 16, 17, 26
Utrecht, Treaty of 130

Vaccaro, Nicola 21
Vaini, Prince Guido 106
Valabrega, Cesare 223
Valesio, Francesco 24, 41–2, 67, 104–5,
  282
Valois y Bethencourt, Bernardo 155
Van Loo, Louis-Michel (1707–71) 196
Veneziano, Gaetano (1656–1716) 10–11,
  20, 40